Poetry
An Introduction

Poetry
An Introduction

Robert DiYanni

Boston   Burr Ridge, IL   Dubuque, IA   Madison, WI
New York   San Francisco   St. Louis
Bangkok Bogotá Caracas Lisbon London Madrid Mexico City
Milan   New Delhi   Seoul   Singapore   Sydney   Taipei   Toronto

McGraw-Hill Higher Education

A Division of The **McGraw-Hill** Companies

POETRY: AN INTRODUCTION

This book is printed on acid-free paper.

1 2 3 4 5 6 7 8 9 0 KPH/KPH 9 0 4 3 2 1 0 9

ISBN 0-07-229507-4 (combined volume)
ISBN 0-07-229509-0 (fiction)
ISBN 0-07-229510-4 (poetry)
ISBN 0-07-229511-2 (drama)

Cover image: *Peterson, Margaret, Three Women
(1938, egg tempera on wood), The Oakland Museum of California*
Editorial director: *Phillip A. Butcher*
Sponsoring editor: *Sarah Touborg Moyers*
Developmental editor: *Alexis Walker*
Editorial assistant: *Bennett Morrison*
Project manager: *Margaret Rathke*
Manager, new book production: *Melonie Salvati*
Designer: *Kiera Cunningham*
Senior photo research coordinator: *Keri Johnson*
Supplement coordinator: *Marc Mattson*
Compositor: *GAC Indianapolis*
Typeface: *10.5/12 Bembo*
Printer: *Quebecor Printing Book Group/Hawkins*

Library of Congress has cataloged an earlier edition as follows

DiYanni, Robert.
    Literature: reading fiction, poetry, and drama / Robert DiYanni.
    — Compact ed.
        p.   cm.
    Includes index.
    ISBN 0-07-229507-4 (combined). — ISBN 0-07-229509-0 (fiction). —
ISBN 0-07-229510-4 (poetry). — ISBN 0-07-229511-2 (drama)
    1. Literature.   2. Literature—Collections.   I. Title.
PN49.D53   2000
808—dc21   99-14165
                                                                                        CIP

www.mhhe.com

About the Author

Robert DiYanni is Professor of English at Pace University, Pleasantville, New York, where he teaches courses in literature, writing, and humanities. He has also taught at Queens College of the City University of New York, at New York University in the Graduate Rhetoric Program, and most recently in the Expository Writing Program at Harvard University. He received his B.A. from Rutgers University (1968) and his Ph.D. from the City University of New York (1976).

Professor DiYanni has written articles and reviews on various aspects of literature, composition, and pedagogy. His books include *The McGraw-Hill Book of Poetry; Women's Voices; Like Season'd Timber: New Essays on George Herbert;* and *Modern American Poets: Their Voices and Visions* (a text to accompany the Public Broadcasting Television series that aired in 1988). With Kraft Rompf, he edited *The McGraw-Hill Book of Poetry* (1993) and *The McGraw-Hill Book of Fiction* (1995). With Janetta Benton he wrote *Arts & Culture: An Introduction to the Humanities* (1998).

*For my students, who have
made the teaching of poetry
a recurring joy*

Contents

ABOUT THE AUTHOR   iii
PREFACE   xvii

CHAPTER ONE   **Reading Poems**   1
The Experience of Poetry   2
Robert Hayden *Those Winter Sundays*   2
The Interpretation of Poetry   4
Robert Frost *Stopping by Woods on a Snowy Evening*   5
The Evaluation of Poetry   8
Adrienne Rich *Aunt Jennifer's Tigers*   11
The Act of Reading Poetry   12
Theodore Roethke *My Papa's Waltz*   12

CHAPTER TWO   **Types of Poetry**   15
Narrative Poetry   15
Lyric Poetry   17

CHAPTER THREE   **Elements of Poetry**   19
Voice: Speaker and Tone   19
Stephen Crane *War Is Kind*   20
Robert Browning *My Last Duchess*   21
Muriel Stuart *In the Orchard*   23
Gerard Manley Hopkins *Thou art indeed just, Lord*   24
Anonymous *Western Wind*   25

ix

Henry Reed *Naming of Parts*   26
Jacques Prévert *Family Portrait*   27

Diction   28
William Wordsworth *I wandered lonely as a cloud*   29
Edwin Arlington Robinson *Miniver Cheevy*   32
William Wordsworth *It is a beauteous evening*   33
Robert Herrick *Delight in Disorder*   34
Adrienne Rich *Rape*   34

Imagery   35
Elizabeth Bishop *First Death in Nova Scotia*   36
William Butler Yeats *The Lake Isle of Innisfree*   39
Robert Browning *Meeting at Night*   40
H. D. (Hilda Doolittle) *Heat*   40
Thomas Hardy *Neutral Tones*   41

Figures of Speech: Simile and Metaphor   42
William Shakespeare *That time of year thou may'st in me
   behold*   43
John Donne *Hymn to God the Father*   44
Robert Wallace *The Double-Play*   45
Louis Simpson *The Battle*   47
Judith Wright *Woman to Child*   47

Symbolism and Allegory   48
Peter Meinke *Advice to My Son*   49
Christina Rossetti *Up-Hill*   51
William Blake *A Poison Tree*   52
Robert Frost *The Road Not Taken*   52
George Herbert *Virtue*   53
Emily Dickinson *Because I could not stop for Death*   54

Syntax   55
John Donne *The Sun Rising*   56
Thomas Hardy *The Man He Killed*   59
William Butler Yeats *An Irish Airman Foresees His Death*   60
Robert Frost *The Silken Tent*   60
E. E. Cummings *"Me up at does"*   61
Stevie Smith *Mother, Among the Dustbins*   62

Sound: Rhyme, Alliteration, Assonance   63
Gerard Manley Hopkins *In the Valley of the Elwy*   65
Thomas Hardy *During Wind and Rain*   67
Alexander Pope *Sound and Sense*   68
May Swenson *The Universe*   69
Bob McKenty *Adam's Song*   70
Helen Chasin *The Word* Plum   70

Rhythm and Meter   71
  Robert Frost *The Span of Life*   72
  George Gordon, Lord Byron *The Destruction of Sennacherib*   77
  Anne Sexton *Her Kind*   78
  William Carlos Williams *The Red Wheelbarrow*   79
Structure: Closed Form and Open Form   79
  John Keats *On First Looking into Chapman's Homer*   81
  Walt Whitman *When I heard the learn'd astronomer*   82
  E. E. Cummings *l(a*   83
  E. E. Cummings *[Buffalo Bill's]*   84
  William Carlos Williams *The Dance*   85
  Denise Levertov *O Taste and See*   86
  Theodore Roethke *The Waking*   87
  C. P. Cavafy *The City*
    Translated by Edmund Keeley and Philip
      Sherrard   88
Theme   88
  Emily Dickinson *Crumbling is not an instant's Act*   89

CHAPTER   *Transformations*   91
FOUR   **Revisions**   91
  William Blake *London* (two versions)   92
  William Butler Yeats *A Dream of Death* (two versions)   95
  Emily Dickinson *The Wind begun to knead [rock] the Grass*
    (two versions)   96
  D. H. Lawrence *[The] Piano* (two versions)   97
Parodies   99
  William Carlos Williams *This Is Just to Say*   99
  Kenneth Koch *Variations on a Theme by William Carlos
    Williams*   100
  Gerard Manley Hopkins *Carrion Comfort*   101
  Gary Layne Hatch *Terrier Torment; or, Mr. Hopkins and
    His Dog*   101
  William Shakespeare *Shall I compare thee to a summer's day*   102
  Howard Moss *Shall I Compare Thee to a Summer's Day*   103
  Robert Frost *Dust of Snow*   103
  Bob McKenty *Snow on Frost*   104
Poems and Paintings   104
  Vincent Van Gogh *The Starry Night*   108
  Anne Sexton *The Starry Night*   108
  Robert Fagles *The Starry Night*   109
  Francesco de Goya *The Third of May, 1808*   110

David Gewanter *Goya's "The Third of May, 1808"*   110
Pieter Breughel the Elder *Landscape with the Fall of Icarus*   111
W. H. Auden *Musée des Beaux Arts*   111
Joseph Langland *Hunters in the Snow: Breughel*   112
Pieter Breughel the Elder *Hunters in the Snow*   113
Edward Hopper *Sunday*   114
E. Ward Herlands *When Edward Hopper Was Painting*   114
William Blake *The Sick Rose* (watercolor)   115
William Blake *The Sick Rose* (poem)   115
Sandro Botticelli *Adoration of the Magi*   116
T. S. Eliot *Journey of the Magi*   116
Giotto di Bondone *Adoration of the Magi*   117
William Butler Yeats *The Magi*   117
Henri Matisse *Dance*   118
Natalie Safir *Matisse's Dance*   118
Pablo Picasso *Girl with a Mandolin*   119
Vinnie-Marie D'Ambrosio *If I Were a Maker I'd*   119
Pablo Picasso *Still Life with Pitcher, Bowl, & Fruit*   120
Gustav Klimt *The Kiss*   121
Lawrence Ferlinghetti *Short Story on a Painting of Gustav Klimt*   121

CHAPTER   **Writing about Poetry**   123
FIVE   **Reasons for Writing about Poetry**   123
          Informal Ways of Writing about Poetry   123
          Robert Hayden *Those Winter Sundays*   124
          Robert Graves *Symptoms of Love*   125
          Formal Ways of Writing about Poetry   126
          Student Papers on Poetry   128
          Questions for Writing about Poetry   133
          Suggestions for Writing   134

CHAPTER   **Three Poets in Context**   137
SIX   **Reading Emily Dickinson, Robert Frost, and
          Langston Hughes in Depth**   137
          Questions for In-Depth Reading   138
          Introduction to Emily Dickinson   139
          Emily Dickinson 326 *I cannot dance upon my Toes*   141
          Emily Dickinson 303 *The Soul selects her own Society*   142
          **Emily Dickinson on Herself and Her First
          Poems**   143
          Letter to Thomas Higginson   143
          Critics on Dickinson   143

Three Poems by Emily Dickinson with Altered Punctuation 148
Emily Dickinson: Poems 149
  199 *I'm "wife"—I've finished that* 149
  214 *I taste a liquor never brewed* 150
  241 *I like a look of Agony* 150
  249 *Wild Nights—Wild Nights!* 151
  258 *There's a certain Slant of light* 151
  280 *I felt a Funeral, in my Brain* 152
  328 *Some keep the Sabbath going to Church* 152
  341 *After great pain, a formal feeling comes* 153
  348 *I dreaded that first Robin, so* 153
  419 *We grow accustomed to the Dark* 154
  435 *Much Madness is divinest Sense* 154
  449 *I died for Beauty—but was scarce* 155
  465 *I heard a Fly buzz—when I died* 155
  536 *The Heart asks Pleasure—first* 156
  585 *I like to see it lap the Miles* 156
  599 *There is a pain—so utter* 157
  632 *The Brain—is wider than the Sky* 157
  650 *Pain—has an element of Blank* 157
  744 *Remorse—is Memory—awake* 158
  754 *My Life had stood—a Loaded Gun* 158
  986 *A narrow Fellow in the Grass* 159
  1068 *Further in Summer than the Birds* 160
  1078 *The Bustle in a House* 160
  1100 *The last Night that She lived* 160
  1129 *Tell all the Truth but tell it slant* 161
  1463 *A Route of Evanescence* 162
  1624 *Apparently with no surprise* 162
  1732 *My life closed twice before its close* 162
Introduction to Robert Frost 163
Critical Comments by Frost 166
  from *The Figure a Poem Makes* 166
  from *"The Constant Symbol"* 167
  from *"The Unmade Word, or Fetching and Far-Fetching"* 168
Critics on Frost 169
Robert Frost: Poems 174
  Mowing 174
  The Tuft of Flowers 174
  Mending Wall 176
  Birches 177
  Home Burial 178
  Hyla Brook 181

Putting in the Seed   181
Fire and Ice   182
For Once, Then, Something   182
Two Look at Two   183
Once by the Pacific   184
Acquainted with the Night   184
Tree at my Window   184
Departmental   185
Desert Places   186
Design   187
Provide, Provide   187
The Most of It   188
Introduction to Langston Hughes   188
Langston Hughes on Harlem   190
A Toast to Harlem   190
Critics on Hughes   191
Langston Hughes: Poems   196
Dream Deferred   196
Same in Blues   197
The Negro Speaks of Rivers   198
Mother to Son   198
I, Too   199
My People   199
The Weary Blues   200
Young Gal's Blues   200
Morning After   201
Trumpet Player   202
Dream Boogie   203
Madam and the Rent Man   204
Theme for English B   205
Aunt Sue's Stories   206
Ballad of the Landlord   207
Let America Be America Again   208

CHAPTER   ***A Collection of Poems***   209
SEVEN   Sappho *To me he seems like a god*   209
            Anonymous *Barbara Allan*   210
            Anonymous *Edward, Edward*   212
            Thomas Wyatt *They flee from me*   213
            Edmund Spenser *One day I wrote her name upon the strand*   214
            Sir Walter Raleigh *The Nymph's Reply to the Shepherd*   215
            Christopher Marlowe *The Passionate Shepherd to His Love*   216
            William Shakespeare *When in disgrace with fortune and men's
                eyes*   216

William Shakespeare *Let me not to the marriage of true
  minds* 217
William Shakespeare *Th' expense of spirit in a waste of
  shame* 217
William Shakespeare *My mistress' eyes are nothing like the
  sun* 218
John Donne *Song* 218
John Donne *The Canonization* 219
John Donne *A Valediction: Forbidding Mourning* 220
John Donne *The Flea* 221
John Donne *Death, be not proud* 222
John Donne *Batter my heart, three-personed God* 223
Ben Jonson *On My First Son* 223
Ben Jonson *Song: To Celia* 224
Robert Herrick *Upon Julia's Clothes* 224
Robert Herrick *To the Virgins, to Make Much of Time* 224
George Herbert *The Altar* 225
John Milton *When I consider how my light is spent* 226
John Milton *On the Late Massacre in Piedmont* 226
Anne Bradstreet *To My Dear and Loving Husband* 227
Andrew Marvell *To His Coy Mistress* 227
Alexander Pope from *An Essay on Man* 229
William Blake *The Clod & the Pebble* 229
William Blake *The Lamb* 230
William Blake *The Tyger* 230
William Blake *The Garden of Love* 231
Robert Burns *A Red, Red Rose* 232
William Wordsworth *The world is too much with us* 232
William Wordsworth *The Solitary Reaper* 233
William Wordsworth *Composed upon Westminster Bridge,
  September 3, 1802* 234
William Wordsworth *Lines Composed a Few Miles above
  Tintern Abbey* 234
Samuel Taylor Coleridge *Kubla Khan* 238
George Gordon, Lord Byron *She walks in beauty* 239
Percy Bysshe Shelley *Ozymandias* 240
Percy Bysshe Shelley *Ode to the West Wind* 240
John Keats *When I have fears that I may cease to be* 243
John Keats *La Belle Dame sans Merci* 243
John Keats *Ode to a Nightingale* 245
John Keats *Ode on a Grecian Urn* 247
Elizabeth Barrett Browning *How do I love thee?* 249
Edgar Allan Poe *To Helen* 249
Edgar Allen Poe *The Raven* 250

Alfred, Lord Tennyson *Ulysses*   253
Alfred, Lord Tennyson *The Eagle*   254
Robert Browning *Soliloquy of the Spanish Cloister*   255
Walt Whitman *A noiseless patient spider*   257
Walt Whitman *Crossing Brooklyn Ferry*   257
Matthew Arnold *Dover Beach*   262
Lewis Carroll *Jabberwocky*   263
Thomas Hardy *The Ruined Maid*   264
Thomas Hardy *Channel Firing*   265
Thomas Hardy *Afterwards*   266
Gerard Manley Hopkins *God's Grandeur*   266
Gerard Manley Hopkins *The Windhover*   267
Gerard Manley Hopkins *Pied Beauty*   267
Gerard Manley Hopkins *Spring and Fall: to a Young Child*   268
A. E. Housman *When I was one-and-twenty*   268
A. E. Housman *To an Athlete Dying Young*   269
William Butler Yeats *The Second Coming*   270
William Butler Yeats *The Wild Swans at Coole*   270
William Butler Yeats *Leda and the Swan*   271
William Butler Yeats *Sailing to Byzantium*   272
Edwin Arlington Robinson *Richard Cory*   273
Paul Laurence Dunbar *We wear the mask*   273
Wallace Stevens *Thirteen Ways of Looking at a Blackbird*   274
William Carlos Williams *Spring and All*   276
William Carlos Williams *Dance Russe*   277
Ezra Pound *The River-Merchant's Wife: A Letter*   277
Marianne Moore *Poetry*   278
T. S. Eliot *The Love Song of J. Alfred Prufrock*   279
John Crowe Ransom *Piazza Piece*   283
Vicente Huidobro *Ars Poetica*
    TRANSLATED BY DAVID M. GUSS   283
Archibald MacLeish *Ars Poetica*   284
Wilfred Owen *Dulce et Decorum Est*   285
E. E. Cummings *anyone lived in a pretty how town*   286
E. E. Cummings *i thank You God for most this amazing*   287
Jean Toomer *Song of the Son*   288
Jean Toomer *Reapers*   288
W. H. Auden *The Unknown Citizen*   289
W. H. Auden *In Memory of W. B. Yeats*   290
Theodore Roethke *Elegy for Jane*   292
Elizabeth Bishop *Sestina*   293
May Swenson *Women*   294

William Stafford *Traveling through the dark* 295
Dylan Thomas *Fern Hill* 295
Dylan Thomas *Do not go gentle into that good night* 297
Gwendolyn Brooks *the mother* 297
Gwendolyn Brooks *First fight. Then fiddle* 298
Lawrence Ferlinghetti *Constantly Risking Absurdity* 299
Richard Wilbur *The Death of a Toad* 300
Philip Larkin *A Study of Reading Habits* 300
Rosario Castellanos *Chess*
    TRANSLATED BY MAUREEN AHERN 301
Galway Kinnell *Saint Francis and the Sow* 302
James Wright *Lying in a Hammock at William Duffy's Farm in Pine Island, Minnesota* 302
James Wright *A Blessing* 303
Anne Sexton *Two Hands* 304

A Selection of Contemporary Poems 305

Donald Hall *My son, my executioner* 305
Gregory Corso *Marriage* 305
Linda Pastan *Ethics* 308
Sylvia Plath *Mirror* 309
Audre Lorde *Hanging Fire* 310
Lucille Clifton *Homage to My Hips* 311
Marge Piercy *A Work of Artifice* 311
Margaret Atwood *This Is a Photograph of Me* 312
Raymond Carver *Photograph of My Father* 313
Seamus Heaney *Mid-Term Break* 313
Seamus Heaney *Digging* 314
Nikki Giovanni *Ego Tripping* 315
Sharon Olds *Size and Sheer Will* 317
Christine Kane Molito *Partial Reflections in Black & Blue* 317
Jane Kenyon *Notes from the Other Side* 318
Yusef Komunyakaa *Facing It* 318
Neal Bowers *Driving Lessons* 319
Kraft Rompf *Waiting Table* 321
Jimmy Santiago Baca from *Meditations on the South Valley XVII* 322
Rita Dove *Canary* 322
Judith Ortiz Cofer *The Idea of Islands* 323
Alberto Rios *A Dream of Husbands* 324
Gertrude Schnackenberg *Signs* 325
Gary Soto *Behind Grandma's House* 325
Louise Erdrich *Indian Boarding School: The Runaways* 326

CHAPTER   *Critical Theory: Approaches to the Analysis and*
EIGHT   *Interpretation of Literature*   327
           Reading for Analysis   327
             Emily Dickinson *I'm "wife"*   327
           The Canon and the Curriculum   328
           Formalist Perspectives   332
           Biographical Perspectives   335
           Historical Perspectives   336
           Psychological Perspectives   339
           Sociological Perspectives   341
           Reader–Response Perspectives   345
           Mythological Perspectives   349
           Structuralist Perspectives   351
           Deconstructive Perspectives   354
           Cultural Studies Perspectives   357
           Using Critical Perspectives as Heuristics   359

CHAPTER   *Writing with Sources*   362
NINE   **Why Do Research about Literature?**   362
           Clarifying the Assignment   363
           Selecting a Topic   363
           Finding and Using Sources   364
           Using Computerized Databases   365
           Using the Internet for Research   366
           Developing a Critical Perspective   367
           Developing a Thesis   367
           Drafting and Revising   368
           Conventions   369
           Documenting Sources   371
           Documenting Electronic Sources   375
           A Student Paper Incorporating Research   378

           APPENDIX: WRITERS' LIVES   381
           GLOSSARY   395
           ACKNOWLEDGMENTS   399
           INDEX   405

Preface

Poetry: An Introduction presents an approach to poems that emphasizes reading as an active enterprise involving thought and feeling. It encourages students to value their emotional reactions and their previous experience with life and with language. Students are introduced to interpretation through illustrated discussions of the elements of poetry. They are invited to consider why they respond as they do and how their responses change during subsequent readings of a poem; they are asked, in short, to relate their experience in reading poems to their experience in living. They are encouraged to see poems as a significant reflection of life and an imaginative extension of its possibilities.

From first page to last, *Poetry* is designed to involve students in the twin acts of reading and analysis. The genre of poetry is introduced by a three-part explanatory overview of the reading process. The introduction is organized around the approach to texts outlined in Robert Scholes's *Textual Power* (Yale University Press, 1985), modified and adapted to my own approach to teaching literature. Scholes identifies three aspects of literary response: reading, interpretation, and criticism. The three-part structure of the introduction breaks down as follows:

the experience of poetry
the interpretation of poetry
the evaluation of poetry

Our *experience* of poetry concerns our impressions of a work, especially our subjective impressions and emotional responses. *Interpretation* involves intellectual and analytical thinking. And the *evaluation* of poetry involves an assessment of aesthetic distinction along with a consideration of a work's social, moral, and cultural values.

Paralleling this schema for the introductory discussion is a similarly or-
ganized introduction to writing about poetry. This chapter describes how to
apply and adapt the approaches presented in the poetry introduction. The
writing chapter includes examples of student writing, sample topics, docu-
mentation procedures, and a general review of the writing process.

For the introduction to poetry, I have also provided a separate illustration of
the "act of reading": a set of annotations for Theodore Roethke's "My Papa's
Waltz" that suggest specific strategies for the critical reading of poems.

In addition to emphasizing the subjective, analytical, and evaluative aspects
of reading poetry, *Poetry* introduces the traditional elements through discussions
tied to specific poems. Throughout these discussions, students are asked to re-
turn to certain works and reconsider them from different perspectives. In
Chapter Three, Elements of Poetry, for example, students are encouraged to
reread particular poems as they study a different element, such as diction, syn-
tax, imagery, or meter. The repetition reinforces the recursive aspect of reading
described in the opening chapter and demonstrates the need to reread poems
for the fullest possible intellectual, emotional, and aesthetic enjoyment.

Poetry broadens the study of the genre with a number of poems in transla-
tion and a special selection of poetic transformations (in Chapter Four), exam-
ples of ways in which poets have modified their own and other artists' works by
means of revision, parody, and adaptation. Of particular interest are the poems
inspired by paintings.

A word about the choice of poems. The classic and contemporary selections
reflect a wide range of styles, voices, subjects, and points of view. Complex and
challenging works appear alongside more readily approachable and accessible
ones. *Poetry,* moreover, contains both in sufficient variety for instructors to as-
sign the more accessible ones for students to read and write about on their
own, while reserving the more ambitious selections for class discussion.

This edition of *Poetry: An Introduction* is based on the fourth edition of *Liter-
ature*. The following features should be highlighted:

- Writing instruction includes a chapter on Writing about Poetry and another
  chapter on Writing with Sources.
- Works are provided with dates of publication or composition.
- The works of three poets are highlighted and contextualized. Multiple selec-
  tions are included for Emily Dickinson, Robert Frost, and Langston Hughes.
  Each of these writers' works is prefaced by an extensive biocritical introduc-
  tion and by critical perspectives written by the writers themselves and by lit-
  erary scholars.
- An extensive chapter on Critical Perspectives has been included in which
  the major schools of literary theory are described and illustrated. Guiding
  questions and brief bibliographies augment the application of ten critical
  approaches.
- An appendix of biographical sketches of the poets has also been included.

This book represents the cooperative efforts of a number of people. This single-
genre spinoff owes its existence ultimately to Steve Pensinger, who encouraged

me to develop the first edition of the four-genre full-size book, *Literature: Reading Fiction, Poetry, Drama, and the Essay,* the predecessor of the newly published compact edition. For both this book and for the compact edition of *Literature,* its parent, I have had the pleasure of working with McGraw-Hill colleagues Sarah Moyers, English editor; Alexis Walker, developmental editor; and Maggie Bogovich, project manager. Each provided me with the kind of high-quality professional assistance I have come to expect from McGraw-Hill. It continues to be a pleasure to work with them and with their publishing colleagues.

I have had the additional pleasure of working with Professor Tom Kitts of St. John's University. Professor Kitts has written a practical and graceful instructor's manual, which serves as a rich and rewarding source of practical and provocative classroom applications.

Finally, I want to thank my wife, Mary, whose loving assistance enabled me to complete this book on schedule.

ROBERT DiYANNI

CHAPTER ONE

Reading Poems

In some ways reading poetry is much like reading fiction and drama: we observe details of action and language, make connections and inferences, and draw conclusions. We also bring to poetry the same intellectual and emotional dispositions, the same general experience with life and literature that we draw on in reading drama and fiction. And yet there is something different about reading poems. The difference, admittedly more one of degree than of kind, involves our being more attentive to the connotations of words, more receptive to the expressive qualities of sound and rhythm in line and stanza, more discerning about details of syntax and punctuation. This increased attention to linguistic detail is necessary because of the density and compression characteristic of poetry. More than fiction or drama, poetry is an art of condensation and implication; poems concentrate meaning and distill feeling.

Learning to read poetry well and to savor its pleasures involves learning to ask questions about how we experience poems, how we interpret them, and how we evaluate them. Such questions include the following:

1. What feelings does the poem evoke? What sensations, associations, and memories does it give rise to?
2. What ideas does the poem express, either directly or indirectly? What sense does it make? What do we understand it to say and suggest?
3. What view of the world does the poet present? Does it agree with your view? What do you think of the poet's view? What value does the poem hold for you as a work of art and as an influence on your way of understanding yourself and others?

Our discussion is divided into three parts: the experience of poetry, the interpretation of poetry, and the evaluation of poetry. In the experience section we will be concerned primarily with subjective responses, with personal reactions. We will reflect on how the poem may be related to our lives. In the

interpretation section our concern will be the intellectual processes that we en-
gage in as we develop an understanding of poetry. Here the focus will be ana-
lytical rather than impressionistic, rational rather than emotional. And in the
evaluation of poetry, we will be concerned with the ways we bring our sense
of who we are and what we believe into our consideration of any poem's sig-
nificance, and with how poems are evaluated aesthetically.

THE EXPERIENCE OF POETRY

We begin by considering the following poem, first from the standpoint of our
experience.

ROBERT HAYDEN
[1913–1980]

Those Winter Sundays

Sundays too my father got up early
and put his clothes on in the blueblack cold,
then with cracked hands that ached
from labor in the weekday weather made
banked fires blaze. No one ever thanked him.   5

I'd wake and hear the cold splintering, breaking.
When the rooms were warm, he'd call,
and slowly I would rise and dress,
fearing the chronic angers of that house,

Speaking indifferently to him,   10
who had driven out the cold
and polished my good shoes as well.
What did I know, what did I know
of love's austere and lonely offices?

Even from a single reading we see that the speaker of "Those Winter Sundays,"
now an adult, is remembering how his father used to get up on cold Sunday
mornings and light the fires that would warm the house for his sleeping fam-
ily. We sense that he regrets how unappreciative of his father he was as a child.
We may wonder what prompts these memories and feelings. Our initial read-
ing may also call up a memory much like the one described in Hayden's poem.
But even if our experience does not echo the speaker's or if our feelings differ
from his, we may respond to the description of waking up on a cold day in a

warm house. Such personal responses, whatever their precise nature, are important to our reading of poetry, for in arriving at a sense of a poem's meaning and value, we often begin with them.

Here is a sampling of one reader's responses to the poem: a set of notes that describe both memories and feelings. Notice how the responses, subjective and impressionistic as they are, nonetheless reveal the reader beginning to reflect on the poem's meaning and values.

> I remember how my father used to wake up at five A.M. to light the furnace so the house would be warm when the rest of the family got up. My strongest memories of this come from my early adolescence, perhaps because it was then that I began to assume this responsibility. I would never have thought to describe the cold as "blue-black" but I like how that makes me remember what the cold felt like at that merciless hour. I also remember the way my father would come and wake us up around 6:30 to get ready for school. By then the floor was warm and the radiators crackled with steam.
>
> Like the rest of my brothers and sisters, I took my father's early morning efforts for granted. We never thought of thanking him. Perhaps we should have. He always knew that we loved him. That wasn't a problem. But as I think back, I don't remember thanking him for much of anything. I guess we were all guilty of speaking indifferently to him, or of not speaking much at all.
>
> A couple of other things about the poem strike me. One is the shoes the father polished for his son. A nice touch, those shoes. I wonder when a boy begins to be responsible for polishing his own shoes. I can't remember when I started polishing mine—high school perhaps—but I do remember often polishing my father's as well—especially on Sundays when he would rush around to get ready for church. A more confusing item is the line about "fearing the chronic angers" of the house. How can a house be angry? Perhaps the writer is referring to the father's anger? I remember my own father becoming angry. He blew his top, as he used to say, pretty regularly, one time punching a hole in the dining room wall, another time ripping the phone off the kitchen wall. I wasn't the target of his anger often, but it was unsettling to see him lose his temper.
>
> The last couple of lines with the repeated question, "What did I know, what did I know," hit me the hardest. I hear regret in them, regret for lost opportunities, regret for understanding too late the motive behind the attentions of the speaker's father. Perhaps there is also regret for the distance that separated father and son. I know a little about that. But I also hear in these lines how love involves sacrifice and that such quiet expressions of love don't always or even often receive the recognition they deserve. For people whose fathers are still alive there is time perhaps to compensate. For me, it's too late.

THE INTERPRETATION OF POETRY

When we interpret a poem, we explain it to ourselves in order to understand it. We makes sense of it, in short. If one of our initial acts is to somehow appropriate the poem personally by relating it to our experience, another is to consider its meaning. When we interpret a poem, we concern ourselves less with how it affects us than with what it means or suggests. Interpretation relies on our intellectual comprehension and rational understanding rather than on our emotional apprehension and response.

The act of interpretation involves essentially four things: observing, connecting, inferring, and concluding. We observe details of description and action, of language and form. We look for connections among these details and begin to establish a sense of the poem's coherence (the way its details fit together in meaningful relationships). On the basis of these connections we make inferences or interpretive guesses about their significance. And finally, we come to a provisional conclusion about the poem's meaning based on our observations, connections, and inferences.

As we continue our discussion of "Those Winter Sundays," we will offer additional observations, inferences, and conclusions, pretty much in that order. This description of the interpretive process makes it seem as if we perform each of these analytical acts in succession. That's not the way it happens. Just as our personal responses and subjective impressions, our memories, sensations, and associations are stirred up *while* we read and *after,* so too all four aspects of interpretation occur simultaneously.

To see what Hayden's poem implies, let's give it a second look. We might notice, for example, that the first words, "Sundays too," indicate that the speaker's father performed his housewarming chores every day, including Sundays. We might notice also that the poem contrasts cold and warmth, with the cold dissipated as the warmth of the fires the father has started suffuses the house. And we might note further that the poem shifts from father to son, from "him" to "I." The first stanza, for example, describes the father's act, the second the boy's awakening to a warm house, while the third records a different kind of awakening—the speaker's realization of his earlier indifference and of his father's love. It is in this third and final stanza that we feel most strongly the contrast between the speaker's past and present, between the then and the now of the poem, between the love that the speaker neither noticed nor acknowledged and the love he later acknowledges and understands.

So far we have centered on the poem's speaker and its subject. (The *speaker* refers to the voice of the character we hear in the poem; the *subject* indicates what the poem is about.) Our first readings of a poem will usually focus on who is speaking about what, and why. In considering speaker and subject, we solidify our sense of what the poem implies, whether its implications concern, primarily, ideas or feelings. When the speaker notes that he feared "the chronic angers of that house," we may sense that he points toward something important. Presumably he feared his father's anger, which on occasion may have been directed at him. But by using the plural form of the word rather than the singular ("angers" rather than "anger") the speaker may be suggesting that there was discord between the father and other members of the family as well. Whatever the specific nature of his fear, the speaker intimates that his fear was the source of his own wariness and indifference toward his father.

The lines that convey the speaker's feeling most intensely, however, are those that end the poem:

> What did I know, what did I know
> of love's austere and lonely offices?

In these lines we sense the speaker's remorse and regret for not being aware of all his father did for him; we sense further that even though he didn't understand and feel the extent of his father's devotion, he certainly does later. Moreover, we sense the intensity of his feelings both in his repetition of the phrase "what did I know," and in the words that describe his father's actions: "love's austere and lonely offices." "Austere" suggests both the rigor and self-discipline of the father's acts and perhaps the stern severity with which he may have performed them. "Lonely" indicates that the father performed his early morning labors alone, without help from the other members of the family. It also suggests that the father was emotionally isolated from the speaker and perhaps from other members of the family.

But the word "offices" conveys other ideas as well. It implies both the duties the father fulfills and the corresponding authority he possesses. In addition, it suggests something done for another, as in the good offices of a friend. Beyond these related meanings, "offices" also refers to the daily prayers recited by clerics. Thus, the words "austere" and "offices" convey the speaker's understanding of his father's sacrifices for him. Moreover, the highly abstract language of the conclusion—so different from the concrete details of the preceding stanzas—may also indicate the speaker's inability to express affection directly (an inadequacy he intimates his father suffered from as well).

To read poetry well we need to slow down enough to observe details of language, form, and sound. By reading slowly and deliberately, we give ourselves a chance to form connections among the poem's details. Read the following poem twice, once straight through without stopping, then again with the interpolated commentary.

ROBERT FROST
[1874–1963]

Stopping by Woods on a Snowy Evening

> Whose woods these are I think I know.
> His house is in the village though;
> He will not see me stopping here
> To watch his woods fill up with snow.

My little horse must think it queer   5
To stop without a farmhouse near
Between the woods and frozen lake
The darkest evening of the year.

He gives his harness bells a shake
To ask if there is some mistake.   10
The only other sound's the sweep
Of easy wind and downy flake.

The woods are lovely, dark and deep,
But I have promises to keep,
And miles to go before I sleep,   15
And miles to go before I sleep.

Read the poem once more, this time along with the comments that follow
each stanza. Attend to the way you make sense of the poem during this read-
ing, particularly in light of the suggestions made in the commentary.

Whose woods these are I think I know.
His house is in the village though;
He will not see me stopping here
To watch his woods fill up with snow.

Comment   Frost's poem opens with a speaker who seems concerned momen-
tarily about who owns the woods. The speaker seems reassured that the owner
can't see him. We might wonder why the speaker should be concerned and
why he bothers to mention it. Does he feel that he is doing something wrong?
The poem doesn't say; instead it paints a picture of man, of woods and snow.
And it raises questions: Why does he stop? What attracts him? Again, the poem
doesn't provide explicit answers.

My little horse must think it queer
To stop without a farmhouse near
Between the woods and frozen lake
The darkest evening of the year.

Comment   In the first stanza the speaker describes the scene and his own ac-
tion. In this stanza, although he further describes this scene and action, he be-
gins by mentioning that his horse is unaccustomed to stopping without a
reason. The first line says that the horse "must" think it queer to stop this way,
indicating that the horse can't really look at the man's action any other way.
Accustomed to stops for food and rest, the horse couldn't possibly understand
the man's impractical reason for stopping. And though the horse is said to
"think," we realize that the horse's thoughts are really the speaker's—that the

speaker projects his thoughts onto the horse because a part of him sees the impracticality of his action.

> He gives his harness bells a shake
> To ask if there is some mistake.
> The only other sound's the sweep
> Of easy wind and downy flake.

Comment   The third stanza continues the emphasis of the second. The speaker interprets the horse's shaking of his harness bells as a signal to move on, as a sign that stopping there serves no useful purpose. We might notice that the poet here emphasizes the stillness of the night, the isolation and privacy of the moment, which is broken only by the sound of the horse's bell. Tension builds in the mind of the speaker: even though he seems to enjoy the stillness of the night and takes pleasure in the "easy wind" and the "downy flake," he also experiences some doubt about what he is doing.

Stanza four:

> The woods are lovely, dark and deep,
> But I have promises to keep,
> And miles to go before I sleep,
> And miles to go before I sleep.

Comment   The opening line summarizes the implications of the details in the preceding stanzas. It's as if the speaker here answers the question why he stopped by the woods. He stopped because he was attracted by their dark beauty. He nevertheless feels a pressure to move on, to return to his responsibilities and obligations.

The final stanza is solemn and serious: Frost slows its pace by including pauses (indicated by punctuation) and by repeating the third line, "And miles to go before I sleep," which he uses to end the poem. In repeating this line, the poet lifts it beyond its literal meaning, inviting us to read "sleep" as the final sleep of death. Once we make this interpretive leap, we can consider "Miles to go" as perhaps the time the speaker has left to live, and "promises" as the obligations and responsibilities he must fulfill before he dies. His stopping to look at the falling snow can be seen as a temporary reprieve from such responsibilities; it might also be seen as a desire to escape them. The essential point, however, seems to be the tug of war going on in the speaker's mind between the two possibilities—stopping to contemplate the beauty of nature, and moving on to return to the active world of work and responsibility.

We have been reading and interpreting the poem one stanza at a time to suggest the way interpretation builds cumulatively as we move through a poem. The process, however, is not simply linear or sequential. For although we interpret later details in light of earlier ones, we also make sense of earlier ones after having interpreted later ones. The act of interpretation, like the experience of reading generally, is recursive. We move back and forth through a text, remembering what we read and anticipating what is to come. The process of interpretation does not end with reading the poem; it continues as we reflect on it afterward. New ideas may come to us, particularly after we have discussed the work with a teacher and classmates or after we have read other works that we can relate to it.

One final point about the interpretation of poetry (and of literature generally): interpretation never really ends. When we interpret a work, we should be concerned less with finding the single right way of understanding it than with arriving at a satisfying explanation, one that makes sense to us, and one whose logic and good sense will appeal to others. Some interpretations, nonetheless, will be more satisfying than others. They will be more convincing, largely because they take into account more of the poem's details, more of its language and form and action. Other interpretations, while perhaps not as convincing, may be valuable for the intellectual stimulation they provide and for the pleasure they afford. Because we invariably bring different experiences of life and of literature to our reading of poems, we will see different things in them and will make different kinds of sense of them. The varying interpretations we make of poems depend largely on what matters to us, what *we* consider vital. It is to this subject, values in poetry, that we turn now.

THE EVALUATION OF POETRY

When we evaluate a poem, we do two different kinds of things. First, we assess its literary quality and make a judgment about how good it is and how successfully it realizes its poetic intentions. We examine its language and structure, for example, and consider how well they work together to embody meaning and convey feeling. Second, we consider how much significance the poem has for us personally, and what significance it may have for other readers—both those who are like us and those who differ in age, race, gender, culture, and ideology. We also consider the significance the poem may have had for the poet, both its general value as part of a body of writing and its particular expression of feelings, attitudes, ideas, and values—its perspective on experience.

Our consideration of a poem's value is a measure of its involvement with our lives, with our way of thinking and being in the actual world. Some poems "speak" to us more than others; some poems mean more to us on some days than on others; and some poems mean both more and less to us at different periods of our lives. In evaluating poems, we explore the how and why of such differences. In doing so, we turn inevitably to a consideration of the various cultural assumptions, moral attitudes, and political convictions that animate particular poems. We consider the perspective from which they were written. Our consideration may involve an investigation into the circumstances of its composition, the external facts and internal experiences of the poet's life, the attitudes and beliefs he or she may have expressed in letters or other comments, the audience and occasion for which a particular poem was written, its publication history and reception by readers past and present.

From even this brief list, we can see how complex literary evaluation can be. Complicating matters even further is how we encounter the poems we evaluate. We come to the poems in this book after many preliminary acts of evaluation by others. The poets who wrote them decided they were valuable enough to preserve. The publishers who put them in print valued them, perhaps more for their potential profit than for the feelings, attitudes, or ideas they express. The editor/author of this book values them, some for how they affect him as a reader, others for their use as illustrations of particular aspects or elements of poetry. Other readers, including the teachers who use them in their courses, also value these poems. But not all readers and teachers value them the same way, and not all for the same reasons.

Does this mean then that we cannot make definitive, final, and absolute evaluations of poems? Probably, since change and variety are the hallmarks of literary evaluation. Our valuing of any poem is therefore subject to change (though not necessarily a radical reevaluation) because the way we see and understand any poem changes as we change. We will find merit in poems whose meaning we understand and whose values are like our own. We will come to value poems whose content we have lived. And we will appreciate poems in relation to other literary works that have had an impact on our lives and our thinking. To put this another way: we can't *not* evaluate the poems we read because we inevitably and automatically measure them against other works we already value. Our evaluation of any poem, moreover, depends not only upon how we understand it (that is, upon how we interpret its meaning), but also upon how we see its relation to our lives at the time we read it.

With these considerations in mind, we can suggest a few general principles upon which to ground preliminary evaluations. First is the realization that an evaluation is essentially a judgment, a set of opinions about a literary work based on a thoughtful consideration of it. We may agree or disagree with the speaker's response to the woods in Frost's "Stopping by Woods." We may confirm or deny the models of experience illustrated in Hayden's "Those Winter Sundays." Invariably, however, we measure the sentiments of a poem against our own. We may or may not appreciate responsibility as much as Frost's speaker seems to. We may or may not cherish our memories of our fathers as Hayden's speaker seems to. And depending on these and other factors, we may arrive at very different assessments of either poem's worth for us as individual readers.

It is important to realize that in evaluating any poem, we appraise it according to our own special combination of cultural, moral, and aesthetic values which derive from our place in family and society. These values are affected by race, gender, and language. Our moral values reflect our ethical norms—what we consider good and evil, right and wrong. They are influenced by our religious beliefs and perhaps by our political convictions as well. Our aesthetic values concern what we see as beautiful or ugly, well or poorly made.

Our response to any poem's outlook (and our opinion of it) is closely related to our interpretation of it. Evaluation depends upon interpretation, for our judgment of a poem depends on how we understand it. That evaluation may be linked to our initial experience of the work, with first impressions conditioning a later response. This is not always the case, fortunately. In fact, one of the benefits of interpretation is its ability to free us from enslavement to our initial responses by enabling us to move beyond them. By bringing our intellect to bear on a work, we may discover meanings in it that were not apparent on initial reading. And while making such interpretive discoveries we may come to feel differently about a poem and derive considerable pleasure from it.

Of the kinds of evaluations we make in reading poetry, those about a poem's aesthetic merit are hardest to discuss. Aesthetic responses are difficult to describe because they involve subjective reactions about what is beautiful or not, what is pleasing or not, what is well-made or not. Our occasional unwillingness to move beyond our initial impressions, our tendency to settle into comfortable judgments and well-worn opinions, further complicates our responses. We may think that as long as we know what we like, that's enough. It's not enough if we are truly interested in developing our capacity for aesthetic appreciation.

Is Frost's "Stopping by Woods" or Hayden's "Those Winter Sundays" a beautiful poem? Does either seem to be a good example of its type—in this case, the lyric poem? What criteria will you use to make a judgment? To answer these questions, you will need to know more about poetry than you are likely to at this point. It would be helpful to have read and absorbed much of the material in Chapter Three, Elements of Poetry. Measuring a poem's achievement requires some knowledge of how poets exploit diction, imagery, syntax, and sound; how they establish form and control tone; how they work within or against a literary tradition.

Admittedly, without a good deal of knowledge about poetry and without considerable practice in reading it, judgments about the aesthetic worth of particular poems need to be made with caution. But we cannot really avoid judging the poems we read any more than we avoid judging the people we meet; the process is natural. What we should strive for in evaluating poems is to understand the merits of different kinds of poems, to judge them fairly against what they were meant to be rather than something we think they should be. Our goal should be, ultimately, to develop a sense of literary tact, the kind of informed and balanced judgment that comes with experience in reading and living, coupled with continued thoughtful reflection on both.

Your evaluation of poetry may very well change as you change. What you consider important criteria now (narrative action, perhaps, or rhymed stanzas) may not be important after you have read many more poems. Poems you dismiss now as irrelevant or uninteresting may mean much more to you if your life changes so that the concerns of those poems become your concerns. As with literary interpretation, so with literary evaluation; it does not remain constant. In the same way that our understanding of literature changes, and in the same way we acknowledge more than one absolute, definitive, and correct interpretation of literary works, so too do we recognize the many ways they may be evaluated.

We can put these ideas to the test by reading Adrienne Rich's "Aunt Jennifer's Tigers" from the standpoint of evaluation. The questions that follow the poem invite you to consider your experience and interpretation, as well as your evaluation of it. To get started, keep these questions in mind during your first couple of readings: What do each of the characters stand for? How would you describe the relationship between the uncle and his wife, Jennifer? Between the men and the tigers? Between Aunt Jennifer and the speaker? And between Aunt Jennifer and the tigers?

ADRIENNE RICH
[b. 1929]

Aunt Jennifer's Tigers

Aunt Jennifer's tigers prance across a screen,
Bright topaz denizens of a world of green.
They do not fear the men beneath the tree;
They pace in sleek chivalric certainty.

Aunt Jennifer's fingers fluttering through her wool   5
Find even the ivory needle hard to pull.
The massive weight of Uncle's wedding band
Sits heavily upon Aunt Jennifer's hand.

When Aunt is dead, her terrified hands will lie
Still ringed with ordeals she was mastered by.   10
The tigers in the panel that she made
Will go on prancing, proud and unafraid.

QUESTIONS FOR REFLECTION

Experience

1. What feelings surfaced as you read this poem?
2. What words, phrases, and details triggered your strongest responses?
3. What associations about your own aunts and uncles do you bring to the poem?
4. Can the situation described here apply to your parents rather than to your aunts and uncles? To both? To neither? Why or why not?

Interpretation

5. What words, phrases, lines, and details may have confused or baffled you? Why?
6. What observations can you make about the poem's details?
7. What words and phrases recur? How? Where? Why?
8. What connections can you establish among the details of action and language?
9. What inferences can you draw from these connections?
10. How, for now at least, do you understand "Aunt Jennifer's Tigers"?

Evaluation

11. What values are associated with Aunt Jennifer? With her husband, the speaker's uncle? With the tigers? With the men who hunt them?
12. What is the relationship among the values associated with these figures?
13. What is the speaker's attitude toward her aunt, her uncle, and the tigers? To what extent do you think the speaker's attitudes are those of the author? On what do you base your view?
14. How do your own ideas and standards influence your experience, interpretation, and evaluation of the poem? Describe how the poem affects you as a reader. Do you like it? Comment on the poem's aesthetic accomplishment.
15. Return to this poem later in the term, after you have had the opportunity to read many more poems, or after you have discussed the poem with teacher(s) and classmates. (Perhaps you can learn something about the life and work of the poet by reading her own poetry and prose or by reading critical studies of her work—or both.) Discuss your initial evaluation and your later evaluation, how they may have changed, and why.

THE ACT OF READING POETRY

Thus far we have read two poems, each followed by comments and questions emphasizing the experience and interpretation of poetry. Next we illustrate active reading—what we actually do when we read and reread a poem. Some of the marginal annotations record observations, others raise questions; all are abbreviated notes that reflect a reading that embodies both thought and feeling. In making notes about a poem in this manner, we become actively engaged in seeing and thinking. Our observations lead us to notice details of language and to think about the poem's implications. As we formulate answers to our questions, however provisional, we find ourselves exploring both the poem's meaning and its value.

The annotations for Theodore Roethke's "My Papa's Waltz" are not concerned with technical matters such as form, rhyme scheme, and meter, or with what such technical features contribute to meaning and feeling. Another set of annotations could be made highlighting these features. In fact, some technical consideration of Roethke's poem appears on page 28. For now, however, we focus on the poem's situation and subject. Here is the poem without annotation:

THEODORE ROETHKE
[1908–1963]

My Papa's Waltz

The whiskey on your breath
Could make a small boy dizzy;

But I hung on like death:
Such waltzing was not easy.

We romped until the pans   5
Slid from the kitchen shelf;
My mother's countenance
Could not unfrown itself.

The hand that held my wrist
Was battered on one knuckle;   10
At every step you missed
My right ear scraped a buckle.

You beat time on my head
With a palm caked hard by dirt,
Then waltzed me off to bed   15
Still clinging to your shirt.

And here it is again with annotations:

My Papa's Waltz

An affectionate term for
his father—papa

The whiskey on your breath
Could make a small boy dizzy;
But I hung on like death:
Such waltzing was not easy.

What kind of waltzing
and who instigated it?

We romped until the pans
Slid from the kitchen shelf;
My mother's countenance
Could not unfrown itself.

"Waltzed" or "danced"
for "romped"?

"Face" or "expression"
for "countenance"?
The mother—angry?
disapproving? mother
as audience—as
non-participant—

The hand that held my wrist
Was battered on one knuckle;
At every step you missed
My right ear scraped a buckle.

The father misses steps but
he can dance—not drunk.

You beat time on my head
With a palm caked hard by dirt,
Then waltzed me off to bed
Still clinging to your shirt.

Clinging—how?
Fearfully? Joyfully? Both?

The boy's father, a manual laborer, is clearly not literally "waltzing" with his
son. His "dance" is more a romp through the house with a stop in the kitchen
and another at the boy's bedroom, where presumably he is unceremoniously

dumped into bed. The mother watches, her frown indicating disapproval, per-
haps even anger.

The dance is somewhat rough because the boy's father has been drinking. It
is also rough because he scrapes the child's ear on his belt buckle as he keeps a
steady rhythm by beating time on the boy's head. The boy is described as
"clinging" to his father's shirt, but the language doesn't clarify whether that
clinging is purely out of terror—or whether it is part of the game father and
son enjoy together. Presumably this bedtime romp is a regular ritual rather than
a one-time occurrence.

The tone of the poem seems nostalgic, though not sentimentally so. The
boy, now a man, remembers his father as "papa," clearly an affectionate term.
The high-spirited bouncing rhythm of the poem seems to counter any indica-
tion that the father's drinking or the son's fear are its central concerns.

CHAPTER TWO

Types of Poetry

Poetry can be classified as narrative or lyric. Narrative poems stress action, and lyrics song. Each of these types has numerous subdivisions: narrative poetry includes the epic, romance, and ballad; lyric poetry includes the elegy and epigraph, sonnet and sestina, aubade and villanelle. Moreover, each major type of poetry adheres to different conventions. *Narrative poems,* for example, tell stories and describe actions; *lyric poems* combine speech and song to express feeling in varying degrees of verbal music.

NARRATIVE POETRY

The grandest of narratives is the epic. *Epics* are long narrative poems that record the adventures of a hero whose exploits are important to the history of a nation. Typically they chronicle the origins of a civilization and embody its central beliefs and values. Epics tend to be larger than life as they recount valorous deeds enacted in vast landscapes. The epic style is as grand as the action; the conventions require that the epic be formal, complex, and serious—suitable to its important subjects.

Among the more famous epics in Western literature are Homer's *Iliad* (about the Greek and Trojan war), Virgil's *Aeneid* (about the founding of Rome), Dante's *Divine Comedy* (a journey through hell, purgatory, and heaven), and Milton's *Paradise Lost* (about the revolt of the angels, and man's creation and fall). For a hint of the epic's subjects and language listen to these opening lines from *The Aeneid* and from *Paradise Lost*. First Virgil:

> I sing of warfare and a man at war.
> From the sea-coast of Troy in early days
> He came to Italy by destiny,
> To our Lavinian western shore,

A fugitive, this captain, buffeted   5
Cruelly on land as on the sea
By blows from powers of the air—behind them
Baleful Juno in her sleepless rage.
And cruel losses were his lot in war,
Till he could found a city and bring home   10
His gods to Latium, land of the Latin race,
The Alban lords, and the high walls of Rome.
Tell me the causes now, O Muse, how galled
In her divine pride, and how sore at heart
From her old wound, the queen of gods compelled him—   15
A man apart, devoted to his mission—
To undergo so many perilous days
And enter on so many trials.

And now Milton:

Of man's first disobedience, and the fruit
Of that forbidden tree whose mortal taste
Brought death into the world, and all our woe,
With loss of Eden, till one greater Man
Restore us, and regain the blissful seat,   5
Sing, Heavenly Muse, that, on the secret top
Of Oreb, or of Sinai, didst inspire
That shepherd who first taught the chosen seed
In the beginning how the Heavens and Earth
Rose out of Chaos: or, if Sion hill   10
Delight thee more, and Siloa's brook that flowed
Fast by the oracle of God, I thence
Invoke thy aid to my adventurous song,
That with no middle flight intends to soar
Above th' Aonian mount, while it pursues   15
Things unattempted yet in prose or rhyme.
And chiefly thou, O Spirit, that dost prefer
Before all temples th' upright heart and pure,
Instruct me, for thou know'st; thou from the first
Wast present, and, with mighty wings outspread,   20
Dovelike sat'st brooding on the vast abyss,
And mad'st it pregnant: what in me is dark
Illumine; what is low, raise and support;
That, to the height of this great argument,
I may assert Eternal Providence,   25
And justify the ways of God to men.

Far less ambitious than epics, *ballads* are perhaps the most popular form of narrative poetry. Originally ballads were meant to be sung or recited. Folk ballads (or popular ballads as they are sometimes called) were passed on orally, only to be written down much later. This accounts for the different versions of many ballads such as "Barbara Allan" and "Edward, Edward" (pages 210 and 212).

In addition to folk ballads of unknown (and sometimes multiple) authorship, there are also literary ballads (of known authorship). One example is "La Belle Dame sans Merci" by John Keats (page 243). Literary ballads imitate the folk ballad by adhering to its basic conventions—repeated lines and stanzas in a refrain, swift action with occasional surprise endings, extraordinary events evoked in direct, simple language, and scant characterization—but are more polished stylistically and more self-conscious in their use of poetic techniques.

Another type of narrative poem is the *romance,* in which adventure is a central feature. The plots of romances tend to be complex, with surprising and even magical actions common. The chief characters are human beings, though they often confront monsters, dragons, and disguised animals in a world that does not adhere consistently to the laws of nature as we know them. Romance in short deals with the marvelous—with, for example, St. George slaying a dragon in a magical forest. Popular during the Middle Ages and Renaissance, the romance as a poetic genre has fallen from favor. Nevertheless, some of its chief characteristics have found expression in popular fictional types such as the western, the adventure story, and the romantic love story.

LYRIC POETRY

Although narrative poems, especially literary ballads, combine story with song, action with emotion, story and action predominate. In lyric poetry, however, story is subordinated to song, and action to emotion. We can define *lyrics* as subjective poems, often brief, that express the feelings and thoughts of a single speaker (who may or may not represent the poet). The lyric is more a poetic manner than a form; it is more variable and less subject to strict convention than narrative poetry.

Lyric poetry is typically characterized by brevity, melody, and emotional intensity. The music of lyrics makes them memorable, and their brevity contributes to the intensity of their emotional expression. Originally designed to be sung to a musical accompaniment (the word *lyric* derives from the Greek *lyre*), lyrics have been the predominant type of poetry in the West for several hundred years.

Forms of lyric poetry range from the *epigram,* a brief witty poem that is often satirical, such as Alexander Pope's "On the Collar of a Dog," to the *elegy,* a lament for the dead, such as Seamus Heaney's "Mid-Term Break" (page 313). Lyric forms also include the *ode,* a long stately poem in stanzas of varied length, meter, and form; and the *aubade,* a love lyric expressing complaint that dawn means the speaker must part from his lover. An example of the ode is John Keats's "Ode to a Nightingale" (page 245); the aubade is represented by John Donne's "The Sun Rising" (page 56).

The tones, moods, and voices of lyric poems are as variable and as complexly intertwined as human feeling, thought, and imagination allow. Generally considered the most compressed poetic type, the lyric poem typically expresses much in little. The *sonnet,* for example, condenses into fourteen lines an expression of emotion or an articulation of idea according to one of two basic patterns: the *Italian* (or *Petrarchan*) and the *English* (or *Shakespearean*). An Italian sonnet is composed of an eight-line octave and a six-line sestet. A Shakespearean sonnet is composed of three four-line quatrains and a concluding two-line couplet (see pages 80–81). The thought and feeling expressed in each sonnet form typically follow the divisions suggested by their structural patterns. Thus an Italian sonnet may state a problem in the octave and present a solution in its sestet. A Shakespearean sonnet will usually introduce a subject in the first quatrain, expand and develop it in the second and third quatrains, and conclude something about it in its final couplet.

Although sonnets reached the height of their popularity during the Renaissance, later writers have continued to be attracted to the form. Some sonnet writers, in fact, like Gerard Manley Hopkins, William Butler Yeats, Robert Frost, and E. E. Cummings have combined the two basic patterns to suit their poetic needs. Occasionally these and other poets have modified the form itself. Robert Frost's "Acquainted with the Night" (page 184), for example, is composed of four tercets and a couplet rather than the familiar three quatrains and a couplet. Frost, moreover, has been known to write fifteen-line sonnets as well.

Less important historically than the sonnet but no less intricate and musical are two other lyric forms, sestina and villanelle, both deriving from French poetry. The *sestina* consists of six stanzas of six lines each followed by a three-line conclusion or *envoy*. The sestina requires a strict pattern of repetition of six key words that end the lines of the first stanza. Elizabeth Bishop's "Sestina" (page 293) is an example.

The *villanelle,* which also relies heavily on repetition, is composed of five three-line tercets and a final four-line quatrain. Its singular feature is the way its first and third lines repeat throughout the poem. The entire first line reappears as the final line of the second and fourth tercets, and the third line of the poem reappears as the third line of the third and fifth tercets and as the concluding line of the poem. Examples include Theodore Roethke's "The Waking" (page 87) and Dylan Thomas's "Do Not Go Gentle into That Good Night" (page 297).

CHAPTER THREE

Elements of Poetry

We can learn to interpret and appreciate poems by understanding their basic elements. The elements of a poem include a *speaker* whose voice we hear in it; its *diction* or selection of words; its *syntax* or the order of those words; its *imagery* or details of sight, sound, taste, smell, and touch; its *figures of speech* or nonliteral ways of expressing one thing in terms of another, such as symbol and metaphor; its *sound effects,* especially rhyme, assonance, and alliteration; its *rhythm and meter* or the pattern of accents we hear in the poem's words, phrases, lines, and sentences; and its *structure* or formal pattern of organization. All the elements of a poem work together harmoniously to convey feeling and embody meaning.

VOICE: SPEAKER AND TONE

When we read or hear a poem, we hear a speaker's voice. It is this voice that conveys the poem's *tone,* its implied attitude toward its subject. Tone is an abstraction we make from the details of a poem's language: the use of meter and rhyme (or lack of them); the inclusion of certain kinds of details and exclusion of other kinds; particular choices of words and sentence pattern, of imagery and figurative language. When we listen to a poem's language and hear the voice of its speaker, we catch its tone and feeling and ultimately its meaning.

In listening to the speaker's voice, for example, in Roethke's "My Papa's Waltz" (in Chapter One), we hear a tone different from that of the speaker in Hayden's "Those Winter Sundays" (Chapter One). Roethke's speaker remembers his father fondly and addresses him ("your breath," "you missed"). He remembers and celebrates their spirited cavorting as a "romp" and a "waltz" and includes such comic details as the mother frowning while pans slide off the kitchen shelves and the father keeping time by steadily patting the boy's head. The poem's complex tone comes from its contrasted details: the boy's hanging on "like death," his ear scraping his father's belt buckle, and his "clinging" to his father's shirt.

The speaker of Hayden's "Those Winter Sundays" admires his father and perhaps feared him as a child. His attitude is suggested by the details he remembers and by the way he meticulously describes his father's attentive labors. But his tone conveys more than admiration; it conveys also a sense of regret, disappointment, and perhaps anguish at having been indifferent toward him as a child. The tone of Hayden's poem has none of the ease and playfulness of Roethke's; it is serious in its portrayal of the speaker's father and solemn in its account of the speaker's subsequent feelings.

The range of tones we find in poems is as various and complex as the range of voices and attitudes we discern in everyday experience. One of the more important and persistent is the *ironic tone* of voice. Irony is a way of speaking that implies a discrepancy or opposition between what is said and what is meant. The following poem by Stephen Crane illustrates this ironic tone of voice.

STEPHEN   CRANE
[*1871–1900*]

War Is Kind

Do not weep, maiden, for war is kind.
Because your lover threw wild hands toward the sky
And the affrighted steed ran on alone,
Do not weep.
War is kind.   5

      Hoarse, booming drums of the regiment,
      Little souls who thirst for fight,
      These men were born to drill and die.
      The unexplained glory flies above them,
      Great is the battle god, great, and his kingdom   10
      A field where a thousand corpses lie.

Do not weep, babe, for war is kind.
Because your father tumbled in the yellow trenches,
Raged at his breast, gulped and died,
Do not weep.   15
War is kind.

      Swift blazing flag of the regiment,
      Eagle with crest of red and gold,
      These men were born to drill and die.

Point for them the virtue of slaughter,   20
Make plain to them the excellence of killing
And a field where a thousand corpses lie.

Mother whose heart hung humble as a button
On the bright splendid shroud of your son,
Do not weep.   25
War is kind.

How do we know that the speaker's attitude towards war is not what his words indicate, that his words are ironic? We know because the details of death in battle are antithetical to the consoling refrain of stanzas one, three, and five: "Do not weep. War is kind." Moreover the details of stanzas two and four also work toward the same ironic end, but in a different way. Instead of the ironic consoling voice of stanzas one, three, and five (which of course offers no real consolation given the brutality described), stanzas two and four sound more supportive of military glory: Crane uses a march-like rhythm along with words connoting military glory in a context that makes them sound hollow and false. The view that war is glorious and that death in battle is honorable is countered with images of slaughter. Compare Crane's poem to another treating the glory of dying for one's country ironically, Wilfred Owen's "Dulce et Decorum Est" (page 285).

Unlike the poems we have been considering in which the speaker is alone, the next poem we will examine contains a speaker who is addressing someone present. A poem in which a speaker addresses a silent listener is called a *dramatic monologue*. As we listen to the speaker's monologue, we usually gain a vivid sense of his character and personality. The following poem, Robert Browning's "My Last Duchess," is a striking example of this form.

ROBERT BROWNING
[*1812–1889*]

My Last Duchess

FERRARA

That's my last Duchess painted on the wall,
Looking as if she were alive. I call
That piece a wonder, now; Frà Pandolf's hands
Worked busily a day, and there she stands.
Will 't please you sit and look at her? I said   5
"Frà Pandolf" by design, for never read
Strangers like you that pictured countenance,
The depth and passion of its earnest glance,

But to myself they turned (since none puts by
The curtain I have drawn for you, but I) 10
And seemed as they would ask me, if they durst,
How such a glance came there; so, not the first
Are you to turn and ask thus. Sir, 'twas not
Her husband's presence only, called that spot
Of joy into the Duchess' cheek; perhaps 15
Frá Pandolf chanced to say, "Her mantle laps
Over my lady's wrist too much," or "Paint
Must never hope to reproduce the faint
Half-flush that dies along her throat." Such stuff
Was courtesy, she thought, and cause enough 20
For calling up that spot of joy. She had
A heart—how shall I say?—too soon made glad,
Too easily impressed; she liked whate'er
She looked on, and her looks went everywhere.
Sir, 'twas all one! My favor at her breast, 25
The dropping of the daylight in the West,
The bough of cherries some officious fool
Broke in the orchard for her, the white mule
She rode with round the terrace—all and each
Would draw from her alike the approving speech, 30
Or blush, at least. She thanked men,—good! but thanked
Somehow—I know not how—as if she ranked
My gift of a nine-hundred-years-old name
With anybody's gift. Who'd stoop to blame
This sort of trifling? Even had you skill 35
In speech—which I have not—to make your will
Quite clear to such an one, and say "Just this
Or that in you disgusts me; here you miss,
Or there exceed the mark"—and if she let
Herself be lessoned so, nor plainly set 40
Her wits to yours, forsooth, and made excuse—
E'en then would be some stooping; and I choose
Never to stoop. Oh sir, she smiled, no doubt,
Whene'er I passed her; but who passed without
Much the same smile? This grew; I gave commands; 45
Then all smiles stopped together. There she stands
As if alive. Will 't please you rise? We'll meet
The company below, then. I repeat,
The Count your master's known munificence
Is ample warrant that no just pretense 50
Of mine for dowry will be disallowed;
Though his fair daughter's self, as I avowed
At starting, is my object. Nay, we'll go
Together down, sir. Notice Neptune, though,
Taming a sea-horse, thought a rarity, 55
Which Claus of Innsbruck cast in bronze for me!

The situation of the poem is this: the Duke of Ferrara, a city-state in Renaissance Italy, is addressing an ambassador who represents a count, the father of a marriageable aristocratic daughter. Although we hear only the duke's voice, we are aware of the ambassador's presence. We probably wonder how the ambassador reacts to what the duke tells him—especially to what he says in lines 45–46. But while the poet hints at the ambassador's actions (lines 12–13; 47–48, for instance) he doesn't reveal his thoughts. Instead he centers our attention on the duke, whose manner, language, gestures, and concerns all reveal the kind of man he is and how he conducted himself in his relations with his last duchess.

The duke reveals himself as a monumental egotist—proud, shrewd, arrogant, and murderous. He shows himself to be a man who will not allow his will to be thwarted or his honor ignored. Intolerant of his former duchess's joy in things other than those he provided, and unwilling to "stoop" to telling her how her behavior insulted him, the duke has had her killed: "I gave commands," he says. "Then all smiles stopped together."

But what has the duchess done to deserve her fate? She expressed joy in compliments given her; she took pleasure in simple things—riding her white mule, watching the sun set, accepting a gift of fruit. Her crime in the duke's eyes was in not recognizing the value of his aristocratic heritage: his name, rank, and pride did not mean enough to her.

Part of our shock in realizing what the duke has done comes from his certainty that he has behaved properly. What else could I do, he seems to say. And part derives perhaps also from the matter-of-fact manner in which the duke turns the conversation from his last duchess to the business at hand, the negotiations about the impending marriage and the dowry. But revealing as these things are, an even stronger index of the duke's egoistic pride is the way he refers to his last duchess as an object, as a possession that has been appropriately added to his prized collection. As a portrait on the wall, the duchess is fully and finally under the duke's control. (He even keeps her portrait behind a curtain so no one can see her without his authority.) The duke's pride in his wife's portrait is equal to his pride in his prized statue of Neptune taming a sea horse.

A few poems notable for their speakers and tones of voice follow. For each identify the speaker and situation. Describe the tone(s) of voice you hear, and consider what the speaker's tone contributes to the ideas and feelings that the poems convey.

MURIEL STUART
[*b. 1889–?*]

In the Orchard

'I thought you loved me.' 'No, it was only fun.'
'When we stood there, closer than all?' 'Well, the harvest moon
Was shining and queer in your hair, and it turned my head.'
'That made you?' 'Yes.' 'Just the moon and the light it made
Under the tree?' 'Well, your mouth, too.' 'Yes, my mouth?'   5

'And the quiet there that sang like the drum in the booth.
You shouldn't have danced like that.' 'Like what?' 'So close,
With your head turned up, and the flower in your hair, a rose
That smelt all warm.' 'I loved you. I thought you knew
I wouldn't have danced like that with any but you.'   10
'I didn't know. I thought you knew it was fun.'
'I thought it was love you meant.' 'Well, it's done.' 'Yes, it's done.
I've seen boys stone a blackbird, and watched them drown
A kitten . . . it clawed at the reeds, and they pushed it down
Into the pool while it screamed. Is that fun, too?'   15
'Well, boys are like that . . . Your brothers . . .' 'Yes, I know.
But you, so lovely and strong! Not you! Not you!'
'They don't understand it's cruel. It's only a game.'
'And are girls fun, too?' 'No, still in a way it's the same.
It's queer and lovely to have a girl . . .' 'Go on.'   20
'It makes you mad for a bit to feel she's your own,
And you laugh and kiss her, and maybe you give her a ring,
But it's only in fun.' 'But I gave you everything.'
'Well, you shouldn't have done it. You know what a fellow thinks
When a girl does that.' 'Yes, he talks of her over his drinks   25
And calls her a—' 'Stop that now. I thought you knew.'
'But it wasn't with anyone else. It was only you.'
'How did I know? I thought you wanted it too.
I thought you were like the rest. Well, what's to be done?'
'To be done?' 'Is it all right?' 'Yes.' 'Sure?' 'Yes, but why?'   30
'I don't know. I thought you were going to cry.
You said you had something to tell me.' 'Yes, I know.
It wasn't anything really . . . I think I'll go.'
'Yes, it's late. There's thunder about, a drop of rain
Fell on my hand in the dark. I'll see you again   35
At the dance next week. You're sure that everything's right?'
'Yes,' 'Well, I'll be going.' 'Kiss me . . .' 'Good night.' . . . 'Good night.'

QUESTIONS FOR REFLECTION

1. What differences exist in the dialogue of the two speakers? How do those differ-
   ences characterize the tone of each speaker's voice?
2. What do the questions, ellipses, and repeated words contribute to the poem's tone?

G E R A R D   M A N L E Y   H O P K I N S

[1844–1889]

Thou art indeed just, Lord

*Justus quidem tu es, Domine, si disputem tecum: verumtamen
justa loquar ad te: Quare via impiorum prosperatur?*[20]

Thou art indeed just, Lord, if I contend
With thee; but, sir, so what I plead is just.
Why do sinners' ways prosper? and why must
Disappointment all I endeavour end?
Wert thou my enemy, O thou my friend,   5
How wouldst thou worse, I wonder, than thou dost
Defeat, thwart me? Oh, the sots and thralls of lust
Do in spare hours more thrive than I that spend,

Sir, life upon thy cause. See, banks and brakes
Now, leavèd how thick! lacèd they are again   10
With fretty chervil, look, and fresh wind shakes

Them; birds build—but not I build; no, but strain,
Time's eunuch, and not breed one work that wakes.
Mine, O thou lord of life, send my roots rain.

QUESTIONS FOR REFLECTION

1. How do the words the speaker uses to address God help establish the tone of the first four lines? What is his attitude toward God here?
2. Lines 5–7 might be paraphrased according to the familiar saying: "with friends like you, who needs enemies." What tone of voice do you hear in those lines? In lines 9–13? In the final line?

ANONYMOUS

Western Wind

Western wind, when will thou blow,
The small rain down can rain?
Christ, if my love were in my arms
And I in my bed again!

QUESTION FOR REFLECTION

What tone bursts through the final couplet? What feeling does the speaker convey? How does the tone of the following alteration compare with the poem's final two lines as written?

Oh God I wish I were in bed
With my lover again.

"*Thou art indeed just, Lord*" **Justus quidem tu es, Domine, si disputem tecum: verumtamen justa loquar ad te: Quare via impiorum prosperatur?** *the first three lines of the poem (up to* prosper) *translate the Latin epigraph.*

HENRY REED

[b. 1914]

Naming of Parts

Today we have naming of parts. Yesterday,
We had daily cleaning. And tomorrow morning,
We shall have what to do after firing. But today,
Today we have naming of parts. Japonica
Glistens like coral in all of the neighboring gardens,   5
        And today we have naming of parts.

This is the lower sling swivel. And this
Is the upper sling swivel, whose use you will see,
When you are given your slings. And this is the piling swivel,
Which in your case you have not got. The branches   10
Hold in the gardens their silent, eloquent gestures,
        Which in our case we have not got.

This is the safety-catch, which is always released
With an easy flick of the thumb. And please do not let me
See anyone using his finger. You can do it quite easy   15
If you have any strength in your thumb. The blossoms
Are fragile and motionless, never letting anyone see
        Any of them using their finger.

And this you can see is the bolt. The purpose of this
Is to open the breech, as you see. We can slide it   20
Rapidly backwards and forwards: we call this
Easing the spring. And rapidly backwards and forwards
The early bees are assaulting and fumbling the flowers:
        They call it easing the Spring.

They call it easing the Spring: it is perfectly easy   25
If you have any strength in your thumb: like the bolt,
And the breech, and the cocking-piece, and the point of balance,
Which in our case we have not got; and the almond-blossom
Silent in all of the gardens and the bees going backwards and forwards,
        For today we have naming of parts.   30

QUESTIONS FOR REFLECTION

1. Each stanza of "Naming of Parts" contains two distinct voices. Where does the first voice end and the second begin? Describe and characterize each voice.
2. Pinpoint the place where the two voices converge. What is the effect of their convergence?

JACQUES PRÉVERT
[1900–1977]

Family Portrait

The mother knits
The son goes to war
She finds it all perfectly natural, Mama
And the father, what is he doing? Papa?
He is making little deals   5
His wife knits
His son goes to war
He is making little deals
He finds it all perfectly natural, Papa
And the son, the son   10
What does the son find?
The son finds absolutely nothing, the son
For the son the war his Mama the knitting his Papa little deals for him the war
When it is all over, that war
He will make little deals, he and his Papa   15
The war continues Mama continues she knits
Papa continues he carries on his activity
The son is killed he no longer carries on
Papa and Mama go to the cemetery
They find it all perfectly natural, Papa and Mama   20
Life continues life with knitting war little deals
Deals war knitting war
Deals deals activity
Life along with the cemetery.

TRANSLATED BY HARRIET ZINNES

QUESTION FOR REFLECTION

Characterize the tone of the first three lines. How is this tone reinforced or altered as the poem develops? What do the repeated words and phrases contribute to the tone?

DICTION

At their most successful, poems include "the best words in the best order," as
Samuel Taylor Coleridge has said. In reading any poem it is necessary to know
what the words mean, but it is equally important to understand what the words
imply or suggest. The *denotation* or dictionary meaning of *dictator,* for example,
is "a person exercising absolute power, especially one who assumes absolute
control without the free consent of the people." But *dictator* also carries addi-
tional *connotations* or associations both personal and public. Beyond its diction-
ary meaning, *dictator* may suggest repressive force and tyrannical oppression; it
may call up images of bloodbaths, purges, executions; it may trigger associations
that prompt us to think of Hitler, for example, or Mussolini. The same kind of
associative resonance occurs with a word like *vacation,* the connotations of
which far outstrip its dictionary definition: "a period of suspension of work,
study, or other activity."

Because poets often hint indirectly at more than their words directly state, it
is necessary to develop the habit of considering the connotations of words as
well as their denotations. Often for both poets and readers the "best words" are
those that do the most work; they convey feelings and indirectly imply ideas
rather than state them outright. Poets choose a particular word because it sug-
gests what they want to suggest. Its appropriateness is a function of both its de-
notation and its connotation. Consider, for example, the second stanza of
Roethke's "My Papa's Waltz":

> We romped until the pans
> Slid from the kitchen shelf;
> My mother's countenance
> Could not unfrown itself.

"Romped" could be replaced by *danced* since the poet is describing a dance,
specifically a waltz. Why "romped" then? For one thing, it means something
different from *danced.* That is, its denotation provides a different meaning, in-
dicating play or frolic of a boisterous nature. Although "romped" is not really a
dance word at all, here it suggests a kind of rough, crude dancing, far less ele-
gant and systematic than waltzing. But it also connotes the kind of vigorous
roughhousing that fathers and sons occasionally engage in and from which
many mothers are excluded—though here, of course, the romp is occasioned
by the father's having had too much to drink. "Romped" then both describes
more precisely the kind of dance and suggests the speaker's attitude toward the
experience.

Perhaps the most unusual words in the stanza, however, are "countenance"
and "unfrown." "Countenance" is less familiar and more surprising than face.
This is also true of "unfrown," a word you won't find in the dictionary. What
makes these words noticeable is not just their uncommonness but their strange-
ness in the context of the stanza. "Countenance," a formal word, contrasts with
the informal language of the two lines before it, lines that describe the infor-
mal romp of a dance; it suggests the mother's formality as she watches the in-

formal play of her husband and son. Although her frown indicates disapproval, perhaps annoyance that her pans are falling, the disapproval and annoyance may be put on, part of an act. It is possible that she is responding as she is expected to respond.

If we look up *countenance* in the *Random House College Dictionary,* here is what we find:

> noun   1. appearance, esp. the expression of the face . . .
>   2. the face; visage
>   3. calm facial expression; composure
>   4. (obsolete) bearing; behavior
> trans. verb   6. to permit or tolerate
>   7. to approve, support, or encourage . . .

Let's consider briefly the implications of these multiple denotations. The second meaning is more general than the first. It is this first meaning to which we gave priority in the discussion above. We determined our sense of the kind of expression on the mother's face from the line, "Could not unfrown itself." But in looking at definitions 3 and 4, we encounter a problem, or at least a complication. Isn't the mother's "frown" a sign of *discomposure* rather than one of the "composure" suggested by a "calm facial expression"? Or is it possible that Roethke has used *countenance* with two meanings in mind: the meaning of "facial expression" on one hand; the meanings of "tolerate and permit, approve and encourage" on the other? This double sense of *countenance* thus parallels the double sense of the experience for the child as both pleasurable and frightening.

Let us look closely at the language of the following poem.

WILLIAM WORDSWORTH
[1770–1850]

I wandered lonely as a cloud

I wandered lonely as a cloud
That floats on high o'er vales and hills,
When all at once I saw a crowd,
A host, of golden daffodils;
Beside the lake, beneath the trees,   5
Fluttering and dancing in the breeze.

Continuous as the stars that shine
And twinkle on the milky way,
They stretched in never-ending line
Along the margin of a bay: 10
Ten thousand saw I at a glance,
Tossing their heads in sprightly dance.

The waves beside them danced; but they
Outdid the sparkling waves in glee:
A poet could not but be gay,   15
In such a jocund company:
I gazed—and gazed—but little thought
What wealth the show to me had brought:

For oft, when on my couch I lie
In vacant or in pensive mood,   20
They flash upon that inward eye
Which is the bliss of solitude;
And then my heart with pleasure fills,
And dances with the daffodils.

The words of the poem are familiar; their meanings should pose no prob-
lems. We might mention that "o'er" in line 2 is an *elision,* the omission of an
unstressed vowel or syllable to preserve the meter, of *over,* and that "oft" in
line 19 is an abbreviated form of *often.* The language, overall, is simple, direct,
and clear.

   We can assure ourselves of the rightness or appropriateness of the poem's
diction by considering the connotations of a few words. We can take lines 3
and 4 as examples.

>   When all at once I saw a crowd,
>   A host, of golden daffodils;

Suppose they had been written this way:

>   When all at once I spied a bunch,
>   A group of yellow daffodils;

Consider the connotations of each version. "Spied" may indicate something se-
cretive or even prying about the speaker's looking. It may also suggest that he
was looking for them. In contrast, "saw" carries less intense and fewer conno-
tations; it merely indicates that the speaker noticed the daffodils, and its tone is
more matter-of-fact. The alternate version's "bunch" and "group" suggest, on
the one hand, a smaller number than Wordsworth's corresponding "crowd"
and, on the other, a less communal sense. "Crowd" and "host," moreover, carry
connotations of a social gathering, of people congregated to share an experi-
ence or simply enjoy one another's company. This implicit humanizing or per-
sonifying of the daffodils (identifying them with human actions and feelings)
brings the daffodils to life: they are described as dancing and as "tossing their
heads" (line 12), and they are called a "jocund company" (line 16). "Company"
underscores the sociality of the daffodils and "jocund" indicates the human
quality of being joyful.

   This emphasis on the happiness of the daffodils and their large number
serves to point up sharply the isolation and disspiritedness of the speaker. Their

vast number is emphasized in the second stanza where they are described as "continuous" and as stretching in a "never-ending line." (And, of course, in the count:"ten thousand.") But this important contrast between the isolation of the speaker and the solidarity of the daffodils, though continued into the second stanza, gives way in stanzas three and four as the speaker imagines himself among the daffodils rather than simply looking at them from a distance. More important, when he remembers them later, he thinks about being "with" them, not literally but imaginatively.

But before we look at words describing the speaker from later stanzas, we should return to the first adjective that describes the flowers:"golden" (line 4). Wordsworth uses "golden," not "yellow," or "amber," or "tawny" because "golden" suggests more than a color; it connotes light (it shines and glitters) and wealth (money and fortune). In fact the speaker uses the word "wealth" in line 18 to indicate how important the experience of seeing the daffodils has been. And in the last two stanzas, we notice that the speaker uses in succession five words denoting *joy* ("glee," "gay," "jocund," "bliss," and "pleasure") in a crescendo that suggests the intensity of the speaker's happiness.

Although Wordsworth uses various words to indicate joy, he occasionally re-peats rather than varies his diction. The repetitions of the words for seeing ("saw," "gazed") inaugurate and sustain the imagery of vision that is central to the poem's meaning; the forms of the verb *to dance* ("dancing," "danced," "dance," and "dances") suggest both that the various elements of nature are in harmony with one another and that nature is also in harmony with man. The poet conveys this by bringing the elements of nature together in pairs: daffodils and wind (stanza one); daffodils and flowers, daffodils and stars (stanza two); wa-ter and wind (stanza three). Nature and man come together explicitly in stanza four when the speaker says that his heart dances with the daffodils.

A different kind of repetition appears in the movement from the loneliness of line one to the solitude of line 22. Both words denote an alone-ness, but they suggest a radical difference in the solitary person's attitude to his state of being alone. The poem moves from the sadly alienated separation felt by the speaker in the beginning to his joy in reimagining the natural scene, a move-ment framed by the words "loneliness" and "solitude." An analogous movement is suggested within the final stanza by the words "vacant" and "fills." The empti-ness of the speaker's spirit is transformed into a fullness of feeling as he re-members the daffodils.

To gain practice in discerning and appreciating diction in poetry, read the following poems with special attention to their words.

EDWIN ARLINGTON ROBINSON
[1869–1935]

Miniver Cheevy

Miniver Cheevy, child of scorn,
    Grew lean while he assailed the seasons;
He wept that he was ever born,
    And he had reasons.

Miniver loved the days of old   5
    When swords were bright and steeds were prancing;
The vision of a warrior bold
    Would set him dancing.

Miniver sighed for what was not,
    And dreamed, and rested from his labors;   10
He dreamed of Thebes° and Camelot,°
    And Priam's neighbors.°

Miniver mourned the ripe renown
    That made so many a name so fragrant;
He mourned Romance, now on the town,   15
    And Art, a vagrant.

Miniver loved the Medici,°
    Albeit he had never seen one;
He would have sinned incessantly
    Could he have been one.   20

Miniver cursed the commonplace
    And eyed a khaki suit with loathing;
He missed the mediæval grace
    Of iron clothing.

Miniver scorned the gold he sought,   25
    But sore annoyed was he without it;
Miniver thought, and thought, and thought,
    And thought about it.

"*Miniver Cheevy*" [11]*Thebes* *Greek city famous in history and legend.* [11]*Camelot* *the seat of King Arthur's court.* [12]*Priam* *king of Troy during the Trojan war.* [17]*The Medici* *family of powerful merchants and bankers, rulers of Florence in the fourteenth, fifteenth, and sixteenth centuries who were known for their patronage of the arts.*

Miniver Cheevy, born too late,
   Scratched his head and kept on thinking;   30
Miniver coughed, and called it fate,
   And kept on drinking.

QUESTIONS FOR REFLECTION

1. List the words in the poem that illustrate what is said in line 5: that "Miniver loved the days of old." List all the verbs that describe Miniver's action or inaction. What do they reveal about him?
2. What are the connotations of "ripe"? (line 13) and "fragrant" (line 14)? What does the combination of each respectively with ideas of fame and nobility suggest about these ideas? And how do the connotations of "on the town" (to describe Romance) and "a vagrant" (to characterize Art) suggest what has happened to Art and Romance?

WILLIAM WORDSWORTH
[1770–1850]

It is a beauteous evening

It is a beauteous evening, calm and free,
The holy time is quiet as a Nun
Breathless with adoration; the broad sun
Is sinking down in its tranquility;
The gentleness of heaven broods o'er the Sea: 5
Listen! the mighty Being is awake,
And doth with his eternal motion make
A sound like thunder—everlastingly.
Dear Child! dear Girl! that walkest with me here,
If thou appear untouched by solemn thought,   10
Thy nature is not therefore less divine:
Thou liest in Abraham's bosom all the year,
And worship'st at the Temple's inner shrine,
God being with thee when we know it not.

QUESTION FOR REFLECTION

What do the following words have in common: *holy, eternal, solemn, divine, nun, adoration, heaven, God?* Which words in the last four lines are congruent with these? And how does this diction reinforce the idea and feeling of the poem?

ROBERT HERRICK
[1591–1667]

Delight in Disorder

A sweet disorder in the dress
Kindles in clothes a wantonness.
A lawn° about the shoulders thrown   fine linen
Into a fine distractiön;
An erring lace, which here and there   5
Enthralls the crimson stomacher;°
A cuff neglectful, and thereby
Ribbons to flow confusedly;
A winning wave, deserving note,
In the tempestuous petticoat;   10
A careless shoestring, in whose tie
I see a wild civility;
Do more bewitch me than when art
Is too precise in every part.

QUESTIONS FOR REFLECTION

1. Examine the connotations of the words suggesting disorder: *thrown, distraction, neg-lectful, confusedly, careless.* Consider especially the connotations and etymology (word origin) of "erring" (line 5) and "tempestuous" (line 10).
2. Consider the words that describe the speaker's reaction to the disordered dress he describes: *sweet, kindles, wantonness, fine, wild, bewitch.* What do the connotations of these words suggest about the speaker?

ADRIENNE RICH
[b. 1929]

Rape

There is a cop who is both prowler and father:
he comes from your block, grew up with your brothers,
had certain ideals.
You hardly know him in his boots and silver badge,
on horseback, one hand touching his gun.   5

"Delight in Disorder" [6]*stomacher a garment worn under the laces of the bodice.*

You hardly know him but you have to get to know him:
he has access to machinery that could kill you.
He and his stallion clop like warlords among the trash,
his ideals stand in the air, a frozen cloud
from between his unsmiling lips.   10

And so, when the time comes, you have to turn to him,
the maniac's sperm still greasing your thighs,
your mind whirling like crazy. You have to confess
to him, you are guilty of the crime
of having been forced.   15

And you see his blue eyes, the blue eyes of all the family
whom you used to know, grow narrow and glisten,
his hand types out the details
and he wants them all
but the hysteria in your voice pleases him best.   20

You hardly know him but now he thinks he knows you:
he has taken down your worst moment
on a machine and filed it in a file.
He knows, or thinks he knows, how much you imagined;
he knows, or thinks he knows, what you secretly wanted.   25

He has access to machinery that could get you put away;
and if, in the sickening light of the precinct,
and if, in the sickening light of the precinct,
your details sound like a portrait of your confessor,
will you swallow, will you deny them, will you lie your way home? 30

QUESTION FOR REFLECTION

The man referred to in the poem is described in line 1 as a "prowler and father," and in line 29 as a "confessor." What are the implications of each? Explain also the implications of line 8: "He and his stallion clop like warlords among the trash."

IMAGERY

Poems are grounded in the concrete and the specific—in details that stimulate our senses—for it is through our senses that we perceive the world. We see daylight break and fade; we hear dogs bark and children laugh; we feel the sting of a bitterly cold wind; we smell the heavy aroma of perfume; we taste the tartness of lemon and the sweetness of chocolate. Poems include such details which trigger our memories, stimulate our feelings, and command our response.

When such specific details appear in poems they are called images. An *image* is a concrete representation of a sense impression, feeling, or idea. Images appeal to one or more of our senses—or, more precisely, they trigger our imaginative reenactment of sensory experience by rendering feeling and thought in concrete details related directly to our physical perception of the world. Images may be visual (something seen), aural (something heard), tactile (something felt), olfactory (something smelled), or gustatory (something tasted).

Tactile images of heat and cold inform Hayden's "Those Winter Sundays" (page 2), in which the speaker's father wakes up early "in the blueblack cold" to make "banked fires blaze." Visual and tactile images appear in Frost's "Stopping by Woods" (page 5), in which the speaker has stopped "between the woods and frozen lake" to listen to "the sweep of easy wind" and watch the fall of "downy" flakes of snow.

We sometimes use the word *imagery* to refer to a pattern of related details in a poem. Shakespeare's sonnet "That time of year thou may'st in me behold," for example (page 43), includes images of darkness and light, cold and warmth, day and night. The images cluster together to describe the passing of time. When images form patterns of related details that convey an idea or feeling beyond what the images literally describe, we call them *metaphorical* or *symbolic*. Such imagistic details suggest a meaning, attitude, or idea—they suggest one thing in terms of another—as for example when images of light are indicative of knowledge or of life and images of darkness are suggestive of ignorance or death.

Poetry describes specific things—daffodils, fires, and finches' wings, for example. And it describes such things in specific terms: the color of the daffodils, the glare of the fire, the beating of the finches' wings. From these and other specific details we derive both meaning and feeling.

For an indication of how images work together to convey feelings and ideas, consider the images in the following poem.

ELIZABETH BISHOP
[*1911–1979*]

First Death in Nova Scotia

In the cold, cold parlor
my mother laid out Arthur
beneath the chromographs:
Edward, Prince of Wales,
with Princess Alexandra,   5
and King George with Queen Mary.
Below them on the table
stood a stuffed loon
shot and stuffed by Uncle
Arthur, Arthur's father.   10

Since Uncle Arthur fired
a bullet into him,
he hadn't said a word.
He kept his own counsel
on his white, frozen lake,   15
the marble–topped table.
His breast was deep and white,
cold and caressable;
his eyes were red glass,
much to be desired.   20

"Come," said my mother,
"Come and say good–bye
to your little cousin Arthur."
I was lifted up and given
one lily of the valley   25
to put in Arthur's hand.
Arthur's coffin was
a little frosted cake,
and the red–eyed loon eyed it
from his white, frozen lake.   30

Arthur was very small.
He was all white, like a doll
that hadn't been painted yet.
Jack Frost had started to paint him
the way he always painted   35
the Maple Leaf (Forever).
He had just begun on his hair,
a few red strokes, and then
Jack Frost had dropped the brush
and left him white, forever.   40

The gracious royal couples
were warm in red and ermine;
their feet were well wrapped up
in the ladies' ermine trains.
They invited Arthur to be   45
the smallest page at court.
But how could Arthur go,
clutching his tiny lily,
with his eyes shut up so tight
and the roads deep in snow?   50

The poem describes a child's view of death. Through images of what the little girl sees and hears, it renders her incomprehension and confused feelings about her cousin Arthur's death. Bishop does this by filtering the child's perceptions through an adult sensibility. In a similar way, the poet presents a voice childlike in its syntactic constructions and adult in its vocabulary. Through the double perspective of the adult/the child we gain a complex inner view of the speaker's impressions and understanding of her experience, vividly rendered in the poem's images.

Our first sense impression is tactile: we imagine "the cold, cold parlor." Immediately after, we see two things: a picture of the British royal family and a stuffed loon, which had been shot by the dead boy's father, also named Arthur. The second stanza describes the loon in more detail. It sits on a marble-topped table, a detail that conveys two tactile impressions, hardness and coldness. This imagery is emphasized in the description of the marble table as the loon's "white, frozen lake."

These visual images are continued in the third stanza in which the speaker sees her dead cousin in his coffin. She holds a long-stemmed white flower which she puts in the dead boy's hand. The images of whiteness and cold (the frozen lake, marble table top, and the dead, stuffed white loon of the previous stanzas) are continued: the speaker describes Arthur's coffin as a "frosted cake." The birthday cake image also indicates the limited extent of the speaker's comprehension of the reality and finality of death.

With the repeated details about the loon's red eyes and its frozen posture and base, the child unconsciously (and the poet consciously) associate the dead boy and the dead loon. This connection is further established by the imagery of the fourth stanza in which Arthur is described as "all white," with "a few red strokes" for his hair. Unlike the maple leaf with its complete and thorough redness, little Arthur is left "unpainted" by Jack Frost (another image of the cold) and is thus left white "forever." On the one hand, such a description clearly indicates the child's fantastic incomprehension of Arthur's death; on the other, it suggests that she intuitively senses that Arthur has been drained of color and of life. A similar combination of intuitive understanding and conscious ignorance is echoed in the speaker's comparison of Arthur with the doll. She sees how similar they look on the surface, but she does not consciously register their similar lifelessness.

The images of the final stanzas recall those of stanza 1. The royal couples of the chromograph are described as dressed in red clothes with white fur trim, details that connect directly with the dead loon. Moreover, the lily of the third stanza (white and short-lived like the boy) reappears clutched in Arthur's hand. The final image is one of whiteness and coldness: deep snow covers the cold ground where Arthur will soon lie.

The poem's concrete details, mostly visual and tactile images, strongly evoke the coldness and lifelessness of the dead child. But they suggest other things as well. The portrait of the royal family and the stuffed loon suggest something of the family's social identity—especially its conservatism and propriety. More importantly, however, these details, along with the others noted above, reveal the limitation of the speaker's understanding. She sees the loon, for example, as quiet: "he hadn't said a word," and "he kept his own counsel." In addition, she fantasizes that the royal family (which she sees as very much alive in their warm furs) have invited little Arthur to serve as "the smallest page at court." Even

though this may be the speaker's way of coping with death, the final two im-
ages of white lily and cold snow, and the tone in which she asks her final ques-
tion all point toward her near acknowledgment of the truth.

 It should prove useful to return at this point to a few of the poems consid-
ered in earlier sections of this introduction and examine their imagery. For fur-
ther practice in responding to poetic images, read the following poems.

WILLIAM BUTLER YEATS
[1865–1939]

The Lake Isle of Innisfree

I will arise and go now, and go to Innisfree,
And a small cabin build there, of clay and wattles° made: interwoven twigs
Nine bean-rows will I have there, a hive for the honey-bee,
And live alone in the bee-loud glade.

And I shall have some peace there, for peace comes dropping slow,   5
Dropping from the veils of the morning to where the cricket sings;
There midnight's all a glimmer, and noon a purple glow,
And evening full of the linnet's wings.

I will arise and go now, for always night and day
I hear lake water lapping with low sounds by the shore;   10
While I stand on the roadway, or on the pavements gray,
I hear it in the deep heart's core.

QUESTION FOR REFLECTION

Identify the images of sound and sight and explain what they contribute to the idea
and feeling of the poem.

ROBERT BROWNING
[1812–1889]

Meeting at Night

The gray sea and the long black land;
And the yellow half-moon large and low;
And the startled little waves that leap
In fiery ringlets from their sleep,
As I gain the cove with pushing prow,   5
And quench its speed i' the slushy sand.

Then a mile of warm sea-scented beach;
Three fields to cross till a farm appears;
A tap at the pane, the quick sharp scratch
And blue spurt of a lighted match,   10
And a voice less loud, through its joys and fears,
Than the two hearts beating each to each!

QUESTION FOR REFLECTION

In a series of images averaging one per line, the poet describes a lover traveling to meet his beloved. Identify each image, the specific sense it stimulates, and the feelings the images evoke.

H. D. (HILDA DOOLITTLE)
[1886–1961]

Heat

O wind, rend open the heat,
cut apart the heat,
rend it to tatters.

Fruit cannot drop
through this thick air—   5
that presses up and blunts
the points of pears
and rounds the grapes.

Cut the heat—
plow through it,   10
turning it on either side
of your path.

QUESTION FOR REFLECTION

By asking the wind to "rend open," "cut apart," and "plow through" the heat, the poet
creates an image of it. Identify this image and explain what stanza two contributes to it.

T H O M A S   H A R D Y
[1840–1928]

Neutral Tones

We stood by a pond that winter day,
And the sun was white, as though chidden of God,
And a few leaves lay on the starving sod;
  —They had fallen from an ash, and were gray.

Your eyes on me were as eyes that rove   5
Over tedious riddles of years ago;
And some words played between us to and fro
  On which lost the more by our love.

The smile on your mouth was the deadest thing
Alive enough to have strength to die;   10
And a grin of bitterness swept thereby
  Like an ominous bird a-wing. . . .

Since then, keen lessons that love deceives,
And wrings with wrong, have shaped to me
Your face, and the God-curst sun, and a tree,   15
  And a pond edged with grayish leaves.

QUESTIONS FOR REFLECTION

1. Examine the images of stanza one. What mood do they create? How do the images
   of stanzas two and three develop and expand those of the opening stanza?
2. What do you notice about the images of the final stanza in relation to those that
   come before?

FIGURES OF SPEECH: SIMILE AND METAPHOR

Language can be conveniently classified as either literal or figurative. When we speak literally, we mean exactly what each word conveys; when we use *figurative language* we mean something other than the actual meaning of the words. "Go jump in the lake," for example, if meant literally would be intended as a command to leave (go) and jump (not dive or wade) into a lake (not a pond or stream). Usually, however, such an expression is not literally meant. In telling someone to go jump in the lake we are telling them something, to be sure, but what we mean is different from the literal meaning of the words. To get lost, perhaps, which is itself a figurative expression.

Rhetoricians have catalogued more than 250 different *figures of speech,* expressions or ways of using words in a nonliteral sense. They include *hyperbole* or exaggeration ("I'll die if I miss that game"); *litotes* or understatement ("Being flayed alive is somewhat painful"); *synecdoche* or using a part to signify the whole ("Lend me a hand"); *metonymy* or substituting an attribute of a thing for the thing itself ("step on the gas"); *personification,* endowing inanimate objects or abstract concepts with animate characteristics or qualities ("the lettuce was lonely without tomatoes and cucumbers for company"). We will not go on to name and illustrate the others but instead will concentrate on two specially important for poetry (and for the other literary genres as well): simile and metaphor.

The heart of both these figures is comparison—the making of connections between normally unrelated things, seeing one thing in terms of another. More than 2,300 years ago Aristotle defined *metaphor* as "an intuitive perception of the similarity in dissimilars." And he suggested further that to be a "master of metaphor" is the greatest of a poet's achievements. In our century, Robert Frost has echoed Aristotle by suggesting that metaphor is central to poetry, and that, essentially, poetry is a way of "saying one thing and meaning another, saying one thing in terms of another."

Although both figures involve comparisons between unlike things, *simile* establishes the comparison explicitly with the words *like* or *as. Metaphor,* on the other hand, employs no such explicit verbal clue. The comparison is *implied* in such a way that the figurative term is substituted for or identified with the literal one. "My daughter dances like an angel" is a simile; "my daughter is an angel" is a metaphor. In this example the difference involves more than the word *like:* the simile is more restricted in its comparative suggestion than is the metaphor. That is, the daughter's angelic attributes are more extensive in the unspecified and unrestricted metaphor. In the simile, however, she only dances like an angel. (There's no suggestion that she possesses other angelic qualities.)

Consider the opening line of Wordsworth's poem about the daffodils: "I wandered lonely as a cloud" (page 29). The simile suggests the speaker's isolation and his aimless wandering. But it doesn't indicate other ways in which cloud and speaker are related. Later the speaker uses another simile to compare the daffodils with stars. This simile specifically highlights one aspect of the connection between stars and flowers: number. It also contains an example of hyperbole in its suggestion that the daffodils stretch in "a never-ending line."

In these examples the poet provides explicit clues that direct us to the comparative connection. He also restricts their application, as we have noted. In a metaphor, Wordsworth writes that the daffodils "flash" upon the "inward eye" of the speaker. The "flash" (an image of light) implies that he sees the flowers in his mind's eye, the inward eye of memory. Moreover, when he "sees" the daffodils in his "inward eye," he realizes the "wealth" they have brought him. This "wealth" is also figurative—Wordsworth uses "wealth" as a metaphor for joy.

These examples of simile and metaphor from Wordsworth's poem are fairly straightforward and uncomplicated. For a more complex example, consider the use of metaphor in the following sonnet by William Shakespeare.

WILLIAM SHAKESPEARE
[1564–1616]

That time of year thou may'st in me behold

That time of year thou may'st in me behold
When yellow leaves, or none, or few, do hang
Upon those boughs which shake against the cold,
Bare ruined choirs where late the sweet birds sang.
In me thou see'st the twilight of such day   5
As after sunset fadeth in the west,
Which by-and-by black night doth take away,
Death's second self that seals up all in rest.
In me thou see'st the glowing of such fire
That on the ashes of his youth doth lie,   10
As the deathbed whereon it must expire,
Consumed with that which it was nourished by.
  This thou perceiv'st, which makes thy love more strong,
  To love that well which thou must leave ere long.

Perhaps the first thing to mention about the poem's metaphorical language is that its images appeal to three senses: sight, hearing, and touch. The images of the first four lines include appeals to each of these senses: we *see* the yellow leaves and bare branches; we *feel* the cold that shakes the boughs; we *hear* (in memory) the singing birds of summer.

But these concrete representations of sensory experience become more than images with emotional reverberations. They become metaphors, ways of talking about one thing in terms of something else. The first image extended into a metaphor is that of autumn, "that time of year" when leaves turn yellow and branches become bare. The fourth line extends the image by describing the tree branches as a choir loft that the birds have recently vacated. Because Shakespeare's speaker says that "you" (we) can behold autumn *in him* ("In me thou see'st the twilight of such day," line 5), we know that he is speaking of more than autumn. We realize that he is talking about one thing in terms of another—about aging in terms of the seasons.

In the next four lines the metaphor of autumn gives way to another: that of twilight ending the day. The sun has set; night is coming on. The "black" night is described as taking away the sun's light (line 7); the sun's setting is seen as a dying of its light. The implied comparison of night with death is directly stated in line 8, where night is called "death's second self"; like death, night "seals up all in rest." Night's rest is, of course, temporary; death's, however, is final. The metaphor is both consoling (death is a kind of restful sleep) and frightening (death "seals up" life in a way that suggests there will be no unsealing).

So far we have noted two extended metaphors of autumn and of evening. Each comparison highlights the way death begins with a prelude: twilight precedes night; autumn precedes winter; illness precedes death. The speaker knows that he is in the autumn of his life, the twilight of his time. This metaphor is continued in a third image: the dying of the fire, which represents the dying out of the speaker's life. This third image emphasizes the extinguishing of light and of heat. The speaker's youth is "ashes," which serve as the "deathbed" on which he will "expire" (line 11). Literally, the lines say that the fire will expire as it burns up the fuel that feeds it. As it does so, it glows with light and heat. The glowing fire is a metaphor for the speaker's life, which is presently still "glowing" but which is beginning to die out as it consumes itself. We might notice that the fire will "expire," a word which means literally to "breathe out . . . to emit the last breath," an image that suggests the termination of breathing in the dying.

The final element of this image of the dying fire is given in line 12: "Consumed with that which it was nourished by." Literally the fire consumes itself by using up its fuel, burning up logs. In its very glowing it burns toward its own extinction. Analogously, the speaker's youthful vitality consumes itself in living. His very living has been and continues to be a dying.

For a few additional examples of how poets employ figurative language, read the following poems. Attend particularly to their figures of comparison and especially to how those comparisons aid your understanding.

JOHN DONNE

[1572–1631]

Hymn to God the Father

1

Wilt thou forgive that sin where I begun,
    Which was my sin though it were done before?
Wilt thou forgive that sin through which I run,

And do run still, though still I do deplore?
   When thou hast done, thou hast not done,   5
   For I have more.

2

Wilt thou forgive that sin by which I've won
   Others to sin, and made my sin their door?
Wilt thou forgive that sin which I did shun
   A year or two, but wallowed in a score?   10
     When thou hast done, thou hast not done,
     For I have more.

3

I have a sin of fear, that when I've spun
   My last thread, I shall perish on the shore;
But swear by thyself that at my death thy son   15
   Shall shine as he shines now, and heretofore;
     And having done that, Thou hast done;
     I fear no more.

QUESTIONS FOR REFLECTION

1. Explain the images in stanza two: the door of sin and wallowing in sin. Relate these two images from stanza three: spinning the last thread and perishing on the shore.
2. The final stanza contains two puns or plays on words. Identify and explain each. What do they contribute to the meaning and tone of the poem?

ROBERT WALLACE
[*b. 1932*]

The Double Play

In his sea-lit
distance, the pitcher winding
like a clock about to chime comes down with

the ball, hit
sharply, under the artificial   5
banks of arc lights, bounds like a vanishing string

over the green
to the shortstop magically
scoops to his right whirling above his invisible

shadows   10
in the dust redirects
its flight to the running poised second baseman

pirouettes
leaping, above the slide, to throw
from mid-air, across the colored tightened interval,   15

to the leaning-
out first baseman ends the dance
drawing it disappearing into his long brown glove

stretches. What
is too swift for deception   20
is final, lost, among the loosened figures

jogging off the field
(the pitcher walks), casual
in the space where the poem has happened.

QUESTIONS FOR REFLECTION

1. As its title suggests the poem describes a double play in baseball—getting two of-
   fensive players out on a single play. Throughout the poem the double play is com-
   pared to a dance. Pinpoint the words and phrases that establish this metaphorical
   connection, and explain what precisely about the double play makes it like a dance.
2. Besides the central metaphor that controls the poem, the poet has introduced other
   comparisons to illuminate and describe aspects or details of the double play. Iden-
   tify and explain these comparisons.
3. In what way has the double play occurred "in the space where the poem has hap-
   pened" (line 24)? How has a double play occurred both on the page and in the poem?

LOUIS SIMPSON
[*b. 1923*]

The Battle

Helmet and rifle, pack and overcoat
Marched through a forest. Somewhere up ahead
Guns thudded. Like the circle of a throat
The night on every side was turning red.

They halted and they dug. They sank like moles   5
Into the clammy earth between the trees.
And soon the sentries, standing in their holes,
Felt the first snow. Their feet began to freeze.

At dawn the first shell landed with a crack.
Then shells and bullets swept the icy woods.   10
This lasted many days. The snow was black.
The corpses stiffened in their scarlet hoods.

Most clearly of that battle I remember
The tiredness in eyes, how hands looked thin
Around a cigarette, and the bright ember   15
Would pulse with all the life there was within.

QUESTION FOR REFLECTION

Identify and explain the figures of speech in the first two stanzas. What impression
does each create? How is the mood they establish enforced by the rest of the poem?

JUDITH WRIGHT
[*b. 1915*]

Woman to Child

You who were darkness warmed my flesh
where out of darkness rose the seed.
Then all a world I made in me;
all the world you hear and see
hung upon my dreaming blood.   5

There moved the multitudinous stars,
and coloured birds and fishes moved.
There swam the sliding continents.
All time lay rolled in me, and sense,
and love that knew not its beloved.   10

O node and focus of the world;
I hold you deep within that well
you shall escape and not escape—
that mirrors still your sleeping shape;
that nurtures still your crescent cell.   15

I wither and you break from me;
yet though you dance in living light
I am the earth, I am the root,
I am the stem that fed the fruit,
the link that joins you to the night.   20

QUESTION FOR REFLECTION

Explain the following figurative expressions:

"All a world I made in me" (line 3)
"All time lay rolled in me" (line 9)
"I hold you deep within that well" (line 12)
"I am the earth, I am the root,
I am the stem that fed the fruit" (lines 18–19)

SYMBOLISM AND ALLEGORY

A *symbol* is any object or action that means more than itself, any object or action that represents something beyond itself. A rose, for example, can represent beauty or love or transience. A tree may represent a family's roots and branches. A soaring bird might stand for freedom. Light might symbolize hope or knowledge or life. These and other familiar symbols may represent different, even opposite things, depending on how they are deployed in a particular poem. Natural symbols like light and darkness, fire and water can stand for contradictory things. Water, for example, which typically symbolizes life (rain, fertility, food, life) can also stand for death (tempests, hurricanes, floods). And fire, which often indicates destruction, can represent purgation or purification. The meaning of any symbol, whether an object, an action, or a gesture, is controlled by its context.

How then do we know if a poetic detail is symbolic? How do we decide whether to leap beyond the poem's literal detail into a symbolic interpretation?

There are no simple answers to these questions. Like any interpretive connections we make in reading, the decision to view something as symbolic depends partly on our skill in reading and partly on whether the poetic context invites and rewards a symbolic reading. The following questions can guide our thinking about interpreting symbols:

1. Is the object, action, gesture, or event important to the poem? Is it described in detail? Does it occur repeatedly? Does it appear at a climactic moment in the poem?
2. Does the poem seem to warrant our granting its details more significance than their immediate literal meaning?
3. Does our symbolic reading make sense? Does it account for the literal details without either ignoring or distorting them?

Even in following such guidelines, there will be occasions when we are not certain that a poem is symbolic. And there will be times when, though we are fairly confident *that* certain details are symbolic, we are not confident about *what* they symbolize. Such uncertainty is due largely to the nature of interpretation, which is an art rather than a science. But these interpretive complications are also due to the differences in complexity and variability with which poets use symbols. The most complex symbols resist definitive and final explanation. We can circle around them, but we neither exhaust their significance nor define their meaning.

As an example of how literal details assume symbolic significance observe their use in the following poem.

PETER MEINKE

[*b. 1932*]

Advice to My Son

The trick is, to live your days
as if each one may be your last
(for they go fast, and young men lose their lives
in strange and unimaginable ways)
but at the same time, plan long range   5
(for they go slow: if you survive
the shattered windshield and the bursting shell
you will arrive
at our approximation here below
of heaven or hell).   10

To be specific, between the peony and the rose
plant squash and spinach, turnips and tomatoes;

beauty is nectar
and nectar, in a desert, saves—
but the stomach craves stronger sustenance   15
than the honied vine.
Therefore, marry a pretty girl
after seeing her mother;
speak truth to one man,
work with another;   20
and always serve bread with your wine.

But, son,
always serve wine.

The concrete details that invite symbolic reading are these: peony and rose; squash, spinach, turnips and tomatoes; bread and wine. If we read the poem literally and assume the advice is meant that way, we learn something about the need to plant and enjoy these flowers and foods. But if we suspect that the speaker is advising his son about more than food and flowers, we will look toward their symbolic implications.

What then do the various plants and the bread and wine symbolize? How is the speaker's advice about them related to the more general advice about living? In the first stanza the general advice implies two contradictory courses of action: (1) live each day to the fullest as if it will be the last; (2) look to the future and plan wisely so your future will not be marred by unwise decisions. By advising his son to plant peonies and roses, the speaker urges him to see the need for beauty and luxury, implying that he needs food for the spirit as well as sustenance for the body.

The symbols of bread and wine suggest a related point. The speaker urges his son to serve both bread and wine as bread is a dietary staple, something basic and common, but wine enhances the bread, making it seem more than mere common fare. Wine symbolizes something festive; it provides a touch of celebration. Thus the speaker's advice about bread and wine parallels his earlier suggestions. In each case, he urges his son to balance and blend, to fulfill both his basic and his spiritual needs. By making his advice concrete the speaker does indeed advocate literally what he says: plant roses and peonies with your vegetables; drink wine with your bread. But by including such specific instructions in a poem that contains other more serious advice about living (live for today, live for the future) the poet invites us to see bread and wine, vegetables and flowers more than literally. If our interpretation of their symbolic dimension is congruent with other parts of the poem, and if it makes sense, then we should feel confident that we are not imposing a symbolic reading where it is not warranted.

Related to symbolism, *allegory* is a form of narrative in which people, places, and happenings have hidden or symbolic meaning; allegory is especially suitable as a vehicle for teaching. In an allegorical work there are most often two levels of meaning, the literal and the symbolic. To understand an allegorical work we must make sense of its details by interpreting their symbolic meaning.

Allegory is thus a type of symbolism. It differs from symbolism in establishing a strict system of correspondences between details of action and a pattern of meaning. Symbolic works that are not allegorical are less systematic and more open-ended in what their symbols mean.

The following allegorical poem describes a journey along an uphill road that ends with the traveler arriving at an inn. We can readily see that the uphill road represents a struggling journey through life, that day and night stand for a life span ending in death. The question-and-answer structure of the poem and its reassuring tone suggest that it can be read as a religious allegory, specifically a Christian one.

CHRISTINA ROSSETTI
[1830–1894]

Up-Hill

Does the road wind up-hill all the way?
    Yes, to the very end.
Will the day's journey take the whole long day?
    From morn to night, my friend.

But is there for the night a resting-place?   5
    A roof for when the slow dark hours begin.
May not the darkness hide it from my face?
    You cannot miss that inn.

Shall I meet other wayfarers at night?
    Those who have gone before.   10
Then must I knock, or call when just in sight?
    They will not keep you standing at that door.

Shall I find comfort, travel-sore and weak?
    Of labor you shall find the sum.
Will there be beds for me and all who seek?   15
    Yea, beds for all who come.

For more exercise in interpreting symbol and allegory, read the following poems with attention to their symbolic and allegorical details. All the poems are symbolic, but not in the same way.

WILLIAM BLAKE
[1757–1827]

A Poison Tree

I was angry with my friend:
I told my wrath, my wrath did end.
I was angry with my foe:
I told it not, my wrath did grow.

And I waterd it in fears,   5
Night & morning with my tears;
And I sunnéd it with smiles,
And with soft deceitful wiles.

And it grew both day and night,
Till it bore an apple bright.   10
And my foe beheld it shine,
And he knew that it was mine,

And into my garden stole,
When the night had veild the pole;
In the morning glad I see   15
My foe outstretchd beneath the tree.

QUESTIONS FOR REFLECTION

1. "A Poison Tree" describes a series of events—it tells a story. Explain your understanding of the story's significance.
2. What does the apple in a garden represent? What difference would it make if it were a peach in an orchard?

ROBERT FROST
[1874–1963]

The Road Not Taken

Two roads diverged in a yellow wood,
And sorry I could not travel both
And be one traveler, long I stood
And looked down one as far as I could
To where it bent in the undergrowth;   5

Then took the other, as just as fair,
And having perhaps the better claim,
Because it was grassy and wanted wear;
Though as for that, the passing there
Had worn them really about the same,   10

And both that morning equally lay
In leaves no step had trodden black.
Oh, I kept the first for another day!
Yet knowing how way leads on to way,
I doubted if I should ever come back.   15

I shall be telling this with a sigh
Somewhere ages and ages hence:
Two roads diverged in a wood, and I—
I took the one less traveled by,
And that has made all the difference.   20

QUESTIONS FOR REFLECTION

1. On one level this is a poem about walking in the woods and choosing one of two paths to follow. What invites us to see the poem as something more? What is this something more?
2. Frost is careful not to specify what the two roads represent: he does not limit their possible symbolic meanings. And yet the nature of the experience he describes does pivot the poem on a central human problem: the inescapable necessity to make choices. Specify some of the choices we all must make that could be represented by the two roads of the poem.

GEORGE HERBERT
[1593–1633]

Virtue

Sweet day, so cool, so calm, so bright,
    The bridal of the earth and sky:
The dew shall weep thy fall tonight;
    For thou must die.

Sweet rose, whose hue, angry and brave,   5
    Bids the rash gazer wipe his eye:
Thy root is ever in its grave,
    And thou must die.

Sweet spring, full of sweet days and roses,
   A box where sweets° compacted lie;   perfumes 10
My music shows ye have your closes,°   musical cadences
   And all must die.

Only a sweet and virtuous soul,
   Like seasoned timber, never gives;
But though the whole world turn to coal,   15
   Then chiefly lives.

QUESTION FOR REFLECTION

The major contrast in the poem is between things that die and the one thing that does not. Identify and comment on the aptness of Herbert's symbols for transience and mortality.

EMILY DICKINSON
[1830–1886]

Because I could not stop for Death

Because I could not stop for Death—
He kindly stopped for me—
The Carriage held but just Ourselves—
And Immortality.

We slowly drove—He knew no haste   5
And I had put away
My labor and my leisure too,
For His Civility—

We passed the School, where Children strove
At Recess—in the Ring—   10
We passed the Fields of Gazing Grain—
We passed the Setting Sun—

Or rather—He passed Us—
The Dews drew quivering and chill—
For only Gossamer, my Gown—   15
My Tippet°—only Tulle—   scarf or stole

We paused before a House that seemed
A Swelling of the Ground—
The Roof was scarcely visible—
The Cornice—in the Ground—   20

Since then—'tis Centuries—and yet
Feels shorter than the Day
I first surmised the Horses' Heads
Were toward Eternity—

QUESTION FOR REFLECTION

Is this poem generally symbolic or is it allegorical? Explain the significance of the details in lines 9–13 and lines 17–20.

SYNTAX

We have previously defined *syntax* as the order of words in sentence, phrase, or clause. From a Greek word meaning "to arrange together," *syntax* refers to the grammatical structure of words in sentences and the deployment of sentences in longer units throughout the poem. Poets use syntax as they use imagery, diction, structure, sound, and rhythm—to express meaning and convey feeling. A poem's syntax is an important element of its tone and a guide to a speaker's state of mind. Speakers who repeat themselves or who break off abruptly in the midst of a thought, for example, reveal something about how they feel.

Let us briefly consider what syntax contributes to the meaning and feeling of a few poems discussed earlier. In "Those Winter Sundays" (page 2), Robert Hayden uses normal word order for each of the poem's four sentences, but he varies their lengths radically. In the first stanza, for example, Hayden follows a long sentence with a short one. The effect is to increase the emphasis on the short sentence: "No one ever thanked him." In the last stanza, Hayden uses a question rather than a statement for the speaker's remembrance of his father's acts of love. Both the question and the repetition of the phrase "What did I know" reveal the intensity of the speaker's regret at his belated understanding.

In "Stopping by Woods on a Snowy Evening" (page 5), Robert Frost achieves emphasis differently through *inversion* or the reversal of the standard order of words in a line or sentence. The word order of the first line of the poem is inverted:

Whose woods these are I think I know.

Normal word order would be:

I think I know whose woods these are.

In the more conversational alternative, emphasis falls on what the speaker knows or thinks he knows. In Frost's line emphasis falls on "the woods," which are more important than what the speaker thinks he knows as he looks at them. Perhaps more important still is the difference in tone between the two versions. Frost's inverted syntax lifts the line, giving it a more even rhythm, slowing it down slightly. The alternate version lacks the rhythmic regularity of Frost's original and reads like a casual statement.

Another aspect of syntax worth noting in Frost's poem is the variations in tempo among the four stanzas. The sentences of the first and last stanzas are the most heavily stopped with punctuation and pauses. The opening stanza contains three pauses before it ends; stanza four includes three in its first line alone and five altogether. In contrast stanza three contains only one stop, halfway through. And stanza two is one long sentence without a single pause or break. Frost carefully controls the movement and speed, the pace and pause of his poem by using punctuation and grammatical form to heighten its expressiveness and to control its tone.

Unlike the inverted and varied syntax of Frost's "Stopping by Woods on a Snowy Evening," William Wordsworth's syntax in "I wandered lonely as a cloud" (page 29) is simple and direct; it does not call attention to itself. The two little syntactic twists that it does contain highlight an important dimension of the poem—visual imagery. One is an inversion: "saw I" (line 11); the other is a repetition: "I gazed—and gazed" (line 17). And consider Walt Whitman's "When I heard the learn'd astronomer" (page 82), which is cast as a single expansive subordinate sentence that sweeps over the first four lines like a wave and then ebbs in the next four. The action of the last four lines is suspended over the first four: we are made to wait for the final simple and important act that Whitman renders in the most direct syntax of any line in the poem: the speaker "look'd up in perfect silence at the stars."

Consider how syntax orders thought and highlights feeling in "The Sun Rising," by John Donne.

JOHN DONNE
[1572–1631]

The Sun Rising

Busy old fool, unruly sun,
    Why dost thou thus,
Through windows, and through curtains call on us?
Must to thy motions lovers' seasons run?
    Saucy pedantic wretch, go chide   5
    Late schoolboys, and sour prentices,
Go tell court-huntsmen that the King will ride,
Call country ants to harvest offices;
Love, all alike, no season knows, nor clime,
Nor hours, days, months, which are the rags of time.   10

Thy beams, so reverend and strong
Why shouldst thou think?
I could eclipse and cloud them with a wink,
But that I would not lose her sight so long;
If her eyes have not blinded thine,   15
Look, and tomorrow late, tell me
Whether both the Indias of spice and mine
Be where thou left'st them, or lie here with me.
Ask for those kings whom thou saw'st yesterday,
And thou shalt hear, All here in one bed lay.   20

She's all states, and all princes, I,
Nothing else is.
Princes do but play us; compared to this,
All's honor's mimic, all wealth alchemy.
Thou, sun, art half as happy as we,   25
In that the world's contracted thus;
Thine age asks ease, and since thy duties be
To warm the world, that's done in warming us.
Shine here to us, and thou art everywhere;
This bed thy center is, these walls, thy sphere.   30

Perhaps the first thing we notice is the dislocation of syntax in the two opening questions. The first question could be rewritten so as to approximate more conventional discourse:

Unruly sun, busy old fool,
Why dost thou thus call on us
Through windows, and through curtains?

Besides an alteration of rhythm, we notice a different emphasis in Donne's lines. The alternate version puts the emphasis on "windows" and "curtains," far less important words than "us," the word Donne's lines emphasize, as the poem is about a pair of lovers.

After another inverted sentence ("Must to thy motions lovers' seasons run") and a short one following the longer opening sentence, we hear a series of tonal shifts. The speed and abruptness of Donne's second question convey the speaker's tone of impatient defiance. The two questions with their emphatic dislocations prepare the way for the series of imperatives that increase our sense of the speaker's authority. This tone gives way abruptly in the last two lines of the stanza to a more leisurely verse movement ("Love, all alike, no season knows, nor clime, / Nor hours, days, months, which are the rags of time"). The dignified and stately tone of these lines derives partly from the simple declarative sentences, partly from the monosyllabic diction, and partly from the frequent pauses marked by punctuation. The overall effect is a slower line and a more exalted tone.

In stanza two the tone shifts back to the playful exaggeration of the beginning of the poem, with similar dislocations of syntax in its opening question. The second sentence (lines 13–18), neither question, statement, nor command, is a statement of possibility. The tone remains playfully defiant ("tell me / Whether both the Indias of spice and mine / Be where thou left'st them"); the speaker continues to exaggerate. The syntax is more convoluted, the sentences more complex than in the first stanza. Again, however, as in the opening stanza, the final line of stanza two resolves into a direct authoritative assertion:

> . . . All here in one bed lay.

Unlike the first two stanzas, the last begins with the declarative syntax and simple, direct assertiveness with which the other two stanzas end. The entire stanza is composed of a series of balanced statements, some parallel, some antithetical. (Not completely, however, since there is something of the complex argument of stanza two midway through this last stanza. And there is also a brief return to the imperative voice in line 29, "Shine here to us.") But from these deviations the speaker quickly returns to the authority of direct declaration, an authority enhanced by the parallel form of the final line, by its slight dislocation of the verbs, and by the tightness of its structure (eliminating a conjunction between the clauses and omitting the implied verb of the second half of the line):

> This bed thy center is, these walls thy sphere.

There are many syntactical possibilities available to poets. For some interesting syntactical forms and their effects see T. S. Eliot's "The Love Song of J. Alfred Prufrock" for its associative syntax (syntax that reflects the mental associations of the speaker [page 279]); Gerard Manley Hopkins's "Thou art indeed just, Lord" (page 24) for its use of fractured or broken syntax; John Milton's "On the Late Massacre in Piedmont" (page 226) for its Latinate syntax; and Alexander Pope's "An Essay on Man," (page 229) for its tightly formal, balanced, and antithetical syntax.

In the poems that follow Thomas Hardy uses broken syntax in "The Man He Killed"; William Butler Yeats uses balanced syntax in "An Irish Airman Foresees His Death"; Robert Frost uses ambiguous syntax so that multiple meanings coexist and coincide in "The Silken Tent"; and E. E. Cummings uses mimetic syntax, which imitates what it describes, in "Me up at does."

THOMAS HARDY
[1840–1928]

The Man He Killed

"Had he and I but met
By some old ancient inn,
We should have sat us down to wet
Right many a nipperkin!

"But ranged as infantry,   5
And staring face to face,
I shot at him as he at me,
And killed him in his place.

"I shot him dead because—
Because he was my foe,   10
Just so: my foe of course he was;
That's clear enough; although

"He thought he'd 'list, perhaps,
Off-hand-like—just as I—
Was out of work—had sold his traps—   15
No other reason why.

"Yes; quaint and curious war is!
You shoot a fellow down
You'd treat if met where any bar is,
Or help to half-a-crown."   20

QUESTIONS FOR REFLECTION

1. The first two stanzas are each a single sentence. Explain their logical and syntactic relationship.
2. Unlike the smooth unbroken sentences of the first two stanzas, we find breaks in the syntax (indicated by dashes) in the next two stanzas. After reading the stanzas aloud, explain what the breaks suggest about the speaker's state of mind.
3. Does the speaker's fluent syntax in the last stanza suggest that he has worked through the state of mind you found evident in stanzas three and four? Explain.

WILLIAM BUTLER YEATS
[1865–1939]

An Irish Airman Foresees His Death

I know that I shall meet my fate
Somewhere among the clouds above;
Those that I fight I do not hate,
Those that I guard I do not love;°
My country is Kiltartan Cross   5
My countrymen Kiltartan's poor,
No likely end could bring them loss
Or leave them happier than before.
Nor law, nor duty bade me fight,
Nor public men, nor cheering crowds,   10
A lonely impulse of delight
Drove to this tumult in the clouds;
I balanced all, brought all to mind,
The years to come seemed waste of breath,
A waste of breath the years behind   15
In balance with this life, this death.

QUESTIONS FOR REFLECTION

1. Point out the ways the syntax of this poem is balanced and controlled. How does the poem's balanced syntax reinforce its meaning?
2. Explain the connection between its syntax and its central idea: the pilot's attitude toward his country, his enemy, his fate.

ROBERT FROST
[1874–1963]

The Silken Tent

She is as in a field a silken tent
At midday when a sunny summer breeze
Has dried the dew and all its ropes relent,

"An Irish Airman Foresees His Death" 3–4 *Those that I fight . . . I do not love; Yeats is referring to the Germans and the English respectively; the war is World War I.*

So that in guys it gently sways at ease,
And its supporting central cedar pole,   5
That is its pinnacle to heavenward
And signifies the sureness of the soul,
Seems to owe naught to any single cord,
But strictly held by none, is loosely bound
By countless silken ties of love and thought   10
To everything on earth the compass round,
And only by one's going slightly taut
In the capriciousness of summer air
Is of the slightest bondage made aware.

QUESTION FOR REFLECTION

Perhaps the most astonishing thing about this sonnet is that it is only a single sentence. Go through the poem again attending to the way the sentence develops. Account for all the conjunctions: *so* (line 4), *and* (line 5), *And* (line 7), *But* (line 9), *And* (line 12). How do those conjunctions help us follow the sentence?

E. E. CUMMINGS
[1894–1962]

"Me up at does"

Me up at does

out of the floor
quietly Stare

a poisoned mouse

still who alive

is asking What
have i done that

You wouldn't have

QUESTIONS FOR REFLECTION

1. Rearrange the syntax of this poem to approximate the normal word order of an English sentence. Where do you have to make the heaviest adjustment?
2. How is Cummings's word order related to the situation the poem describes? What does Cummings gain by ordering his words as he does?

STEVIE SMITH
[1902–1971]

Mother, Among the Dustbins

Mother, among the dustbins and the manure
I feel the measure of my humanity, an allure
As of the presence of God. I am sure

In the dustbins, in the manure, in the cat at play,
Is the presence of God, in a sure way   5
He moves there. Mother, what do you say?

I too have felt the presence of God in the broom
I hold, in the cobwebs in the room,
But most of all in the silence of the tomb.

Ah! but that thought that informs the hope of our kind   10
Is but an empty thing, what lies behind?—
Naught but the vanity of a protesting mind

That would not die. This is the thought that bounces
Within a conceited head and trounces
Inquiry. Man is most frivolous when he pronounces.   15

Well Mother, I shall continue to think as I do,
And I think you would be wise to do so too,
Can you question the folly of man in the creation of God?
    Who are you?

QUESTION FOR REFLECTION

Examine the way the poet uses balanced phrasing, primarily repeated phrases throughout the poem. Notice the play of long sentence against short, of question against statement. What do these syntactic elements contribute to the tone and attitude of the poem?

SOUND: RHYME, ALLITERATION, ASSONANCE

The most familiar element of poetry is *rhyme,* which can be defined as the matching of final vowel and consonant sounds in two or more words. When the corresponding sounds occur at the ends of lines we have *end rhyme;* when they occur within lines we have *internal rhyme.* The opening stanza of Edgar Allan Poe's "The Raven" illustrates both:

> Once upon a midnight dreary, while I pondered weak and weary,
> Over many a quaint and curious volume of forgotten lore—
> While I nodded nearly napping, suddenly there came a tapping,
> As of some one gently rapping, rapping at my chamber door.
> "'Tis some visitor," I muttered, "tapping at my chamber door—
> Only this and nothing more."

For the reader rhyme is a pleasure, for the poet a challenge. Part of its pleasure for the reader is in anticipating and hearing a poem's echoing song. Part of its challenge for the poet is in rhyming naturally, without forcing the rhythm, the syntax, or the sense. When the challenge is met successfully, the poem is a pleasure to listen to; it sounds natural to the ear, and its rhyme makes it easier to remember.

Robert Frost's "Stopping by Woods on a Snowy Evening" is one such rhyming success. Reread it once more, preferably aloud, and listen to its music.

> Whose woods these are I think I know.
> His house is in the village, though;
> He will not see me stopping here
> To watch his woods fill up with snow.
>
> My little horse must think it queer
> To stop without a farmhouse near
> Between the woods and frozen lake
> The darkest evening of the year.
>
> He gives his harness bells a shake
> To ask if there is some mistake.
> The only other sound's the sweep
> Of easy wind and downy flake.
>
> The woods are lovely, dark and deep,
> But I have promises to keep,
> And miles to go before I sleep,
> And miles to go before I sleep.

Notice how in each of the first three stanzas, three of the four lines rhyme (lines 1, 2, and 4), and Frost picks up the nonrhymed sound of each stanza (the

third line) and links it with the rhyming sound of the stanza that follows it, un-
til the fourth stanza when he closes with four matching rhymes. Part of our
pleasure in Frost's rhyming may derive from the pattern of departure and return
it voices. Part may stem also from the way the rhyme pattern supports the
poem's meaning. The speaker is caught between his desire to remain still,
peacefully held by the serene beauty of the woods, and his contrasting need to
leave, to return to his responsibilities. In a similar way, the poem's rhyme is
caught between a surge forward toward a new sound and a return to a sound
repeated earlier. The pull and counterpull of the rhyme reflect the speaker's
ambivalence.

The rhymes in Frost's poem are *exact* or *perfect rhymes:* that is, the rhyming
words share corresponding sounds and stresses and a similar number of sylla-
bles. While Frost's poem contains perfect rhymes ("know," "though," and
"snow," for example), we sometimes hear in poems a less exact, *imperfect, ap-
proximate,* or *slant rhyme.* Emily Dickinson's "Crumbling is not an instant's Act"
(page 89) includes both exact rhyme ("dust"-"rust") and slant rhyme ("slow"-
"law"). Theodore Roethke's "My Papa's Waltz" (page 12) contains a slant
rhyme on (*"dizzy"-"easy"*), which also exemplifies *feminine rhyme.* In feminine
rhyme the final syllable of a rhymed word is unstressed; in *masculine rhyme* the
final syllable is stressed—or the words rhymed are each only one syllable.

Besides rhyme, two other forms of sound play prevail in poetry: *alliteration*
or the repetition of consonant sounds, especially at the beginning of words,
and *assonance* or the repetition of vowel sounds. In his witty guide to poetic
technique, *Rhyme's Reason,* John Hollander describes alliteration and asso-
nance like this:

> Assonance is the spirit of a rhyme,
> A common vowel, hovering like a sigh
> After its consonantal body dies. . . .
>
>   . . .
> Alliteration lightly links
> Stressed syllables with common consonants.

Walt Whitman's "When I heard the learn'd astronomer" (page 82) though lack-
ing in end rhyme, possesses a high degree of assonance. The long *i*'s in lines 1,
3, and 4 accumulate and gather force as the poem glides into its last four lines:
"*I,*" "tired," "rising," "gliding," "*I,*" "myself," "night," "time to time," and "si-
lence." This assonance sweetens the sound of the second part of the poem,
highlighting its radical shift of action and feeling.

Both alliteration and assonance are clearly audible in "Stopping by Woods,"
particularly in the third stanza:

> He gives his harness bells a shake
> To ask if there is some mistake.
> The only other sound's the sweep
> Of easy wind and downy flake.

Notice that the long *e* of "sweep" is echoed in "*ea*-sy" and "down-*y*," and that the *ow* of "do*w*ny" echoes the same sound in "so*u*nd's." These repetitions of sound accentuate the images the words embody, aural images (wind–blow and snow–fall), tactile images (the soft fluff of down and the feel of the gently blowing wind), and visual images (the white flakes of snow).

The alliterative *s*'s in "*s*ome," "*s*ound," and "*s*weep" are supported by the internal and terminal *s*'s: "Give*s*," "hi*s*," "harne*ss* bell*s*," and "i*s*," and also by mid-word *s*'s: "a*s*k," "mi*s*take," and "ea*s*y." Some of these sounds are heavier than others—the two similar heavy *s*'s of "easy" and "his" contrast the lighter softer "*s*" in "harness" and "mistake."

Listen to the sound effects of rhyme, alliteration, and assonance, in the following poem. Try to determine what *sound* contributes to the poem's meaning.

GERARD MANLEY HOPKINS
[1844–1889]

In the Valley of the Elwy

I remember a house where all were good
   To me, God knows, deserving no such thing:
   Comforting smell breathed at very entering,
Fetched fresh, as I suppose, off some sweet wood.
That cordial air made those kind people a hood   5
   All over, as a bevy of eggs the mothering wing
   Will, or mild nights the new morsels of Spring:
Why, it seemed of course; seemed of right it should.

Lovely the woods, waters, meadows, combes, vales,
All the air things wear that build this world of Wales;   10
   Only the inmate does not correspond:

God, lover of souls, swaying considerate scales,
Complete thy creature dear O where it fails,
   Being mighty a master, being a father and fond.

We note first that the rhyme scheme reveals a Petrarchan sonnet: *abba, abba, ccd, ccd* (see page 80). Also we might note that its rhyme pattern corresponds to its sentence structure: the octave splits into two sentences, lines 1–4 and 5–8; the sestet, though only one sentence, splits into two equal parts, lines 9–11 and 12–14. Hopkins's use of the Italian rhyme scheme keeps similar sounds repeating throughout: *good, wood, hood, should; thing, entering, wing, Spring; vales, Wales, scales, fails; correspond, fond.* (The rhyme pattern of the Shakespearean or English sonnet, by contrast, as heard in "That time of year," [page 43] contains fewer rhyming repetitions, as it uses a greater number of different sounds.)

Besides extensive rhyme, Hopkins uses alliteration and assonance—lightly in the octave and more heavily in the sestet. Lines 3–6, for example, collect short *e*'s in "sm*e*ll," "*ve*ry," "*e*ntering," "f*e*tched" and "fr*e*sh," "b*e*vy" and "*e*ggs." Lines 4–8 begin an alliterative use of *w*, which is more elaborately sounded in lines 9–10 of the sestet; in lines 4–8 we hear: "s*w*eet *w*ood," "*w*ing *W*ill," and "*w*hy." In addition, in line 7 "m*i*ld n*i*ghts" picks up the long *i* of "Wh*y*," which finds an echo in the rhyme on "r*i*ght." This seventh line also contains what we might call a reversed or crisscrossed alliteration in "*m*ild *n*ights" and "*n*ew *m*orsels."

But these sound effects are only a pale indication of what we hear in the sestet. Perhaps the most musical lines of the entire poem are the opening lines of the sestet (lines 9–10). *L*'s frame both of these lines: "*L*ovely . . . va*l*es" and "A*ll* . . . Wa*l*es." *L*'s are further sounded in "bui*l*d this wor*l*d." The *w*, which as we noted ended the octave, is carried into the sestet in "*w*oods," "*w*aters," "mead-o*w*s," "*w*ear," "*w*orld," and "*W*ales." The sestet also includes a variety of vowels: l*o*v*e*ly, w*oo*ds, w*a*t*e*r, m*ea*d*o*ws, c*o*mbes, v*a*les, *a*ll, *ai*r, w*ea*r, th*a*t, b*u*ild, th*i*s, w*o*rld, W*a*les.

Hopkins sounds a similarly varied vowel music in the last line, where he also uses alliteration and repetition to call attention to important attributes of God:

> Being mighty a master, being a father and fond.

One line, however, especially lacks music: line 11. Coming amidst such splendid sounds, it stands out even more sharply:

> Only the inmate does not correspond.

This expressive use of sound variation supports the idea that the line conveys: that in this beautiful natural world, the "inmate," the speaker in the guise of prisoner, does not fit. He feels out of place, out of harmony with his environment. In the lines that follow (12–14), he asks God to "complete" him, to make him whole, to integrate him into the world. And he prays in language that immediately picks up the sound play of assonance and alliteration that had been momentarily suspended in line 11. The speaker's harmony and wholeness are thus restored in the poem's beauty of sound.

To further develop your ear for sound in poetry, listen to the poems that follow:

THOMAS HARDY

[1840–1928]

During Wind and Rain

They sing their dearest songs—
He, she, all of them—yea,
Treble and tenor and bass,
   And one to play;
With the candles mooning each face. . . .   5
   Ah, no; the years O!
How the sick leaves reel down in throngs!

They clear the creeping moss—
Elders and juniors—aye,
Making the pathway neat   10
   And the garden gay;
And they build a shady seat. . . .
   Ah, no; the years, the years;
See, the white stormbirds wing across!

They are blithely breakfasting all—   15
Men and maidens—yea,
Under the summer tree,
   With a glimpse of the bay,
While pet fowl come to the knee. . . .
   Ah, no; the years O!   20
And the rotten rose is ripped from the wall.

They change to a high new house,
He, she, all of them—aye,
Clocks and carpets, and chairs
   On the lawn all day,   25
And brightest things that are theirs. . . .
   Ah, no; the years, the years;
Down their carved names the rain drop ploughs.

QUESTIONS FOR REFLECTION

1. Chart the poem's rhyme scheme. Note the repetitions of lines ("Ah no: the years")
and of words ("O," "aye," and "yea"). What do these repetitions contribute to the
idea and feeling of the poem?
2. Identify examples of alliteration and comment on their effect.

ALEXANDER POPE
[1688–1744]

Sound and Sense

True ease in writing comes from art, not chance,
As those move easiest who have learned to dance.
'Tis not enough no harshness gives offense,
The sound must seem an echo to the sense:
Soft is the strain when Zephyr° gently blows,   5
And the smooth stream in smoother numbers flows;
But when loud surges lash the sounding shore,
The hoarse, rough verse should like the torrent roar.
When Ajax° strives, some rock's vast weight to throw,
The line too labors, and the words move slow;   10
Not so, when swift Camilla° scours the plain,
Flies o'er th' unbending corn, and skims along the main.
Hear how Timotheus'° varied lays surprise,
And bid alternate passions fall and rise!
While, at each change, the son of Libyan Jove,°   15
Now burns with glory, and then melts with love;
Now his fierce eyes with sparkling fury glow,
Now sighs steal out, and tears begin to flow;
Persians and Greeks like turns of nature found,
And the world's victor stood subdued by sound!   20
The pow'r of music all our hearts allow,
And what Timotheus was, is DRYDEN now.

QUESTIONS FOR REFLECTION

1. How does the poet enact verbally what he asserts in line 4, that "the sound must seem an echo to the sense"?
2. What contrast is described and imitated in sound effects in lines 5–6 and 7–8? Between lines 9–10 and lines 11–12?

"Sound and Sense" ⁵*Zephyr* the west wind. ⁹*Ajax* a strong Greek warrior in the Trojan War. ¹¹*Camilla* an ancient Volcian queen noted for her speed and lightness of step. ¹³*Timotheus* a musician in John Dryden's poem "Alexander's Feast." ¹⁵*the son of Libyan Jove* Alexander the Great (356–323 B.C.), king of Macedonia and military conqueror who spread Greek culture throughout the ancient world.

MAY SWENSON
[1919–1989]

The Universe

What
  is it about,
the universe,
the universe about us stretching out?
We, within our brains,   5
within it,
  think
we must unspin
the laws that spin it.
  We think *why*   10
because we think
because.
Because we think,
we think
the universe about us.   15

But does it think,
the universe?
 Then what about?
  About us?
If not,   20
must there be cause
in the universe?
Must it have laws?
And what
if the universe   25
is not about us?
Then what?
What
is it about?
And what   30
about *us?*

QUESTION FOR REFLECTION

Is this poem merely a witty game of repeating words or does it employ sound effects
to sound effect? Consider especially lines 10–15 and 24–31.

BOB MCKENTY
[b. 1935]

Adam's Song

Come live with me and be my love.
Come romp with me in Eden's grove
In unabated joy, not shy
But unabashed by nudity,
Where you can bare—sans shame—your breast   5
Until the fell Forbidden Feast.
Thereafter I shall toil and sweat
To earn whatever bread we eat
And you, in bearing children, shall
Know pain and suffering. The Fall   10
Will bring us sickness, death, and fear,
Embarrassment and underwear
(For which the Fig donates its leaf)
And poets who are surely deaf.

QUESTION FOR REFLECTION

Identify the sound effects at play in "Adam's Song." Consider especially the poem's rhymes.

HELEN CHASIN
[b. 1938]

The Word *Plum*

The word *plum* is delicious

pout and push, luxury of
self-love, and savoring murmur

full in the mouth and falling
like fruit   5

   taut skin
   pierced, bitten, provoked into
   juice, and tart flesh

question
and reply, lip and tongue   10
of pleasure.

QUESTIONS FOR REFLECTION

1. How is the word *p-l-u-m* sounded and resounded in the poem? Look at and listen
   to lines 2–3 in particular.
2. Map out the poem's patterns of alliteration and vowel repetition.

RHYTHM AND METER

Rhythm refers to the regular recurrence of the accent or stress in poem or
song. It is the pulse or beat we feel in a phrase of music or a line of poetry. We
derive our sense of rhythm from everyday life and from our experience with
language and music. We experience the rhythm of day and night, the seasonal
rhythms of the year, the beat of our hearts, and the rise and fall of our chests as
we breathe in and out.

Perhaps our earliest memories of rhythm in language are associated with
nursery rhymes like

> JACK and JILL went UP the HILL★
> to FETCH a PAIL of WAter.

Later we probably learned songs like "America," whose rhythm we might indi-
cate like this:

> MY COUN-TRY 'tis of THEE
> SWEET LAND of LIberTY
> Of THEE i SING.

Since then we have developed an ear for the rhythm of language in everyday
speech:

> I THINK I'll HIT the HAY
> Did you SEE that?
> Or: Did you see THAT?
> or: GO and DON'T come BACK.

★Capitalization indicates stressed syllables, lowercase letters unstressed ones.

Poets rely heavily on rhythm to express meaning and convey feeling. In "The Sun Rising" John Donne puts words together in a pattern of stressed and unstressed syllables:

> BUsy old FOOL, unRULy SUN
> WHY DOST THOU THUS
> Through WINdows, and through CURtains, CALL on US?

Donne uses four accents per line—even in the second more slowly paced short line. Later in the stanza, he retards the tempo further. Listen to the accents in the following lines:

> LOVE, all aLIKE, no SEAson knows, nor CLIME,
> Nor HOURS, DAYS, MONTHS, which ARE the RAGS of TIME.

The accents result partly from Donne's use of monosyllabic words and partly from pauses within the line (indicated by commas). Such pauses are called *caesuras* and are represented by a double slash (//). The final couplet of Donne's poem illustrates a common use of caesura—to split a line near its midpoint:

> Shine here to us, // and thou art everywhere;
> This bed thy center is, // these walls thy sphere.

Marking the accents as well, we get this:

> SHINE HERE to US, // and THOU art EVeryWHERE;
> THIS BED thy CENter IS, // THESE WALLS thy SPHERE.

Notice again how the monosyllabic diction and the balanced phrasing combine with the caesuras to slow the lines down. The stately rhythm enforces the speaker's dignified tone and serious point: "Here is everywhere; this room is a world in itself; it is all that matters to us."

In the following brief poem by Robert Frost, you can readily hear and feel the contrasting pace and rhythms of its two lines:

The Span of Life

> The OLD DOG BARKS BACKward withOUT GETting UP.
> I can reMEMber when HE was a PUP.

The first line is slower than the second. It is harder to pronounce and takes longer to say because Frost clusters the hard consonants, *d, k,* and *g* sounds, in the first line, and because the first line contains seven stresses to the four accents of the second. Three of the seven stresses fall at the beginning of the line, which gets it off to a slow start, whereas the accents of the second line are evenly spaced. The contrasting rhythms of the lines reinforce their contrasting images and sound effects. More importantly, however, the differences in the sounds and rhythms in the two lines echo their contrast of youth and age.

But we cannot proceed any further in this discussion of rhythm without introducing more precise terms to refer to the patterns of accents we hear in a poem. If rhythm is the pulse or beat we hear in the line, then we can define *meter* as the measure or patterned count of a poetic line. Meter is a count of the stresses we feel in the poem's rhythm. By convention the unit of poetic meter in English is the *foot*, a unit of measure consisting of stressed and unstressed syllables. A poetic foot may be either *iambic* or *trochaic, anapestic* or *dactylic.* An iambic line is composed primarily of *iambs,* an *iamb* being defined as an unaccented syllable followed by an accented one as in the word "preVENT" or "conTAIN." Reversing the order of accented and unaccented syllables we get a *trochee,* which is an accented syllable followed by an unaccented one, as in "FOOTball" or "LIquor." We can represent an accented syllable by a ' and an unaccented syllable by a ˘: thus, prĕvent(˘ '), an iamb, and lí'quŏr ('˘), a trochee. Because both iambic and trochaic feet contain two syllables per foot, they are called *duple* (or double) meters. These duple meters can be distinguished from *triple* meters (three-syllable meters) like anapestic and dactylic meters. An *anapest* (˘˘ ') consists of two unaccented syllables followed by an accented one as in cŏmprĕHE'ND or iñtĕrVE'NE. A *dactyl* reverses the anapest, beginning with an accented syllable followed by two unaccented ones. DA'Ngĕroŭs and CHE'ERfŭllў are examples. So is the word AN'ăpĕst.

Three additional points must be noted about poetic meter. First, anapestic (˘˘ ') and iambic (˘ ') meters move from an unstressed syllable to a stressed one. For this reason they are called *rising* meters. (They "rise" to the stressed syllable.) Lines in anapestic or iambic meter frequently end with a stressed syllable. Trochaic ('˘) and dactylic ('˘˘) meters, on the other hand, are said to be *falling* meters because they begin with a stressed syllable and decline in pitch and emphasis. (Syllables at the ends of trochaic and dactylic lines are generally unstressed.)

Second, the regularity of a poem's meter is not inflexible. In a predominantly iambic poem (Shakespeare's sonnet "That time of year thou may'st in me behold," for example, or Frost's "Stopping by Woods"), every line will not usually conform exactly to the strict metrical pattern. Frost's poem is much more regular in its iambic meter than is Shakespeare's, but Frost avoids metrical monotony by subtly altering his rhythm. And in one important instance Frost departs from the pattern slightly. We can divide the last stanza of Frost's poem into metrical feet and mark the accents in this manner, separating the feet with slashes.

> Thĕ woo'ds / ărĕ lo've / lў da'rk / ăñd de'ep. /
> Bŭt I' / ha've pr'o / mĭsĕs / tŏ ke'ep,
> Añd mil'es / tŏ g'o /bĕfo're / Ĭ sle'ep,
> Añd mil'es / tŏ g'o /bĕfo're / Ĭ sle'ep,

If we regard the pattern of this stanza and the pattern of the poem as a whole as regularly, even insistently, iambic, then the second line of this final stanza marks a slight deviation from that norm. The second and third feet of the line can be read as two accented syllables followed by two unaccented syllables, a spondaic foot followed by a pyrrhic. That's the way I've marked them. Two accented syllables together is called a *spondee* (KNI'CK-KNA'CK); two unaccented ones, a *pyrrhic* (ŏf thĕ). Both spondaic and pyrrhic feet serve as substitute feet for iambic and trochaic feet. Neither can serve as the metrical norm of an English poem.

Third, we give names to lines of poetry based on the number of feet they contain. You may have noticed in looking back at "Stopping by Woods on a Snowy Evening" that it consists of eight-syllable or *octosyllabic* lines. Since the meter is iambic (˘ ´) with two syllables per foot, the line contains four iambic feet and is hence called a *tetrameter* line (from the Greek word for *four*). Thus Frost's poem is written in *iambic tetrameter*, unlike Shakespeare's sonnet "That time of year thou may'st in me behold," for example, which contains ten-syllable lines, also predominantly iambic. Such five-foot lines are named *pentameters* (from the Greek "penta" for five), making the sonnet a poem in *iambic pentameter.*

Here is a chart of the various meters and poetic feet.

	Foot	Meter	Example
Rising or Ascending Feet	iamb	iambic	prevent
	anapest	anapestic	comprehend
Falling or Descending Feet	trochee	trochaic	football
	dactyl	dactylic	cheerfully
Substitute Feet	spondee	spondaic	knick-knack
	pyrrhic	pyrrhic	(light) of the
			(world)

Duple Meters: two syllables per foot: iambic and trochaic

Triple Meters: three syllables per foot: anapestic and dactylic

Number of feet per line

one foot	monometer
two feet	dimeter
three feet	trimeter
four feet	tetrameter
five feet	pentameter
six feet	hexameter
seven feet	heptameter
eight feet	octameter

You should now be better able to discern the meter and rhythm of a poem. You can make an instructive comparison for yourself by taking the measure of two poems in the same meter: Shakespeare's sonnet "That time of year thou may'st in me behold" (page 43) and Hopkins's "In the Valley of the Elwy," (page 65) both written in iambic pentameter. In Hopkins's sonnet, see if you can account for the speed of the octave and the slower pace of the sestet: look to changes in the basic iambic pattern; look for caesuras; and watch for *enjambed* or run-on lines, whose sense and grammar runs over and into the next line. You should be alert in both poems for how parallel sentence structure and the sound play of alliteration and assonance collaborate with rhythm and meter to support each poem's feeling and meaning. Listen carefully, especially to the last line of the octave and sestet of Hopkins's sonnet and to Shakespeare's concluding couplet.

Metrical Variation

We noted earlier that Frost's "Stopping by Woods" is written in strict iambic pentameter with only one slight variation in line 14. How then does Frost manage to avoid the monotony of fifteen lines of ta TUM / ta TUM / ta TUM / ta TUM / ? One way is by varying the reader's focus on different details: woods, snow, and speaker (stanza one); horse and darkness (stanza two); horse and snow (stanza three); woods and darkness and speaker (stanza four). Another is to vary the syntax, as he does with the inversion of the opening line. A third is simply to use a familiar diction in a normal speaking voice. Fourth and perhaps most important is Frost's masterful control of tempo. Of the four stanzas none carry the same pattern of end stopping. Stanza one is end-stopped at the first, second, and fourth lines, with line 3 enjambed. Stanza three is the closest to the second stanza, with two end-stopped lines and two enjambed lines. Stanza four is heavily stopped with two caesuras in its initial line and with end stops at every line. (It is here that we are slowed down to feel the seductive beauty of the woods; it is here that the symbolic weight of the poem is heaviest.) But we should not overlook the contrasting second stanza, which is cast as a single flowing sentence. The iambic pattern inhabits this stanza as it beats in the others. But as a result of the variety of technical resources Frost displays in the poem, we hear the iambic beat but are not overwhelmed by it.

Frost's rhythmical variations can be compared with Whitman's expressive use of metrical variation in "When I heard the learn'd astronomer" (page 82), a poem in *free verse,* verse without a fixed metrical pattern. Whitman's poem is characteristic of much free verse in its varying line lengths and accents per line, and in its imitation of the cadences of speech. The poem's final line ("Look'd up in perfect silence at the stars"), however, differs from the others, as Paul Fussell has pointed out in *Poetic Meter and Poetic Form.*★ It is written in strict iambic pentameter, a variation which carries considerable expressive power, coming after the seemingly casual metrical organization of the previous lines. Because Whitman's line must be read in the context of the whole poem for its expressive impact to be felt, you should turn to it, preferably to read it aloud. Consider whether, as some readers have suggested, the poem is not really in free verse at all, but rather in *blank verse,* unrhymed iambic pentameter.

Besides this expressive use of metrical variation, Whitman's poem exhibits additional elements of rhythmic control: in its consistency of end-stopped lines; in its flexible use of caesura (lines 2, 3, and 7); in its absence of caesura from the shorter lines (1, and 4–8). We can perhaps gain a greater appreciation of Whitman's rhythmical accomplishment by recasting his lines like this:

★Paul Fussell, *Poetic Meter and Poetic Form* (New York: Random House, 1979), p. 85.

> When I heard the learn'd astronomer,
> When the proofs, the figures
> Were ranged in columns before me,
> When I was shown the charts and diagrams
> To add, divide, and measure them,
> When I sitting heard the astronomer
> Where he lectured to much applause
> In the lecture-room. . . .

Or like this:

> When I heard
> The learn'd astronomer,
> When the proofs,
> The figures were ranged
> In columns
> Before me,
> When I was shown
> The charts and diagrams
> To add, divide and
> Measure them. . . .

Both versions destroy the poem: they eliminate the sweep of its long lines, destroying its cadences and rhythm, and ultimately inhibiting its expressiveness.

Before leaving the poem, we should note that Whitman's rhythmic effects work together with other devices of sound, structure, and diction. In the same way, for example, that the strict iambic pentameter of the last line varies the prevailing meter expressively, so too does its assonance (the long *i*'s) deviate expressively from the poem's previously established avoidance of vowel music. In addition, the meter of the final line stresses *si'leňce* and *sta'rs,* both of which the speaker values. Finally, the iambic rhythm of the line has us looking U'P and A'T the stars, an unusual metrical effect since prepositions are almost always unstressed.

Throughout these comments on the rhythm and meter of the poems by Whitman and Frost, we have been engaged in the act of *scansion,* measuring verse, identifying its prevailing meter and rhythm, and accounting for deviations from the metrical pattern. In scanning a poem, we try to determine its dominant rhythm and meter, and to account for variations from the norm. The pattern we hear as dominant will influence how we read lines that do not conform metrically, and also how we interpret and respond to those lines. Consider, for example, the words "at a glance" abstracted from their place in a line of Wordsworth's "I wandered lonely as a cloud." Do you hear them as anapestic: ǎt ǎ gla'nce? This is a likely way to hear the words outside the context of the poem. But when we return them to the poem, we may hear them another way:

> Těn tho'usǎnd sa'w Ĭ a't ǎ gla'nce.

In such a case we will probably hear both the rhythmic pattern of the normal speaking voice (aĭ ă glá́nce) and the metrical pattern of iambic pentameter (át ă glá́nce). Our experience of rhythm thus will often involve a tension between the two patterns as we hear one superimposed on the other.

One last note about rhythm and meter. Without the turn of the poetic line, without the division of words into lines, we have no poem. For what distinguishes poetry from prose is the line; it is the line that makes verse what it is (from the Latin *versus,* to turn). And as the poet Wendell Berry has pointed out, it is the line of verse that "checks the merely impulsive flow of speech, subjects it to another pulse, to measure."★ Without the measure of meter, without the turn of the line, there is no music and no poem. Meter and rhythm are not merely technical elements, no more than diction and imagery, syntax and structure and sound. All of these interrelated elements of poetry have effects on readers, do things to readers. We sense them and feel them and thereby understand a poem, not just with our minds, but also with our eyes and ears.

Here are a few additional poems for rhythmic and metrical consideration.

GEORGE GORDON, LORD BYRON
[*1788–1824*]

The Destruction of Sennacherib°

The Assyrian came down like the wolf on the fold,
And his cohorts were gleaming in purple and gold;
And the sheen of their spears was like stars on the sea,
When the blue wave rolls nightly on deep Galilee.

Like the leaves of the forest when summer is green,   5
That host with their banners at sunset were seen:
Like the leaves of the forest when autumn hath blown,
That host on the morrow lay withered and strown.

For the Angel of Death spread his wings on the blast,
And breathed in the face of the foe as he passed;   10
And the eyes of the sleepers waxed deadly and chill,
And their hearts but once heaved—and for ever grew still!

And there lay the steed with his nostril all wide,
But through it there rolled not the breath of his pride;
And the foam of his gasping lay white on the turf,   15
And cold as the spray of the rock-beating surf.

★Wendell Berry, *Standing By Words* (San Francisco: North Point Press, 1983), p. 28.

And there lay the rider distorted and pale,
With the dew on his brow, and the rust on his mail;
And the tents were all silent, the banners alone,
The lances unlifted, the trumpet unblown.   20

And the widows of Ashur are loud in their wail,
And the idols are broke in the temple of Baal;
And the might of the Gentile, unsmote by the sword,
Hath melted like snow in the glance of the Lord!

QUESTIONS FOR REFLECTION

1. Identify the poem's meter. What kind of movement and rhythm does the meter create?
2. How is it appropriate to the action and idea of the poem?

ANNE SEXTON
[1928–1974]

Her Kind

I have gone out, a possessed witch,
haunting the black air, braver at night;
dreaming evil, I have done my hitch
over the plain houses, light by light:
lonely thing, twelve-fingered, out of mind.   5
A woman like that is not a woman, quite.
I have been her kind.
I have found the warm caves in the woods,
filled them with skillets, carvings, shelves,
closets, silks, innumerable goods;   10
fixed the suppers for the worms and the elves:
whining, rearranging the disaligned.
A woman like that is misunderstood.
I have been her kind.

I have ridden in your cart, driver,   15
waved my nude arms at villages going by,
learning the last bright routes, survivor
where your flames still bite my thigh
and my ribs crack where your wheels wind.
A woman like that is not ashamed to die.   20
I have been her kind.

" The Destruction of Sennacherib" **The Destruction of Sennacherib**   *the poem is based on the biblical account*
(II Kings 19:35) of the Assyrian king, Sennacherib, whose army was destroyed by the angel of the Lord in an invasion
of Jerusalem.

QUESTIONS FOR REFLECTION

1. Identify the prevailing meter of the poem. How does Sexton keep the poem moving?
2. Examine her uses of caesura and enjambment, and comment on their effect on the poem's rhythm.

WILLIAM CARLOS WILLIAMS
[*1883–1963*]

The Red Wheelbarrow

so much depends
upon

a red wheel
barrow

glazed with rain   5
water

beside the white
chickens

QUESTIONS FOR REFLECTION

1. Mark the poem's meter. Which lines match each other metrically?
2. What is the effect of the breaks between lines 3 and 4 and between lines 5 and 6?

STRUCTURE: CLOSED FORM AND OPEN FORM

When we analyze a poem's structure, we focus on its patterns of organization. *Form* exists in poems on many levels from patterns of sound and image to structures of syntax and of thought; it is as much a matter of phrase and line as of stanza and whole poem.

Among the most popular forms of poetry has been the *sonnet,* a fourteen-line poem usually written in iambic pentameter (see pp. 73–75). Because the form of the sonnet is strictly constrained, it is considered a *closed* or *fixed form.* We can recognize poems in fixed forms such as the sonnet, sestina, and vil-lanelle by their patterns of rhyme, meter, and repetition; they reveal their struc-tural patterns both aurally and visually. We see the shapes of their stanzas and the patterns of their line lengths; we feel their metrical beat, and we hear their play of sound.

The *Shakespearean* or *English sonnet* falls into three *quatrains* or four-line sections with the rhyme pattern *abab cdcd efef* followed by a *couplet* or pair of rhymed lines with the pattern *gg*. Let us reread Shakespeare's sonnet, "That time of year thou may'st in me behold."

That time of year thou may'st in me behold	*a*	
When yellow leaves, or none, or few, do hang	*b*	
Upon those boughs which shake against the cold,	*a*	
Bare ruined choirs, where late the sweet birds sang.	*b*	
In me thou see'st the twilight of such day	*c*	5
As after sunset fadeth in the west;	*d*	
Which by-and-by black night doth take away,	*c*	
Death's second self that seals up all in rest.	*d*	
In me thou see'st the glowing of such fire	*e*	
That on the ashes of his youth doth lie,	*f*	10
As the deathbed whereon it must expire,	*e*	
Consumed with that which it was nourished by.	*f*	
This thou perceiv'st, which makes thy love more strong,	*g*	
To love that well which thou must leave ere long.	*g*	

Each of the three quatrains of the poem is a single sentence, as is the couplet. This organization of the poem's sentences corresponds to its rhyme and images, which are also arranged in three quatrains and a final couplet. The pattern is reinforced, moreover, by the use of repeated words in the three quatrains: "In me behold"; "In me thou see'st"; "In me thou see'st."

There is a progression in the imagery in the sonnet: daylight becomes twilight; twilight turns into night. And there is a countermovement from images of longer duration to those of shorter: from the dying of a season to the dying of a day to the dying of a fire. In addition, within each image there is a movement from optimism to pessimism. Each image begins more hopefully than it ends: the yellow leaves become "bare ruined choirs" (lines 1–4); the twilight gives way to "Death's second self" (lines 5–8); the "glowing . . . fire" becomes "ashes" on a "deathbed" (lines 9–12).

The couplet is both a logical and an emotional response to the three quatrains that precede it. In the couplet is an implied *therefore* or *because* that can be heard by reversing the word order of its first line: Since you perceive this, it makes your love more strong. The last line is both a plea and a command to "love that well which thou must leave ere long," with "which" carrying the force of *because*.

Not every sonnet Shakespeare wrote is structured as tightly as this one. Look at the sonnets on pages 216–218 to see how Shakespeare varies this pattern, how, for example, he uses the couplet not only to respond to the quatrains, but to summarize their point or extend their implications as well.

An alternative to the Shakespearean sonnet is the *Petrarchan* or *Italian sonnet,* which falls into two parts: an *octave* of eight lines and a *sestet* of six. The octave rhyme pattern is *abba abba* (two sets of four lines); the sestet's lines are more variable: *cde cde;* or *ced ced;* or *cd cd cd.* The following is an example of the Italian form:

JOHN KEATS
[1795–1821]

On First Looking into Chapman's Homer°

Much have I traveled in the realms of gold	*a*	
And many goodly states and kingdoms seen;	*b*	
Round many western islands have I been	*b*	
Which bards in fealty° to Apollo° hold.	*a*	allegiance
Oft of one wide expanse had I been told	*a*	5
That deep-browed Homer ruled as his demesne;°	*b*	domain
Yet never did I breathe its pure serene°	*b*	atmosphere
Till I heard Chapman speak out loud and bold:	*a*	
Then felt I like some watcher of the skies	*c*	
When a new planet swims into his ken;	*d*	10
Or like stout Cortez° when with eagle eyes	*c*	
He stared at the Pacific—and all his men	*d*	
Looked at each other with a wild surmise—	*c*	
Silent, upon a peak in Darien.	*d*	

Perhaps the most notable structural feature of the Italian sonnet is the way it turns on the ninth line. The first eight lines of Keats's sonnet describe the speaker's wide reading and compare reading with traveling. Lines 9–14 dramatically convey the speaker's feelings upon first reading Chapman's translation of Homer's great epic poems, *The Iliad* and *The Odyssey*. The speaker's excitement appears in lines 12 and 13, whose broken syntax contrasts with the smooth fluency of the first part of the sonnet. In addition, the octave and sestet differ in diction as well. The diction of the octave is elevated and formal, employing archaic words like "goodly" and "bards," and roundabout expressions like "realms of gold." Such words and phrases create an impression of the remoteness of the past, of its grandeur and dignity. In the sestet the diction is simpler and more direct. Keats's use of figures of comparison in the sestet contributes to the striking change in diction. The two major comparisons, both similes, convey the excitement of discovery. By means of descriptions of action (they "looked" and "stared") and reaction (their "wild surmise" and stunned silence) Keats conveys vividly the speaker's feeling of elation and excitement. Keats capitalizes on the structural possibilities of the Italian sonnet by reserving this elation for the sestet and by varying the diction of octave and sestet.

But not all poems are written in fixed forms. Many poets have resisted the limitations inherent in using a consistent and specific metrical pattern or in

---

"On First Looking into Chapman's Homer" **Chapman's Homer** *translation of Homer's Odyssey by George Chapman, a contemporary of Shakespeare.* [4]***Apollo** god of the sun and poetic inspiration.* [11–14]***Cortez . . . Darien Cortez,** Spanish conqueror of Mexico. Balboa, not Cortez, however, was the first European to see the Pacific from Darien in Panama.*

rhyming lines in a prescribed manner. As an alternative to the strictness of fixed form, they developed and discovered looser, more *open* and *free forms. Open* or *free form* does not imply formlessness. It suggests, instead, that poets capitalize on the freedom either to create their own forms or to use the traditional fixed forms in more flexible ways. An example of a poem in open form by Walt Whitman follows.

WALT WHITMAN
[1819–1892]

When I heard the learn'd astronomer

When I heard the learn'd astronomer,
When the proofs, the figures, were ranged in columns before me,
When I was shown the charts and diagrams, to add, divide, and measure them,
When I sitting heard the astronomer where he lectured with much applause in the
      lecture-room,
How soon unaccountable I became tired and sick,   5
Till rising and gliding out I wander'd off by myself,
In the mystical moist night-air, and from time to time,
Look'd up in perfect silence at the stars.

     Although Whitman's poem is arranged as a single sentence, it can be divided into two parts, each of four lines. The two-part division accumulates a set of contrasts: the speaker with other people and the speaker alone; the speaker sitting inside and the speaker standing outside looking at the stars; the noise inside and the silence outside; the lecturer's activity and the speaker's passivity; the clutter of details in lines 1–4 and the spareness of details in lines 5–8.

     These contrasts reflect the poem's movement from one kind of learning about nature to another: from passive listening to active observation; from indirect factual knowledge to direct mystical apprehension. Whether the poet rejects the first form of knowledge for the second, or whether he suggests that both are needed is not directly stated. The emphasis, nevertheless, is on the speaker's need to be alone and to experience nature directly.

     More elaborate departures from fixed form include poems such as this unusual configuration of E. E. Cummings:

E. E. CUMMINGS
[1894–1962]

l (a

l(a

le
af
fa

ll

s)
one
l

iness

Perhaps the first things to notice are the lack of capital letters and the absence of punctuation (except for the parentheses). What we don't see is as important as what we do. We don't see any recognizable words or sentences, to say nothing of traditional stanzas or lines of poetry. The poem strikes the eye as a series of letters that stream down the page, for the most part two to a line. Rearranging the letters horizontally we find these words: *(a leaf falls) loneliness.* (The first *l* of *loneliness* appears before the parenthesis, like this: *l (a leaf falls) oneliness;* to get *loneliness* you have to move the *l* in front of *oneliness.*

A single falling leaf is a traditional symbol of loneliness; this image is not new. What is new, however, is the way Cummings has coupled the concept with the image, the way he has formed and shaped them into a nontraditional poem. But what has the poet gained by arranging his poem this way? By breaking the horizontal line of verse into a series of fragments (from the horizontal viewpoint), Cummings illustrates visually the separation that is the primary cause of loneliness. Both the word *loneliness* and the image described in *a leaf falls* are broken apart, separated in this way. In addition, by splitting the initial letter from *loneliness,* the poet has revealed the hidden *one* in the word. It's as if he is saying: loneliness is *one*-liness. This idea is further corroborated in the visual ambiguity of "l." Initially we are not sure whether this symbol "l" is a number—*one*—or the letter *l.* By shaping and arranging his poem this way, Cummings unites form and content, structure and idea. He also invites us to play the poetry game with him by remaking the poem as we put its pieces together. In doing so we step back and see in the design of the poem a leaf falling

d

o

w

n

the page. By positioning the letters as he does; Cummings pictures a
leaf fall:

le

af

fa

ll

s.

If "l(a" is a poem for the eye, the following poem, also by Cummings, is
arranged for voice. From the standpoint of traditional poetic form, it too ex-
hibits peculiarities of sound and structure, line and stanza.

E. E. CUMMINGS
[1894–1962]

[Buffalo Bill's]

Buffalo Bill's
defunct
    who used to
    ride a watersmooth-silver
                            stallion   5
and break onetwothreefourfive pigeons justlikethat
                          Jesus

he was a handsome man
                and what i want to know is
how do you like your blueeyed boy   10
Mister Death

    Before we listen closely to the voice of the poem, let's glance at how it hits
the eye. "Buffalo Bill's," "stallion," "defunct," "Jesus," and "Mister Death" are all
set on separate lines *as* complete lines. "Buffalo Bill's," "Mister Death," and "Je-
sus" are the only words capitalized. "Buffalo Bill's and "Mister Death" frame
the poem; "Jesus" is set off on its own as far to the right as the line will go.
Other words also receive a visual stress. At two points in line 6, Cummings
buncheswordstogetherlikethis. Both of these visual effects are translated from
eye to voice to ear so that we read the poem acknowledging the stress in each
case. Cummings has used typography as a formal way of laying out language
on the page to direct our reading. To see and hear what he has accomplished
in this respect, read aloud the following rearranged version, which deliberately
flattens the special effects Cummings highlights.

Buffalo Bill's defunct,
Who used to ride
a water-smooth silver stallion
and break one, two, three, four, five
pigeons just like that
Jesus he was a handsome man
And what I would like to know is
how do you like your
blueeyed boy, Mister Death?

Let us, finally, summarize our remarks about structure and form. By discerning a poem's structure, we gain a clue to its meaning. We can increase our ability to apprehend a poem's organization by doing the following:

1. Looking and listening for changes of diction and imagery, tone and mood, rhythm and rhyme, time and place and circumstance.
2. Watching for repeated elements: words, images, patterns of syntax, rhythm and rhyme.
3. Remembering that structure is an aspect of meaning. It is not something independent of meaning, but works with other poetic elements to embody meaning, to formulate it. A poem's structure, its form, is part of what the poem says, part of how it means what it does.

Test out these ideas by analyzing the form of the following poems.

WILLIAM CARLOS WILLIAMS
[1883–1963]

The Dance

In Breughel's° great picture, The Kermess,
the dancers go round, they go round and
around, the squeal and the blare and the
tweedle of bagpipes, a bugle and fiddles
tipping their bellies (round as the thick-   5
sided glasses whose wash they impound)
their hips and their bellies off balance
to turn them. Kicking and rolling about
the Fair Grounds, swinging their butts, those
shanks must be sound to bear up under such   10
rollicking measures, prance as they dance
in Breughel's great picture, The Kermess.

"The Dance" ¹**Breughel** *Pieter Breughel the Elder (1525–1569), Flemish painter of peasant life. The Kermess is a painting of a peasant wedding dance. See pp. 111–113 for reproductions of two of Breughel's paintings and the poems they inspired.*

QUESTIONS FOR REFLECTION

1. What kind of dance does the poem describe? What kind of action does the first long sentence imitate (lines 1–8)?
2. Comment on the relationship between the first and last lines.

DENISE LEVERTOV

[*b. 1923*]

O Taste and See

The world is
not with us enough.
O taste and see

the subway Bible poster said,
meaning The Lord, meaning   5
if anything all that lives
to the imagination's tongue,

grief, mercy, language,
tangerine, weather, to
breathe them, bite,   10
savor, chew, swallow, transform

into our flesh our
deaths, crossing the street, plum, quince,
living in the orchard and being

hungry, and plucking   15
the fruit.

QUESTION FOR REFLECTION

Imagine this poem written as a single stanza. What is the advantage of the poet's having structured it as she has?

THEODORE ROETHKE
[1908–1963]

The Waking

I wake to sleep, and take my waking slow.
I feel my fate in what I cannot fear.
I learn by going where I have to go.

We think by feeling. What is there to know?
I hear my being dance from ear to ear. 5
I wake to sleep, and take my waking slow.

Of those so close beside me, which are you?
God bless the Ground! I shall walk softly there,
And learn by going where I have to go.

Light takes the Tree; but who can tell us how? 10
The lowly worm climbs up a winding stair;
I wake to sleep, and take my waking slow.

Great Nature has another thing to do
To you and me; so take the lively air,
And, lovely, learn by going where to go. 15

This shaking keeps me steady. I should know.
What falls away is always. And is near.
I wake to sleep, and take my waking slow.
I learn by going where I have to go.

QUESTION FOR REFLECTION

Describe the patterns of repetition that prevail in the poem. Consider repeated rhyme
and repeated lines. What is their effect on the poem's tone and feeling?

C. P. CAVAFY
[1863–1933]

The City

You said: "I'll go to another country, go to another shore,
find another city better than this one.
Whatever I try to do is fated to turn out wrong
and my heart lies buried as though it were something dead.
How long can I let my mind moulder in this place?   5
Wherever I turn, wherever I happen to look,
I see the black ruins of my life, here,
where I've spent so many years, wasted them, destroyed
     them totally."

You won't find a new country, won't find another shore.   10
This city will always pursue you. You will walk
the same streets, grow old in the same neighborhoods,
will turn gray in these same houses.
You will always end up in this city. Don't hope for things
     elsewhere: 15
there is no ship for you, there is no road.
As you've wasted your life here, in this small corner,
you've destroyed it everywhere else in the world.

TRANSLATED BY EDMUND KEELEY AND PHILIP SHERRARD

QUESTION FOR REFLECTION

Why is the poem divided the way it is?

THEME

Theme is an abstraction or generalization drawn from the details of a literary
work; theme refers to an idea or intellectually apprehensible meaning inherent
and implicit in a work. In determining a poem's theme we should be careful
neither to oversimplify the poem nor to distort its meaning. To suggest that the
theme of Hayden's "Those Winter Sundays," for example, is a father's loving
concern for his family is to highlight only part of the poem's meaning, for it
does not take into account the speaker's remorse about his indifference to his
father. Analogously, if we see Roethke's "My Papa's Waltz" as a statement about

a child's terror at his father's horseplay, we misrepresent the complexity of the speaker's response to his memories of his father and their bedtime ritual.

We should also recognize that poems can have multiple themes: poems can be interpreted from more than one perspective and there is more than one way to state or explain a poem's meaning. Let us briefly reconsider Frost's "Stopping by Woods on a Snowy Evening" (page 5).

We can say, for example, that the theme of Frost's poem is the necessity to face the responsibilities inherent in adult life. We can go on to say that the poem centers on a tension in our lives between our desire for rest and peace and our need to fulfill responsibilities and meet obligations. But we shouldn't remain satisfied with this explanation. For, as we have previously stated, the speaker's "miles to go" before he "sleeps" metaphorically describes all he must accomplish before he dies. The final stanza reveals a tension between the speaker's desire to continue and an impulse to stay at rest, to ease himself into the peace of death. We might further interpret the seductiveness of death as an attractive way of escaping the pressures of circumstance and the weight of responsibility.

We can abstract yet another theme: the ability of man to appreciate beauty, particularly the beauty of nature. We might argue, for example, that Frost contrasts man's capacity for taking pleasure in watching the snow fall in a dark wood with an animal's inability to enjoy either the spectacular beauty of the scene or its serenity. Presumably, animals, unlike men, do not possess an aesthetic faculty, the ability to appreciate beauty.

Consider the subject and theme of the following poem.

E M I L Y   D I C K I N S O N
[*1830–1886*]

Crumbling is not an instant's Act

Crumbling is not an instant's Act,
A fundamental pause
Dilapidation's processes
Are organized Decays.

'Tis first a Cobweb on the Soul,   5
A Cuticle of Dust,
A Borer in the Axis,
An Elemental Rust—

Ruin is formal—Devil's work,
Consecutive and slow—   10
Fail in an instant, no man did
Slipping—is Crash's law.

The central idea of the poem is expressed in its opening line. We might para-
phrase it this way: crumbling does not happen instantaneously; it is a gradual
process, occurring slowly, cumulatively over time. The remainder of the first
stanza further establishes this idea by accenting how "crumbling" is a conse-
quence of dilapidation, which is a result of "decay." The deterioration that re-
sults is progressive; it is an organized, systematic process: one stage of decay
leads to the next until destruction inevitably follows.

The gradual nature of decay is emphasized in the final stanza with the state-
ment that no one ever failed in an "instant," that the catastrophe occurs after,
and as a consequence of, a series of failures. We can thus read the poem as a
statement about the process of ruin (personal, emotional, financial) as well as a
description of the process of decay. And we can summarize its theme thus: fail-
ure and destruction can be traced to small-scale elements that precede and
cause them in the sense of natural law ("Crash's law").

The theme is illustrated in the second stanza's four images of decay: cobweb,
rust, dust, and the borer in the axis. These images are all accompanied by bits
of specifying detail. The dust is a "cuticle," an image with suggestions of some-
thing at the edges, of something on the outside and also of something human;
the "Cobweb on the Soul" suggests *spiritual* deterioration ("cobwebs" suggest
neglect); the "elemental" rust puts decay at the heart of things, at the center and
vital core where the "borer" is operating. The poet applies each of these images
of decay to a person, particularly to his or her soul: the dust encircling it, the
cobweb netting it, the borer eating into it, and the rust corrupting it. Such an
interpretation of spiritual decay seems further warranted by the first line of the
third stanza: "Ruin is formal—devil's work." *Ruin* is perhaps the word most
strongly suggestive of human and spiritual collapse; "Devil's work" is a grand,
"old-fashioned" image of active evil. Thus, a statement of the poem's theme
must accommodate the idea of spiritual decay.

Centering on a poem's theme then, we work toward understanding a poem's
significance—what it says, what it implies, what it means.

CHAPTER FOUR

Transformations

REVISIONS

Unlike the goddess Athena, who sprang full-grown from the head of Zeus, poems rarely emerge fully formed from poets' heads. When they do, however, it is often because the poet worked on them both consciously and subconsciously before putting a word on paper. The product of labor as well as inspiration, good poems are the result of considerable care, of repeated efforts to find the right words and put them in the right order.

And yet for all the effort involved, the words and lines of a poem should seem natural, even inevitable. The great modern Irish poet William Butler Yeats put it this way:

> . . . A line will take us hours maybe;
> Yet if it does not seem a moment's thought,
> Our stitching and unstitching has been nought.

We suspect that these lines and the complete poem from which they are taken, "Adam's Curse," took more than a few moments to compose. So too did the following lines in which John Keats describes a woman preparing for bed. Keats's notebook reveals his struggle to bring them to the point where he felt satisfied with them. Here are the lines as published in his "The Eve of St. Agnes":

> . . . her vespers done,
> Of all its wreathed pearls her hair she frees
> Unclasps her warmed jewels one by one;
> Loosens her fragrant bodice; by degrees
> Her rich attire creeps rustling to her knees . . .

Other less successful renderings, however, preceded this final version of the description. Previously, for example, Keats had written "her praying done" rather than "her vespers done." And before that he had written: "her prayers said." Both of these versions are less precise and less musical than the final one. "Vespers," which means evening prayers, is more precise than "prayers"; it is also more musical, echoing the *e* of "her." For "frees" Keats had previously written "strips," a word with quite different connotations and sound. For "warmed" he had written "bosom," and for "rich," "sweet." Of her dress he had also written that it "falls light" instead of "creeps rustling" to her knees. In each case Keats worked toward phrases that possess greater sensuousness and that are richer in sound and imagistic effects. But it is in the fourth line that we can see Keats struggle hardest before he settles on "Loosens her fragrant bodice; by degrees." Here are his earlier attempts:

1. Loosens her bursting, her bodice from her
2. Loosens her bodice lace string
3. Loosens her bodice and her bosom bare
4. Loosens her fragrant bodice and doth bare/Her
5. Loosens her fragrant bodice: and down slips

We have only to consider the images and connotations of "bursting bodice" and "bosom bare" to see how different an effect is achieved with "fragrant bodice." Keats deliberately avoids the stronger sexual overtones of the earlier versions, replacing words suggesting physical sensuality with others of a sensuous rather than a sensual nature.

We can see the process of revision at work more fully in the following poem by William Blake, reprinted in two versions.

WILLIAM BLAKE
[1757–1827]

London

I wander thro' each dirty street,
Near where the dirty Thames does flow,
And [see] mark in every face I meet
Marks of weakness, marks of woe.

In every cry of every man   5
In [every voice of every child] every infant's cry of fear
In every voice, in every ban
The [german] mind forg'd [links I hear] manacles I hear.

[But most] How the chimney sweeper's cry
[Blackens o'er the churches' walls]
Every black'ning church appalls,   10
And the hapless soldier's sigh
Runs in blood down palace walls.

[But most the midnight harlot's curse
From every dismal street I hear,
Weaves around the marriage hearse   15
And blasts the new born infant's tear.]

[Alternate fourth stanza]
But most [from every] thro' wintry streets I hear
How the midnight harlot's curse
Blasts the new born infant's tear,   20
And [hangs] smites with plagues the marriage hearse.

London

I wander thro' each charter'd street,
Near where the charter'd Thames does flow,
And mark in every face I meet
Marks of weakness, marks of woe.

In every cry of every Man,   5
In every Infant's cry of fear,
In every voice, in every ban,
The mind-forg'd manacles I hear.

How the Chimney-sweeper's cry
Every black'ning Church appalls;   10
And the hapless Soldier's sigh
Runs in blood down Palace walls.

But most thro' midnight streets I hear
How the youthful Harlot's curse
Blasts the new born Infant's tear,   15
And blights with plagues the Marriage hearse.

Let's consider the changes in "London" stanza by stanza to determine the implications of each alteration and to estimate how the accumulated changes affect the tone and meaning of the poem as Blake published it.

Stanza One In line 1 "charter'd" replaces "dirty." Although both words are trochaic, the sound of "charter'd" echoes "wander." More important than this use of assonance are the meanings of "charter'd." It denotes something for lease or hire, something established by a charter (a written certificate defining the legal conditions under which a corporate body is organized). The applicable meaning seems to be "hired out." The word's connotations include something defined, planned, laid out, bounded, limited by law, perhaps fixed or determined by decree. Both the street and the river Thames are described as "charter'd," as hired out and bound.

The second alteration in this stanza is Blake's substitution of "mark" for "see." "Mark" means "to take notice of; to give attention; to consider." But it also suggests a more emotionally moving seeing, a more intense noticing than "see." This use of *mark* as a verb in line 3 is further intensified with its appearance as a noun in the next line. Two denotations of the word there seem applicable: "something appearing distinctly on a surface, as a line, spot, scar, or dent" and "something indicative of one's condition, feelings."

Stanza Two   "Man" replaces "man" and "Infant's" replaces "infant's." How important, in each case, is the difference? The early version of the second line has "voice" of a "child." Why do you think Blake changed these words to the "cry" of an infant, and a "cry of fear" at that? "German" in the fourth line means "germane," suggesting something closely related or akin. This word gives way in the later version to "mind-forg'd." "Links" is replaced by "manacles." Consider the denotations and connotations of the words of the later version. How does the meaning of "manacles" support the meanings of "charter'd" and "marks"? How can "manacles" be "mind-forg'd"? And why "forg'd" and not some other word like "made"?

Stanza Three   Consider the implications of the second line in both versions. In the early version the blackening is attributed to the chimney sweeper's cry. In the revised version Blake makes "black'ning" an adjective modifying Church. How can the church's walls be blackened by the cry of a chimney sweeper? And, why does Blake use the adjective "black'ning" to modify "Church"? Reflect on the connotations of "black," "blacken," and "black'ning," and consider the denotations and connotations of "appalls."

Stanza Four   Here we have more than revisions of words or lines. Though many details from the early version are carried over to the later one, they are rearranged, recombined, and rethought. In addition, some details disappear and others emerge. The rhymes, though the same, are reversed, with "hear-tear" ending the early version and "curse-hearse" concluding the final one. In the later version "the midnight harlot" has become "the youthful Harlot"—the word *youthful* a detail that intensifies our emotional response. The "curse" of the second line is both the curse that the harlot passes on to her infant, blinding it at birth with the effects of venereal disease, and the curse of the harlot's own life. Her position echoes the implications of "charter'd" and "wandered" of stanza one. She wanders the streets, but she is hardly free. She is bound, fixed, a body for hire. The final line of the stanza is the most heavily altered. "Blights" and "plagues" suggest not only the ruin of the harlot and her child, but also the destruction of the social order: marriage is cursed, innocent children suffer, soldiers die senselessly, and in general the London populace exhibits signs of desperate suffering.

Blake's revisions intensify his indictment of the institutions—moral, military, and legal—responsible for the human squalor and the misery suffered by innocent people. His revisions increase the emotional intensity of the poem as they darken its view of the lives of the people of London and, by extension, the lives of other urban inhabitants.

Below you will find two versions of three different poems. For each pair examine changes in diction, imagery, syntax, structure, sound, rhythm, meter, and meaning. Explain the significance of the changes and indicate which version of each pair you prefer and why.

W I L L I A M   B U T L E R   Y E A T S
[*1865–1939*]

A Dream of Death

I dreamed that one had died in a strange place
Near no accustomed hand,
And they had nailed the boards above her face
The peasants of that land,

And wondering planted by her solitude   5
A cypress and a yew.
I came and wrote upon a cross of wood—
Man had no more to do—

'She was more beautiful than thy first love,
This lady by the trees';   10
And gazed upon the mournful stars above,
And heard the mournful breeze.

A Dream of Death

I dreamed that one had died in a strange place
Near no accustomed hand;
And they had nailed the boards above her face,
The peasants of that land,
Wondering to lay her in that solitude,   5
And raised above her mound
A cross they had made out of two bits of wood,
And planted cypress round;

And left her to the indifferent stars above
Until I carved these words: 10
She was more beautiful than thy first love,
But now lies under boards.

QUESTIONS FOR REFLECTION

1. Compare the tone of the last four lines of each version. Consider especially the difference between "mournful stars" and "indifferent stars."
2. What details have disappeared in the second version and what has been added? To what effect?

EMILY   DICKINSON
[1830–1886]

The Wind begun to knead the Grass

The Wind begun to knead the Grass—
As Women do a Dough—
He flung a Hand full at the Plain—
A Hand full at the Sky—
The Leaves unhooked themselves from Trees—   5
And started all abroad—
The Dust did scoop itself like Hands—
And throw away the Road—
The Wagons quickened on the Street—
The Thunders gossiped low—   10
The Lightning showed a Yellow Head—
And then a livid Toe—
The Birds put up the Bars to Nests—
The Cattle flung to Barns—
Then came one drop of Giant Rain—   15
And then, as if the Hands
That held the Dams—had parted hold—
The Waters Wrecked the Sky—
But overlooked my Father's House—
Just Quartering a Tree—   20

The Wind begun to rock the Grass

The Wind begun to rock the Grass
With threatening Tunes and low—
He threw a Menace at the Earth—
A Menace at the Sky.

The Leaves unhooked themselves from Trees—   5
And started all abroad
The Dust did scoop itself like Hands
And threw away the Road.

The Wagons quickened on the Streets
The Thunder hurried slow—   10
The Lightning showed a Yellow Beak
And then a livid Claw.

The Birds put up the Bars to Nests—
The Cattle fled to Barns—
There came one drop of Giant Rain   15
And then as if the Hands

That held the Dams had parted hold
The Waters Wrecked the Sky,
But overlooked my Father's House—
Just quartering a Tree—   20

QUESTIONS FOR REFLECTION

1. Comment on the change in the organization. Does the poem's appearance in stan-
   zas make it easier or more difficult to read?
2. Compare the tone of the first four lines of each version.
3. In lines 11–12 of each version, which image is more consistent and more vivid?

D. H. LAWRENCE

[*1885–1930*]

The Piano

Somewhere beneath that piano's superb sleek black
Must hide my mother's piano, little and brown, with the back
That stood close to the wall, and the front's faded silk both torn,
And the keys with little hollows, that my mother's fingers had worn.

Softly, in the shadows, a woman is singing to me   5
Quietly, through the years I have crept back to see
A child sitting under the piano, in the boom of the shaking strings
Pressing the little poised feet of the mother who smiles as she sings.

The full throated woman has chosen a winning, living song
And surely the heart that is in me must belong   10
To the old Sunday evenings, when darkness wandered outside
And hymns gleamed on our warm lips, as we watched mother's fingers glide.

Or this is my sister at home in the old front room
Singing love's first surprised gladness, alone in the gloom.
She will start when she sees me, and blushing, spread out her hands   15
To cover my mouth's raillery, till I'm bound in her shame's heart-spun bands

A woman is singing me a wild Hungarian air
And her arms, and her bosom, and the whole of her soul is bare,
And the great black piano is clamouring as my mother's never could clamour
And my mother's tunes are devoured of this music's ravaging glamour.   20

Piano

Softly, in the dusk, a woman is singing to me;
Taking me back down the vista of years, till I see
A child sitting under the piano, in the boom of the tingling strings
And pressing the small, poised feet of a mother who smiles as she sings.

In spite of myself, the insidious mastery of song   5
Betrays me back, till the heart of me weeps to belong
To the old Sunday evenings at home, with winter outside
And hymns in the cosy parlour, the tinkling piano our guide.

So now it is vain for the singer to burst into clamour
With the great black piano appassionato. The glamour   10
Of childish days is upon me, my manhood is cast
Down in the flood of remembrance, I weep like a child for the past.

QUESTIONS FOR REFLECTION

1. Which details have been eliminated from the second version? Which have been
   added?
2. Discuss the difference in tone and idea between the two versions of the poem.

PARODIES

A *parody* is a humorous, mocking imitation of another work. A parodic poem ridicules by distorting and exaggerating aspects of the poem it imitates. There may be distortions of the tone and purpose of the original poem or exaggerations of its stylistic mannerisms. The best parodists respect the works they parody, for to write parody well writers must understand and appreciate what they poke fun at. Good parodies catch the special manner and flavor of the originals. In them we hear echoes of the voice of the earlier poem. By extending the original beyond its limits, a parodist can point to the virtues of the poem he or she parodies. The following parody of William Carlos Williams's "This Is Just to Say" seems to do this. First, Williams's poem.

WILLIAM CARLOS WILLIAMS
[1883–1963]

This Is Just to Say

I have eaten
the plums
that were in
the icebox

and which 5
you were probably
saving
for breakfast

Forgive me
they were delicious 10
so sweet
and so cold

Now Kenneth Koch's parody:

KENNETH KOCH
[b. 1925]

Variations on a Theme by William Carlos Williams

1

I chopped down the house that you had been saving to live in next summer.
I am sorry, but it was morning, and I had nothing to do
and its wooden beams were so inviting.

2

We laughed at the hollyhocks together
And then I sprayed them with lye.   5
Forgive me. I simply do not know what I am doing.

3

I gave away the money that you had been saving to live on for the next ten years.
The man who asked for it was shabby
and the firm March wind on the porch was so juicy and cold.

4

Last evening we went dancing and I broke your leg.   10
Forgive me. I was clumsy, and
I wanted you here in the wards, where I am the doctor!

QUESTIONS FOR REFLECTION

1. Explain Koch's title.
2. Would his parody be as effective if he cut it down to one or two stanzas? If the four stanzas were rearranged? How long, in comparison, is Williams's poem, and why do you think Koch made his parody four times as long?
3. What do the four "variations" have in common?
4. Does the parody seem fair to Williams? Is it a coherent and engaging poem in its own right?

The following poem and its parodic counterpart are sonnets. Gary Hatch follows G. M. Hopkins closely as he parodies "Carrion Comfort," imitating the earlier poet's syntax strictly in some lines and more loosely in others.

GERARD MANLEY HOPKINS
[*1844–1889*]

Carrion Comfort

Not, I'll not, carrion comfort, Despair, not feast on thee;
Not untwist—slack they may be—these last strands of man
In me ór, most weary, cry *I can no more.* I can;
Can something, hope, wish day come, not choose not to be.

But ah, but O thou terrible, why wouldst thou rude on me   5
Thy wring-world right foot rock? lay a lionlimb against me? scan
With darksome devouring eyes my bruisèd bones? and fan,
O in turns of tempest, me heaped there; me frantic to avoid thee and flee?

Why? That my chaff might fly; my grain lie, sheer and clear.
Nay in all that toil, that coil, since (seems) I kissed the rod,   10
Hand rather, my heart lo! lapped strength, stole joy, would laugh, chéer.
Cheer whom though? The hero whose heaven-handling flung me, fóot tród
Me? or me that fought him? O which one? is it each one? That night, that year
Of now done darkness I wretch lay wrestling with (my God!) my God.

GARY LAYNE HATCH
[*b. 1964*]

Terrier Torment; or, Mr. Hopkins and his Dog

(FROM THE LESSER-KNOWN TERRIER SONNETS)

Put, stay put, Terrier Torment, Heel! I'll put on thee—
Quick though thou be—this leash. And,
Most wary, try to hold you still. I can;
Plan something—hold, wash dog, (come!) not choose to let you flee.

But ow! but oh thou terrier, why wouldst thou, wet on me,   5
Thy bark-loud-mutt-mouth munch? put a puppy paw against me? You plan
With funsome, frolicking eyes to dodge my dives and land
(Ow!) in squalls of squiggling—dog-piled there—wiggling to get free.

Why? That thy hair might dry, thy fur lie sheen and clean.
In all that toil, that soil, since (seems) I washed the dog,   10
(Dried rather) his hide (oh!) gobbed grime, caked crud.
I could wash, clean. Clean whom though? Him whose water-wiggling soused me,
    sud
Soaked me? or me that caught him? O which one? is it each one? That hour, that
    day
That soap-sick Saturday when I (drench) lay wrestling with my doggone dog.

(1995)

In the next pair of poems you hear two very different voices. Account for the difference in tone between them. Explain how Howard Moss's poem parodies Shakespeare's sonnet. Consider, finally, the sense the later poem makes on its own, unrelated to the sonnet.

WILLIAM SHAKESPEARE
[1564–1616]

Shall I compare thee to a summer's day

Shall I compare thee to a summer's day?
Thou art more lovely and more temperate:
Rough winds do shake the darling buds of May,
And summer's lease hath all too short a date;
Sometime too hot the eye of heaven shines,   5
And often is his gold complexion dimm'd;
And every fair from fair sometime declines,
By chance or nature's changing course untrimm'd:
But thy eternal summer shall not fade
Nor lose possession of that fair thou ow'st;   10
Nor shall Death brag thou wand'rest in his shade,
When in eternal lines to time thou grow'st;
So long as men can breathe or eyes can see,
So long lives this, and this gives life to thee.

HOWARD MOSS
[*b. 1922*]

Shall I Compare Thee to a Summer's Day?

Who says you're like one of the dog days?
You're nicer. And better.
Even in May, the weather can be gray,
And a summer sub–let doesn't last forever.
Sometimes the sun's too hot;   5
Sometimes it is not.
Who can stay young forever?
People break their necks or just drop dead!
But you? Never!
If there's just one condensed reader left   10
Who can figure out the abridged alphabet
   After you're dead and gone,
   In this poem you'll live on!

Finally, consider again the following brief poem by Robert Frost and an equally brief parody by Bob McKenty.

ROBERT FROST
[*1874–1963*]

Dust of Snow

The way a crow
Shook down on me
The dust of snow
From a hemlock tree

Has given my heart   5
A change of mood
And saved some part
Of a day I had rued.

BOB MCKENTY
[b. 1935]

Snow on Frost

A wayward crow
Shook down on him
The dust of snow
From a hemlock limb.

Amused (I recall)   5
The poet stopped,
Delighted that's all
The black bird dropped.

QUESTION FOR REFLECTION

In what ways does McKenty's parody mimic Frost's poem? In what ways does the parody depart from the original?

POEMS AND PAINTINGS

In Roman times and again during the Renaissance, poems were characterized as speaking pictures and painting as silent poetry. A poem, that is, was seen as a visual image given speech, a painting as a silent visual poem. Earlier, in our discussion of structure, we noted that the shape of a poem, its arrangement on the page, is an important dimension of its effect.

Here, however, we will consider another dimension of the relationship between words and visual images. On the pages that follow you will find poems paired with the paintings that inspired them. Three of the paintings are accompanied by more than one poem so you will have a chance to compare different interpretations and "translations" of a painting into a poem. As you consider each pair, spend some time looking carefully at the painting. Take an inventory of its details; observe its color and texture, its organization and perspective, its line, and its form. Think about the implications of its title; examine the action or scene it depicts. Then read the poem(s) as interpretation(s) and translation(s) of the painting. Notice what the poets include, what they omit, what they alter.

Even though you will be comparing poem with painting and poem with poem, remember that each poem is a separate and individual work. Read each the way you would read any other poem, giving careful attention to its formal

elements. Consider whether the poems can stand alone without their corre-
sponding paintings. And finally, observe how each poet has transformed the
painting to create a new work, one which conveys its own feelings and bears its
own implications.

QUESTIONS FOR REFLECTION

Vincent Van Gogh, *The Starry Night*

1. About the series of poems he wrote based on Van Gogh's paintings, Robert Fagles
   has written: "I wanted to try my hand at a kind of translation I hadn't done before,
   not from a foreign language, but from a group of paintings." What has Fagles trans-
   lated from the painting into the poem?
2. Does either Fagles's poem or Sexton's help you to see things in the painting that
   you had overlooked? Why or why not?
3. Does either poem seem to emphasize the painting more than the painter? Does it
   present a neutral description of the work? Does it imply or state a judgment about
   either the artist or his painting?
4. Compare Fagles's poem with Anne Sexton's "The Starry Night." Consider tone,
   imagery, structure, and feeling.

Francesco de Goya, *The Third of May, 1808*

1. Compare Gewanter's use of Goya with Fagles's use of Van Gogh. How does each
   poet convey the sense of the art he describes? How does each use that art for his
   own purposes?
2. Is Gewanter's poem comprehensible without the *painting*? Why or why not? How
   does the poem help you to see and understand Goya's art better?

Pieter Breughel the Elder, *Landscape with the Fall of Icarus*

1. Where is Icarus mentioned in Auden's poem? What does Auden end with and what
   does that ending imply?
2. How does Auden's poem offer us a clue to its intentions from the beginning?
   Would it matter if Auden's stanzas were reversed? Why or why not?
3. "Museé des Beaux Arts" can be divided into two parts. What is their relationship?
4. How does the title of Auden's poem reflect its author's preoccupations with the
   painting?

Pieter Breughel the Elder, *Hunters in the Snow*

1. How does Langland's poem better help you to see the details of the painting? How
   does the poem help you to better understand its symbolic implications?

2. Where does the poem depart from the details of the painting? In what ways and for what purposes?
3. What is emphasized in the opening stanza and the ending?
4. Langland's poem neither rhymes nor uses a consistent metrical pattern, yet it does exhibit formal organization. What devices of form, sound, and rhythm does it include? What do they contribute to the meaning and feeling of the work?

Edward Hopper, *Sunday*

1. How would you characterize the mood of Hopper's painting? What details contribute to or help establish that mood?
2. What does the poet E. Ward Herlands do with Hopper's painting? How does her treatment differ from that of the other poets inspired by paintings?
3. What is different about the form of Herlands's piece, a "prose poem"? What qualities make it poetic, and what qualities make it prosaic?

William Blake, *The Sick Rose*

1. How does Blake's art help you to understand his poem? How does it enable you to see something about the poem you may have overlooked, or to make connections you may have missed?
2. To what extent, if any, does Blake's illustration channel your reading of the poem, limiting the way you interpret it? Is it possible that the poem was written to illustrate the painting, or do you think the painting was designed to parallel the poem?

Sandro Botticelli, Giotto di Bondone, *Adoration of the Magi*

1. Compare the two paintings as stories. What does Botticelli emphasize? What does Giotto focus on? Identify figures common to both paintings and explain their significance.
2. Compare Eliot's and Yeats's poems as treatments of the general subject of the Magi. What is Yeats's concern and what is Eliot's? Do you think either poem was inspired by a painting? Why or why not?
3. Consider the poetic styles of Eliot and Yeats. Characterize each by focusing on the poet's uses of language and detail, rhythm and structure.
4. Who is the speaker in Eliot's poem? In Yeats's? Which line or lines in each poem best reveal the speaker's attitude toward what he describes?

Henri Matisse, *Dance*

1. How would you characterize the mood and spirit of the painting? What elements contribute most to these?
2. What is the significance of the ring of dancers and of the space between two of them?

3. Describe the relationship between Matisse's painting and Natalie Safir's poem. To what extent do the two works share a common theme and tone?
4. Why do you think Matisse used large patches of bold simple colors against which to set his human figures? How detailed is his rendering of the human figures? What is the effect of that rendering?

Pablo Picasso, *Girl with Mandolin*

1. What do you see when you look at Picasso's painting? What is the effect of the painter's transforming and combining objects in the manner he has done here?
2. What is the relation of Vinnie D'Ambrosio's poem to Picasso's painting?
3. Consider the language D'Ambrosio employs, especially the sounds of the words she uses. Why does she choose the sounds she does?
4. Do you prefer this painting of Picasso or the next one? Why?

Pablo Picasso, *Still Life with Pitcher, Bowl, & Fruit*

1. What elements of Picasso's painting are echoed in the poem?
2. To what extent does D'Ambrosio's poem suggest Picasso's style of painting?
3. If you could devise an alternative title for this painting, what would it be? Why?
4. Identify elements of sound play in Vinnie D'Ambrosio's poem. What do they contribute to the tone of the poem? What feeling do you come away with from reading "If I Were a Maker I'd"?

Gustav Klimt, *The Kiss*

1. What is your initial impression upon looking at Klimt's painting? How would you characterize the painting's style? its emphasis?
2. What effect does Ferlinghetti's poem have on your subsequent viewing of the painting? Why?
3. To what extent is Ferlinghetti's poem a description of Klimt's painting? To what extent is his poem an interpretation of the painting? Where is this interpretive inclination strongest?
4. Do you think the title of the poem and that of the painting are aptly chosen? Why or why not?

ANNE SEXTON
[1928–1975]

The Starry Night

That does not keep me from having a terrible need of—shall I say the word—religion.
Then I go out at night to paint the stars.

VINCENT VAN GOGH in a letter to his brother

The town does not exist
except where one black-haired tree slips
up like a drowned woman into the hot sky.
The town is silent. The night boils with eleven stars
Oh starry starry night! This is how   5
I want to die.

It moves. They are all alive.
Even the moon bulges in its orange irons
to push children, like a god, from its eye.
The old unseen serpent swallows up the stars.   10
Oh starry starry night! This is how
I want to die:

into that rushing beast of the night,
sucked up by that great dragon, to split
from my life with no flag,   15
no belly,
no cry.

The Starry Night

Long as I paint
I feel myself
less mad
the brush in my hand
a lightning rod to madness   5

But never ground that madness
execute it ride the lightning up
from these benighted streets and steeple up
with the cypress look its black is burning green

I am that I am it cries   10
it lifts me up the nightfall up
the cloudrack coiling like a dragon's flanks
a third of the stars of heaven wheeling in its wake
wheels in wheels around the moon that cradles round the sun

and if I can only trail these whirling eternal stars   15
with one sweep of the brush like Michael's sword if I can
cut the life out of the beast—safeguard the mother and the son
all heaven will hymn in conflagration blazing down
              the night the mountain ranges down
the claustrophobic valleys of the mad   20

              Madness
       is what I have instead of heaven
       God deliver me—help me now deliver
       all this frenzy back into your hands
       our brushstrokes burning clearer into dawn   25

DAVID GEWANTER
[b. 1954]

Goya's "The Third of May, 1808"

I'll show you:
onto the dirt-grey
canvas he's smeared—
jam on bread—
a sticky red for blood   5
oozed from the broken
heads and shot-up bodies
heaped near the cowering group
agape at soldiers hunched above
their knived rifles.   10
The air is oil-black,
smokeless, the whole scene
painted right before the guns
report, and more killed;
see the soldiers bend   15
in careful aim, bent
like mothers nursing—
one geometry of care:
exact angle for Madonna,
for men aiming murder—   20
and yet suspended,
the crisis held up for us

to observe at leisure—
in "The Resurrection" by
Grünewald, think how Christ   25
has bolted from his tomb,
rising, splendid,
while blinded soldiers
hurl themselves down,
never landing—   30
all are trapped in place:
one can't reach heaven,
the others never fall—
and here, before the dull wedge
representing *hill,*   35
one of Goya's victims
raises his arms up,
waiting always—
you know him, his shirt
blank as a page—   40
here, hand me a butterknife
to scrape with, I'll show you how
he painted bullets
inside the painted guns.

Pieter Breughel the Elder, Landscape with the Fall of Icarus (c. 1558). MUSÉES ROYAUX DES BEAUX–ARTS, BRUSSELS. SCALA/ART RESOURCE, NY.

W. H. AUDEN
[1907—1973]
Musée des Beaux Arts

About suffering they were never wrong,
The old Masters: how well they understood
Its human position: how it takes place
While someone else is eating or opening a window or just walking dully along;
How, when the aged are reverently, passionately waiting   5
For the miraculous birth, there always must be
Children who did not specially want it to happen, skating
On a pond at the edge of the wood:
They never forgot
That even the dreadful martyrdom must run its course   10
Anyhow in a corner, some untidy spot
Where the dogs go on with their doggy life and the torturer's horse
Scratches its innocent behind on a tree.

In Breughel's *Icarus,* for instance: how everything turns away
Quite leisurely from the disaster; the ploughman may   15
Have heard the splash, the forsaken cry,
But for him it was not an important failure; the sun shone
As it had to on the white legs disappearing into the green
Water, and the expensive delicate ship that must have seen
Something amazing, a boy falling out of the sky,   20
Had somewhere to get to and sailed calmly on.

JOSEPH LANGLAND
[b. 1917]

Hunters in the Snow: Breughel

Quail and rabbit hunters with tawny hounds,
Shadowless, out of late afternoon
Trudge toward the neutral evening of indeterminate form.
Done with their blood-annunciated day
Public dogs and all the passionless mongrels   5
Through deep snow
Trail their deliberate masters
Descending from the upper village home in lowering light.
Sooty lamps
Glow in the stone-carved kitchens.   10

This is the fabulous hour of shape and form
When Flemish children are gray-black-olive
And green-dark-brown
Scattered and skating informal figures
On the mill ice pond.   15
Moving in stillness
A hunched dame struggles with her bundled sticks,
Letting her evening's comfort cudgel her
While she, like jug or wheel, like a wagon cart
Walked by lazy oxen along the old snowlanes,   20
Creeps and crunches down the dusky street.
High in the fire-red dooryard
Half unhitched the sign of the Inn
Hangs in wind
Tipped to the pitch of the roof.   25
Near it anonymous parents and peasant girl,
Living like proverbs carved in the alehouse walls,
Gather the country evening into their arms
And lean to the glowing flames.

Now in the dimming distance fades   30
The other village; across the valley
Imperturbable Flemish cliffs and crags
Vaguely advance, close in loom
Lost in nearness. Now
The night-black raven perched in branching boughs   35
Opens its early wing and slipping out
Above the gray-green valley
Weaves a net of slumber over the snow-capped homes.
And now the church, and then the walls and roofs
Of all the little houses are become   40

Close kin to shadow with small lantern eyes.
And now the bird of evening
With shadows streaming down from its gliding wings
Circles the neighboring hills
Of Hertogenbosch, Brabant.   45

Darkness stalks the hunters,
Slowly sliding down,
Falling in beating rings and soft diagonals.
Lodged in the vague vast valley the village sleeps.

Pieter Breughel the Elder, Hunters in the Snow (1565). KUNSTHISTORISCHES MUSEUM, VIENNA. ART RESOURCE, NY.

Edward Hopper, Sunday, (1926). OIL ON CANVAS, 29 × 34. THE PHILLIPS COLLECTION, WASHINGTON, D.C.

E. WARD HERLANDS
[b. 1925]

When Edward Hopper Was Painting

I like to think that on a Sunday afternoon when Edward Hopper was painting his lone man seated on a street curb, with shaft of light warming that man's right arm & right cheek, I like to think that on that very same day I was there, somewhere round that corner, dressed in a Wedgewood-blue velvet-collared English wool coat, (incongruous elegance for a workingman's child) offspring of a proud Austro-Hungarian immigrant & a first generation American. I like to believe that in the minutes just after the seated man arose from his head-bowed position, that my father came strolling down the very same street pushing me in my gray straw perambulator & when his path & ours were parallel & as that man approached, I like to think that the lone man in the Hopper painting looked down at me, smiled & said, Nice kid you've got there, Dad.

WILLIAM BLAKE

[1757–1827]

The Sick Rose

O Rose, thou art sick!
The invisible worm
That flies in the night,
In the howling storm,

Has found out thy bed
Of crimson joy,
And his dark secret love
Does thy life destroy.

Sandro Botticelli, Adoration of the Magi (c. 1475).
UFFIZI GALLERY, FLORENCE. SCALA/ART RESOURCE, NY.

T. S. ELIOT

[*1888–1965*]

Journey of the Magi

'A cold coming we had of it,
Just the worst time of the year
For a journey, and such a long journey:
The ways deep and the weather sharp,
The very dead of winter.'   5
And the camels galled, sore-footed, refractory,
Lying down in the melting snow.
There were times we regretted
The summer palaces on slopes, the terraces,
And the silken girls bringing sherbet.   10
Then the camel men cursing and grumbling
And running away, and wanting their liquor and women,
And the night-fires going out, and the lack of shelters,
And the cities hostile and the towns unfriendly
And the villages dirty and charging high prices: 15
A hard time we had of it.
At the end we preferred to travel all night,
Sleeping in snatches,
With the voices singing in our ears, saying
That this was all folly.   20

Then at dawn we came down to a temperate valley,
Wet, below the snow line, smelling of vegetation;
With a running stream and a water-mill beating the darkness,
And three trees on the low sky,

And an old white horse galloped away in the meadow.   25
Then we came to a tavern with vine-leaves over the lintel,
Six hands at an open door dicing for pieces of silver,
And feet kicking the empty wine-skins.
But there was no information, and so we continued
And arrived at evening, not a moment too soon   30
Finding the place; it was (you may say) satisfactory.

All this was a long time ago, I remember,
And I would do it again, but set down
This set down
This: were we led all that way for   35
Birth or Death? There was a Birth, certainly,
We had evidence and no doubt. I had seen birth and death,
But had thought they were different; this Birth was
Hard and bitter agony for us, like Death, our death.
We returned to our places, these Kingdoms,   40
But no longer at ease here, in the old dispensation,
With an alien people clutching their gods.
I should be glad of another death.

Giotto di Bondone, Adoration of the Magi (1313).
SCROVEGNI CHAPEL, PADUA. SCALA/ART RESOURCE.

WILLIAM BUTLER YEATS
[*1865–1939*]

The Magi

Now as at all times I can see in the mind's eye,
In their stiff, painted clothes, the pale unsatisfied ones
Appear and disappear in the blue depth of the sky
With all their ancient faces like rain-beaten stones,
And all their helms of silver hovering side by side,   5
And all their eyes still fixed, hoping to find once more,
Being by Calvary's turbulence unsatisfied,
The uncontrollable mystery on the bestial floor.

Henri Matisse, Dance (first version). Paris. (March 1909). OIL ON CANVAS, 8′ 6½″ × 12′ 9½″. MUSEUM OF MODERN ART, NEW YORK. GIFT OF NELSON A. ROCKEFELLER IN HONOR OF ALFRED H. BARR, JR.

NATALIE SAFIR

[*b. 1935*]

Matisse's Dance

A break in the circle dance of naked women,
dropped stitch between the hands
of the slender figure stretching too hard
to reach her joyful sisters.

Spirals of glee sail from the arms   5
of the tallest woman. She pulls the circle
around with her fire. What has she found
that she doesn't keep losing,
her torso a green-burning torch?

Grass mounds curve ripely beneath   10
two others who dance beyond the blue.
Breasts swell and multiply and
rhythms rise to a gallop.

Hurry, frightened one, and grab on—before
the stitch is forever lost, before the dance   15
unravels and a black sun swirls from that space.

Pablo Picasso, Girl with a Mandolin (Fanny Tellier). Paris (late spring 1910). OIL ON CANVAS 39½″ × 29″. THE MUSEUM OF MODERN ART, NEW YORK. NELSON A. ROCKEFELLER BEQUEST.

VINNIE-MARIE D'AMBROSIO
[b. 1928]

If I Were a Maker I'd

make a melon
            orange in yellow
add a rod
fret it   and string it

and trim a pick   5
from a suppleplump pit.

My tools would burgeon
bunches of grapes and

then ghosts in motley
no–shaped and graced   10
would pin the grapes

to their pointed shoes   and ring-a-ling them.

One shade would dandle my banjo gently—
and soon

you'd see a melon roll through air!   15
you'd see grapes leaping and lighting!

and you'd hear my mooncurled song!

Pablo Picasso, Still Life with Pitcher, Bowl, & Fruit (1931). PRIVATE COLLECTION.
GIRAUDON/ART RESOURCE, NY.

Gustav Klimt, The Kiss (1907–1908). KUNSTHISTORICHES MUSEUM, VIENNA. ERICK LESSING/ART RESOURCE, NY.

LAWRENCE FERLINGHETTI
[*b. 1919*]

Short Story on a Painting of Gustav Klimt

They are kneeling upright on a flowered bed
   He
      has just caught her there
            and holds her still
  Her gown   5
      has slipped down
            off her shoulder
  He has an urgent hunger
       His dark head
           bends to hers   10
              hungrily
And the woman the woman
  turns her tangerine lips from his
      one hand like the head of a dead swan
        draped down over   15
            his heavy neck
     the fingers
       strangely crimped
         tightly together
  her other arm doubled up   20
    against her tight breast

her hand a languid claw
                clutching his hand
    which would turn her mouth
                      to his   25
her long dress made
      of multicolored blossoms
          quilted on gold
her Titian hair
      with blue stars in it   30
And his gold
      harlequin robe
          checkered with
            dark squares
Gold garlands   35
      stream down over
          her bare calves &
          tensed feet
Nearby there must be
    a jeweled tree   40
      with glass leaves aglitter
      in the gold air
It must be
    morning
      in a faraway place somewhere   45
They
   are silent together
          as in a flowered field
   upon the summer couch
        which must be hers   50
And he holds her still
      so passionately
  holds her head to his
      so gently so insistently
   to make her turn   55
      her lips to his
Her eyes are closed
      like folded petals
She
  will not open   60
    He
      is not the One

CHAPTER FIVE

Writing about Poetry

REASONS FOR WRITING ABOUT POETRY

Why write about poetry? One reason is to find out what you think about a poem. Another is to induce yourself to read a poem more carefully. You may write about a work of poetry because it engages you, and you may wish to celebrate it or to argue with its implied ideas and values. Still another reason is that you may simply be required to do so as a course assignment.

Whatever your reasons for writing about poetry, a number of things happen when you do. First, in writing about a poem you tend to read it more attentively, noticing things you might overlook in a more casual reading. Second, since writing stimulates thinking, when you write about poetry you find yourself thinking more about what a particular work means and why you respond to it as you do. And third, you begin to acquire power over the works you write about, making them more meaningful to you.

INFORMAL WAYS OF WRITING ABOUT POETRY

When you write about a poem, you may write for yourself or you may write for others. Writing for yourself, writing to discover what you think, often takes casual forms such as annotation and freewriting. These less formal kinds of writing are useful for helping you focus on your reading of poetry. They are also helpful in studying for tests about poetry and can serve as preliminary forms of writing when you write more formal essays and papers.

Annotation

When you annotate a text, you make notes about it, usually in the margins or at the top and bottom of pages—or both. Annotations can also be made within the text, as underlined words, circled phrases, and bracketed sentences or para-graphs. Annotations may also assume the form of arrows, question marks, and various other marks.

Annotating a literary work offers a convenient and relatively painless way to begin writing about it. Annotating can get you started zeroing in on what you think interesting or important. You can also annotate to signal details that puzzle or disconcert you.

Your markings serve to focus your attention and clarify your understanding of a poem. Your annotations can save you time in rereading or studying a work. And they can also be used when you write a more formal paper.

Annotations for the following poem illustrate the process.

ROBERT HAYDEN

Those Winter Sundays

Sundays <u>too my father</u> got up early
and put <u>his</u> clothes on in the <u>blueblack</u>
  cold,
then with cracked hands that ached
from labor in the weekday weather made
banked fires blaze. <u>No one ever thanked</u>
  him.

<u>I'd</u> wake and hear the cold splintering,
  breaking,
When the rooms were warm, <u>he'd</u> call,
and slowly <u>I</u> would rise and dress,
<u>fearing</u> the chronic angers of that house,

Speaking <u>indifferently</u> to him,
who had driven out the <u>cold</u>
and polished my good shoes as well.
<u>What did I know, what did I know</u> of
  love's austere and <u>lonely</u> offices?

*This father gets up early
every day—even on
Sundays.*

How can cold be
"blueblack"?

*No one? Not other family
members? Not the
speaker?*

Stanza one emphasizes the
speaker's father; stanza two
shifts emphasis to the
speaker himself.

Speaker remembers his
fear. Fear of what? His
father's anger? Was it
directed at him?

Father drives out the
cold—warms the house,
literally. Is the father
himself a "warm" person,
or "cold"?

Repeats the question.
Tone? Feeling? Speaker
knows *now* what he did
not know then.

Father's loneliness/father's
love.

Freewriting

Freewriting is a kind of informal writing you do for yourself. In freewriting you explore a text to find out what you think about it and how you respond to it. When you freewrite, you do not know ahead of time what your ideas about the work will be. Freewriting leads you to explore your memories and experi-ence as well as aspects of the text itself. You sometimes wander from the details of the poem you are writing about. In the process you may discover thoughts and feelings you didn't know you had or were only dimly aware of. You can use freewriting to explore all your responses to a work. You can also use the technique to see where it leads you in thinking about the work itself.

First read Robert Graves's "Symptoms of Love," then look at some sample responses written by students who had heard Graves's poem read aloud and then read it once to themselves.

ROBERT GRAVES
[1895–1985]

Symptoms of Love

Love is a universal migraine,
A bright stain on the vision
Blotting out reason.

Symptoms of true love
Are leanness, jealousy,   5
Laggard dawns;

Are omens and nightmares—
Listening for a knock,
Waiting for a sign:

For a touch of her fingers   10
In a darkened room,
For a searching look.

Take courage, lover!
Could you endure such pain
At any hand but hers?   15

COLLEGE FRESHMAN: This lover is really bitter. He thinks love is a headache (migraine) and sees love mainly as negative and frightening. I noticed he talked about "omens and nightmares." He could have said "promises and dreams" or something like that, but he didn't. So as far as I am concerned, this speaker is a person who does not see any hope or possibility of growing better because of love. This is all pessimistic.

COLLEGE SOPHOMORE: Not that I haven't seen many failed relationships, but as a "thirty-something" male, I think the speaker in this poem (who also seems to be male) is very young. He sees "true love" as something that "blots out reason" and is always jealously waiting for a sign that the lady returns his feelings. I think as most people get older, they do not spend so much time thinking about "how is she (or he, in the case of a woman) going to react to me?" Instead they are looking for someone who will not cause them pain, someone who will be on the same wavelength.

COLLEGE JUNIOR: The first thing I thought when I was listening to the poem being read was that it was a terrible way to look at love. Like a migraine headache. Then when I read it myself, it made me smile some at the end. It was a sad smile—or maybe an ironic smile is what I mean. Because at the end, the speaker advises other lovers to "Take courage," so I thought that showed that he was at least willing to try again. He seemed to be saying that, yes, love is painful but it is a pain that can be worth it if you get rewarded with that "searching look" while the two of you are "in a darkened room." What he is talking about is that "chemistry" between two people who are really attracted to each other, but maybe they aren't meant for each other because of their opposing personalities. But the physical attraction is something that you just can't always push away.

COLLEGE FRESHMAN: A man wrote this poem and the character in the poem is a man, but the feelings are something I can really understand. I think more of women or girls being the ones who wait around for signs or who stay up all night or lose weight because they are in love with someone who isn't responding. I can certainly understand watching for every look and trying to figure out what it might mean and whether it might be saying that this person likes you. I've had plenty of headaches waiting for the phone to ring. Graves is right on target when he says "Love is a universal migraine."

The responses show the wide variety of reactions readers have when they encounter the same text. Note that the second reader and the fourth reader, particularly, include thoughts and feelings related to their own circumstances.

FORMAL WAYS OF WRITING ABOUT POETRY

Among the more common formal ways of writing about poetry is analysis. In writing an analytical essay about a poem, your goal is to explain how one or more particular aspects or issues in the work contribute to its overall meaning. You might analyze the dialogue in Stuart's "In the Orchard" or the voices in Reed's "Naming of Parts," for example, in explaining what the verbal exchanges between characters or the difference in voices contributes to each poem's meaning. You might analyze the imagery of H. D.'s "Heat" or Hardy's "Neutral Tones" to see what that imagery suggests about the speaker's perspective or the author's attitude. Or you might analyze the syntax of Frost's "The

Silken Tent" or Cummings's "Me up at does" for what that syntax reveals about each poem's theme.

In addition to analyzing these and other poetic elements in a single poem, you might also write to compare two poems, perhaps by focusing on their symbolism, sound effects, rhythm and meter, structure, or figures of speech. Or, instead of focusing on literary elements per se, you might write to see how a particular critical perspective (see our discussion in Chapter Eight) illuminates a poem. For example, you might consider the ways reader–response criticism contributes to your understanding of Piercy's "A Work of Artifice" (page 311) or new historicism contributes to your understanding of Poe's "To Helen" (page 249).

The following brief analysis of Plath's "Mirror" (page 309) focuses on the poem's imagery and its structure. The writer considers how Plath's language and organization convey an implied idea about women.

Student Papers on Poetry

Jennifer Stepkowski
Professor O'Leary

Reflections on Sylvia Plath's "Mirror"

Sylvia Plath's poem, "Mirror," presents a portrayal of
womanhood that is both accurate and upsetting. The mirror in
Plath's poem reflects honestly both inanimate objects and the
faces of those who peer into it. To convey the mirror's
uncompromising accuracy in reflecting what shows in its glass
surface, Plath uses such words as "exact," "truthful,"
"really," and "faithfully." Plath personifies her mirror and
makes it the poem's speaker. "I am silver and exact," the
speaker begins. "I have no preconceptions" (1.1). This
exactness of the mirror's reflection of reality coupled with
Plath's precise diction present a harsh reality in which women
grow old inexorably. Women have old age to look forward to,
and old age in which the young girls they once were have been
"drowned" (1.17).

The image of drowning follows logically from the opening of
the poem's second stanza in which the mirror is compared to a
lake. It is in this lake (or mirror as lake) that a woman
searches for her self, reaching, as Plath writes, "for what
she really is" (1.11). What the woman finds, however, so
disconcerts her that she responds with "an agitation of hands"
(1.14), which calls up a vision of the woman's hands in
flurried motion around her face. Yet even though she is upset
by what she sees in the mirror, the woman returns repeatedly,
for as the mirror says, "I am important to her" (1.15).

Plath is uncompromising in portraying women's need to see
themselves, a need fed by a powerful concern with their
appearance. She also conveys without compromise the inevitable
process of aging, rendered powerfully in the simile that
concludes the poem. Plath conveys a sense of the woman at
three stages of life: as she is now, growing older in the
poem's present; as she was once as a young girl; and as she
will be as an old woman who "rises toward her day after day,
like a terrible fish" (1.18).

The images of the second stanza—of lake and tears and
agitated hands of a drowning girl and old woman rising like a
fish—reflect concretely the first stanza's general

statements. There Plath describes the mirror as having "no
preconceptions" (1.1), as "swallow[ing] immediately just as it
is," whatever it sees, "unmisted by love or dislike." Soon the
woman will be swallowed by the mirror as it has swallowed the
young girl she once was. Only the old woman remains, coming
and going from the mirror, staring into it and looking for the
middle-aged woman and the young girl who will have long since
vanished.

A Paper That Compares Two Versions of a Poem

In the following paper Amanda Ackerman compares an early version of Blake's
"London" with the published version (pages 92–93). The writer carefully ana-
lyzes Blake's diction and selection of detail to arrive at an interpretation of the
later version. Seeing what words Blake rejected and changed helped her un-
derstand what Blake's published poem emphasizes.

Ackerman, Amanda
DiYanni
8/3/92
Third Essay

The Sad World of "London"

In William Blake's "London," the speaker takes a midnight walk
through London's dismal streets. As the speaker travels, he
remarks on the depravity, the weakness, and the sad
restrictions which abound in the London society. However,
because of Blake's affinity for perfection in his poetry, the
speaker's footsteps are thoughtfully planned. In fact, it was
necessary for Blake to make several revisions within his first
draft of "London" before he was satisfied with the final
version. Each change that Blake makes bears significance,
whether it is as subtle as the capitalization of one letter,
or as dramatic as the complete revision of an entire stanza.
With each change, the poem becomes richer with connotations of
restraint, with imagery far more vivid and alarming, and with
an expression of a devastation ultimately more heart-felt.
   The majority of the changes that Blake makes within the
first three stanzas of the poem are deceptively minute, yet
their impact is anything but insignificant. For example, by
simply replacing three words within the first stanza of the
original version, Blake allows the second version of "London"
to immediately take on an altogether different feeling. In the
earlier version of the poem, Blake expresses his discontent by
describing the Thames and the London streets as "dirty." By
sharp contrast, in the later version Blake describes the same
scene as "charter'd," a word that denotes boundaries and
restrictions: "I wander through each charter'd street, Near
where the charter'd Thames does flow . . ." (lines 1-2).
Instead of providing the reader with a vague and somewhat
cryptic idea of London's decay, Blake instantly alerts the
reader to the sad reality of London's restrictions. London is
a world so devastated by repression that even the "free
flowing" Thames and the city streets themselves are weakened.
Nothing and no one is left untouched by London's all-consuming
restrictions, for the reader "sees in every face [he] meets,
Marks of weakness, marks of woe." This image, although
disturbing, cannot compare to the deeper despair expressed in
the second version, for in this version the speaker "marks in
every face [he] meets, Marks of weakness, marks of woe . . ."
The grief of those that the speaker sees becomes much more
terrifying, for their faces are so miserable and weak that
they are able to leave a permanent impression on those who see

them. This is a much more powerful image than that of a person despondently "seeing" the sad faces of those around him. Also, by changing "see" to "mark," Blake creates a haunting repetition which not only enhances the fluidity of the poem, but more importantly "marks" the reader himself by echoing the dismal truth.

Again, Blake makes revisions in the second stanza which appear small, but nonetheless which add tremendously to the impact of the poem. To begin with, Blake makes what appears to be a simple grammatical change; he capitalizes words such as "Man" and "Infant" in the second version. By doing this, Blake makes those unknown people that he describes seem much more frighteningly human, for he capitalizes their names just as we would capitalize the name of an individual person. Also, the striking image of a grown man crying becomes much more devastating when that "man" becomes "Man"—a universal representation for all mankind. In addition, the capitalized letters of these words allow them to stand out, and thus magnify their impact. Blake also makes another significantly effective change within the second stanza; he changes "In every voice of every child" to "In every Infant's cry of fear," a line much richer in impact and feeling. The first line gives a somewhat vague picture of the sadness in the lives of many faceless children, whereas the second line evokes a much more specific and alarming image, for it is the purest and most innocent of all human beings—the newborn baby—which even in its naivete feels the pain of repression so intensely that it "cries out."

As frightening as that image is, Blake affects the reader even more deeply by revealing the two terrifying sources of London's restricted freedom—one being the human mind. The already unnerving image of the human mind being its own means of imprisonment is made much more vivid when Blake changes the "mind forg'd links" described in the first version, to the "mind-forg'd manacles" of the second. The word "manacles" is a word so rich with connotations of restraint and imprisonment that the reader is given a both alarming and sickening image of the mind itself—the only possession of man thought to be truly incapable of being barred or restricted—eating away at its own freedom. Blake also reveals the other source of London's grief and repressed freedom in a bold protest against the leadership of his time—Blake identifies the leaders themselves as the source of London's anguish. Again, by capitalizing certain words and by changing one line in the third stanza, Blake makes his attack on the leadership of his time all the more forceful and justifiable. In the second version, Blake capitalizes words such as "Chimney-sweeper's,"

"Church," "Soldier's," and "Palace" in order to display his discontent much more emphatically. The reader ultimately takes much more notice of the young Chimney-sweeper's cry, and of the unfortunate Soldier whose own lifeblood is "running down the walls" of the buildings where the incompetent leaders reside. Blake further stresses the heartlessness of London's leaders through another significant revision; he changes the line "Blacken's o'er the church walls" to "Every black'ning Church appalls." In the second version, the Church of England—thought to be a sacred place of sanctuary and of guidance—instead of providing its people with any kind of relief, is actively "appalling" or denunciating the efforts of its impoverished people, particularly the poor child-laborers who must sweep chimneys in order to survive. This is a much more horrifying image than that of the first.

However, in the last stanza Blake provides the reader with perhaps the most alarming imagery of all, as London has been reduced to a state where nothing at all is sacred. In the last stanza, Blake brings about a marked difference in the impact of the poem through several dramatic changes. The earlier version of the poem uses imagery which vaguely connotes the sadness and the depravity found in the London society. However, Blake expresses this detestable human condition much more forcefully in the final version. Instead of the "midnight harlot," "dismal street," and "curses weaving and blasting," Blake uses much more powerful words and imagery. A strong image such as a "midnight street" brings a much darker and ominous feeling to the poem. Also, in an astonishing paradox, Blake refers to the harlot as "youthful." By doing this, Blake brings about a much more alarming image of the corrupted and devastated innocence of a child. Also, the "curses" of the harlot appear to be much more cruel and hurtful as they "blight with plagues" rather than "weave" around a marriage hearse. In this second image a youthful mother is trying to destroy her own infant's tears—no sooner has the infant experienced its first moments of life in the world, than it is feeling the sickness of repression. Nothing is sacred any longer in the dismal world of London, certainly not the bond between mother and child, and not even marriage. Blake ends the final version of his poem with the lasting impression of a "Marriage Hearse." This last image leaves the reader devastated, as it is marriage—probably considered the most sacred and beautiful institution of man—which itself is dead and on its way to being buried.

Although the reader encounters feelings of deep sadness, corruption, and repression within the lines of Blake's first version of "London," the walk that the reader takes through

London's dreary streets in the final version of the poem
provides the reader with a much more heart-felt insight into
London's miserable reality. Regardless of the size of each
revision, each change that Blake makes within his poem
produces a more powerful understanding and a more profound
idea: specifically, the idea of restriction, the idea that man
himself has created a world in which he has stifled his own
expression and put boundaries on his growth—in the sad world
of London.

QUESTIONS FOR WRITING ABOUT POETRY

In writing about the elements of poetry, the following questions can help you focus
your thinking and prepare yourself for writing analytical essays and papers. Use the
questions as a checklist to guide you to important aspects of any poem you read.

Voice: Speaker and Situation

1. Who is the speaker of the poem? How would you characterize this speaker?
2. Where does the speaker reveal his or her attitude toward the poem's subject? Do
   the speaker's attitude or feelings change at any point? If so, where and with what
   implications?
3. What is the speaker's situation? What is happening in the poem?

Diction and Imagery

4. Do you understand the denotations of all the words used in the poem? Look up
   any words you are not completely sure of.
5. Which words convey the richest connotations? What do these connotations con-
   tribute to your understanding of the poem?
6. What kinds of imagery does the poem include? Do you detect any patterns
   among the images? What do the images collectively suggest?

Figures of Speech

7. What kinds of figures of speech occur in the poem? How important are figures of
   comparison—simile and metaphor?
8. How do the poem's figures of speech contribute to the poem's vividness and con-
   creteness? What do they contribute to its feeling and meaning?

Symbolism and Allegory

9. What details of language and action carry symbolic implications? How do you know?
10. Does the poem exhibit a pattern of linked allegorical details?

Syntax and Structure

11. What kinds of sentences does the poet use? What kinds of structure and pattern do the poem's sentences exhibit?
12. What does the poem's syntax reveal about the state of mind of its speaker?
13. How is the poem organized? How do its stanzas or major sections develop?
14. How are the stanzas or major sections of the poem related?

Sound, Rhythm, and Meter

15. Does the poem rhyme? Does it employ assonance, alliteration, onomatopoeia, or other forms of sound play? With what effects?
16. What kinds of rhythm and meter does the poem include? Does the rhythm change or is the meter varied at any point? With what effects?

Theme

17. How do the poetic elements create and convey the poem's meaning(s)?
18. Do you think there is more than one theme? Why or why not?
19. Is the theme of the poem explicit or implicit? Is it conveyed more clearly in one part of the poem than another?

Critical Perspectives

20. Which of the critical perspectives (Chapter 8) best helps you make sense of the poem? Why?
21. To what extent do the poem's language and details convey its meaning? To what extent do you need to go outside the poem for an understanding of its allusions, its historical or biographical implications, or other kinds of information?
22. To what extent does the poem confirm or support, confute or contradict your personal values, beliefs, attitudes, or dispositions? Why?

Suggestions for Writing

The Experience of Poetry

1. Write a paper in which you recount your experience of reading a particular poem or a series of poems by the same author. You may want to compare your initial experience of reading the poem(s) with your subsequent experience.
2. Relate the action or situation of a poem to your experience. Explain how the poem is relevant to your situation, and comment on how

reading and thinking about it may have helped you view your own situation and experience more clearly.

The Interpretation of Poetry

3. Characterize the speaker of any poem. Present a sketch of the speaker's character by referring to the language of the poem. Consider not only what the speaker says but the manner in which it is said and what it reveals about the speaker.

4. Describe the narrative element in any poem. Consider how important its "story" or narrative material is, and what would be gained or lost without it. Consider also how the narrative dimension of the poem would work as a story, play, or essay.

5. Explicate the opening lines of a poem. Explain the significance of the lines in the context of the poem overall.

6. Explicate the closing lines of a poem. Consider how they can be related to earlier lines.

7. Select two or more key lines from a short poem (or groups of lines from longer ones). Explain their significance and consider their relationship to one another.

8. Read five or more poems by the same poet and discuss the features they have in common.

9. Analyze a single poem that is representative of a poet's work. Explain what makes the poem representative.

10. Analyze the diction or word choices of a poem. Consider other words the poet could have chosen. Examine the denotations and connotations of the words the poet chose. Use your analysis of the diction to develop an interpretation of the poem.

11. Analyze the imagery of a poem. List the poem's significant details (if a long poem) or all the details if it's short. Discuss what the images contribute to the poem's tone, feeling, and/or meaning.

12. Analyze the figurative language of a poem. Identify and explain each figure of speech and discuss its function in the poem overall.

13. Discuss the ironic dimensions of a poem. Identify examples of irony, and explain their significance and effect.

14. Identify the allusions in a poem and explain what they contribute to your understanding of it.

15. Analyze the structure of a poem. Consider both its overall structure and its small-scale structure—how the individual parts themselves are organized. Identify the main parts of the poem and comment on their relationship to each other.

16. Analyze the sound effects of a poem. Explain how sound contributes to its sense and spirit.

17. Analyze the rhythm and meter of a poem. Identify its prevailing metrical pattern. Acknowledge any deviations from this meter and

comment on the significance of these deviations. Consider what the poem's rhythm and meter contribute to its overall meaning and feeling.

The Evaluation of Poetry

18. Discuss the values exemplified in one or more poems. Consider, that is, the cultural, moral, social, or ethical norms that either appear explicitly in the poem(s) or are implied by it. Identify those values, relate them to your own, and comment on their significance.
19. Compare two poems, evaluating their literary and linguistic merit. Explain what the two poems have in common, how they differ, and why one is superior to the other.
20. Evaluate a poem from the standpoint of its literary excellence. Explain why you consider it to be an effective or ineffective poem.

To Research or Imagine

21. Develop an alternative ending for a poem, changing the outcome of its action, altering its pattern of rhythm or rhyme, or making other changes. Be prepared to defend your alternative version as a reasonable possibility. Consider why the poet chose to end the poem as he or she did.
22. Read some letters or essays by a poet whose poetry you know and enjoy. Consider how your reading of the poet's prose aids your understanding or increases your enjoyment.
23. Read a full-scale biography of a poet whose work you admire. Write a paper explaining how the poet's life is or is not reflected in the poetic work.
24. Write a paper in which you examine how a particular poet worked within and/or against the prevailing social attitudes, moral beliefs, or cultural dispositions of his or her time.
25. Read a critical study of any poet you would like to learn more about. Write a paper explaining how reading the book has increased your understanding and/or appreciation of the poetry.

C H A P T E R   S I X

Three Poets in Context

READING EMILY DICKINSON, ROBERT FROST, AND LANGSTON HUGHES IN DEPTH

The primary context for reading any single poem is other poems by the same poet. Additional contexts include other poems by contemporary poets and by poets with similar thematic preoccupations or stylistic inclinations. Emily Dickinson's poems, for example, can be read in relation to those of her contemporary Walt Whitman. Dickinson's poems can also be read in relation to seventeenth-century metaphysical poetry, especially the poems of George Herbert and John Donne, with whom Dickinson shared religious interests and some stylistic traits.

Additional contexts for reading Dickinson's poetry include her letters and her life. To some extent at least, a poet's work reflects his or her life. Knowing at least the broad outlines of poets' lives can be helpful in gaining additional perspectives on their poetry.

The context of poets' lives is naturally extended by their culture and environment. Knowing something of nineteenth-century New England culture enhances a reader's understanding of Dickinson's poetry. Knowing something about the development of literary modernism and about Robert Frost's and Langston Hughes's relationship to that movement situates their poetry in the context of their time and delineates it sharply against that backdrop.

Moreover, what is true for the life of Dickinson is also true for the life of Frost and Hughes. Knowing the facts of their lives enhances our reading of their poetry. This having been said, however, it is the inner lives of these poets rather than their external lives that are of interest in their poems. Thus, primary emphasis in reading Dickinson, Frost, and Hughes should be on their artistry, on how they deploy language to create art, rather than on how their poems manifest aspects of their lives.

Still another context for reading Dickinson, Frost, and Hughes is provided by their comments on the art and craft of poetry. Dickinson discusses poetry in her letters, Frost in both letters and essays. Neither poet provides interpretations of their poems. Frost, in fact, often had fun with audiences who asked about the meanings of particular poems, frequently teasing them with irrelevant information (only occasionally accurate) about how his poems were composed. Nonetheless poets' comments on the art of poetry generally and on their particular poetic intentions can be helpful in approaching their work. Frost's interest in how a poem can convey the intonational qualities of the spoken voice is a case in point. For Langston Hughes's poems, readers should attend both to their speech and to their song, particularly to the feeling of the blues they so often invoke

Dickinson, Frost, and Hughes have attracted a wide range of critical interpretation, providing still another context for their work. A sample of that criticism is included in this chapter.

QUESTIONS FOR IN-DEPTH READING

1. What general or overall thematic connections can you make between different works?
2. What stylistic similarities do you notice between and among different works?
3. How do the works differ in emphasis, tone, and style?
4. Once you have identified a writer's major preoccupations, place each work on a spectrum or a grid that represents the range of the writer's concerns.
5. What connections and disjunctions do you find among the following literary elements as they are embodied in different poems by the same writer?
   a. speaker and situation
   b. diction and imagery
   c. figures of speech
   d. symbolism and allegory
   e. syntax and structure
   f. sound and sense
   g. rhythm and meter
   h. theme and thought
6. To what extent are your responses to and perceptions of different works by the same writer shared by others—by critics, by classmates, and by the writers themselves?
7. What relationships and differences do you see between the work of one writer and that of another who shares similar thematic interests, stylistic proclivities, or cultural, religious, or social values?
8. Which of the critical perspectives seem most useful as analytical tools for approaching the body of work of particular writers?

INTRODUCTION TO EMILY DICKINSON

[1830–1886]

Emily Dickinson's external life was remarkably circumscribed. Born in 1830 in Amherst, Massachusetts, and educated at Amherst Academy, she lived there her entire life, except for a brief stay at what was later to become Mount Holyoke College. She lived a life of seclusion, leaving Massachusetts only once and rarely leaving her father's house during the last fifteen years of her life. She died in the house where she was born.

If Dickinson's external life was unadventurous, her interior life was not. Her mind was anything but provincial. She read widely in English literature and thought deeply about what she read. She expressed a particular fondness for the poetry of John Keats and Robert Browning, the prose of John Ruskin and Sir Thomas Browne, and the novels of George Eliot and Charlotte and Emily Brontë. And although she disclaimed knowledge of Whitman's work, she treasured a book that significantly influenced both Whitman's poetry and her own: the King James translation of the Bible. She especially liked the Book of Revelation.

Dickinson is often bracketed with Whitman as a cofounder of modern American poetry. Each brought to poetry something new, fresh, and strikingly original. But their poems, however prototypically modern, could not be more different. A mere glance at the page reveals a significant visual difference. Whitman's poems are large and expansive. The lines are long and the poems are typically ample and open. Dickinson's poems, by contrast, are highly compressed. They squeeze moments of intensely felt life and thought into tight four-line stanzas that compress feeling and condense thought.

The openness of Whitman's form is paralleled by the openness of his stance, his public outgoing manner. Dickinson's poetry is much more private, tending toward inwardness. Hers is a more meditative poetry than Whitman's, a poetry rooted partly in the metaphysical poetry of such seventeenth-century writers as John Donne and George Herbert. More directly influential on Dickinson's poetry than the metaphysical poets, however, was the tradition of Protestant hymnology. Her poems frequently employ the meter of hymns and follow their typical stanzaic pattern. Here, for example, is the opening verse of "Our God, Our Help in Ages Past," its accented syllables marked with ´.

> Oŭr Go´d, oŭr he´lp iň a´gĕs pa´st,
> Oŭr ho´pe fŏr ye´ars tŏ co´me,
> Oŭr she´ltĕr fro´m tŏe sto´rmў bla´st,
> Aňd ou´r ĕte´rnăl ho´me.

The hymn's meter and formal structure are highly regular. The first and third lines are in iambic tetrameter, the second and fourth in iambic trimeter. The lack of metrical variation results in a steady, predictable rhythm, essential for singing. Dickinson varies this standard pattern to suit her poetic purpose. Her numerous variations amply testify to the ingenious and stunning uses to which she put this familiar meter. Consider, for example, "I felt a Funeral, in my Brain," "I like a look of Agony," "I died for Beauty—but was scarce," and "I heard a Fly buzz—when I died."

Dickinson's adaptation of hymn meter accords with her adaptation of the traditional religious doctrines of orthodox Christianity. For although her poems reflect a Calvinist heritage—particularly in their probing self-analysis, in which an intensely religious disposition intersects with profound psychological experience—she was not an orthodox Christian. Her religious ideas, like her life and poetry, were distinctive and individual. And even when her views tend toward orthodox teaching, as in her attitude toward immortality, her literary expression of such a belief is strikingly original. In addition, Dickinson's mischievous wit contrasts sharply with the brooding solemnity characteristic of much Calvinist-inspired religious writing. Finally, her love for nature separates her from her Puritan precursors, allying her instead with such transcendentalist contemporaries as Emerson, Whitman, and Thoreau, though her vision of life is starker than theirs.

Dickinson's poetry requires repeated and careful readings. Her diction is frequently surprising. Her elliptical syntax occasionally departs from the normal pattern. Readers must consequently fill in the gaps her language creates. Her taut lines need to be loosened; her tight poems need to be opened up. Words, phrases, lines cry out for the expansion of interpretive paraphrase.

Though a dictionary is necessary to identify the meanings of many of the words in Dickinson's poems, we need to attend to their richness of connotation as well. In "A narrow Fellow in the Grass," for example, we can explore the connotations of "Fellow," "transport," "cordiality," and "Zero at the Bone," considering how they fuse thought and feeling. In "The Bustle in a House," we can be alert for the fresh treatment of metaphor in the second stanza and attentive to the connotations of "industries," "Morning," and "Enacted" from the opening lines. And in "Tell all the Truth but tell it slant," we can discover the general idea implied by the poem and then apply it to specific areas of our experience. In doing so we will discover how Dickinson treats both nature and human experience obliquely and indirectly. To read her poems requires, in addition, a willingness to wait for the poem's possibilities of meaning to reveal themselves. Since many of her poems are cast as riddles, we must be willing to accept uncertainty, ambiguity, and partial understanding in interpreting them.

We also have to extend our notion of what constitutes acceptable poetic technique—something her contemporaries found nearly impossible. Dickinson was criticized for using inexact rhymes, rough rhythms, and colloquial diction, and for taking liberties with grammar. Her odd punctuation—heavy on dashes—and her peculiar use of capitalization were also unappreciated. But Dickinson exploited these and other poetic resources to convey complex states of mind and feeling. She employed these and other poetic idiosyncrasies not for their own sake, but for emotional and psychological impact.

In his extensive biography of Dickinson, Richard B. Sewall describes her resolve to portray the state of her mind and being in all their unorthodox complexity. He also describes Dickinson's early and futile hopes for publication and appreciation as well as her resignation to what she termed her "barefoot rank: of anonymity." Sewall also reveals her determination to pursue truth and to make poems her way. When Thomas Wentworth Higginson, an influential contemporary critic, advised her to write a more polite poetry, less indirect and metaphoric, smoother in rhythm and rhyme, simpler in thought, and less colloquial in idiom, she replied with a poem. Her answer is that although she could have written otherwise, she chose to write as she did.

I cannot dance upon my Toes

I cannot dance upon my Toes—
No Man instructed me—
But oftentimes, among my mind,
A Glee possesseth me,

That had I Ballet knowledge—   5
Would put itself abroad
In Pirouette to blanch a Troupe—
Or lay a Prima, mad,

And though I had no Gown of Gauze—
No ringlet, to my Hair,   10
Nor hopped to Audiences—like Birds,
One claw upon the Air,

Nor tossed my shape in Eider Balls,
Nor rolled on wheels of snow
Till I was out of sight, in sound,   15
The House encore me so—

Nor any know I know the Art
I mention—easy—Here—
Nor any Placard boast me—
It's full as Opera   20

(#326)

Sewall describes how Dickinson's poems reflect her poetic vocation. He demonstrates how basic religious texts such as the Bible and Thomas à Kempis's *The Imitation of Christ* sustained her both spiritually and poetically. Though allowing that Dickinson's decision to cloister herself in her chamber could have had its roots in neurosis, he argues that her firm resolve was motivated by a commitment to the art of poetry akin to the ascetic discipline of religious devotion. In fact, he suggests that one of her more famous poems—one usually interpreted as a love poem—can be read as a dedication to the spiritual or poetic life. It can also be read as a celebration of individual choice.

The Soul selects her own Society

The Soul selects her own Society—
Then—shuts the Door—
To her divine Majority—
Present no more—

Unmoved—she notes the Chariots—pausing—   5
At her low Gate—
Unmoved—an Emperor be kneeling
Upon her Mat—

I've known her—from an ample nation—
Choose One—   10
Then—close the Valves of her attention—
Like Stone—

(#303)

    Sewall's central point about the relationship between Dickinson's life and art is that although we may not be certain which interpretation to favor when considering this and many other poems, we can remain satisfied with our uncertainty because such ambiguity is central to her art. She writes metaphorically, concealing as much as she reveals. As readers we share in apprehending the nature of the experience she describes—in the poem above, the experience of making a decisive choice involving commitment and renunciation. In doing so, however, we also supply specific details from our own lives to render the decision specific and significant. Dickinson's poetry, in other words, conveys the essence of an experience, its heart and core. Her poems, as Sewall aptly notes, do not tell us so much how to live as what it feels like to be alive.

    Emily Dickinson's poems do not encompass a wide range of experience; instead they probe deeply into a few of life's major experiences—love, death, doubt, and faith. In examining her experience, Dickinson makes a scrupulous effort to tell the truth, but she tells it "slant." Part of her originality and artistry includes the way she invites us to share in her search for truth. The qualified assertions we frequently find in her poems, their riddles and uncertainties, and their questioning stance demand our participation and response. In considering her representation of intensely felt moments of consciousness, we experience for ourselves her explosive power. And in learning to share Dickinson's acute perceptions and feelings, we also come to understand our own.

EMILY DICKINSON ON HERSELF AND HER FIRST POEMS

Letter to Thomas Higginson

Mr Higginson,

   Your kindness claimed earlier gratitude—but I was ill—and write today, from my pillow.

   Thank you for the surgery—it was not so painful as I supposed. I bring you others—as you ask—though they might not differ—

   While my thought is undressed—I can make the distinction, but when I put them in the Gown—they look alike, and numb.

   You asked how old I was? I made no verse—but one or two—until this winter—Sir—

   I had a terror—since September—I could tell to none—and so I sing, as the Boy does by the Burying Ground—because I am afraid—You inquire my Books—For Poets—I have Keats—and Mr and Mrs Browning. For Prose—Mr Ruskin—Sir Thomas Browne—and the Revelations. I went to school—but in your manner of the phrase—had no education. When a little Girl, I had a friend, who taught me Immortality—but venturing too near, himself—he never returned—Soon after, my Tutor, died—and for several years, my Lexicon—was my only companion—Then I found one more—but he was not contented I be his scholar—so he left the Land.

   You ask of my Companions Hills—Sir—and the Sundown—and a Dog—large as myself, that my Father bought me—They are better than Beings—because they know—but do not tell—and the noise in the Pool, at Noon—excels my Piano. I have a Brother and Sister—My Mother does not care for thought—and Father, too busy with his Briefs—to notice what we do—He buys me many Books—but begs me not to read them—because he fears they joggle the Mind. They are religious—except me—and address an Eclipse, every morning—whom they call their "Father." But I fear my story fatigues you—I would like to learn—Could you tell me how to grow—or is it unconveyed—like Melody—or Witchcraft?

(from a letter to Thomas Wentworth Higginson, April 25, 1862)

CRITICS ON DICKINSON

ALLEN TATE

Dickinson and Knowledge

from *"Emily Dickinson,"* in Collected Essays

Dickinson pursues that knowledge wherever it is to be found, no matter how it makes her feel. She reports her pursuit, seemingly as it occurs, with such profound attention that her poems offer exhilaration, no matter how sombre their topic.

To see Dickinson as an epistemological poet, a poet who advances a theory of knowledge in her work, doesn't mean that she is exclusively, or even primarily, an intellectual poet. She was brilliant, well educated, and confident in her use of conceptual, scientific, legal and linguistic terminology, but the truly remarkable quality of mind in her poetry comes from her refusal to separate this mind from the body and emotions which temper it. Dickinson writes close to the traditions of post-Romantic poetry and women's poetry in that her poetry expresses strong emotion. She stands to the side of it to the extent that the drive for knowledge dominates, and the affairs of the heart are seen as part of that knowledge, not separate. Hers is an epistemology of feeling. It is actually quite difficult to locate Dickinson's refusal to sublimate in literary-historical terms, because it is so alien to our usual structuring of dualism. Dickinson has the direct access to emotion which is thought to be—and is—a characteristic of much women's poetry. She doesn't, however, soften those emotions into acceptability or use poetry as an escape, either for herself or for her reader. Perhaps her knowledge has gone unrecognized for just this reason: she doesn't present it as a solution to human loss and pain. Rather, it is a way of experiencing fully and with utmost clarity whatever must be experienced.

Emily Dickinson's poetry runs the full emotive range from ecstatic celebration to numb despair. Huge shifts of perspective, imagery of thresholds, gems, open and closed space, stars, planets and firmaments mark Dickinson's sublime. In a few, very striking, poems she sees both human and writerly desires as capable of fulfilment. Imagery of plentitude—wine, feasting, nectar, flood and luxury—accompanies Dickinson's joyous knowledge. In these poems, her tone is often highly erotic:

> Wild Nights—Wild Nights!
> Were I with thee
> Wild Nights should be
> Our luxury!

As Dickinson would have known, the Latin word *luxus,* from which 'luxury' stems, means sensual excess or debauchery. Her declaration is actually redundant, further emphasizing its ecstatic triumph by the repetition of 'Wild Nights'. It is as if sensuous bliss is a state in which everything means the same thing, which is itself. The second stanza of 'Wild Nights—Wild Nights!' develops this oceanic emotion into a nautical metaphor as Dickinson, somewhat more conventionally, declares that 'Winds' are 'futile' 'To a Heart in port—'. Nor will this mariner need 'Compass' or 'Chart' to guide herself.

The poem's last stanza takes off from this hint of exultant freedom. The sexual beat of the rower's oars gives way to sheer exclamation:

> Rowing in Eden—
> Ah, the Sea!
> Might I but moor—Tonight—
> In Thee!

The last image may look like gender reversal, with the speaker seeing herself as the active partner, but Dickinson isn't concerned with whether or not her ecstasy fits

Victorian convention. The image is one of choosing to be contained by the lover. Mooring tonight is a way of remaining eternally in the oceanic paradise of Eros.

JUDITH FARR

On "Wild Nights"

from *The Passion of Emily Dickinson*

"Wild Nights," its theatrical opening spondees worthy of turbulence and storm, justifies Dickinson's heritage as an admirer of Emily Brontë and *Wuthering Heights.* The seas that separate or unite Charlotte Brontë's heroines and their "masters" also come to mind. Here is a scene reminiscent not only of the intensity of the Brontës' world but also of hundreds of dark canvases by the Hudson River and Luminist painters. Cole's *Tornado in an American Forest* (1835), like his *Expulsion from Eden,* had made the frenzy of storm synonymous with *passio*—distress or love—while seascapes like Fitz Hugh Lane's *Ships and an Approaching Storm off Owl's Head, Maine* (1860) or Heade's *Approaching Storm: Beach Near Newport* (1860) made angry seas expressive of the sea of feeling. Furthermore, Dickinson's image of the rowboat was conceived during the 1860s, when the idea of the lone boat in contest with high seas was particularly popular. There were many studies like Church's *An Old Boat* (1850), in which failure and loss were described by an abandoned rowboat at the edge of brimming, light-filled waters. Whistler expressed *The Sea* (1865) of defeat by picturing a rowboat stranded at the edge of sullen tides. Dickinson's lyrics about the "Edifice of Ocean" with its "tumultuous Rooms" (1217) would find analogues in the vehement seascapes of Winslow Homer, for whom the ocean could also be a metaphor of grandeur and grief. As a favorite nineteenth-century sport, however, rowing on smooth water was described by Thomas Eakins' Luminist paintings: for example, the famous *Max Schmitt in a Single Scull* (1871), which has a serene if rather triste formality.

Having said all this, it is equally important to say that "Wild Nights" is among the most Dickinsonian of the lyrics: ironic, paradoxical, voluptuous, and terse all at once. At first it projects a tumultuous nocturnal seascape, the wildness Nature's. But the next three lines of the first quatrain propose this as a luxury: that is, a rare experience to be enjoyed. Thus the imagined wildness is also human, internal, joyous. The next quatrain, spoken from the vantage point of one who has felt winds, declares how futile they would be in port, at rest, where neither they nor a compass or chart—the scientific instruments of explorers—are needed. By the closing quatrain, the speaker is "Rowing in Eden," her visionary desire having triumphed over the course of a life's voyage. Dickinson may have been remembering Bowles's rowing in Eden and all those betrothed nineteenth-century lovers so often depicted rowing together as one stroke in the same boat. (Thus in chapter 41 of *Little Women,* to give a popular example, Amy and Laurie row their boat "smoothly through the water" opposite Chillon, then decide to marry.) In Eden Dickinson finds a sea of love that is pleasurable, not frightening, and a Thee in which she might safely moor or harbor. Dickinson's inclusion of a sea in Eden, a garden, reminds us that the book of Genesis provides a river in Eden that waters the garden (2:10). (Other poems, such as "My River runs to thee" [162], may be related to her imagery of primal—sexual—waters. That poem was sent in a letter to Mary Bowles in August 1861; but like most of her words to Mary, it was probably intended for her husband.) In *Expulsion from Eden* Cole included a placid lake and a gentle waterfall in his Eden. When Dickinson's first quatrain is taken together with the last in poem 249, however, the reader realizes that she means to "moor" in passion, to luxuriate in wildness. For though hers is a boat that rows rather than rides the waters, her satisfaction in "Wild Nights" comes from strong delight. Even in Eden, she hears the sea. To moor is still to be wild for this prohibited voice that prays "Might I . . ."

ALLEN TATE

On *"Because I Could Not Stop for Death"*

from *"Emily Dickinson,"* in Collected Essays

If the word "great" means anything in poetry, this poem is one of the greatest in the English language. The rhythm charges with movement the pattern of suspended action back of the poem. Every image is precise and, moreover, not merely beautiful, but fused with the central idea. Every image extends and intensifies every other. The third stanza especially shows Miss Dickinson's power to fuse, into a single order of perception, a heterogeneous series: the children, the grain, and the setting sun (time) have the same degree of credibility; the first subtly preparing for the last. The sharp *gazing* before *grain* instills into nature a cold vitality of which the qualitative richness has infinite depth. The content of death in the poem eludes explicit definition. He is a gentleman taking a lady out for a drive. But note the restraint that keeps the poet from carrying this so far that it becomes ludicrous and incredible; and note the subtly interfused erotic motive, which the idea of death has presented to most romantic poets, love being a symbol interchangeable with death. The terror of death is objectified through this figure of the genteel driver, who is made ironically to serve the end of Immortality. This is the heart of the poem: she has presented a typical Christian theme in its final irresolution, without making any final statements about it. There is no solution to the problem; there can be only a presentation of it in the full context of intellect and feeling. A construction of the human will, elaborated with all the abstracting powers of the mind, is put to the concrete test of experience: the idea of immortality is confronted with the fact of physical disintegration. We are not told what to think; we are told to look at the situation.

The framework of the poem is, in fact, the two abstractions, mortality and eternity, which are made to associate in equality with the images: she sees the ideas, and thinks the perceptions. She did, of course, nothing of the sort; but we must use the logical distinctions, even to the extent of paradox, if we are to form any notion of this rare quality of mind. She could not in the proper sense think at all, and unless we prefer the feeble poetry of moral ideas that flourished in New England in the eighties, we must conclude that her intellectual deficiency contributed at least negatively to her great distinction. Miss Dickinson is probably the only Anglo-American poet of her century whose work exhibits the perfect literary situation—in which is possible the fusion of sensibility and thought. Unlike her contemporaries, she never succumbed to her ideas, to easy solutions, to her private desires. . . .

Neither the feeling nor the style of Miss Dickinson belongs to the seventeenth century; yet between her and Donne there are remarkable ties. Their religious ideas, their abstractions, are momently toppling from the rational plane to the level of perception. The ideas, in fact, are no longer the impersonal religious symbols created anew in the heat of emotion, that we find in poets like Herbert and Vaughan. They have become, for Donne, the terms of personality; they are mingled with the miscellany of sensation. In Miss Dickinson, as in Donne, we may detect a singularly morbid concern, not for religious truth, but for personal revelation. The modern word is self-exploitation. It is egoism grown irresponsible in religion and decadent in morals. In religion it is blasphemy; in society it means usually that culture is not self-contained and sufficient, that the spiritual community is breaking up. This is, along with some other features that do not concern us here, the perfect literary situation.

HELEN MCNEIL

Dickinson's Method

from *Emily Dickinson*

Many Victorian poems describe unexamined abstractions, as if society agreed about what constituted sorrow or love. These could be personified, and their attributes could be listed and elaborated metaphorically. Dickinson takes on a frightening abstraction and evolves its attributes from experience, not tradition. In poetry and philosophy, the subject—the experiencing person—may wonder about the existence of other minds. Dickinson wrote many poems on this problem. In 'Pain—has an Element of Blank,' she contemplates the possibility that there may be circumstances in which the perceiving consciousness also does not exist, erased by its own emotion. 'The Soul has

Bandaged moments—' she begins another poem; the abstract soul is a bandaged body, in a metaphor which denies dualism. Time is also represented physically, bound up by pain. As Dickinson concludes at the end of 'The Soul has Bandaged moments—,' such recognitions 'are not brayed of Tongue—' in the public discourse of her society, or, for that matter, our society either.

Dickinson wrote about feeling, but out of feeling she constructed a theory of knowledge—not *beyond* feeling, or free from it, or in any way separate, but using it as a kind of knowing. In effect—though not in conventional terms—she is an epistemological poet, a poet who advances a theory of knowledge. Dickinson made this concern explicit. After the forms of the verb 'to be,' 'know' is the most frequently used verb in Dickinson's poetry, appearing 230 times, more even than any noun except 'day.'

Dickinson's constant pressure towards knowing means that she can treat even the most tormented situations with great calm. She can begin by writing 'I felt a Funeral, in my Brain,' or 'Pain—has an Element of Blank—' or 'I felt my life with both my hands—' and then proceed to delineate that state with a commanding accuracy. In a manner more resembling the Metaphysical poets than her Victorian contemporaries, male or female, she uses emotionally heightened states as occasions for clarity.

American poetry characteristically embodies acts of process: the Dickinsonian 'process' is passionate investigation. Her investigative process often implies narrative by taking speaker and reader through a sequence of rapidly changing images, even when all the action is interior. These investigations structure Dickinson's poetry; I suspect that the flexibility of her investigative movement is the major reason why Dickinson generally was contented with common metre. She may even have enjoyed the way her condensed discoveries press against the limits of a small form.

THREE POEMS BY EMILY DICKINSON WITH ALTERED PUNCTUATION

After her death, Emily Dickinson's poems were published with their punctuation changed to conform to the conventional usage of the time. Compare these versions with Dickinson's originals in the next section of this chapter.

Pain has an element of blank

Pain has an element of blank;
It cannot recollect
When it began, or if there were
A day when it was not.

It has no future but itself,
Its infinite realms contain
Its past, enlightened to perceive
New periods of pain.

The brain is wider than the sky

The brain is wider than the sky,
For, put them side by side,
The one the other will include
With ease, and you beside.

The brain is deeper than the sea
For, hold them, blue to blue,
The one the other will absorb,
As sponges, buckets do.

The brain is just the weight of God,
For, lift them, pound for pound,
And they will differ, if they do,
As syllable from sound.

The soul selects her own society

The soul selects her own society,
Then shuts the door;
On her divine majority
Obtrude no more.

Unmoved, she notes the chariot's pausing
At her low gate;
Unmoved, an emperor is kneeling
Upon her mat.

I've known her from an ample nation
Choose one;
Then close the valves of her attention
Like stone.

EMILY DICKINSON: POEMS

I'm "wife"—I've finished that

I'm "wife"—I've finished that
That other state—
I'm Czar—I'm "Woman" now—
It's safer so—

How odd the Girl's life looks   5
Behind this soft Eclipse—
I think that Earth feels so
To folks in Heaven—now—

This being comfort—then
That other kind—was pain—   10
But why compare?
I'm "Wife"! Stop there!

(#199, 1860, 1890)

I taste a liquor never brewed

I taste a liquor never brewed—
From Tankards scooped in Pearl—
Not all the Vats upon the Rhine
Yield such an Alcohol!

Inebriate of Air—am I—   5
And Debauchee of Dew—
Reeling—thro endless summer days—
From inns of Molten Blue—

When "Landlords" turn the drunken Bee
Out of the Foxglove's door—   10
When Butterflies—renounce their "drams"—
I shall but drink the more!

Till Seraphs swing their snowy Hats—
And Saints—to windows run—
To see the little Tippler   15
Leaning against the—Sun—

(#214, 1860, 1861)

I like a look of Agony

I like a look of Agony,
Because I know it's true—
Men do not sham Convulsion,
Nor simulate, a Throe—

The Eyes glaze once—and that is Death—   5
Impossible to feign
The Beads upon the Forehead
By homely Anguish strung.

(#241, 1861, 1890)

Wild Nights—Wild Nights!

Wild Nights—Wild Nights!
Were I with thee
Wild Nights should be
Our luxury!

Futile—the Winds— 5
To a Heart in port—
Done with the Compass—
Done with the Chart!

Rowing in Eden—
Ah, the Sea! 10
Might I but moor—Tonight—
In Thee!

(#249, 1861, 1891)

There's a certain Slant of light

There's a certain Slant of light,
Winter Afternoons—
That oppresses, like the Heft
Of Cathedral Tunes—

Heavenly Hurt, it gives us— 5
We can find no scar,
But internal difference,
Where the Meanings, are—

None may teach it—Any—
'Tis the Sea Despair— 10
An imperial affliction
Sent us of the Air—

When it comes, the Landscape listens—
Shadows—hold their breath—
When it goes, 'tis like the Distance 15
On the look of Death—

(#258, 1861, 1890)

I felt a Funeral, in my Brain

I felt a Funeral, in my Brain,
And Mourners to and fro
Kept treading—treading—till it seemed
That Sense was breaking through—

And when they all were seated,   5
A Service, like a Drum—
Kept beating—beating—till I thought
My Mind was going numb—

And I heard them lift a Box
And creak across my Soul   10
With those same Boots of Lead, again,
Then Space—began to toll,

As all the Heavens were a Bell,
And Being, but an Ear,
And I, and Silence, some strange Race   15
Wrecked, solitary, here—

And then a Plank in Reason, broke,
And I dropped down, and down—
And hit a World, at every plunge,
And Finished knowing—then—   20

(#280, 1861, 1896)

Some keep the Sabbath going to Church

Some keep the Sabbath going to Church—
I keep it, staying at Home—
With a Bobolink for a Chorister—
And an Orchard, for a Dome—

Some keep the Sabbath in Surplice—   5
I just wear my Wings—
And instead of tolling the Bell, for Church,
Our little Sexton—sings.

God preaches, a noted Clergyman—
And the sermon is never long,   10
So instead of getting to Heaven, at last—
I'm going, all along.

(#328, 1862, 1891)

After great pain, a formal feeling comes

After great pain, a formal feeling comes—
The Nerves sit ceremonious, like Tombs—
The stiff Heart questions was it He, that bore,
And Yesterday, or Centuries before?

The Feet, mechanical, go round—   5
Of Ground, or Air, or Ought—
A Wooden way
Regardless grown,
A Quartz contentment, like a stone—

This is the Hour of Lead—   10
Remembered, if outlived,
As Freezing persons, recollect the Snow—
First—Chill—then Stupor—then the letting go—

(#341, 1862, 1929)

I dreaded that first Robin, so

I dreaded that first Robin, so,
But He is mastered, now,
I'm some accustomed to Him grown,
He hurts a little, though—

I thought if I could only live   5
Till that first Shout got by—
Not all Pianos in the Woods
Had power to mangle me—

I dared not meet the Daffodils—
For fear their Yellow Gown   10
Would pierce me with a fashion
So foreign to my own—

I wished the Grass would hurry—
So—when 'twas time to see—
He'd be too tall, the tallest one   15
Could stretch—to look at me—

I could not bear the Bees should come,
I wished they'd stay away
In those dim countries where they go,
What word had they, for me?   20

They're here, though; not a creature failed—
No Blossom stayed away
In gentle deference to me—
The Queen of Calvary—

Each one salutes me, as he goes,   25
And I, my childish Plumes,
Lift, in bereaved acknowledgment
Of their unthinking Drums—

                                            (#348, 1862, 1891)

We grow accustomed to the Dark

We grow accustomed to the Dark—
When Light is put away—
As when the Neighbor holds the Lamp
To witness her Goodbye—

A Moment—We uncertain step   5
For newness of the night—
Then—fit our Vision to the Dark—
And meet the Road—erect—

And so of larger—Darknesses—
Those Evenings of the Brain—   10
When not a Moon disclose a sign—
Or Star—come out—within—

The Bravest—grope a little—
And sometimes hit a Tree
Directly in the Forehead—   15
But as they learn to see—

Either the Darkness alters—
Or something in the sight
Adjusts itself to Midnight—
And Life steps almost straight.   20

                                            (#419, 1862, 1935)

Much Madness is divinest Sense

Much Madness is divinest Sense—
To a discerning Eye—
Much Sense—the starkest Madness—

'Tis the Majority
In this, as All, prevail— 5
Assent—and you are sane—
Demur—you're straightway dangerous—
And handled with a Chain—

(#435, 1862, 1935)

I died for Beauty—but was scarce

I died for Beauty—but was scarce
Adjusted in the Tomb
When One who died for Truth, was lain
In an adjoining Room—

He questioned softly "Why I failed?" 5
"For Beauty," I replied—
"And I—for Truth—Themself are One—
We Brethren, are," He said—

And so, as Kinsmen, met a Night—
We talked between the Rooms— 10
Until the Moss had reached our lips—
And covered up—our names—

(#449, 1862, 1890)

I heard a Fly buzz—when I died

I heard a Fly buzz—when I died—
The Stillness in the Room
Was like the Stillness in the Air—
Between the Heaves of Storm—

The Eyes around—had wrung them dry— 5
And Breaths were gathering firm
For that last Onset—when the King
Be witnessed—in the Room—

I willed my Keepsakes—Signed away
What portion of me be 10
Assignable—and then it was
There interposed a Fly—

With Blue—uncertain stumbling Buzz—
Between the light—and me—
And then the Windows failed—and then   15
I could not see to see—

(#465, 1862, 1896)

The Heart asks Pleasure—first

The Heart asks Pleasure—first—
And then—Excuse from Pain—
And then—those little Anodynes
That deaden suffering—

And then—to go to sleep—   5
And then—if it should be
The will of its Inquisition
The privilege to die—

(#536, 1862, 1890)

I like to see it lap the Miles

I like to see it lap the Miles—
And lick the Valleys up—
And stop to feed itself at Tanks—
And then—prodigious step

Around a Pile of Mountains—   5
And supercilious peer
In Shanties—by the sides of Roads—
And then a Quarry pare

To fit its Ribs
And crawl between   10
Complaining all the while
In horrid—hooting stanza—
Then chase itself down Hill—

And neigh like Boanerges—
Then—punctual as a Star   15
Stop—docile and omnipotent
At its own stable door—

(#585, 1862, 1891)

There is a pain—so utter

There is a pain—so utter—
It swallows substance up—
Then covers the Abyss with Trance—
So Memory can step
Around—across—upon it—   5
As one within a Swoon—
Goes safely—where an open eye—
Would drop Him—Bone by Bone.

(#599, 1862, 1929)

The Brain—is wider than the sky—

The Brain—is wider than the Sky—
For—put them side by side—
The one the other will contain
With ease—and You—beside—

The Brain is deeper than the sea—
For—hold them—Blue to Blue—
The one the other will absorb—
As Sponges—Buckets—do—

The Brain is just the weight of God—
For—Heft them—Pound for Pound—
And they will differ—if they do—
As Syllable from Sound—

(#632, 1862, 1896)

Pain—has an Element of Blank

Pain—has an Element of Blank—
It cannot recollect
When it begun—or if there were
A time when it was not—

It has no Future—but itself—   5
Its Infinite contain
Its Past—enlightened to perceive
New Periods—of Pain.

(#650, 1862, 1890)

Remorse—is Memory—awake

Remorse—is Memory—awake—
Her Parties all astir—
A Presence of Departed Acts—
At window—and at Door—

Its Past—set down before the Soul   5
And lighted with a Match—
Perusal—to facilitate—
And help Belief to stretch—

Remorse is cureless—the Disease
Not even God—can heal—   10
For 'tis His institution—and
The Adequate of Hell—

(#744, 1863, 1891)

My Life had stood—a Loaded Gun

My Life had stood—a Loaded Gun—
In Corners—till a Day
The Owner passed—identified—
And carried Me away—

And now We roam in Sovereign Woods—   5
And now We hunt the Doe—
And every time I speak for Him—
The Mountains straight reply—

And do I smile, such cordial light
Upon the Valley glow—   10
It is as a Vesuvian face
Had let its pleasure through—

And when at Night—Our good Day done—
I guard My Master's Head—
'Tis better than the Eider-Duck's   15
Deep Pillow—to have shared—

To foe of His—I'm deadly foe—
None stir the second time—
On whom I lay a Yellow Eye—
Or an emphatic Thumb—   20

Though I than He—may longer live
He longer must—than I—
For I have but the power to kill,
Without—the power to die—

(#754, 1863, 1929)

A narrow Fellow in the Grass

A narrow Fellow in the Grass
Occasionally rides—
You may have met Him—did you not
His notice sudden is—

The Grass divides as with a Comb—   5
A spotted shaft is seen—
And then it closes at your feet
And opens further on—

He likes a Boggy Acre
A floor too cool for Corn—   10
Yet when a Boy, and Barefoot—
I more than once at Noon
Have passed, I thought, a Whip lash
Unbraiding in the Sun
When stooping to secure it   15
It wrinkled, and was gone—

Several of Nature's People
I know, and they know me—
I feel for them a transport
Of cordiality—   20

But never met this Fellow
Attended, or alone
Without a tighter breathing
And Zero at the Bone—

(#986, 1865, 1866)

Further in Summer than the Birds

Further in Summer than the Birds
Pathetic from the Grass
A minor Nation celebrates
Its unobtrusive Mass.

No Ordinance be seen   5
So gradual the Grace
A pensive Custom it becomes
Enlarging Loneliness.

Antiquest felt at Noon
When August burning low   10
Arise this spectral Canticle
Repose to typify

Remit as yet no Grace
No Furrow on the Glow
Yet a Druidic Difference   15
Enhances Nature now

(#1068, 1866, 1891)

The Bustle in a House

The Bustle in a House
The Morning after Death
Is solemnest of industries
Enacted upon Earth—

The Sweeping up the Heart   5
And putting Love away
We shall not want to use again
Until Eternity.

(#1078, 1866, 1890)

The last Night that She lived

The last Night that She lived
It was a Common Night
Except the Dying—this to Us
Made Nature different

We noticed smallest things—   5
Things overlooked before
By this great light upon our Minds
Italicized—as 'twere.

As We went out and in
Between Her final Room   10
And Rooms where Those to be alive
Tomorrow were, a Blame

That Others could exist
While She must finish quite
A Jealousy for Her arose   15
So nearly infinite—

We waited while She passed—
It was a narrow time—
Too jostled were Our Souls to speak
At length the notice came.   20

She mentioned, and forgot—
Then lightly as a Reed
Bent to the Water, struggled scarce—
Consented, and was dead—

And We—We placed the Hair—   25
And drew the Head erect—
And then an awful leisure was
Belief to regulate—

(#1100, 1866, 1890)

Tell all the Truth but tell it slant

Tell all the Truth but tell it slant—
Success in Circuit lies
Too bright for our infirm Delight
The Truth's superb surprise

As Lightning to the Children eased   5
With explanation kind
The Truth must dazzle gradually
Or every man be blind—

(#1129, 1868, 1945)

A Route of Evanescence

A Route of Evanescence
With a revolving Wheel—
A Resonance of Emerald—
A Rush of Cochineal—
And every Blossom on the Bush   5
Adjusts its tumbled Head—
The mail from Tunis, probably,
An easy Morning's Ride—

(#1463, 1879, 1891)

Apparently with no surprise

Apparently with no surprise
To any happy Flower
The Frost beheads it at its play—
In accidental power—
The blonde Assassin passes on—   5
The Sun proceeds unmoved
To measure off another Day
For an Approving God.

(#1624, 1884, 1890)

My life closed twice before its close

My life closed twice before its close—
It yet remains to see
If Immortality unveil
A third event to me

So huge, so hopeless to conceive   5
As these that twice befell.
Parting is all we know of heaven,
And all we need of hell.

(#1732, 1896)

INTRODUCTION TO ROBERT FROST

[1874–1963]

Like Walt Whitman before him, Robert Frost yearned to become America's foremost poet. Aiming for both critical and popular acclaim, Frost hoped to achieve recognition as a major poet and to reach the widest possible audience. And although he did succeed in becoming a popular poet (perhaps the most popular in America's history), in the minds of some readers his very popularity diminished his critical stature. Frost himself, however, was partly responsible for this. The image he projected—folksy, lovable, homespun—undercut his reputation as a major poet. Even today, with Frost's poetic stature widely acknowledged, he is occasionally seen as a less serious, less impressive, less demanding, and hence less important poet than his contemporaries Ezra Pound, T. S. Eliot, and Wallace Stevens.

There is a measure of truth in this assessment, perhaps, but only a small measure. Frost's poems are easier to read than those of Pound, Eliot, or Stevens: his familiar vocabulary and traditional forms enhance their accessibility. But his poems are neither simple nor easy to understand. Their diction is more richly allusive and connotative than at first may appear. Their paraphrasable thought is subtler and more profound than an initial reading might suggest. Moreover, their form, though traditional, is more intricately wrought and more decisively experimental than is generally recognized. Before turning to consider these claims, we should be aware of the course of Frost's poetic career, particularly of his popularity as an honored national poet, who, ironically, was first recognized abroad rather than at home.

Although Robert Frost is considered a New England farmer-poet who captures in his verse the tang of Yankee speech, he was born in San Francisco and lived there until the age of eleven, when his family moved to Lawrence, Massachusetts. He attended high school in Lawrence and was covaledictorian of his graduating class with Elinor White, whom he later married. Frost continued his education at Dartmouth College, where he remained for only one term, and later at Harvard University, where he studied for two years without taking a degree. After working at a succession of odd jobs including farming and factory work, Frost taught at Pinkerton Academy, where from 1906 to 1910 he reformed the English syllabus, directed theatrical productions, and wrote many of the poems later included in his first book, *A Boy's Will.*

In 1911, in an attempt to attract the attention of prominent and influential members in the literary world, he sold his farm in Derry, New Hampshire, and moved with his family to England. There he met and received the support of Ezra Pound, who helped secure publication of his first two volumes of poems, and of Edward Thomas, who reviewed them perceptively. Having launched his career, Frost returned to America in 1915 and quickly secured an American publisher—Henry Holt and Co.—for the two books published in England, *A Boy's Will* (1913) and *North of Boston* (1914), and for subsequent volumes as well. With the publication in 1916 of *Mountain Interval,* Frost's fame grew. In 1917, and periodically thereafter, he was poet in residence at Amherst College and served in a similar capacity at various other colleges and universities including Dartmouth, Wesleyan, Michigan, Harvard, and Yale. Frost received awards and prizes, among them the Bollingen Poetry Prize (1963) and four Pulitzer Prizes (1924, 1931, 1937, and 1943). In addition many honorary degrees, including ones from Oxford and Cambridge universities, were conferred on him. Although Frost was fond of joking that he could make a blanket of the many academic hoods he had acquired, he valued them, particularly those from the British institutions. Later in his life Frost was appointed goodwill emissary to South America and the Soviet Union. At the time he was also the only American poet honored with an invitation to read his work at a presidential inauguration. In January 1961, at the inauguration of John F. Kennedy, Frost read "The Gift Outright" and another poem he had composed for the occasion.

This brief summary of Frost's career, however, oversimplifies what was in reality a more complex and arduous process. Initially an obscure writer, Frost experienced difficulty in breaking into print in a significant way. He later struggled with the decline of his poetic powers, most of his best work having been produced when he was younger. And more tragically, he suffered the deaths of his wife and three of his children, one of whom committed suicide. He also saw his sister and one of his daughters succumb to mental illness. And finally, despite his many prizes and awards, Frost was bitter that he never won a Nobel Prize. He died in 1963, two weeks short of his eighty-ninth birthday.

What accounts for Frost's fame and popularity? Three things, at least: his shrewd management of his career, including the cultivation of his poetic image; his use of familiar subjects, especially the natural world and people engaged in recognizable activities; and his accessible language and apparent simplicity of thought. From the beginning, Frost skillfully managed his poetic career, going abroad to England to win the approval of the prominent poets and critics of his day. Frost, of course, did not plan every step of his rise to fame; rather he trusted to his highly developed instinct for sizing up opportunities and capitalizing on them. As William Pritchard explains in *Robert Frost: A Literary Life Reconsidered,* Frost retrospectively structured his literary life as one of adversity overcome. The most important aspect of this biographical semifictionalizing was Frost's portrayal of himself as a literary exile unappreciated in his home country. Allied with this biographical mythmaking was Frost's control over his public image. He refused, for example, to read his darker, more skeptical poems in public, preferring instead to reveal his more congenial, folksy side. And he carefully masked from public exposure his hunger for fame and an occasional nasty denigration of those poets he considered his strongest rivals.

More important to his popularity than his masterly manipulation of his public persona, however, is the readability of his poetry. Frost avoids obscure language, preferring the familiar word and the idiomatic phrase. He also shuns foreign words and shies away from all but the scantiest of references to economic, literary, and political history. And instead of the structural openness, fragmentation, and discontinuity favored by some of his contemporaries, Frost used traditional poetic forms characterized by coherence and continuity.

That Frost's poems are relatively easy to read does not mean that they are necessarily easy to understand. Frost is a master of concealment, of saying one thing in terms of another, and especially of saying two or more things simultaneously. Even his most accessible poems such as "Birches," "Mending Wall," and "The Road Not Taken" contain clear invitations to consider their symbolic ramifications. The symbolic nature of these poems doesn't manifest itself immediately. To appreciate the fullness of Frost's achievement, we need to read with attention to their symbolic detail, whether we are reading the meditative blank verse of "Birches" or "Mending Wall" or the lyrical descriptions of "Desert Places" or "Stopping by Woods on a Snowy Evening."

It is also a mistake to assume, on the basis of a familiarity with a few of Frost's more famous lyrics, that his poetry lacks either drama or humor. "Departmental" reveals Frost's humorous side, while "Home Burial" shows him at work in a longer, more dramatic form. Though his poems are certainly serious, they are not solemn. This is as true of "Stopping by Woods" and "The Road Not Taken" as it is for "The Silken Tent," a witty extended comparison between a woman and a pitched tent; "Provide, Provide," a pragmatic set of admonitions about how to get on in the world; and "A Considerable Speck," a satirical jab at human limitations, particularly the performances of writers. Moreover, Frost himself warned us against taking him too seriously. Although we cannot completely trust him in such matters since he enjoyed teasing his audiences, we can at least regard his work as a mixture of playfulness and seriousness. "If it is with outer seriousness," he once remarked, "it must with inner humor; if with inner seriousness, then with outer humor."

Complicating matters further is Frost's view of nature. More often than not, nature appears as a powerful, dangerous, and cruel force, its purpose and design not immediately apparent. Frost avoids a simple representation of the relationship between the natural and human worlds. He does not share Emerson's belief in nature as a moral teacher. He does not believe, for example, that in reading nature we discover moral and spiritual truths. That romantic view is questioned in poems like "Desert Places" and "The Most of It," where nature seems to express "nothing" to the human observer. Yet other poems, such as "The Tuft of Flowers" and "Two Look at Two," are entirely compatible with Emersonian and Whitmanesque transcendentalist ideas, in which nature and man form part of a harmonious whole.

Frost's response to nature is, essentially, to wonder skeptically just how much "meaning" in nature there really is for human beings. A poem like "Tree at My Window" explores this issue. In the first part of the poem, there seems to be a definite connection between nature (trees) and people; the human and the natural worlds intersect. But the last stanza suggests that there are radical differences between the two worlds, differences that separate them more than their similarities bind them.

The complexity and richness of Frost's vision of nature are paralleled by the subtlety of his technical achievement. Though he worked in traditional forms— sonnet, heroic couplet, blank verse, four-line stanza—the effects he wrought in them are remarkable for their range and versatility. To take just one example, consider his sonnets, which include poems in both of the traditional forms,

Shakespearean and Petrarchan. "Putting in the Seed" is constructed according to the Shakespearean, or English, pattern with three quatrains and a concluding couplet (though Frost alters the rhyme pattern slightly). "Design" follows the Petrarchan model: an octave of eight lines followed by a sestet of six. The octave of "Design" describes a natural scene (a white spider finding on a white flower a white moth that it kills and devours). The sestet explores the significance of the event. Though conventional in logical organization, "Design" exhibits a variation from the Petrarchan rhyme scheme: *abba abba cde cde* (or *cd cd cd*). Frost's poem uses only three rhymes throughout both octave and sestet: *abba abba acc caa*.

Frost's sonnets often diverge in some way from the traditional sonnet and thus make something new and fresh of the form. "Mowing," for example, while composed according to the Petrarchan structure, contains a strong concluding couplet more characteristic of the Shakespearean sonnet. It also varies from the rhyme scheme of both traditional patterns, though using the same number of different sounds as the Shakespearean form: *abca bdec dfeg fg*. The poem displays a curious use of overlapping sound effects that Frost worked out more elaborately and systematically in other lyrics. Other sonnet variations appear in "The Silken Tent," which is constructed as a single sentence spun out over the fourteen lines in a Shakespearean pattern. Working against that rhyme scheme, however, is a logical structure more characteristic of the Petrarchan division into two major sections, with a turn at the ninth line. Such hybrid sonnets are accompanied by other sonnet experiments such as "Once by the Pacific," in seven couplets rhyming *aa bb cc dd ee ff gg,* and "Acquainted with the Night," composed in the interlocking rhymes of *terza rima: aba bcb cdc ded ee.*

Frost was a skilled wordsmith who cared about the sounds of his sentences. He noted more than once how "the sentence sound says more than the words"; how "tones of voice" can "mean more than words." In such voice tones Frost heard the sounds of sense and captured them in his verse, heightening their expressiveness by combining the inflections of ordinary speech with the measured regularity of meter. Because Frost's achievement in this regard surpasses that of most other modern American poets, we should be particularly attentive to the way he makes poetry out of the spoken word. His poems often mask the most elegant and subtle of his technical accomplishments. Perhaps the best way to read Frost's poems is to approach them as performances, as poetic acts of skillful daring, of risks taken, of technical dangers overcome. In doing so we may share the pleasure Frost took in poetic performance. In addition, we can see how Frost's poetry often "begins in delight and ends in wisdom," offering along the way what he called "a momentary stay against confusion."

CRITICAL COMMENTS BY FROST

from *The Figure a Poem Makes*

The figure a poem makes. It begins in delight and ends in wisdom. The figure is the same as for love. No one can really hold that the ecstasy should be static and stand still in one place. It begins in delight, it inclines to the impulse, it assumes direction with the first line laid down, it runs a course of lucky events, and ends in a clarification of life—not necessarily a great clarification, such as sects and cults are founded on, but in a momentary stay against confusion. It has denouement. It has an outcome that though unforeseen was predestined from the first image of the original mood—and indeed from the very mood. It is but a trick poem and no poem at all if the best of it was thought of first and saved for the last. It finds its own name as it goes and discovers the best waiting for it in some final phrase at once wise and sad—the happy-sad blend of the drinking song.

No tears in the writer, no tears in the reader. No surprise for the writer, no surprise for the reader. For me the initial delight is in the surprise of remembering something I didn't know I knew. I am in a place, in a situation, as if I had materialized from cloud or risen out of the ground. There is a glad recognition of the long lost and the rest follows. Step by step the wonder of unexpected supply keeps growing. The impressions most useful to my purpose seem always those I was unaware of and so made no note of at the time when taken, and the conclusion is come to that like giants we are always hurling experience ahead of us to pave the future with against the day when we may want to strike a line of purpose across it for somewhere. The line will have the more charm for not being mechanically straight. We enjoy the straight crookedness of a good walking stick. Modern instruments of precision are being used to make things crooked as if by eye and hand in the old days. . . .

More than once I should have lost my soul to radicalism if it had been the originality it was mistaken for by its young converts. Originality and initiative are what I ask for my country. For myself the originality need be no more than the freshness of a poem run in the way I have described: from delight to wisdom. The figure is the same as for love. Like a piece of ice on a hot stove the poem must ride on its own melting. A poem may be worked over once it is in being, but may not be worried into being. Its most previous quality will remain its having run itself and carried away the poet with it. Read it a hundred times: it will forever keep its freshness as a metal keeps its fragrance. It can never lose its sense of a meaning that once unfolded by surprise as it went.

from *"The Constant Symbol"*

I give you a new definition of a sentence:

A sentence is a sound in itself on which other sounds called words may be strung.

You may string words together without a sentence-sound to string them on just as you may tie clothes together by the sleeves and stretch them without a clothes line between two trees, but—it is bad for the clothes.

The number of words you may string on one sentence-sound is not fixed but there is always danger of overloading.

The sentence-sounds are very definite entities. (This is no literary mysticism I am preaching.) They are as definite as words. It is not impossible that they could be collected in a book though I don't at present see on what system they would be catalogued.

They are apprehended by the ear. They are gathered by the ear from the vernacular and brought into books. Many of them are already familiar to us in books. I think no writer invents them. The most original writer only catches them fresh from talk, where they grow spontaneously.

A man is all a writer if *all* his words are strung on definite recognizable sentence sounds. The voice of the imagination, the speaking voice must know certainly how to behave how to posture in every sentence he offers.

A man is a marked writer if his words are largely strung on the more striking sentence sounds.

A word about recognition: In literature it is our business to give people the thing that will make them say, "Oh yes I know what you mean." It is never to tell them something they don't know, but something they know and hadn't thought of saying. It must be something they recognize. . . .

The sentence as a sound in itself apart from the word sounds is no mere figure of speech. I shall show the sentence sound saying all that the sentence conveys with little or no help from the meaning of the words. I shall show the sentence sound opposing the sense of the words as in irony. And so till I establish the distinction between the grammatical sentence and the vital sentence. The grammatical sentence is merely accessory to the other and chiefly valuable as furnishing a clue to the other. You recognize the sentence sound in this: *You, you*—! It is so strong that if you hear it as I do you have to pronounce the two you's differently. Just so many sentence sounds belong to man as just so many vocal runs belong to one kind of bird. We come into the world with them and create none of them.

There are many other things I have found myself saying about poetry, but the chiefest of these is that it is metaphor, saying one thing and meaning another, saying one thing in terms of another, the pleasure of ulteriority. Poetry is simply made of metaphor. So also is philosophy—and science, too, for that matter, if it will take the soft impeachment from a friend. Every poem is a new metaphor inside or it is nothing. And there is a sense in which all poems are the same old metaphor always.

from *"The Unmade Word, Or Fetching and Far-Fetching"*

There are two kinds of language: the spoken language and the written language—our everyday speech which we call the vernacular; and a more literary, sophisticated, artificial, elegant language that belongs to books. We often hear it said that a man talks like a book in this second way. We object to anybody's talking in this literary, artificial English; we don't object to anybody's writing in it; we rather expect people to write in a literary, somewhat artificial style. I, myself, could get along very well without this bookish language altogether. I agree with the poet who visited this country not long ago when he said that all our literature has got to come down, sooner or later, to the talk of everyday life. William Butler Yeats says that all our words, phrases, and idioms to be effective must be in the manner of everyday speech.

We've got to come down to this speech of everyday, to begin with—the hard everyday word of the street, business, trades, work in summer—to begin with; but there is some sort of obligation laid on us, to lift the words of every day, to give them a metaphorical turn. No, you don't want to use that term—give the words a poetic touch. I'll show you what I mean by an example: take for example the word "lemon," that's a good practical word with no literary associations—a word that you use with the grocer and in the kitchen; it has no literary associations at all; "Peach" is another one; but you boys have taken these two words and given them a poetic twist.

CRITICS ON FROST

N O R M A N   H O L L A N D

Reading Frost

from *The Brain of Robert Frost*

We can explore the workings of Frost's brain—or mind—through one of his better-known poems, "Once by the Pacific" [see page 184 of this text]. I think this poem had at the core of its creation a widespread and well-known childhood fear. I find it of particular interest therefore, because it allows us to see how Frost defended himself against fears we may well have experienced ourselves. As I put the poem together for myself, I respond most immediately to its violence, to words like "rage," "din," or the menacing phrase, "dark intent." The first substantial word I hear is "shattered" and the final rhyme is "broken," although, to be sure, it is only "water" that is shattered and broken, a water that is (ironically) "Pacific"—peaceful.

This night is unique: the waves "thought of doing something to the shore/That water never did to land before." And immense. I imagine huge dimensions from phrases like "great waves," "ocean-water," or words like "land," "continent," or (in time) "an age." I find these sizes made still bigger by a pattern of buttressing, doubling, and increasing. The shore is backed by cliff, and the cliff is backed by continent. "There would be *more* than ocean-water broken." Waves looked over *other* waves. This was not just a night, but an age. And finally, the poem, having begun with the storm, ends with God and the Last Judgment, a final doubling, a bigness bigger than even waves and continent, an immensity of words called forth by words. In reciting this poem, one of the critics recalls, Frost would drop into a deep voice for God's words at the end.

I hear about a "misty din," and waves think of "doing something." "Someone had better be prepared." I get a feeling of indefiniteness from these phrases. "You could not tell" exactly, but you surmise a "dark intent." "More than ocean-water" would be broken—but what? "Something," Stanley Burnshaw points out, is "the most significant single word in the poems." It occurs 137 times in the Frost canon, "someone" 77 times, and "somehow" 8 times. They are all part of what Frost called in an essay of his, "Extravagance," the going beyond domestic boundaries to find something wild and, here, ominous.

"Someone" is going to be a victim, and in "some*one*," I find yet another tendency, one that works along with the vagueness, namely, personification. Frost gives the whole scene human attributes. The sea "looked" and "thought." The night has an "intent," and the land is "lucky" because it is backed by other land. One critic, Judith P. Saunders, is "amused to see waves and clouds endowed with the motives and appearance of stock villains in a Grade B movie." Most see it as beginning ominously and becoming still more ominous.

One would think that personification would counter the sense of indefiniteness, but somehow, in my mind, at any rate, it makes it still more ominous: the people are huge and vague and therefore all the more menacing. Intimations of warring personalities reach a height for me in lines 6 and 7, when the poem pivots from "the gleam of eyes" associated with the skies to a direct "you." It is as if the interpersonal conflict comes about precisely because *you looked*. Finally, at the end of the poem, there is God who seems to be both the instigator of violence and the one who puts an end to it. Possibly, C. Hines Edwards suggests, Blake's picture of God inspired Frost's imagining here. . . .

Here, it seems to me, we are coming very close to the nature of Frost's creativity as a poet, perhaps the creativity of all poets. Language occupies a special, pivotal place in Frost's psychic economy. He can use words two ways: to call up the kind of thing he most fears (being overpowered, unmanned, unselved, fused into another) and to manage that same fantasy. He can use words both to evoke a fantasy that feels particularly dangerous to him and to limit that same fantasy. To the extent we can re-create in our own terms our equivalent for that fearful fantasy and manage it using *his* words (because we share Frost's language), we say his poem succeeds. We award its author the accolade of "creativity."

In effect, language serves Frost as an agent both of fantasy and of mastery. In "Once by the Pacific," he uses a poetic form that resembles a familiar defense mechanism: projection. He starts with a storm, but it turns out to be more than a storm. In this poem, he starts with a wall but it turns out not to be "just a wall." In both instances, his language enables him and us to build a process of projection: "something" doesn't like the wall; its gaps have a mysterious quality ("No one has seen them made or heard them made"); it seems to be engaged in a struggle between human beings (as the high waves by the Pacific were). In effect, Frost's language projects (in a paranoid way that probably accounts for the faint *frisson* I feel at this poem) human attributes onto the inanimate world. His words put the dangerous wishes and fears within himself out into the world around him. Then his poem explores those mental states in the guise of physically dealing with the actualities of a New England farm or the San Francisco coast.

WILLIAM PRITCHARD

On "Stopping by Woods"

from *Robert Frost: A Literary Life Reconsidered*

With respect to his most anthologized poem, "Stopping by Woods . . ." which he called "my best bid for remembrance," such "feats" are seen in its rhyme scheme, with the third unrhyming line in each of the first three stanzas becoming the rhyme word of each succeeding stanza until the last one, all of whose end words rhyme and whose final couplet consists of a repeated "And miles to go before I sleep." Or they can be heard in the movement of the last two lines of stanza three:

> He gives his harness bells a shake
> To ask if there is some mistake.
> The only other sound's the sweep
> Of easy wind and downy flake.

As with "Her early leaf's a flower," the contraction effortlessly carries us along into "the sweep/Of easy wind" so that we arrive at the end almost without knowing it.

Discussion of this poem has usually concerned itself with matters of "content" or meaning (What do the woods represent? Is this a poem in which suicide is contemplated?). Frost, accordingly, as he continued to read it in public made fun of efforts to draw out or fix its meaning as something large and impressive, something to do with man's existential loneliness or other ultimate matters. Perhaps because of these efforts, and on at least one occasion—his last appearance in 1962 at the Ford Forum in Boston—he told his audience that the thing which had given him most pleasure in composing the poem was the effortless sound of that couplet about the horse and what it does when stopped by the woods: "He gives his harness bells a shake / To ask if there is some mistake." We might guess that he held these lines up for admiration because they are probably the hardest ones in the poem out of which to make anything significant: regular in their iambic rhythm and suggesting nothing more than they assert, they establish a sound against which the "other sound" of the following lines can, by contrast, make itself heard. Frost's fondness for this couplet suggests that however much he cared about the "larger" issues or questions which "Stopping by Woods . . ." raises and provokes, he wanted to direct his readers away from solemnly debating them; instead he invited them simply to be pleased with how he had put it. He was to say later on about Edwin Arlington Robinson something which could more naturally have been said about himself—that his life as a poet was "a revel in the felicities of labguage." "Stopping by Woods . . . " can be appreciated only by removing it from its pedestal and noting how it is a miniature revel in such felicities.

RICHARD POIRIER

On "Stopping by Woods on a Snowy Evening"

from *Robert Frost: The Work of Knowing*

As its opening words suggest—"Whose woods these are I think I know"—["Stopping by Woods on a Snowy Evening"] is a poem concerned with ownership and also with someone who cannot be or does not choose to be very emphatic even about owning himself. He does not want or expect to be seen. And his reason, aside from being on someone else's property, is that it would apparently be out of character for him to be there, communing alone with a woods fast filling up with snow. He is, after all, a man of business who has promised his time, his future to other people. It would appear that he is not only a scheduled man but a fairly convivial one. He knows who owns which parcels of land, or thinks he does, and his language has a sort of pleasant neighborliness, as in the phrase "stopping by." It is no wonder that his little horse would think his actions "queer" or that he would let the horse, instead of himself, take responsibility for the judgment. He is in danger of losing himself; and his language by the end of the third stanza begins to carry hints of a seductive luxuriousness unlike anything preceding it—"Easy wind and downy flake . . . lovely, dark and deep." Even before the somnolent repetition of the last two lines, he is ready to drop off. His opening question about who owns the woods becomes, because of the very absence from the poem of any man "too exactly himself," a question of whether the woods are to "own" him. With the drowsy repetitiousness of rhymes in the last stanza, four in a row, it takes some optimism to be sure that (thanks mostly to his little horse, who makes the only assertive sound in the poem) he will be able to keep his promises. At issue, of course, is really whether or not he will be able to "keep" his life.

RICHARD POIRIER

On "Mending Wall"

from *Robert Frost: The Work of Knowing*

The limits, boundaries, or customs which define a "home," a personal property, are often taken, that is, as an occasion for freedom rather than for confinement. The real significance of the famous poem "Mending Wall" is that it suggests how much for Frost freedom is contingent upon some degree of restriction. More specifically, it can be said that restrictions, or forms, are a precondition for expression. Without them, even nature ceases to offer itself up for a reading. Forms of any sort have been so overwhelmed in "Desert Places," for example, that the prospect is for "a blanker whiteness of benighted snow / With no expression, nothing to express," the world as a blank sheet of paper enveloped in darkness.

Natural forces in "Mending Wall," having each year to encounter the human imposition of a freshly repaired wall, tend to become expressive in a quite selective way. Whatever it is "that doesn't love a wall," "*sends* the frozen-ground-swell under it/And *spills* the upper boulders in the sun, / And *makes* gaps even two can pass abreast" (my italics). More important, this active response to human structurings prompts a counterresponse and activity from people who are committed to the making and remaking of those structures. And who are such people? The point usually missed, along with most other things importantly at work in this poem, is that it is not the neighbor, described as "an old-stone savage armed," a man who can only dully repeat, "Good fences make good neighbors"—that it is not he who initiates the fence-making. Rather it is the far more spirited, lively, and "mischievous" speaker of the poem. While admitting that they do not need the wall, it is he who each year "lets my neighbor know beyond the hill" that it is time to do the job anyway, and who will go out alone to fill the gaps made in the wall by hunters: "I have come after them and made repairs / When they have left not one stone on a stone." Though the speaker may or may not think that good neighbors are made by good fences, it is abundantly clear that he likes the yearly ritual, the yearly "outdoor game" by which fences are made. Because if fences do not "make good neighbors" the *"making"* of fences can. More is "made" in this "outdoor game" than fences. The two men also "make" talk, or at least that is what the speaker tries to do as against the reiterated assertions of his companion, which are as heavy and limited as the wall itself. So hopeless is this speaker of any response, that all his talk may be only to himself. He is looking for some acknowledgment of those forces at work which are impatient of convention and of merely repeated forms; but he is looking in vain.

YVOR WINTERS

Robert Frost: Or, the Spiritual Drifter as Poet

from *The Function of Criticism*

Frost writes of rural subjects, and the American reader of our time has an affection for rural subjects which is partly the product of the Romantic sentimentalization of "nature," but which is partly also a nostalgic looking back to the rural life which predominated in this nation a generation or two ago; the rural life is somehow regarded as the truly American life. I have no objection to the poet's employing rural settings; but we should remember that it is the poet's business to evaluate human experience, and the rural setting is no more valuable for this purpose than any other or than no particular setting, and one could argue with some plausibility that an exclusive concentration on it may be limiting.

Frost early began his endeavor to make his style approximate as closely as possible the style of conversation, and this endeavor has added to his reputation: it has helped to make him seem "natural." But poetry is not conversation, and I see no reason why poetry should be called upon to imitate conversation. Conversation is the most careless and formless of human utterance; it is spontaneous and unrevised, and its vocabulary is commonly limited. Poetry is the most difficult form of human utterance; we revise poems carefully in order to make them more nearly perfect. The two forms of expression are extremes, they are not close to each other. We do not praise a violinist for playing as if he were improvising; we praise him for playing well. And when a man plays well or writes well, his audience must have intelligence, training, and patience in order to appreciate him. We do not understand difficult matters "naturally." . . .

Frost, as far as we have examined him, then, is a poet who holds the following views: he believes that impulse is trustworthy and reason contemptible, that formative decisions should be made casually and passively, that the individual should retreat from cooperative action with his kind, should retreat not to engage in intellectual activity but in order to protect himself from the contamination of outside influence, that affairs manage themselves for the best if left alone, that ideas of good and evil need not be taken very seriously. These views are sure to be a hindrance to self-development, and they effectually cut Frost off from any really profound understanding of human experience, whether political, moral, metaphysical, or religious. The result in the didactic poems is the perversity and incoherence of thought; the result in the narrative poems is either slightness of subject or a flat and uninteresting apprehension of the subject; the result in the symbolic lyrics is a disturbing dislocation between the descriptive surface, which is frequently lovely, and the ultimate meaning, which is usually sentimental and unacceptable. The result in nearly all the poems is a measure of carelessness in the style, sometimes small and sometimes great, but usually evident: the conversational manner will naturally suit a poet who takes all experience so casually, and it is only natural that the conversational manner should often become very conversational indeed.

ROBERT FROST: POEMS

Mowing

There was never a sound beside the wood but one,
And that was my long scythe whispering to the ground.
What was it it whispered? I knew not well myself;
Perhaps it was something about the heat of the sun,
Something, perhaps, about the lack of sound—   5
And that was why it whispered and did not speak.
It was no dream of the gift of idle hours,
Or easy gold at the hand of fay or elf:
Anything more than the truth would have seemed too weak
To the earnest love that laid the swale in rows,   10
Not without feeble-pointed spikes of flowers
(Pale orchises), and scared a bright green snake.
The fact is the sweetest dream that labor knows.
My long scythe whispered and left the hay to make.

(1913)

The Tuft of Flowers

I went to turn the grass once after one
Who mowed it in the dew before the sun.

The dew was gone that made his blade so keen
Before I came to view the leveled scene.

I looked for him behind an isle of trees;   5
I listened for his whetstone in the breeze.

But he had gone his way, the grass all mown,
And I must be, as he had been,—alone,

"As all must be," I said within my heart,
"Whether they work together or apart."   10

But as I said it, swift there passed me by
On noiseless wing a bewildered butterfly,

Seeking with memories grown dim o'er night
Some resting flower of yesterday's delight.

And once I marked his flight go round and round,   15
As where some flower lay withering on the ground.

And then he flew as far as eye could see,
And then on tremulous wing came back to me.

I thought of questions that have no reply,
And would have turned to toss the grass to dry;   20

But he turned first, and led my eye to look
At a tall tuft of flowers beside a brook,

A leaping tongue of bloom the scythe had spared
Beside a reedy brook the scythe had bared.

The mower in the dew had loved them thus,   25
By leaving them to flourish, not for us,

Nor yet to draw one thought of ours to him,
But from sheer morning gladness at the brim.

The butterfly and I had lit upon,
Nevertheless, a message from the dawn,   30

That made me hear the wakening birds around,
And hear his long scythe whispering to the ground,

And feel a spirit kindred to my own;
So that henceforth I worked no more alone;

But glad with him, I worked as with his aid,   35
And weary, sought at noon with him the shade;

And dreaming, as it were, held brotherly speech
With one whose thought I had not hoped to reach.

"Men work together," I told him from the heart,
"Whether they work together or apart."   40

                                                          (1913)

Mending Wall

Something there is that doesn't love a wall,
That sends the frozen-ground-swell under it,
And spills the upper boulders in the sun;
And makes gaps even two can pass abreast.
The work of hunters is another thing: 5
I have come after them and made repair
Where they have left not one stone on a stone,
But they would have the rabbit out of hiding,
To please the yelping dogs. The gaps I mean,
No one has seen them made or heard them made,   10
But at spring mending-time we find them there.
I let my neighbor know beyond the hill;
And on a day we meet to walk the line
And set the wall between us once again.
We keep the wall between us as we go.   15
To each the boulders that have fallen to each.
And some are loaves and some so nearly balls
We have to use a spell to make them balance:
"Stay where you are until our backs are turned!"
We wear our fingers rough with handling them.   20
Oh, just another kind of outdoor game,
One on a side. It comes to little more:
There where it is we do not need the wall:
He is all pine and I am apple orchard.
My apple trees will never get across   25
And eat the cones under his pines, I tell him.
He only says, "Good fences make good neighbors."
Spring is the mischief in me, and I wonder
If I could put a notion in his head:
"Why do they make good neighbors? Isn't it   30
Where there are cows? But here there are no cows.
Before I built a wall I'd ask to know
What I was walling in or walling out,
And to whom I was like to give offense.
Something there is that doesn't love a wall,   35
That wants it down." I could say "Elves" to him,
But it's not elves exactly, and I'd rather
He said it for himself. I see him there
Bringing a stone grasped firmly by the top
In each hand, like an old-stone savage armed.   40
He moves in darkness as it seems to me,
Not of woods only and the shade of trees.
He will not go behind his father's saying,
And he likes having thought of it so well
He says again, "Good fences make good neighbors."   45
                                                                         (1914)

Birches

When I see birches bend to left and right
Across the lines of straighter darker trees,
I like to think some boy's been swinging them.
But swinging doesn't bend them down to stay
As ice-storms do. Often you must have seen them   5
Loaded with ice a sunny winter morning
After a rain. They click upon themselves
As the breeze rises, and turn many-colored
As the stir cracks and crazes their enamel.
Soon the sun's warmth makes them shed crystal shells   10
Shattering and avalanching on the snow-crust—
Such heaps of broken glass to sweep away
You'd think the inner dome of heaven had fallen.
They are dragged to the withered bracken by the load,
And they seem not to break; though once they are bowed   15
So low for long, they never right themselves:
You may see their trunks arching in the woods
Years afterwards, trailing their leaves on the ground
Like girls on hands and knees that throw their hair
Before them over their heads to dry in the sun.   20
But I was going to say when Truth broke in
With all her matter-of-fact about the ice-storm,
I should prefer to have some boy bend them
As he went out and in to fetch the cows—
Some boy too far from town to learn baseball,   25
Whose only play was what he found himself,
Summer or winter, and could play alone.
One by one he subdued his father's trees
By riding them down over and over again
Until he took the stiffness out of them,   30
And not one but hung limp, not one was left
For him to conquer. He learned all there was
To learn about not launching out too soon
And so not carrying the tree away
Clear to the ground. He always kept his poise   35
To the top branches, climbing carefully
With the same pains you use to fill a cup
Up to the brim, and even above the brim.
Then he flung outward, feet first, with a swish,
Kicking his way down through the air to the ground.   40
So was I once myself a swinger of birches.
And so I dream of going back to be.
It's when I'm weary of considerations,
And life is too much like a pathless wood

Where your face burns and tickles with the cobwebs   45
Broken across it, and one eye is weeping
From a twig's having lashed across it open.
I'd like to get away from earth awhile
And then come back to it and begin over.
May no fate willfully misunderstand me   50
And half grant what I wish and snatch me away
Not to return. Earth's the right place for love:
I don't know where it's likely to go better.
I'd like to go by climbing a birch tree,
And climb black branches up a snow-white trunk   55
Toward heaven, till the tree could bear no more,
But dipped its top and set me down again.
That would be good both going and coming back.
One could do worse than be a swinger of birches.

(1916)

Home Burial

He saw her from the bottom of the stairs
Before she saw him. She was starting down,
Looking back over her shoulder at some fear.
She took a doubtful step and then undid it
To raise herself and look again. He spoke   5
Advancing toward her: "What is it you see
From up there always—for I want to know."
She turned and sank upon her skirts at that,
And her face changed from terrified to dull.
He said to gain time: "What is it you see"   10
Mounting until she cowered under him.
"I will find out now—you must tell me, dear."
She, in her place, refused him any help
With the least stiffening of her neck and silence.
She let him look, sure that he wouldn't see,   15
Blind creature; and awhile he didn't see.
But at last he murmured, "Oh," and again, "Oh."

"What is it—what?" she said.
    "Just that I see."

"You don't," she challenged. "Tell me what it is."

"The wonder is I didn't see at once.   20
I never noticed it from here before.
I must be wonted to it—that's the reason.

The little graveyard where my people are!
So small the window frames the whole of it.
Not so much larger than a bedroom, is it?   25
There are three stones of slate and one of marble,
Broad-shouldered little slabs there in the sunlight
On the sidehill. We haven't to mind *those*.
But I understand: it is not the stones,
But the child's mound—"

    "Don't, don't, don't, don't," she cried.   30

She withdrew shrinking from beneath his arm
That rested on the banister, and slid downstairs;
And turned on him with such a daunting look,
He said twice over before he knew himself:
"Can't a man speak of his own child he's lost?"   35

"Not you! Oh, where's my hat? Oh, I don't need it!
I must get out of here. I must get air.
I don't know rightly whether any man can."

"Amy! Don't go to someone else this time.
Listen to me. I won't come down the stairs."   40
He sat and fixed his chin between his fists.
"There's something I should like to ask you, dear."
"You don't know how to ask it."
    "Help me, then."

Her fingers moved the latch for all reply.

"My words are nearly always an offense.   45
I don't know how to speak of anything
So as to please you. But I might be taught
I should suppose. I can't say I see how.
A man must partly give up being a man
With women-folk. We could have some arrangement   50
By which I'd bind myself to keep hands off
Anything special you're a-mind to name.
Though I don't like such things 'twixt those that love.
Two that don't love can't live together without them.
But two that do can't live together with them."   55
She moved the latch a little. "Don't—don't go.
Don't carry it to someone else this time.
Tell me about it if it's something human.
Let me into your grief. I'm not so much
Unlike other folks as your standing there   60
Apart would make me out. Give me my chance.
I do think, though, you overdo it a little.

What was it brought you up to think it the thing
To take your mother-loss of a first child
So inconsolably—in the face of love.   65
You'd think his memory might be satisfied—"

"There you go sneering now!"
          "I'm not, I'm not!
You make me angry. I'll come down to you.
God, what a woman! And it's come to this,
A man can't speak of his own child that's dead."   70

"You can't because you don't know how to speak.
If you had any feelings, you that dug
With your own hand—how could you?—his little grave;
I saw you from that very window there,
Making the gravel leap and leap in air,   75
Leap up, like that, like that, and land so lightly
And roll back down the mound beside the hole.
I thought, Who is that man? I didn't know you.
And I crept down the stairs and up the stairs
To look again, and still your spade kept lifting.   80
Then you came in. I heard your rumbling voice
Out in the kitchen, and I don't know why,
But I went near to see with my own eyes.
You could sit there with the stains on your shoes
Of the fresh earth from your own baby's grave   85
And talk about your everyday concerns.
You had stood the spade up against the wall
Outside there in the entry, for I saw it."

"I shall laugh the worst laugh I ever laughed.
I'm cursed. God, if I don't believe I'm cursed."   90

"I can repeat the very words you were saying.
'Three foggy mornings and one rainy day
Will rot the best birch fence a man can build.'
Think of it, talk like that at such a time!
What had how long it takes a birch to rot   95
To do with what was in the darkened parlor?
You *couldn't* care! The nearest friends can go
With anyone to death, comes so far short
They might as well not try to go at all.
No, from the time when one is sick to death,   100
One is alone, and he dies more alone.
Friends make pretense of following to the grave,
But before one is in it, their minds are turned
And making the best of their way back to life

And living people, and things they understand. 105
But the world's evil. I won't have grief so
If I can change it. Oh, I won't, I won't!"

"There, you have said it all and you feel better.
You won't go now. You're crying. Close the door.
The heart's gone out of it: why keep it up. 110
Amy! There's someone coming down the road!"

"*You*—oh, you think the talk is all. I must go—
Somewhere out of this house. How can I make you—"

"If—you—do!" She was opening the door wider.
"Where do you mean to go? First tell me that. 115
I'll follow and bring you back by force. I *will!*—"

(1914)

Hyla Brook

By June our brook's run out of song and speed.
Sought for much after that, it will be found
Either to have gone groping underground
(And taken with it all the Hyla breed
That shouted in the mist a month ago, 5
Like ghost of sleigh bells in a ghost of snow)—
Or flourished and come up in jewelweed,
Weak foliage that is blown upon and bent
Even against the way its waters went.
Its bed is left a faded paper sheet 10
Of dead leaves stuck together by the heat—
A brook to none but who remember long.
This as it will be seen is other far
Than with brooks taken otherwhere in song.
We love the things we love for what they are. 15

(1916)

Putting in the Seed

You come to fetch me from my work tonight
When supper's on the table, and we'll see
If I can leave off burying the white
Soft petals fallen from the apple tree
(Soft petals, yes, but not so barren quite, 5
Mingled with these, smooth bean and wrinkled pea),

And go along with you ere you lose sight
Of what you came for and become like me,
Slave to a springtime passion for the earth.
How Love burns through the Putting in the Seed   10
On through the watching for that early birth
When, just as the soil tarnishes with weed,
The sturdy seedling with arched body comes
Shouldering its way and shedding the earth crumbs.

(1916)

Fire and Ice

Some say the world will end in fire,
Some say in ice.
From what I've tasted of desire
I hold with those who favor fire.
But if it had to perish twice,   5
I think I know enough of hate
To say that for destruction ice
Is also great
And would suffice.

(1923)

For Once, Then, Something

Others taunt me with having knelt at well-curbs
Always wrong to the light, so never seeing
Deeper down in the well than where the water
Gives me back in a shining surface picture
Me myself in the summer heaven godlike   5
Looking out of a wreath of fern and cloud puffs.
Once, when trying with chin against a well-curb,
I discerned, as I thought, beyond the picture,
Through the picture, a something white, uncertain,
Something more of the depths—and then I lost it.   10
Water came to rebuke the too clear water.
One drop fell from a fern, and lo, a ripple
Shook whatever it was lay there at bottom,
Blurred it, blotted it out. What was that whiteness?
Truth? A pebble of quartz? For once, then, something.   15

(1923)

Two Look at Two

Love and forgetting might have carried them
A little further up the mountainside
With night so near, but not much further up.
They must have halted soon in any case
With thoughts of the path back, how rough it was   5
With rock and washout, and unsafe in darkness;
When they were halted by a tumbled wall
With barbed-wire binding. They stood facing this,
Spending what onward impulse they still had
In one last look the way they must not go,   10
On up the failing path, where, if a stone
On earthside moved at night, it moved itself;
No footstep moved it. "This is all," they sighed,
"Good-night to woods." But not so; there was more.
A doe from round a spruce stood looking at them   15
Across the wall, as near the wall as they.
She saw them in their field, they her in hers.
The difficulty of seeing what stood still,
Like some up-ended boulder split in two,
Was in her clouded eyes: they saw no fear there.   20
She seemed to think that two thus they were safe.
Then, as if they were something that, though strange,
She could not trouble her mind with too long,
She sighed and passed unscared along the wall.
"This, then, is all. What more is there to ask?"   25
But no, not yet. A snort to bid them wait.
A buck from round the spruce stood looking at them
Across the wall, as near the wall as they.
This was an antlered buck of lusty nostril,
Not the same doe come back into her place.   30
He viewed them quizzically with jerks of head,
As if to ask, "Why don't you make some motion?
Or give some sign of life? Because you can't.
I doubt if you're as living as you look."
Thus till he had them almost feeling dared   35
To stretch a proffering hand—and a spell-breaking.
Then he too passed unscared along the wall.
Two had seen two, whichever side you spoke from.
"This *must* be all." It was all. Still they stood,
A great wave from it going over them,   40
As if the earth in one unlooked-for favor
Had made them certain earth returned their love.

(1923)

Once by the Pacific

The shattered water made a misty din.
Great waves looked over others coming in,
And thought of doing something to the shore
That water never did to land before.
The clouds were low and hairy in the skies,   5
Like locks blown forward in the gleam of eyes.
You could not tell, and yet it looked as if
The shore was lucky in being backed by cliff,
The cliff in being backed by continent;
It looked as if a night of dark intent   10
Was coming, and not only a night, an age.
Someone had better be prepared for rage.
There would be more than ocean-water broken
Before God's last *Put out the Light* was spoken.

(1928)

Acquainted with the Night

I have been one acquainted with the night.
I have walked out in rain—and back in rain.
I have outwalked the furthest city light.

I have looked down the saddest city lane.
I have passed by the watchman on his beat   5
And dropped my eyes, unwilling to explain.

I have stood still and stopped the sound of feet
When far away an interrupted cry
Came over houses from another street,

But not to call me back or say good-by;   10
And further still at an unearthly height
One luminary clock against the sky

Proclaimed the time was neither wrong nor right.
I have been one acquainted with the night.

(1928)

Tree at my Window

Tree at my window, window tree,
My sash is lowered when night comes on;
But let there never be curtain drawn
Between you and me.

Vague dream-head lifted out of the ground, 5
And thing next most diffuse to cloud,
Not all your light tongues talking aloud
Could be profound.

But, tree, I have seen you taken and tossed,
And if you have seen me when I slept, 10
You have seen me when I was taken and swept
And all but lost.

That day she put our heads together,
Fate had her imagination about her,
Your head so much concerned with outer, 15
Mine with inner, weather.

(1928)

Departmental

An ant on the tablecloth
Ran into a dormant moth
Of many times his size.
He showed not the least surprise.
His business wasn't with such. 5
He gave it scarcely a touch,
And was off on his duty run.
Yet if he encountered one
Of the hive's enquiry squad
Whose work is to find out God 10
And the nature of time and space,
He would put him onto the case.
Ants are a curious race;
One crossing with hurried tread
The body of one of their dead 15
Isn't given a moment's arrest—
Seems not even impressed.
But he no doubt reports to any
With whom he crosses antennae,
And they no doubt report 20
To the higher up at court.
Then word goes forth in Formic:
"Death's come to Jerry McCormic,
Our selfless forager Jerry.
Will the special Janizary 25
Whose office it is to bury
The dead of the commissary

Go bring him home to his people.
Lay him in state on a sepal.
Wrap him for shroud in a petal.   0
Embalm him with ichor of nettle.
This is the word of your Queen."
And presently on the scene
Appears a solemn mortician:
And taking formal position   35
With feelers calmly atwiddle,
Seizes the dead by the middle,
And heaving him high in the air,
Carries him out of there.
No one stands round to stare.   40
It is nobody else's affair.

It couldn't be called ungentle.
But how thoroughly departmental.

(1936)

Desert Places

Snow falling and night falling fast, oh, fast
In a field I looked into going past,
And the ground almost covered smooth in snow,
But a few weeds and stubble showing last.

The woods around it have it—it is theirs.   5
All animals are smothered in their lairs.
I am too absent-spirited to count;
The loneliness includes me unawares.

And lonely as it is, that loneliness
Will be more lonely ere it will be less—   10
A blanker whiteness of benighted snow
With no expression, nothing to express.

They cannot scare me with their empty spaces
Between stars—on stars where no human race is.
I have it in me so much nearer home   15
To scare myself with my own desert places.

(1936)

Design

I found a dimpled spider, fat and white,
On a white heal-all, holding up a moth
Like a white piece of rigid satin cloth—
Assorted characters of death and blight
Mixed ready to begin the morning right,   5
Like the ingredients of a witches' broth—
A snow-drop spider, a flower like a froth,
And dead wings carried like a paper kite.

What had that flower to do with being white,
The wayside blue and innocent heal-all?   10
What brought the kindred spider to that height,
Then steered the white moth thither in the night?
What but design of darkness to appall?—
If design govern in a thing so small.

(1936)

Provide, Provide

The witch that came (the withered hag)
To wash the steps with pail and rag,
Was once the beauty Abishag,

The picture pride of Hollywood.
Too many fall from great and good   5
For you to doubt the likelihood.

Die early and avoid the fate.
Or if predestined to die late,
Make up your mind to die in state.

Make the whole stock exchange your own!   10
If need be occupy a throne,
Where nobody can call *you* crone.

Some have relied on what they knew;
Others on being simply true.
What worked for them might work for you.   15

No memory of having starred
Atones for later disregard
Or keeps the end from being hard.

Better to go down dignified
With boughten friendship at your side   20
Than none at all. Provide, provide!

(1936)

The Most of It

He thought he kept the universe alone;
For all the voice in answer he could wake
Was but the mocking echo of his own
From some tree-hidden cliff across the lake.
Some morning from the boulder-broken beach   5
He would cry out on life, that what it wants
Is not its own love back in copy speech,
But counter-love, original response.
And nothing ever came of what he cried
Unless it was the embodiment that crashed   10
In the cliff's talus on the other side,
And then in the far-distant water splashed,
But after a time allowed for it to swim,
Instead of proving human when it neared
And someone else additional to him,   15
As a great buck it powerfully appeared,
Pushing the crumpled water up ahead,
And landed pouring like a waterfall,
And stumbled through the rocks with horny tread,
And forced the underbrush—and that was all.   20

(1942)

INTRODUCTION TO LANGSTON HUGHES

[1902–1967]

"Poetry," Langston Hughes once remarked, "should be direct, comprehensible, and the epitome of simplicity." His poems illustrate these guidelines with remarkable consistency. Avoiding the obscure and the difficult, Hughes wrote poems that could be understood by readers and listeners who had little prior experience with poetry. He sought to write poems that were immediately understandable, poems that express concretely the concerns of daily life.

Hughes's poetry offers a transcription of urban life through a portrayal of the speech, habits, attitudes, and feelings of an oppressed people. The poems do more, however, than reveal the pain of poverty. They also illustrate racial pride and dignity. Hughes's poems cling, moreover, to the spoken language. They derive from an oral tradition in which folk poetry is recited and performed, rather than published in written form. In the oral tradition poems are passed down from one generation to the next through performance and recitation. As a result Hughes's poems, more than most, need to be read aloud to be fully appreciated. Hughes himself became famous for his public readings, which were sometimes accompanied by a glee club or jazz combo.

Music, in fact, is a central feature of Hughes's poetry. And the kind of music most evident in his work is the blues, an important influence in the work of many modern black writers, especially those associated with the Harlem Renaissance, a flowering of artistic activity among black artists and writers of Harlem in the 1920s. Hughes once described the blues as "sad funny songs— too sad to be funny and too funny to be sad," songs that contain "laughter and pain, hunger and heartache." The bittersweet tone and view of life reflected in Hughes's perspective on the blues is consistently mirrored in his poems, which sometimes adapt the stanza form of the typical blues song. This stanza includes two nearly identical lines followed by a third that contrasts with the first two. "Same in Blues" exhibits this characteristic with only slight modifications. In this and other poems, Hughes succeeds in grafting the inflections of the urban black dialect onto the rhythms of the blues.

But the blues is not the only musical influence on Hughes's poetry; his work also makes use of jazz as both subject and style, though Hughes's jazz poems are freer and looser in form than his blues poems. This difference reflects the improvisatory nature of jazz as well as its energy and vitality, which contrast with the more controlled idiom of the blues. The aggressive exuberance of jazz, its relaxed but vigorous informality is evident in poems like "Trumpet Player."

Hughes was a prolific writer whose published books span forty years (1926–1967). His output includes sixteen volumes of poems; two novels; three collections of short stories; four documentary works; three historical works; twenty dramatic pieces, including plays, musicals, and operettas; two volumes of autobiography; eight children's books; and twelve radio and television scripts. In addition, Hughes edited seven books—mostly collections of poems by black writers—and translated four others, including the poems of the renowned modern Spanish poet Federico García Lorca. Such versatility established Hughes as an important man of letters, contributing to his stature as a leading figure in the arts, especially the theater, whose audience Hughes was instrumental in enlarging.

The writers who influenced Hughes included Paul Dunbar, whose poems re-created the black vernacular, and W. E. B. DuBois, whose collection of essays on Afro-American life, *The Souls of Black Folk,* exerted a lasting influence on many writers, including novelists Richard Wright and James Baldwin. Hughes was also strongly influenced by the democratic idealism of Walt Whitman and the populism of Carl Sandburg, whom Hughes designated his "guiding star." From Sandburg, Hughes learned to write free verse. From Dunbar, he learned a method of incorporating local dialect into poems. And from DuBois, he derived what later came to be called black pride. These influences were combined and amalgamated in myriad ways, resulting in poems that provided insight into urban life.

Hughes's life was as varied as his writing. Born in Joplin, Missouri, in 1902, Hughes lived in Kansas and Ohio before studying at Columbia University in New York and later and more fully at Lincoln University in Pennsylvania. He worked as a seaman and as a newspaper correspondent and columnist for the *Chicago Defender,* the *Baltimore Afro-American,* and the *New York Post.* He also worked briefly as a cook at a fashionable restaurant in

France and as a busboy in a Washington, D.C., hotel. It was there that Hughes left three of his poems beside the plate of a hotel dinner guest, the poet Vachel Lindsay, who recognized their merit and helped Hughes to secure their publication.

Hughes also founded theaters on both coasts—the Harlem Suitcase Theatre (New York, 1938) and, in the Midwest, the Skyloft Players (Chicago, 1941). He traveled extensively, visiting and at various times living in Africa and Europe, especially Italy and France, as well as in Cuba, Haiti, Russia, Korea, and Japan. His life and travels are richly and engagingly chronicled in his two volumes of autobiography, *The Big Sea* (1940) and *I Wonder As I Wander* (1956).

As a writer who believed it was his vocation to "explain and illuminate the Negro condition in America," Hughes captured the experience as "the hurt of their lives, the monotony of their jobs, and the veiled weariness of their songs." He accomplished this in poems remarkable not only for their directness and simplicity but for their economy, lucidity, and wit. Whether he was writing poems of racial protest like "Dream Deferred" and "Ballad of the Landlord" or poems of racial affirmation like "Mother to Son" and "The Negro Speaks of Rivers," Hughes was able to find language and forms to express not only the pain of urban life but also its splendid vitality.

LANGSTON HUGHES ON HARLEM

A Toast to Harlem

Quiet can seem unduly loud at times. Since nobody at the bar was saying a word during a lull in the bright blues-blare of the Wishing Well's usually overworked juke box, I addressed my friend Simple.

"Since you told me last night you are an Indian, explain to me how it is you find yourself living in a furnished room in Harlem, my brave buck, instead of on a reservation?"

"I am a colored Indian," said Simple.

"In other words, a Negro."

"A Black Foot Indian, daddy-o, not a red one. Anyhow, Harlem is the place I always did want to be. And if it wasn't for landladies, I would be happy. That's a fact! I love Harlem."

"What is it you love about Harlem?"

"It's so full of Negroes," said Simple. "I feel like I got protection."

"From what?"

"From white folks," said Simple. "Furthermore, I like Harlem because it belongs to me."

"Harlem does not belong to you. You don't own the houses in Harlem. They belong to white folks."

"I might not own 'em," said Simple, "but I live in 'em. It would take an atom bomb to get me out."

"Or a depression," I said.

"I would not move for no depression. No, I would not go back down South, not even to Baltimore. I am in Harlem to stay! You say the houses ain't mine. Well, the sidewalk is—and don't nobody push me off. The cops don't even say, 'Move on,' hardly no more. They learned something from them Harlem riots. They used to beat your head right in public, but now they only beat it after they get you down to the station-house. And they don't beat it then if they think you know a colored congressman."

"Harlem has few Negro leaders," I said.

"Elected by my *own* vote," said Simple. "Here I ain't scared to vote—that's another thing I like about Harlem. I also like it because we've got subways and it does not take all day to get downtown, neither are you Crowed on the way. Why, Negroes is running some of these subway trains. This morning I rode the A Train down to 34th street. There were a Negro driving it, making ninety miles a hour. That cat *were really driving* that train! Every time he flew by one of them local stations looks like he was saying, 'Look at me! This train is mine!' That cat were gone, ole man. Which is another reason why I like Harlem! Sometimes I run into Duke Ellington on 125th Street and I say, 'What you know there, Duke?' Duke says, 'Solid, ole man.' He does not know me from Adam, but he speaks. One day I saw Lena Horne coming out of the Hotel Theresa and I said, 'Huba! Huba!' Lena smiled. Folks is friendly in Harlem. I feel like I got the world in a jug and the stopper in my hand! So drink a toast to Harlem!"

Simple lifted his glass of beer:

> "Here's to Harlem!
> They say Heaven is Paradise.
> If Harlem ain't Heaven,
> Then a mouse ain't mice!"

(1950)

CRITICS ON HUGHES

ARNOLD RAMPERSAD

Langston Hughes as Folk Poet

from *Langston Hughes*

Hughes was often called and sometimes called himself, a folk poet. To some people this means that his work is almost artless and thus possibly beneath criticism. The truth indeed is that Hughes published many poems that are doggerel. To reach his primary audience—the black masses—he was prepared to write "down" to them. Some of the pieces in this volume were intended for public recitation mainly; some started as song lyrics. Like many democratic poets, such as William Carlos Williams, he believed that the full range of his poetry should reach print as soon as possible; poetry is a form of social action. However, for Hughes, as for all serious poets, the writing of poetry was

virtually a sacred commitment. And while he wished to write no verse that was be-
yond the ability of the masses of people to understand, his poetry, in common with
that of other committed writers, is replete with allusions that must be respected and
understood if it is to be properly appreciated. To respect Hughes's work, above all one
must respect the African American people and their culture, as well as the American
people in general and their national culture.

If Hughes kept at the center of his art the hopes and dreams, as well as the actual
lived conditions, of African Americans, he almost always saw these factors in the con-
text of the eternally embattled but eternally inspiring American democratic tradition,
even as changes in the world order, notably the collapse of colonialism in Africa, re-
defined experiences of African peoples around the world. Almost always, too, Hughes
attempted to preserve a sense of himself as a poet beyond race and other corrosive so-
cial pressures. By his absolute dedication to his art and to his social vision, as well as
to his central audience, he fused his unique vision of himself as a poet to his produc-
tion of art.

"What is poetry?" Langston Hughes was asked near his death. He answered, "It is
the human soul entire, squeezed like a lemon or a lime, drop by drop, into atomic
words." He wanted no definition of the poet that divorced his art from the immedi-
acy of life. "A poet is a human being," he declared. "Each human being must live
within his time, with and for his people, and within the boundaries of his country."
Hughes constantly called upon himself for the courage and the endurance necessary
to write according to these beliefs. "Hang yourself, poet, in your own words," he
urged all those who would take up the mantle of the poet and dare to speak to the
world. "Otherwise, you are dead."

ONWUCHEKWA JEMIE

Hughes and the Evolution of
Consciousness in Black Poetry

from *Langston Hughes: An Introduction to the Poetry*

W. E. B. DuBois's formulation of the dilemma of the black artist was one of the earli-
est and is still, perhaps, the most lucid. As he stated it, the black artist's problem was in
deciding whether to reflect "the beauty revealed to him . . . the soul-beauty of a race
which his larger audience despised," or to "articulate the message of another people."
As Afro-American history is in part the history of a people caught between two con-
flicting worlds, and of their efforts to reconcile those worlds, to bring an end their
"double-consciousness" by merging their African and American selves into a single,
undivided whole, so is Afro-American literary history in part a record of the black
writer's choices between revealing the soul-beauty of his own people and articulating
the message of another people; so is it the history of his efforts to bring to an end the
very need for choice by somehow bringing the two things together.

The literary beauty revealed to the black writer is contained in his oral folk tradition with its vast universe of themes and images and its smooth and complex strategies of delivery. The "message of another people," on the other hand, is carried in the forms and attitudes, themes and styles and sensibilities of white American and European culture and literature. In another sense, the black writer's problem is as much one of medium as of ethos: his problem is how to actualize the oral tradition in written form, how to recreate the vital force, the sights and sounds and smells of the performance-event on dumb, flat, one-dimensional paper. This problem of *media transfer* is one which the black musician, for instance, does not have, for his art operates within the continuum of the oral medium. The black writer's problem is further complicated by the fact that he has no long written tradition of his own to emulate; and for him to abandon the effort to translate into written form that oral medium which is the full reservoir of his culture would be to annihilate his identity and become a zombie, a programmed vehicle for "the message of another people."

Hardly any black writer of any generation has found it easy, or even possible, to avoid making a choice. And as might be expected, the choices have been neither uniform nor consistent in any era. In every generation, some writers have chosen to reveal the soul-beauty of their own people, some to carry the message of another people. Sometimes the writer vacillates, yielding to the one imperative at one time or in one work, to the other in another, or attempting to answer to both imperatives at the same time and in the same works. Or the writer may undercut the self-acceptance evident in his works with actions and pronouncements indicating reservations and self-doubt.

RICHARD K. BARKSDALE

On Hughes's "Ballad of the Landlord"

from *Langston Hughes: The Poet and His Critics*

An interesting prelude to the social, economic, and political concerns expressed in his poems about Harlem in the 1940s was Hughes's *Ballad of the Landlord,* first published in *Opportunity* (Dec. 1940) and then included as one of the poems in *Jim Crow's Last Stand* (1943) and later in *Montage of a Dream Deferred*. In 1940, the poem was a rather innocuous rendering of an imaginary dialogue between a disgruntled tenant and a tight-fisted landlord. In creating a poem about two such social archetypes, the poet was by no means taking any new steps in dramatic poetry. The literature of most capitalist and noncapitalist societies often pits the haves against the have-nots, and not infrequently the haves are wealthy men of property who "lord" it over improvident men who own nothing. So the confrontation between tenant and landlord was in 1940 just another instance of the social malevolence of a system that punished the powerless and excused the powerful. In fact, Hughes's tone of dry irony throughout the poem leads one to suspect that the poet deliberately overstated a situation and that some sardonic humor was supposed to be squeezed out of the incident. Says the Tenant in furious high dudgeon:

What? You gonna get eviction orders?
You gonna cut off my heat?
You gonna take my furniture and
Throw it in the street?

Um-huh! You talking high and mighty.
Talk on—till you get through.
You ain't gonna be able to say a word
If I land my fist on you.

The Man of Property, in fear and trembling, invokes the symbols of law and order:

Police! Police!
Come and get this man!
He's trying to ruin the government
And overturn the land!

Ironically, this poem, which in 1940 depicted a highly probable incident in American urban life and was certainly not written to incite an economic revolt or promote social unrest, became, by the mid-1960s, a verboten assignment in a literature class in a Boston high school. In his Langston Hughes headnote in *Black Voices* (1967), Abraham Chapman reported that a Boston high school English teacher named Jonathan Kozol was fired for assigning it to his students. By the mid-sixties, Boston and many other American cities had become riot-torn, racial tinderboxes, and their ghettos seethed with tenant anger and discontent. So the poem gathered new meanings reflecting the times, and the word of its tenant persona bespoke the collective anger of thousands of black have-nots. In his review of Gwendolyn Brooks's "Street in Bronzeville" in *Opportunity* (Fall 1945), Hughes praised that young poet's initial volume of poems for its incisive social and political statements and for its "picture-power." His conclusion was that "Poets often say these things better than politicians." Such a comment aptly fits "Ballad of the Landlord." At least, someone on the Boston School Committee evidently thought so.

ONWUCHEKWA JEMIE

On "The Negro Speaks of Rivers"

from *Langston Hughes: An Introduction to the Poetry*

"The Negro Speaks of Rivers" is perhaps the most profound of these poems of heritage and strength. Composed when Hughes was a mere 17 years old, and dedicated to W. E. B. DuBois, it is a sonorous evocation of transcendent essences so ancient as to appear timeless, predating human existence, longer than human memory. The rivers are part of God's body, and participate in his immortality. They are the earthly analogues of eternity: deep, continuous, mysterious. They are named in the order of their association with black history. The black man has drunk of their life-giving essences, and thereby borrowed their immortality. He and the rivers have become one. The magical transformation of the Mississippi from mud to gold by the sun's radiance is mirrored in the transformation of slaves into free men by Lincoln's Proclamation (and, in Hughes's poems, the transformation of shabby cabarets into gorgeous palaces, dancing girls into queens and priestesses by the spell of black music). As the rivers deepen with time, so does the black man's soul; as their waters ceaselessly flow, so will the black soul endure. The black man has seen the rise and fall of civilizations from the earliest times, seen the beauty and death-changes of the world over the thousands of years, and will survive even this America. The poem's meaning is related to Zora Neale Hurston's judgment of the mythic High John de Conquer, whom she held as a symbol of the triumphant spirit of black America: that John was of the "Be" class. "*Be* here when the ruthless man comes, and *be* here when he is gone." In a time and place where black life is held cheap and the days of black men appear to be numbered, the poem is a majestic reminder of the strength and fullness of history, of the source of that life which transcends even ceaseless labor and burning crosses.

JAMES A. EMANUEL

On "Trumpet Player"

from *Langston Hughes*

The meaning of jazz to the musician is combined with racial background in "Trumpet Player" in *Fields of Wonder.* Jazz is "honey/Mixed with liquid fire"; and the trumpet player, says the poet at the end, never knows "upon what riff the music slips/Its hypodermic needle/To his soul." Finally, to the musician, trouble "Mellows to a golden note." The first third of the poem outlines the Negro musician, tired eyes smoldering with memories of slavery, hair "tamed down." The weakest stanza shows the Negro's longing for the moon and sea as "old desire" distilled into rhythm. The quoted lines and a few others reveal the true distillation, jazz made precious by its long and sacrificial birth.

   While writing "Trumpet Player," Hughes was fully abreast of the new be-bop music emerging from Minton's Playhouse in Harlem. Among the poems inspired by be-bop— a rhythmically complex and experimental kind of jazz characterized by dissonance, improvisation, and unusual lyrics—the best is the leadoff "Dream Boogie" in *Montage of a Dream Deferred* (1951):

> Good morning, daddy!
> Ain't you heard
> The boogie-woogie rumble
> Of a dream deferred?

Listen closely:
You'll hear their feet
Beating out and beating out a —

You think
It's a happy beat?

Listen to it closely:
Ain't you heard
something underneath
like a —

What did I say?

Sure,
I'm happy!
Take it away!

Hey, pop!
Re-bop!
Mop!

Y-e-a-h!

Keeping up with a changing Harlem, Hughes is alert to the "hip" insider's elastic jargon as well as the generations-old truth of Negro life—the dream deferred. "Dream Boogie" perfectly fulfills its purpose, wasting no word. It has variations in mood: ease, irony, sarcasm, and terse joviality. It mixes old devices of the dramatic monologue with a contemporary boogiewoogie beat. Its rough-hewn grace adds power to its clarity.

LANGSTON HUGHES: POEMS

Dream Deferred

What happens to a dream deferred?

Does it dry up
like a raisin in the sun?
Or fester like a sore—
And then run?
Does it stink like rotten meat?
Or crust and sugar over—
like a syrupy sweet?

Maybe it just sags
like a heavy load.

Or does it explode?

Same in Blues

I said to my baby,
Baby, take it slow
I can't, she said, I can't!
I got to go!

> There's a certain   5
> amount of traveling
> in a dream deferred.

Lulu said to Leonard,
I want a diamond ring.
Leonard said to Lulu,   10
You won't get a goddamn thing!

> A certain
> amount of nothing
> in a dream deferred.

Daddy, daddy, daddy,   15
All I want is you.
You can have me, baby—
but my lovin' days is through.

> A certain
> amount of impotence   20
> in a dream deferred.

Three parties
On my party line—
But that third party,
Lord, ain't mine!   25

> There's liable
> to be confusion
> in a dream deferred.

From river to river
Uptown and down,   30
There's liable to be confusion
when a dream gets kicked around.

You talk like
they don't kick
dreams around   35
Downtown.

I expect they do—
But I'm talking about
Harlem to you!
Harlem to you!   40
Harlem to you!
Harlem to you!

The Negro Speaks of Rivers

I've known rivers:
I've known rivers ancient as the world and older than the flow
    of human blood in human veins.
My soul has grown deep like the rivers.

I bathed in the Euphrates when dawns were young.
I built my hut near the Congo and it lulled me to sleep.   5
I looked upon the Nile and raised the pyramids above it.
I heard the singing of the Mississippi when Abe Lincoln
        went down to New Orleans, and I've seen its muddy
        bosom turn all golden in the sunset.

I've known rivers:
Ancient, dusky rivers.

My soul has grown deep like the rivers.   10

Mother to Son

Well, son, I'll tell you:
Life for me ain't been no crystal stair.
It's had tacks in it,
And splinters,
And boards torn up,   5
And places with no carpet on the floor—
Bare.
But all the time
I'se been a–climbin' on,
And reachin' landin's,   10
And turnin' corners,
And sometimes goin' in the dark

Where there ain't been no light.
So boy, don't you turn back.
Don't you set down on the steps   15
'Cause you finds it's kinder hard.
Don't you fall now—
For I'se still goin', honey,
I'se still climbin',
And life for me ain't been no crystal stair.   20

I, Too

I, too, sing America.

I am the darker brother.
They send me to eat in the kitchen.
When company comes,
But I laugh,   5
And eat well,
And grow strong.

Tomorrow,
I'll be at the table
When company comes.   10
Nobody'll dare
Say to me,
"Eat in the kitchen,"
Then.

Besides,   15
They'll see how beautiful I am
And be ashamed—
I, too, am America.

My People

The night is beautiful,
So the faces of my people.

The stars are beautiful,
So the eyes of my people.

Beautiful, also, is the sun.   5
Beautiful, also, are the souls of my people.

The Weary Blues

Droning a drowsy syncopated tune,
Rocking back and forth to a mellow croon,
    I heard a Negro play.
Down on Lenox Avenue the other night
By the pale dull pallor of an old gas light   5
    He did a lazy sway. . . .
    He did a lazy sway. . . .
To the tune o' those Weary Blues.
With his ebony hands on each ivory key
He made that poor piano moan with melody.   10
    O Blues!
Swaying to and fro on his rickety stool
He played that sad raggy tune like a musical fool.
    Sweet Blues!   15
Coming from a black man's soul.
    O Blues!
In a deep song voice with a melancholy tone
I heard that Negro sing, that old piano moan—
    "Ain't got nobody in all this world,
    Ain't got nobody but ma self.   20
    I's gwine to quit ma frownin'
    And put ma troubles on the shelf."
Thump, thump, thump, went his foot on the floor.
He played a few chords then he sang some more—
    "I got the Weary Blues   25
    And I can't be satisfied.
    Got the Weary Blues
    And can't be satisfied—
    I ain't happy no mo'
    And I wish that I had died."   30
And far into the night he crooned that tune.
The stars went out and so did the moon.
The singer stopped playing and went to bed
While the Weary Blues echoed through his head
He slept like a rock or a man that's dead.

Young Gal's Blues

    I'm gonna walk to the graveyard
    'Hind ma friend Miss Cora Lee.
    Gonna walk to the graveyard
    'Hind ma dear friend Cora Lee.
    Cause when I'm dead some   5
    Body'll have to walk behind me.

I'm goin' to the po' house
To see ma old Aunt Clew.
Goin' to the po' house
To see ma old Aunt Clew.   10
When I'm old an' ugly
I'll want to see somebody, too.

The po' house is lonely
An' the grave is cold.
O, the po' house is lonely,   15
The graveyard grave is cold.
But I'd rather be dead than
To be ugly an' old.

When love is gone what
Can a young gal do?   20
When love is gone, O,
What can a young gal do?
Keep on a–lovin' me, daddy,
Cause I don't want to be blue.

Morning After

I was so sick last night I
Didn't hardly know my mind.
So sick last night I
Didn't know my mind.
I drunk some bad licker that   5
Almost made me blind.
Had a dream last night I
Thought I was in hell.
I drempt last night I
Thought I was in hell.   10
Woke up and looked around me—
Babe, your mouth was open like a well.
I said, Baby! Baby!
Please don't snore so loud.
Baby! Please!   15
Please don't snore so loud.
You jest a little bit o' woman but you
Sound like a great big crowd.

Trumpet Player

The Negro
With the trumpet at his lips
Has dark moons of weariness
Beneath his eyes
Where the smoldering memory   5
Of slave ships
Blazed to the crack of whips
About his thighs.

The Negro
With the trumpet at his lips   10
Has a head of vibrant hair
Tamed down,
Patent-leathered now
Until it gleams
Like jet—   15
Were jet a crown.

The music
From the trumpet at his lips
Is honey
Mixed with liquid fire.   20
The rhythm
From the trumpet at his lips
Is ecstasy
Distilled from old desire—

Desire   25
That is longing for the moon
Where the moonlight's but a spotlight
In his eyes,
Desire
That is longing for the sea   30
Where the sea's a bar-glass
Sucker size.

The Negro
With the trumpet at his lips
Whose jacket   35
Has a *fine* one-button roll,
Does not know
Upon what riff the music slips
Its hypodermic needle
To his soul—   40

But softly
As the tune comes from his throat
Trouble
Mellows to a golden note.

Dream Boogie

Good morning, daddy!
Ain't you heard
The boogie-woogie rumble
Of a dream deferred?

Listen closely: 5
You'll hear their feet
Beating out and beating out a—

     You think
     It's a happy beat?

Listen to it closely: 10
Ain't you heard
something underneath
like a—

     What did I say?

Sure,   15
I'm happy!
Take it away!

     Hey, pop!
     Re-bop!
     Mop!   20

     Y-e-a-h!

     What don't bug
     them white kids
     sure bugs me:
     We knows everybody   25
     ain't free!

Some of these young ones is cert'ly bad—
One batted a hard ball right through my window
and my gold fish et the glass.

What's written down   30
for white folks
ain't for us a-tall:
"Liberty And Justice—
Huh—For All."

Oop-pop-a-da!   35
Skee! Daddle-de-do!
Be-bop!

Salt'peanuts!

De-dop!

Madam and the Rent Man

The rent man knocked.
He said, Howdy-do?
I said, What
Can I do for you?
He said, You know   5
Your rent is due.

I said, Listen,
Before I'd pay
I'd go to Hades
And rot away!   10

The sink is broke,
The water don't run,
And you ain't done a thing
You promised to've done.

Back window's cracked,   15
Kitchen floor squeaks,
There's rats in the cellar,
And the attic leaks.

He said, Madam,
It's not up to me.   20
I'm just the agent,
Don't you see?

I said, Naturally,
You pass the buck.
If it's money you want   25
You're out of luck.

He said, Madam,
I ain't pleased!
I said, Neither am I.

So we agrees!   30

Theme for English B

The instructor said,

> *Go home and write*
> *a page tonight.*
> *And let that page come out of you—*
> *Then, it will be true.*   5

I wonder if it's that simple?

I am twenty-two, colored, born in Winston-Salem.
I went to school there, then Durham, then here
to this college on the hill above Harlem.
I am the only colored student in my class.   10
The steps from the hill lead down into Harlem,
through a park, then I cross St. Nicholas,
Eighth Avenue, Seventh, and I come to the Y,
the Harlem Branch Y, where I take the elevator
up to my room, sit down, and write this page: 15

It's not easy to know what is true for you or me
at twenty-two, my age. But I guess I'm what
I feel and see and hear. Harlem, I hear you:
hear you, hear me—we two—you, me, talk on this page.
(I hear New York, too.) Me—who?   20

Well, I like to eat, sleep, drink, and be in love.
I like to work, read, learn, and understand life.
I like a pipe for a Christmas present,
or records—Bessie, bop, or Bach.
I guess being colored doesn't make me *not* like   25
the same things other folks like who are other races.

So will my page be colored that I write?
Being me, it will not be white.
But it will be
a part of you, instructor.   30
You are white—
yet a part of me, as I am a part of you.

That's American.
Sometimes perhaps you don't want to be a part of me.
Nor do I often want to be a part of you.   35
But we are, that's true!
As I learn from you,
I guess you learn from me—
although you're older—and white—
and somewhat more free.   40

This is my page for English B.

Aunt Sue's Stories

Aunt Sue has a head full of stories.
Aunt Sue has a whole heart full of stories.
Summer nights on the front porch
Aunt Sue cuddles a brown-faced child to her bosom
And tells him stories.   5

Black slaves
Working in the hot sun,
And black slaves
Walking in the dewy night,
And black slaves   10
Singing sorrow songs on the banks of a mighty river
Mingle themselves softly
In the flow of old Aunt Sue's voice,
Mingle themselves softly
In the dark shadows that cross and recross   15
Aunt Sue's stories.

And the dark-faced child, listening,
Knows that Aunt Sue's stories are real stories.
He knows that Aunt Sue never got her stories
Out of any book at all,   20
But that they came
Right out of her own life.

The dark-faced child is quiet
Of a summer night
Listening to Aunt Sue's stories.   25

Ballad of the Landlord

Landlord, landlord,
My roof has sprung a leak.
Don't you 'member I told you about it
Way last week?

Landlord, landlord,   5
These steps is broken down.
When you come up yourself
It's a wonder you don't fall down.

Ten Bucks you say I owe you?
Ten Bucks you say is due?   10
Well, that's Ten Bucks more'n I'll pay you.
Till you fix this house up new.

What? You gonna get eviction orders?
You gonna cut off my heat?
You gonna take my furniture and   15
Throw it in the street?

Um-huh! You talking high and mighty.
Talk on—till you get through.
You ain't gonna be able to say a word
If I land my fist on you.   20

   Police! Police!
   Come and get this man!
   He's trying to ruin the government
   And overturn the land!

Copper's whistle!   25
Patrol bell!
Arrest.

Precinct Station.
Iron cell.
Headlines in press:

MAN THREATENS LANDLORD

TENANT HELD NO BAIL

JUDGE GIVES NEGRO 90 DAYS IN COUNTY JAIL

[1949]

Let America Be America Again

Let America be America again.
Let it be the dream it used to be.
Let it be the pioneer on the plain
Seeking the home where he himself is free.

(America never was America to me.)   5

Let America be the dream the dreamers dreamed—
Let it be that great strong land of love
Where never kings connive nor tyrants scheme
That any man be crushed by one above.

(It never was America to me.)   10

CHAPTER SEVEN

A Collection of Poems

The forms of things unknown, the poet's pen / Turns them to shapes, and gives to airy nothing / A local habitation and a name.
WILLIAM SHAKESPEARE

A good poem is a contribution to reality. The world is never the same once a good poem has been added to it.
DYLAN THOMAS

SAPPHO
[7th–6th century B.C.]

To me he seems like a god

To me he seems like a god
as he sits facing you and
hears you near as you speak
softly and laugh
in a sweet echo that jolts   5
the heart in my ribs. For now
as I look at you my voice
is empty and

can say nothing as my tongue
cracks and slender fire is quick   10
under my skin. My eyes are dead
to light, my ears

pound, and sweat pours over me.
I convulse, paler than grass,
and feel my mind slip as I   15
go close to death

[but must suffer all, being poor.]

TRANSLATED BY WILLIS BARNSTONE

(c. 6th century B.C.*)*

ANONYMOUS

Barbara Allan

1

It was in and about the Martinmas time,°
   When the green leaves were a falling,
That Sir John Græme, in the West Country,
   Fell in love with Barbara Allan.

2

He sent his man down through the town,   5
   To the place where she was dwelling:
"O haste and come to my master dear,
   Gin° ye be Barbara Allan."   if

3

O hooly,° hooly rose she up,   gently
   To the place where he was lying,   10
And when she drew the curtain by:
   "Young man, I think you're dying."

4

"O it's I'm sick, and very, very sick,
   And 'tis a' for Barbara Allan."
"O the better for me ye s'° never be,   shall   15
   Though your heart's blood were a-spilling.

"Barbara Allan"   [1]***Martinmas***   *Mass (or feast) of St. Martin (d. 655) on November 11.*

5

"O dinna ye mind,° young man," said she,
   "When ye was in the tavern a drinking,
That ye made the healths gae° round and round,   go
   And slighted Barbara Allan?"   20

6

He turned his face unto the wall,
   And death was with him dealing:
"Adieu, adieu, my dear friends all,
   And be kind to Barbara Allan."

7

And slowly, slowly raise she up,   25
   And slowly, slowly left him,
And sighing said, she could not stay,
   Since death of life had reft° him.   deprived

8

She had not gane° a mile but twa,°   gone/two
   When she heard the dead-bell ringing,   30
And every jow° that the dead-bell geid,°   beat/gave
   It cried, "Woe to Barbara Allan!"

9

"O mother, mother, make my bed!
   O make it saft and narrow!
Since my love died for me to-day,   35
   I'll die for him to-morrow."

(c. 14th century)

---

[17]*dinna ye mind*   *don't you remember.*

ANONYMOUS

Edward, Edward

1

"Why does your brand° sae° drap wi' bluid,   sword/so
        Edward, Edward,
Why does your brand sae drap wi' bluid,
    And why sae sad gang° ye, O?"   go
"O I ha'e killed my hawk sae guid,   5
        Mither, mither,
O I ha'e killed my hawk sae guid,
    And I had nae mair but he, O."

2

"Your hawk's bluid was never sae reid,°   red
        Edward, Edward,   10
Your hawk's bluid was never sae reid,
    My dear son, I tell thee, O."
"O I ha'e killed my reid-roan steed,
        Mither, mither,
O I ha'e killed my reid-roan steed,   15
    That erst was sae fair and free, O."

3

"Your steed was auld, and ye ha'e gat mair,
        Edward, Edward,
Your steed was auld, and ye ha'e gat mair,
    Some other dule° ye drie°, O."   grief/suffer   20
"O I ha'e killed my fader dear,
        Mither, mither,
O I ha'e killed my fader dear,
    Alas, and wae° is me, O!"   woe

4

"And whatten° penance wul ye dree for that,   what kind of   25
        Edward, Edward?
And whatten penance wul ye dree for that,
    My dear son, now tell me O?"
"I'll set my feet in yonder boat,
        Mither, mither,   30
I'll set my feet in yonder boat,
    And I'll fare over the sea, O."

5

"And what wul ye do wi' your towers and your ha',
    Edward, Edward?
And what wul ye do wi' your towers and your ha',   35
    That were sae fair to see, O?"
"I'll let them stand tul they down fa',
    Mither, mither,
I'll let them stand tul they down fa',
    For here never mair maun° I be, O."   must   40

6

"And what wul ye leave to your bairns° and your wife,   children
    Edward, Edward?
And what wul ye leave to your bairns and your wife,
    Whan ye gang over the sea, O?"
"The warlde's room, let them beg thrae° life,   through 45
    Mither, mither,
The warlde's room, let them beg thrae life,
    For them never mair wul I see, O."

7

"And what wul ye leave to your ain mither dear,
    Edward, Edward?   50
And what wul ye leave to your ain mither dear,
    My dear son, now tell me, O?"
"The curse of hell frae° me sall° ye bear,   from/shall
    Mither, mither,
The curse of hell frae me sall ye bear,   55
    Sic° counsels ye gave to me, O."   such

(c. 14th century)

THOMAS WYATT
[1503–1542]

They flee from me

They flee from me, that sometime did me seek,
With naked foot stalking in my chamber.
I have seen them, gentle, tame, and meek,
That now are wild, and do not remember
That sometime they put themselves in danger   5
To take bread at my hand; and now they range,
Busily seeking with a continual change.

Thanked be Fortune it hath been otherwise,
Twenty times better; but once in special,
In thin array, after a pleasant guise,   10
When her loose gown from her shoulders did fall,
And she me caught in her arms long and small,°   thin
And therewith all sweetly did me kiss
And softly said, "Dear heart, how like you this?"

It was no dream, I lay broad waking.   15
But all is turned, thorough° my gentleness,   through
Into a strange fashion of forsaking;
And I have leave to go, of her goodness,
And she also to use newfangleness.
But since that I so kindely am served,   20
I fain would know what she hath deserved.

(1557)

EDMUND SPENSER
[1552–1599]

One day I wrote her name upon the strand

One day I wrote her name upon the strand,°   beach
But came the waves and washéd it away:
Agayne I wrote it with a second hand,
But came the tyde, and made my paynes his pray.
"Vayne man," sayd she, "that doest in vaine assay,   5
A mortall thing so to immortalize,
For I my selve shall lyke to this decay,
And eek° my name bee wypéd out lykewize."   also
"Not so," quod° I, "let baser things devize°   said/devise
To dy in dust, but you shall live by fame: 10
My verse your vertues rare shall eternize,
And in the hevens wryte your glorious name.
Where whenas death shall all the world subdew,
Our love shall live, and later life renew."

(1595)

SIR WALTER RALEIGH
[*c. 1552–1618*]

The Nymph's Reply to the Shepherd

If all the world and love were young,
And truth in every shepherd's tongue,
These pretty pleasures might me move
To live with thee and be thy love.

Time drives the flocks from field to fold   5
When rivers rage and rocks grow cold,
And Philomel° becometh dumb;
The rest complains of cares to come.

The flowers do fade, and wanton fields
To wayward winter reckoning yields;   10
A honey tongue, a heart of gall,
Is fancy's spring, but sorrow's fall.

Thy gowns, thy shoes, thy beds of roses,
Thy cap, thy kirtle,° and thy posies   long dress
Soon break, soon wither, soon forgotten—   15
In folly ripe, in reason rotten.

Thy belt of straw and ivy buds,
Thy coral clasps and amber studs,
All these in me no means can move
To come to thee and be thy love.   20

But could youth last and love still breed,
Had joys no date° nor age no need,   end
Then these delights my mind might move
To live with thee and be thy love.

"The Nymph's Reply to the Shepherd"   [7]*Philomel*   *the nightingale. According to Ovid's* Metamorphoses,
Philomel's brother-in-law Tereus had her tongue cut out to prevent her from revealing that he had raped her. See also
Bob McKenty's "Adam's Song," page 70.

CHRISTOPHER MARLOWE
[1564–1593]

The Passionate Shepherd to His Love

Come live with me and be my love,
And we will all the pleasures prove°   try
That valleys, groves, hills, and fields,
Woods, or steepy mountain yields.

And we will sit upon the rocks,   5
Seeing the shepherds feed their flocks,
By shallow rivers to whose falls
Melodious birds sing madrigals.

And I will make thee beds of roses
And a thousand fragrant posies,   10
A cap of flowers, and a kirtle°   a long dress
Embroidered all with leaves of myrtle;

A gown made of the finest wool
Which from our pretty lambs we pull;
Fair lined slippers for the cold,   15
With buckles of the purest gold;

A belt of straw and ivy buds,
With coral clasps and amber studs:
And if these pleasures may thee move,   20
Come live with me, and be my love.

The shepherds' swains shall dance and sing
For they delight each May morning:
If these delights thy mind may move,
Then live with me and be my love.

WILLIAM SHAKESPEARE
[1564–1616]

When in disgrace with fortune and men's eyes

When, in disgrace with fortune and men's eyes,
I all alone beweep my outcast state,
And trouble deaf heaven with my bootless° cries,   useless

And look upon myself, and curse my fate,
Wishing me like to one more rich in hope,   5
Featured like him, like him with friends possessed,
Desiring this man's art and that man's scope,
With what I most enjoy contented least;
Yet in these thoughts myself almost despising,
Haply I think on thee—and then my state,   10
Like to the lark at break of day arising
From sullen earth, sings hymns at heaven's gate;
For thy sweet love remembered such wealth brings
That then I scorn to change my state with kings.

(1609)

Let me not to the marriage of true minds

Let me not to the marriage of true minds
Admit impediments.° Love is not love   hindrances
Which alters when it alteration finds,
Or bends with the remover to remove:
Oh, no! it is an ever-fixéd mark,   5
That looks on tempests and is never shaken;
It is the star to every wandering bark,°   ship
Whose worth's unknown, although his height be taken.°
Love's not Time's fool, though rosy lips and cheeks
Within his bending sickle's compass come;   10
Love alters not with his brief hours and weeks,
But bears° it out even to the edge of doom.°   lasts/judgment day
If this be error and upon me proved,
I never writ, nor no man ever loved.

(1609)

Th' expense of spirit in a waste of shame

Th' expense of spirit in a waste of shame
Is lust in action; and till action, lust
Is perjured, murderous, bloody, full of blame,
Savage, extreme, rude, cruel, not to trust;
Enjoyed no sooner but despiséd straight: 5
Past reason hunted; and no sooner had,
Past reason hated, as a swallowed bait,
On purpose laid to make the taker mad:
Mad in pursuit, and in possession so;

"Let me not to the marriage of true minds"   [8]**height be taken**   *its elevation be measured.*

Had, having, and in quest to have, extreme; 10
A bliss in proof,° and proved, a very woe; in the experience
Before, a joy proposed; behind, a dream.
All this the world well knows; yet none knows well
To shun the heaven that leads men to this hell.

(1609)

My mistress' eyes are nothing like the sun

My mistress' eyes are nothing like the sun;
Coral is far more red than her lips' red;
If snow be white, why then her breasts are dun;
If hairs be wires, black wires grow on her head.
I have seen roses damasked,° red and white, variegated 5
But no such roses see I in her cheeks;
And in some perfumes is there more delight
Than in the breath that from my mistress reeks.
I love to hear her speak, yet well I know
That music hath a far more pleasing sound; 10
I grant I never saw a goddess go;° walk
My mistress, when she walks, treads on the ground.
And yet, by heaven, I think my love as rare
As any she belied with false compare.

(1609)

JOHN DONNE
[1572–1631]

Song

Go, and catch a falling star,
   Get with child a mandrake root,°
Tell me, where all past years are,
   Or who cleft the devil's foot,
Teach me to hear mermaids singing 5
Or to keep off envy's stinging,
     And find
     What wind
Serves to advance an honest mind.

"Song" ²**mandrake root** *Resembling a human body, the forked root of the mandrake was used as a medicine to induce conception.*

If thou beest born to strange sights,   10
    Things invisible to see,
Ride ten thousand days and nights,
    Till age snow white hairs on thee;
Thou, when thou return'st, wilt tell me
All strange wonders that befell thee,   15
      And swear,
      No where
Lives a woman true, and fair.

If thou find'st one, let me know:
    Such a pilgrimage were sweet.   20
Yet do not, I would not go,
    Though at next door we might meet:
Though she were true when you met her,
And last till you write your letter,
      Yet she   25
      Will be
False, ere I come, to two, or three.

                  (1633)

The Canonization

For God's sake hold your tongue, and let me love,
    Or chide my palsy, or my gout,
My five gray hairs, or ruined fortune, flout,
    With wealth your state, your mind with arts improve,
      Take you a course,° get you a place,°   direction/appointment   5
      Observe His Honor, or His Grace,
Or the King's real, or his stampéd face°   on a coin
      Contémplate; what you will, approve,°   try
    So you will let me love.

Alas, alas, who's injured by my love?   10
    What merchant's ships have my sighs drowned?
Who says my tears have overflowed his ground?
    When did my colds a forward spring remove?
      When did the heats which my veins fill
      Add one more to the plaguy bill?°   list of victims   15
Soldiers find wars, and lawyers find out still
    Litigious men, which quarrels move,
    Though she and I do love.

Call us what you will, we're made such by love;
    Call her one, me another fly,   20

We're tapers too, and at our own cost die,°
    And we in us find th' eagle and the dove
        The phoenix riddle° hath more wit°   sense
    By us: we two being one, are it.
So, to one neutral thing both sexes fit.   25
    We die and rise the same, and prove
    Mysterious by this love.

We can die by it, if not live by love,
    And if unfit for tombs and hearse
Our legend be, it will be fit for verse;   30
    And if no piece of chronicle we prove,
        We'll build in sonnets pretty rooms;
        As well a well-wrought urn becomes
The greatest ashes, as half-acre tombs;
        And by these hymns, all shall approve   35
    Us canonized for love:

And thus invoke us: You whom reverend love
    Made one another's hermitage;
You, to whom love was peace, that now is rage;
        Who did the whole world's soul contract, and drove   40
        Into the glasses of your eyes
        (So made such mirrors, and such spies,
That they did all to you epitomize)
    Countries, towns, courts: Beg from above
    A pattern of your love!

                                (1633)

A Valediction: Forbidding Mourning

As virtuous men pass mildly away,
    And whisper to their souls to go,
Whilst some of their sad friends do say,
    "The breath goes now," and some say, "No,"

So let us melt, and make no noise,   5
    No tear-floods, nor sigh-tempests move;
    'Twere profanation of our joys
        To tell the laity our love.

"The Canonization"   **21 at our own cost die**   *Death was a metaphor for sexual intercourse; each act of sexual congress supposedly shortened one's life by a day.*   **23 the phoenix riddle**   *a legendary, mythological bird, the only one of its kind. It is consumed in fire and then resurrected from the ashes to begin life anew.*

Moving of the earth° brings harms and fears,   earthquakes
    Men reckon what it did and meant;   10
But trepidation of the spheres,°
    Though greater far, is innocent.

Dull sublunary° lovers' love   earthly
    (Whose soul is sense) cannot admit
Absence, because it doth remove   15
    Those things which elemented° it.   composed

But we, by a love so much refined
    That our selves know not what it is,
Inter-assured of the mind,
    Care less, eyes, lips, and hands to miss.   20

Our two souls therefore, which are one,
    Though I must go, endure not yet
A breach, but an expansion,
    Like gold to airy thinness beat.

If they be two, they are two so   25
    As stiff twin compasses° are two:
Thy soul, the fixed foot, makes no show
    To move, but doth, if the other do;

And though it in the center sit,
    Yet when the other far doth roam,   30
It leans, and hearkens after it,
    And grows erect, as that comes home.

Such wilt thou be to me, who must,
    Like the other foot, obliquely run;
Thy firmness makes my circle just,   35
    And makes me end where I begun.

                                                         (1633)

The Flea

Mark but this flea, and mark in this
How little that which thou deny'st me is;
It sucked me first, and now sucks thee,
And in this flea our two bloods mingled be;

"A Valediction"   [11] *trepidation of the spheres*   movement in the outermost of the heavenly spheres. In Ptolemy's astronomy these outer spheres caused others to vary from their orbits.   [26] *twin compasses*   the two feet of a mathematical compass used for drawing circles.

Thou know'st that this cannot be said   5
A sin, nor shame, nor loss of maidenhead;
    Yet this enjoys before it woo,
    And pampered swells with one blood made of two,
    And this, alas, is more than we would do.

Oh stay, three lives in one flea spare,   10
Where we almost, yea, more than married are.
This flea is you and I, and this
Our marriage bed and marriage temple is;
Though parents grudge, and you, we are met
And cloistered in these living walls of jet.   15
    Though use° make you apt to kill me,   custom
    Let not to that, self-murder added be,
    And sacrilege, three sins in killing three.

Cruel and sudden, hast thou since
Purpled thy nail in blood of innocence?   20
Wherein could this flea guilty be,
Except in that drop which it sucked from thee?
Yet thou triumph'st and say'st that thou
Find'st not thyself, nor me the weaker now.
    'Tis true. Then learn how false fears be: 25
    Just so much honor, when thou yield'st to me,
    Will waste, as this flea's death took life from thee.

                                    (1633)

Death, be not proud

Death, be not proud, though some have callèd thee
Mighty and dreadful, for thou are not so;
For those whom thou think'st thou dost overthrow
Die not, poor Death, nor yet canst thou kill me.
From rest and sleep, which but thy pictures be,   5
Much pleasure; then from thee much more must flow,
And soonest our best men with thee do go,
Rest of their bones, and soul's delivery.
Thou art slave to fate, chance, kings, and desperate men,
And dost with poison, war, and sickness dwell,   10
And poppy or charms can make us sleep as well
And better than thy stroke; why swell'st thou then?
One short sleep past, we wake eternally
And death shall be no more; Death, thou shalt die.

                                    (1633)

Batter my heart, three-personed God

Batter my heart, three-personed God; for You
As yet but knock, breathe, shine, and seek to mend;
That I may rise and stand, o'erthrow me, and bend
Your force to break, blow, burn, and make me new.
I, like an usurped town, to another due,   5
Labor to admit You, but O, to no end;
Reason, Your viceroy in me, me should defend,
But is captíved, and proves weak or untrue.
Yet dearly I love You, and would be lovéd fain,°   gladly
But am betrothed unto Your enemy.   10
Divorce me, untie or break that knot again;
Take me to You, imprison me, for I,
Except You enthrall me, never shall be free,
Nor ever chaste, except You ravish me.

(1633)

BEN JONSON
[1573–1637]

On My First Son

Farewell, thou child of my right hand,° and joy;
My sin was too much hope of thee, loved boy:
Seven years thou wert lent to me, and I thee pay,
Exacted by thy fate, on the just day.°
O could I lose all father now! for why   5
Will man lament the state he should envý,
To have so soon 'scaped world's and flesh's rage,
And, if no other misery, yet age?
Rest in soft peace, and asked, say, "Here doth lie
Ben Jonson his best piece of poetry."   10
For whose sake henceforth all his vows be such
As what he loves may never like too much.

(1616)

"On My First Son" ¹*child of my right hand* *the literal meaning, in Hebrew, of Benjamin, the boy's name.*
⁴*the just day* *Jonson's son died on his seventh birthday.*

Song: To Celia

Drink to me only with thine eyes,
And I will pledge with mine;
Or leave a kiss but in the cup,
And I'll not look for wine.
The thirst that from the soul doth rise,   5
Doth ask a drink divine:
But might I of Jove's nectar sup,
I would not change for thine.

I sent thee late a rosy wreath,
Not so much honoring thee,   10
As giving it a hope, that there
It could not withered be.
But thou thereon did'st only breathe,
And sent'st it back to me;
Since when it grows and smells, I swear,   15
Not of itself, but thee.

(1606)

ROBERT HERRICK
[1591–1674]

Upon Julia's Clothes

Whenas in silks my Julia goes,
Then, then, methinks, how sweetly flows
That liquefaction of her clothes.

Next, when I cast mine eyes and see
That brave vibration each way free,   5
O how that glittering taketh me!

(1648)

To the Virgins, to Make Much of Time

Gather ye rosebuds while ye may:
    Old Time is still a-flying;
And this same flower that smiles today,
    Tomorrow will be dying.

The glorious lamp of heaven, the sun,   5
  The higher he's a-getting,
The sooner will his race be run,
  And nearer he's to setting.

That age is best which is the first,
  When youth and blood are warmer;   10
But being spent, the worse, and worst
  Times, still succeed the former.

Then be not coy, but use your time;
  And while ye may, go marry:
For, having lost but once your prime,   15
  You may for ever tarry.

                                                    (1648)

G E O R G E   H E R B E R T
[1593–1633]

The Altar

A broken ALTAR, Lord, Thy servant rears,
Made of a heart and cemented with tears;
  Whose parts are as Thy hand did frame;
  No workman's tool hath touched the same.
        A   HEART   alone   5
        Is   such   a   stone,
        As   nothing   but
        Thy power doth cut.
        Wherefore each part
        Of my hard heart   10
        Meets in this frame
        To praise Thy name,
  That if I chance to hold my peace,
  These stones to praise Thee may not cease.
Oh, let Thy blessed SACRIFICE be mine,
And sanctify this ALTAR to be Thine.   15

                                                    (1633)

JOHN MILTON
[1608–1674]

When I consider how my light is spent°

When I consider how my light is spent
 Ere half my days, in this dark world and wide,
 And that one talent° which is death to hide
 Lodged with me useless, though my soul more bent
To serve therewith my Maker, and present   5
 My true account, lest he returning chide;
 "Doth God exact day-labor, light denied?"
 I fondly° ask; but Patience to prevent   foolishly
That murmur, soon replies, "God doth not need
 Either man's work or his own gifts; who best   10
 Bear his mild yoke, they serve him best. His state
Is kingly. Thousands at his bidding speed
 And post o'er land and ocean without rest:
 They also serve who only stand and wait."

                 (1673)

On the Late Massacre in Piedmont°

Avenge, O Lord, thy slaughtered saints, whose bones
 Lie scattered on the Alpine mountains cold,
 Even them who kept thy truth so pure of old
 When all our fathers worshiped stocks° and stones idols
Forget not: in thy book record their groans   5
 Who were thy sheep and in their ancient fold
 Slain by the bloody Piedmontese that rolled
 Mother with infant down the rocks. Their moans
The vales redoubled to the hills, and they
 To Heaven. Their martyred blood and ashes sow 10
 O'er all th' Italian fields where still doth sway
The triple tyrant:° that from these may grow
 A hundredfold, who having learnt thy way
 Early may fly the Babylonian woe.

                 (1673)

"When I consider how my light is spent" *Milton went blind in 1651.* [3]*one talent* *an allusion to Jesus's parable of the talents, in which the servant who buried the talent given him by his master was cast into the darkness (Matthew 25:14–30).* "On the Late Massacre" *The Duke of Savoy in 1655 massacred 1,700 Waldensians, members of a Protestant sect.* [12]***The triple tyrant*** *the pope, whose tiara contains three crowns.*

ANNE BRADSTREET
[1612–1672]

To My Dear and Loving Husband

If ever two were one, then surely we.
If ever man were loved by wife, then thee;
If ever wife was happy in a man,
Compare with me, ye women, if you can.
I prize thy love more than whole mines of gold   5
Or all the riches that the East doth hold.
My love is such that rivers cannot quench,
Nor aught but love from thee give recompense.
Thy love is such I can no way repay,
The heavens reward thee manifold, I pray.   10
Then while we live, in love let's so perséver
That when we live no more, we may live ever.

(1678)

ANDREW MARVELL
[1621–1678]

To His Coy Mistress

   Had we but world enough, and time,
This coyness, lady, were no crime.
We would sit down, and think which way
To walk, and pass our long love's day.
Thou by the Indian Ganges' side   5
Shoudst rubies° find; I by the tide
Of Humber° would complain. I would
Love you ten years before the flood,
And you should, if you please, refuse
Till the conversion of the Jews.°   10
My vegetable love° should grow
Vaster than empires and more slow;
An hundred years should go to praise
Thine eyes, and on thy forehead gaze;

"To His Coy Mistress"   °**rubies**   *associated with virginity.*   ⁷**Humber**   *the river that runs through Marvell's native town, Hull.*   ¹⁰**the conversion of the Jews**   *supposedly to occur at the end of time.*   ¹¹**vegetable love** a reference to the idea that vegetables have the power to grow but lack consciousness.*

Two hundred to adore each breast,   15
But thirty thousand to the rest;
An age at least to every part,
And the last age should show your heart.
For, lady, you deserve this state,
Nor would I love at lower rate.   20
    But at my back I always hear
Time's wingéd chariot hurrying near;
And yonder all before us lie
Deserts of vast eternity.
Thy beauty shall no more be found;   25
Nor, in thy marble vault, shall sound
My echoing song; then worms shall try
That long-preserved virginity,
And your quaint° honor turn to dust,   overscrupulous
And into ashes all my lust: 30
The grave's a fine and private place,
But none, I think, do there embrace.
    Now therefore, while the youthful hue
Sits on thy skin like morning dew
And while thy willing soul transpires°   breathes forth   35
At every pore with instant fires,
Now let us sport us while we may,
And now, like amorous birds of prey,
Rather at once our time devour
Than languish in his slow-chapped° power.   slow-jawed   40
Let us roll all our strength and all
Our sweetness up into one ball,
And tear our pleasures with rough strife
Through the iron gates of life:
Thus, though we cannot make our sun   45
Stand still, yet we will make him run.

                                              (1681)

ALEXANDER POPE
[1688–1744]

from *An Essay on Man*

FROM *EPISTLE II*

I. Know then thyself, presume not God to scan;°   scrutinize
The proper study of mankind is Man.
Placed on this isthmus of a middle state,
A being darkly wise, and rudely° great;   crudely
With too much knowledge for the Sceptic side,   5
With too much weakness for the Stoic's pride,
He hangs between; in doubt to act, or rest,
In doubt to deem himself a god, or beast;
In doubt his mind or body to prefer,
Born but to die, and reasoning but to err;   10
Alike in ignorance, his reason such,
Whether he thinks too little, or too much:
Chaos of thought and passion, all confused;
Still by himself abused, or disabused;
Created half to rise, and half to fall;   15
Great lord of all things, yet a prey to all;
Sole judge of truth, in endless error hurled:
The glory, jest, and riddle of the world!

(1711)

WILLIAM BLAKE
[1757–1827]

The Clod & the Pebble

"Love seeketh not Itself to please,
Nor for itself hath any care;
But for another gives its ease,
And builds a Heaven in Hell's despair."

    So sang a little Clod of Clay,   5
    Trodden with the cattle's feet;
    But a Pebble of the brook,
    Warbled out these metres meet:

"Love seeketh only Self to please,
To bind another to its delight,   10
Joys in another's loss of ease,
And builds a Hell in Heaven's despite."

                                                          (1794)

The Lamb

   Little Lamb, who made thee?
     Dost thou know who made thee?
Gave thee life & bid thee feed,
By the stream & o'er the mead;
Gave thee clothing of delight,   5
Softest clothing wooly bright;
Gave thee such a tender voice,
Making all the vales rejoice!
     Little Lamb who made thee?
     Dost thou know who made thee?   10

   Little Lamb I'll tell thee,
     Little Lamb I'll tell thee!
He is callèd by thy name,
For he calls himself a Lamb:
He is meek & he is mild,   15
He became a little child:
I a child & thou a lamb,
We are callèd by his name.
     Little Lamb God bless thee.
     Little Lamb God bless thee.   20

                                                          (1789)

The Tyger

Tyger! Tyger! burning bright
In the forests of the night,
What immortal hand or eye
Could frame thy fearful symmetry?

In what distant deeps or skies   5
Burnt the fire of thine eyes?
On what wings dare he aspire?
What the hand, dare seize the fire?

And what shoulder, & what art,
Could twist the sinews of thy heart? 10
And when thy heart began to beat,
What dread hand? & what dread feet?

What the hammer? what the chain?
In what furnace was thy brain?
What the anvil? what dread grasp 15
Dare its deadly terrors clasp?

When the stars threw down their spears,
And water'd heaven with their tears,
Did he smile his work to see?
Did he who made the Lamb make thee? 20

Tyger! Tyger! burning bright
In the forests of the night,
What immortal hand or eye
Dare frame thy fearful symmetry?

(1794)

The Garden of Love

I went to the Garden of Love,
And saw what I never had seen:
A Chapel was built in the midst,
Where I used to play on the green.

And the gates of this Chapel were shut, 5
And "Thou shalt not" writ over the door;
So I turn'd to the Garden of Love,
That so many sweet flowers bore,

And I saw it was filled with graves,
And tomb-stones where flowers should be: 10
And Priests in black gowns were walking their rounds,
And binding with briars my joys & desires.

(1794)

ROBERT BURNS
[1759–1796]

A Red, Red Rose

O my luve's like a red, red rose,
   That's newly sprung in June;
O my luve's like the melodie
   That's sweetly played in tune.

As fair art thou, my bonnie lass,   5
   So deep in luve am I;
And I will luve thee still, my dear,
   Till a' the seas gang dry.

Till a' the seas gang dry, my dear,
   And the rocks melt wi' the sun: 10
O I will love thee still, my dear,
   While the sands o' life shall run.

And fare thee weel, my only luve,
   And fare thee weel awhile!
And I will come again, my luve,   15
   Though it were ten thousand mile.

                              (1796)

WILLIAM WORDSWORTH
[1770–1850]

The world is too much with us

The world is too much with us; late and soon,
Getting and spending, we lay waste our powers;
Little we see in Nature that is ours;
We have given our hearts away, a sordid boon!°   gift
This Sea that bares her bosom to the moon,   5
The winds that will be howling at all hours,
And are up-gathered now like sleeping flowers,
For this, for everything, we are out of tune;
It moves us not.—Great God! I'd rather be
A Pagan suckled in a creed outworn;   10

So might I, standing on this pleasant lea,
Have glimpses that would make me less forlorn;
Have sight of Proteus rising from the sea;
Or hear old Triton° blow his wreathéd horn.

(1807)

The Solitary Reaper

Behold her, single in the field,
Yon solitary Highland Lass!
Reaping and singing by herself;
Stop here, or gently pass!
Alone she cuts and binds the grain,   5
And sings a melancholy strain;
O listen! for the Vale profound
Is overflowing with the sound.

No Nightingale did ever chaunt
More welcome notes to weary bands   10
Of travelers in some shady haunt,
Among Arabian sands;
A voice so thrilling ne'er was heard
In springtime from the Cuckoo bird,
Breaking the silence of the seas   15
Among the farthest Hebrides.

Will no one tell me what she sings?—
Perhaps the plaintive numbers flow
For old, unhappy, far-off things,
And battles long ago;   20
Or is it some more humble lay,
Familiar matter of today?
Some natural sorrow, loss, or pain,
That has been, and may be again?

Whate'er the theme, the Maiden sang   25
As if her song could have no ending;
I saw her singing at her work,
And o'er the sickle bending—
I listened, motionless and still;
And, as I mounted up the hill,   30
The music in my heart I bore,
Long after it was heard no more.

(1807)

"The world is too much with us"   13–14**Proteus . . . Triton**   *classical sea gods. Triton's conch-shell horn calmed the waves.*

Composed upon Westminster Bridge, September 3, 1802

Earth has not anything to show more fair:
Dull would he be of soul who could pass by
A sight so touching in its majesty;
This City now doth, like a garment, wear
The beauty of the morning; silent, bare,   5
Ships, towers, domes, theaters, and temples lie
Open unto the fields, and to the sky;
All bright and glittering in the smokeless air.
Never did sun more beautifully steep
In his first splendor, valley, rock, or hill;   10
Ne'er saw I, never felt, a calm so deep!
The river glideth at his own sweet will:
Dear God! the very houses seem asleep;
And all that mighty heart is lying still!

(1807)

Lines

COMPOSED A FEW MILES ABOVE TINTERN ABBEY ON REVISITING THE BANKS OF THE
WYE DURING A TOUR, JULY 13, 1798

Five years have passed; five summers, with the length
Of five long winters! and again I hear
These waters, rolling from their mountain-springs
With a soft inland murmur. Once again
Do I behold these steep and lofty cliffs,   5
That on a wild secluded scene impress
Thoughts of more deep seclusion; and connect
The landscape with the quiet of the sky.
The day is come when I again repose
Here, under this dark sycamore, and view   10
These plots of cottage ground, these orchard tufts,
Which at this season, with their unripe fruits,
Are clad in one green hue, and lose themselves
Mid groves and copses.° Once again I see   thickets
These hedgerows, hardly hedgerows, little lines   15
Of sportive wood run wild; these pastoral farms,
Green to the very door; and wreaths of smoke
Sent up, in silence, from among the trees!
With some uncertain notice, as might seem
Of vagrant dwellers in the houseless woods,   20
Or of some Hermit's cave, where by his fire
The Hermit sits alone.
                        These beauteous forms,
Through a long absence, have not been to me

As is a landscape to a blind man's eye;
But oft, in lonely rooms, and 'mid the din   25
Of towns and cities, I have owed to them,
In hours of weariness, sensations sweet,
Felt in the blood, and felt along the heart;
And passing even into my purer mind
With tranquil restoration—feelings too   30
Of unremembered pleasure; such, perhaps,
As have no slight or trivial influence
On that best portion of a good man's life,
His little, nameless, unremembered, acts
Of kindness and of love. Nor less, I trust,   35
To them I may have owed another gift,
Of aspect more sublime; that blessed mood,
In which the burthen of the mystery,
In which the heavy and the weary weight
Of all this unintelligible world,   40
Is lightened—that serene and blessed mood,
In which the affections gently lead us on—
Until, the breath of this corporeal frame
And even the motion of our human blood
Almost suspended, we are laid asleep   45
In body, and become a living soul;
While with an eye made quiet by the power
Of harmony, and the deep power of joy,
We see into the life of things.

                    If this
Be but a vain belief, yet, oh! how oft—   50
In darkness and amid the many shapes
Of joyless daylight; when the fretful stir
Unprofitable, and the fever of the world,
Have hung upon the beatings of my heart—
How oft, in spirit, have I turned to thee,   55
O sylvan Wye! thou wanderer through the woods,
How often has my spirit turned to thee!

   And now, with gleams of half-extinguished thought,
With many recognitions dim and faint,
And somewhat of a sad perplexity,   60
The picture of the mind revives again;
While here I stand, not only with the sense
Of present pleasure, but with pleasing thoughts
That in this moment there is life and food
For future years. And so I dare to hope,   65
Though changed, no doubt, from what I was when first
I came among these hills; when like a roe

I bounded o'er the mountains, by the sides
Of the deep rivers, and the lonely streams,
Wherever nature led—more like a man   70
Flying from something that he dreads than one
Who sought the thing he loved. For nature then
(The coarser pleasures of my boyish days,
And their glad animal movements all gone by)
To me was all in all.—I cannot paint   75
What then I was. The sounding cataract
Haunted me like a passion; the tall rock,
The mountain, and the deep and gloomy wood,
Their colors and their forms, were then to me
An appetite; a feeling and a love,   80
That had no need of a remoter charm,
By thought supplied, nor any interest
Unborrowed from the eye.—That time is past,
And all its aching joys are now no more,
And all its dizzy raptures. Not for this   85
Faint I, nor mourn nor murmur; other gifts
Have followed; for such loss, I would believe,
Abundant recompense. For I have learned
To look on nature, not as in the hour
Of thoughtless youth, but hearing oftentimes   90
The still, sad music of humanity,
Nor harsh nor grating, though of ample power
To chasten and subdue. And I have felt
A presence that disturbs me with the joy
Of elevated thoughts; a sense sublime   95
Of something far more deeply interfused,
Whose dwelling is the light of setting suns,
And the round ocean and the living air,
And the blue sky, and in the mind of man:
A motion and a spirit, that impels   100
All thinking things, all objects of all thought,
And rolls through all things. Therefore am I still
A lover of the meadows and the woods,
And mountains; and of all that we behold
From this green earth; of all the mighty world   105
Of eye, and ear—both what they half create,
And what perceive; well pleased to recognize
In nature and the language of the sense
The anchor of my purest thoughts, the nurse,
The guide, the guardian of my heart, and soul   110
Of all my moral being.

            Nor perchance,
If I were not thus taught, should I the more
Suffer my genial spirits° to decay: powers

For thou art with me here upon the banks
Of this fair river; thou my dearest Friend,° 115
My dear, dear Friend; and in thy voice I catch
The language of my former heart, and read
My former pleasures in the shooting lights
Of thy wild eyes. Oh! yet a little while
May I behold in thee what I was once, 120
My dear, dear Sister! and this prayer I make,
Knowing that Nature never did betray
The heart that loved her; 'tis her privilege,
Through all the years of this our life, to lead
From joy to joy: for she can so inform°   give form to 125
The mind that is within us, so impress
With quietness and beauty, and so feed
With lofty thoughts, that neither evil tongues,
Rash judgments, nor the sneers of selfish men,
Nor greetings where no kindness is, nor all 130
The dreary intercourse of daily life,
Shall e'er prevail against us, or disturb
Our cheerful faith, that all which we behold
Is full of blessings. Therefore let the moon
Shine on thee in thy solitary walk; 135
And let the misty mountain winds be free
To blow against thee: and, in after years,
When these wild ecstasies shall be matured
Into a sober pleasure; when thy mind
Shall be a mansion for all lovely forms, 140
Thy memory be as a dwelling place
For all sweet sounds and harmonies; oh! then,
If solitude, or fear, or pain, or grief
Should be thy portion, with what healing thoughts
Of tender joy wilt thou remember me, 145
And these my exhortations! Nor, perchance—
If I should be where I no more can hear
Thy voice, nor catch from thy wild eyes these gleams
Of past existence—wilt thou then forget
That on the banks of this delightful stream 150
We stood together; and that I, so long
A worshiper of Nature, hither came
Unwearied in that service; rather say
With warmer love—oh! with far deeper zeal
Of holier love. Nor wilt thou then forget, 155
That after many wanderings, many years
Of absence, these steep woods and lofty cliffs,
And this green pastoral landscape, were to me
More dear, both for themselves and for thy sake!

(1798)

"Lines Composed a Few Miles above Tintern Abbey"   [115]***Friend***   *Wordsworth's sister, Dorothy.*

SAMUEL TAYLOR COLERIDGE
[1772–1834]

Kubla Khan°

OR A VISION IN A DREAM. A FRAGMENT

In Xanadu did Kubla Khan
A stately pleasure dome decree:
Where Alph, the sacred river, ran
Through caverns measureless to man
   Down to a sunless sea.   5

So twice five miles of fertile ground
With walls and towers were girdled round:
And there were gardens bright with sinuous rills,
Where blossomed many an incense-bearing tree;
And here were forests ancient as the hills,   10
Enfolding sunny spots of greenery.

But oh! that deep romantic chasm which slanted
Down the green hill athwart a cedarn cover!
A savage place! as holy and enchanted
As e'er beneath a waning moon was haunted   15
By woman wailing for her demon lover!
And from this chasm, with ceaseless turmoil seething,
As if this earth in fast thick pants were breathing,
A mighty fountain momently was forced:
Amid whose swift half-intermitted burst   20
Huge fragments vaulted like rebounding hail,
Or chaffy grain beneath the thresher's flail:
And 'mid these dancing rocks at once and ever
It flung up momently the sacred river.
Five miles meandering with a mazy motion   25
Through wood and dale the sacred river ran,
Then reached the caverns measureless to man,
And sank in tumult to a lifeless ocean:
And 'mid this tumult Kubla heard from far
Ancestral voices prophesying war!   30

   The shadow of the dome of pleasure
   Floated midway on the waves;

"Kubla Khan"   *the first ruler of the Mongol dynasty in thirteenth-century China. Coleridge's topography and place names are imaginary.*

Where was heard the mingled measure
From the fountain and the caves.
It was a miracle of rare device,   35
A sunny pleasure dome with caves of ice!

A damsel with a dulcimer
In a vision once I saw:
It was an Abyssinian maid,
And on her dulcimer she played,   40
Singing of Mount Abora.
Could I revive within me
Her symphony and song,
To such a deep delight 'twould win me,
That with music loud and long,   45
I would build that dome in air,
That sunny dome! those caves of ice!
And all who heard should see them there,
And all should cry, Beware! Beware!
His flashing eyes, his floating hair!   50
Weave a circle round him thrice,
And close your eyes with holy dread,
For he on honey-dew hath fed,
And drunk the milk of Paradise.

(1798)

GEORGE GORDON, LORD BYRON
[1788–1824]

She walks in beauty

1

She walks in beauty, like the night
    Of cloudless climes and starry skies;
And all that's best of dark and bright
    Meet in her aspect and her eyes:
Thus mellowed to that tender light   5
    Which heaven to gaudy day denies.

2

One shade the more, one ray the less,
    Had half impaired the nameless grace
Which waves in every raven tress,
    Or softly lightens o'er her face;   10
Where thoughts serenely sweet express
    How pure, how dear their dwelling place.

3

And on that cheek, and o'er that brow,
    So soft, so calm, yet eloquent,
The smiles that win, the tints that glow,   15
    But tell of days in goodness spent,
A mind at peace with all below,
    A heart whose love is innocent!

                                              (1815)

PERCY BYSSHE SHELLEY
[1792–1822]

Ozymandias°

I met a traveler from an antique land
Who said: Two vast and trunkless legs of stone
Stand in the desert . . . Near them, on the sand,
Half sunk, a shattered visage lies, whose frown,
And wrinkled lip, and sneer of cold command,   5
Tell that its sculptor well those passions read
Which yet survive, stamped on these lifeless things,
The hand that mocked them, and the heart that fed:
And on the pedestal these words appear:
"My name is Ozymandias, king of kings: 10
Look on my works, ye Mighty, and despair!"
Nothing beside remains. Round the decay
Of that colossal wreck, boundless and bare
The lone and level sands stretch far away.

                                              (1818)

Ode to the West Wind

1

O wild West Wind, thou breath of Autumn's being,
Thou, from whose unseen presence the leaves dead
Are driven, like ghosts from an enchanter fleeing,

Yellow, and black, and pale, and hectic red,
Pestilence-stricken multitudes: O thou,   5
Who chariotest to their dark wintry bed

"Ozymandias"   *Greek name for the Egyptian ruler Rameses II, who erected a huge statue in his own likeness, among numerous other monuments.*

The wingéd seeds, where they lie cold and low,
Each like a corpse within its grave, until
Thine azure sister of the Spring shall blow

Her clarion° o'er the dreaming earth, and fill   trumpet call   10
(Driving sweet buds like flocks to feed in air)
With living hues and odors plain and hill:

Wild Spirit, which art moving everywhere;
Destroyer and preserver; hear, oh, hear!

2

Thou on whose stream, mid the steep sky's commotion,   15
Loose clouds like earth's decaying leaves are shed,
Shook from the tangled boughs of Heaven and Ocean,

Angels° of rain and lightning: there are spread   messengers
On the blue surface of thine aëry surge,
Like the bright hair uplifted from the head   20

Of some fierce Maenad,° even from the dim verge
Of the horizon to the zenith's height,
The locks of the approaching storm. Thou dirge

Of the dying year, to which this closing night
Will be the dome of a vast sepulcher,   25
Vaulted with all thy congregated might

Of vapors, from whose solid atmosphere
Black rain, and fire, and hail will burst: oh, hear!

3

Thou who didst waken from his summer dreams
The blue Mediterranean, where he lay,   30
Lulled by the coil of his crystálline streams,

Beside a pumice isle in Baiae's bay,
And saw in sleep old palaces and towers
Quivering within the wave's intenser day,

All overgrown with azure moss and flowers   35
So sweet, the sense faints picturing them! Thou
For whose path the Atlantic's level powers

"Ode to the West Wind"   [21]**Maenad**   *frenzied female worshipper of Dionysus, god of wine and fertility.*

Cleave themselves into chasms, while far below
The sea-blooms and the oozy woods which wear
The sapless foliage of the ocean, know   40

Thy voice, and suddenly grow gray with fear,
And tremble and despoil themselves: oh, hear!

4

If I were a dead leaf thou mightest bear;
If I were a swift cloud to fly with thee;
A wave to pant beneath thy power, and share   45

The impulse of thy strength, only less free
Than thou, O uncontrollable! If even
I were as in my boyhood, and could be

The comrade of thy wanderings over Heaven,
As then, when to outstrip thy skyey speed   50
Scarce seemed a vision; I would ne'er have striven

As thus with thee in prayer in my sore need.
Oh, lift me as a wave, a leaf, a cloud!
I fall upon the thorns of life! I bleed!

A heavy weight of hours has chained and bowed   55
One too like thee: tameless, and swift, and proud.

5

Make me thy lyre,° even as the forest is: small harp
What if my leaves are falling like its own!
The tumult of thy mighty harmonies

Will take from both a deep, autumnal tone,   60
Sweet though in sadness. Be thou, Spirit fierce,
My spirit! Be thou me, impetuous one!

Drive my dead thoughts over the universe
Like withered leaves to quicken a new birth!
And, by the incantation of this verse,   65

Scatter, as from an unextinguished hearth
Ashes and sparks, my words among mankind!
Be through my lips to unawakened earth

The trumpet of a prophecy! O Wind,
If Winter comes, can Spring be far behind?   70

                                                        (1820)

JOHN KEATS
[1795–1821]

When I have fears that I may cease to be

When I have fears that I may cease to be
  Before my pen has gleaned my teeming brain,
Before high-piléd books, in charact'ry,°   written symbols
  Hold like rich garners the full-ripened grain;
When I behold, upon the night's starred face,   5
  Huge cloudy symbols of a high romance,
And think that I may never live to trace
  Their shadows, with the magic hand of chance;
And when I feel, fair creature of an hour,
  That I shall never look upon thee more,   10
Never have relish in the faery° power   magical
  Of unreflecting love!—then on the shore
Of the wide world I stand alone, and think
Till Love and Fame to nothingness do sink.

(1818, 1848)

La Belle Dame sans Merci°

O what can ail thee, Knight at arms,
  Alone and palely loitering?
The sedge has withered from the Lake
  And no birds sing!

O what can ail thee, Knight at arms,   5
  So haggard, and so woebegone?
The squirrel's granary is full
  And the harvest's done.

I see a lily on thy brow
  With anguish moist and fever dew,   10
And on thy cheeks a fading rose
  Fast withereth too.

"I met a Lady in the Meads,°   meadows
  Full beautiful, a faery's child,
Her hair was long, her foot was light   15
  And her eyes were wild.

"I made a Garland for her head,
 And bracelets too, and fragrant Zone;°   girdle
She looked at me as she did love
 And made sweet moan.   20

"I set her on my pacing steed
 And nothing else saw all day long,
For sidelong would she bend and sing
 A faery's song.

"She found me roots of relish sweet,   25
 And honey wild, and manna dew,
And sure in language strange she said
 'I love thee true.'

"She took me to her elfin grot
 And there she wept and sighed full sore,   30
And there I shut her wild wild eyes
 With kisses four.

"And there she lulléd me asleep,
 And there I dreamed, Ah Woe betide!
The latest dream I ever dreamt   35
 On the cold hill side.

"I saw pale Kings, and Princes too,
 Pale warriors, death-pale were they all;
They cried, 'La belle dame sans merci
 Hath thee in thrall!'   40

"I saw their starved lips in the gloam
 With horrid warning gapéd wide,
And I awoke, and found me here
 On the cold hill's side.

"And this is why I sojourn here,   45
 Alone and palely loitering;
Though the sedge is withered from the Lake
 And no birds sing."

                 (1819, 1888)

"La Belle Dame sans Merci" *the beautiful lady without mercy.*

Ode to a Nightingale

1

My heart aches, and a drowsy numbness pains
   My sense, as though of hemlock° I had drunk,
Or emptied some dull opiate to the drains°   dregs
   One minute past, and Lethe-wards° had sunk:
'Tis not through envy of thy happy lot,   5
   But being too happy in thine happiness—
      That thou, light-wingéd Dryad° of the trees,   tree nymph
         In some melodious plot
Of beechen green, and shadows numberless,
   Singest of summer in full-throated ease.   10

2

O, for a draught of vintage! that hath been
   Cooled a long age in the deep-delvéd earth,
Tasting of Flora° and the country green,
   Dance, and Provençal song,° and sunburnt mirth!
O for a beaker full of the warm South,   15
   Full of the true, the blushful Hippocrene,°
      With beaded bubbles winking at the brim,
         And purple-stainéd mouth;
That I might drink, and leave the world unseen,
   And with thee fade away into the forest dim: 20

3

Fade far away, dissolve, and quite forget
   What thou among the leaves hast never known,
The weariness, the fever, and the fret
   Here, where men sit and hear each other groan;
Where palsy shakes a few, sad, last gray hairs,   25
   Where youth grows pale, and specter-thin, and dies,
      Where but to think is to be full of sorrow
         And leaden-eyed despairs,
Where Beauty cannot keep her lustrous eyes,
   Or new Love pine at them beyond tomorrow.   30

"Ode to a Nightingale" [2]*hemlock* *opiate; poisonous in large quantities.*   [4]**Lethe-wards** *towards Lethe,*
the river of forgetfulness.   [13]**Flora** *goddess of the flowers.*   [14]**Provençal song** *Provence, in southern France,*
home of the troubadours.   [16]**true . . . Hippocrene** *wine. A fountain on Mount Helicon in Greece, whose waters*
reputedly stimulated poetic imagination.

4

Away! away! for I will fly to thee,
  Not charioted by Bacchus and his pards,°
But on the viewless° wings of Poesy,   invisible
  Though the dull brain perplexes and retards:
Already with thee! tender is the night,   35
  And haply° the Queen-Moon is on her throne,   perhaps
    Clustered around by all her starry Fays;°   fairies
      But here there is no light,
Save what from heaven is with the breezes blown
  Through verdurous glooms and winding mossy ways.   40

5

I cannot see what flowers are at my feet,
  Nor what soft incense hangs upon the boughs,
But, in embalméd° darkness, guess each sweet   scented
  Wherewith the seasonable month endows
The grass, the thicket, and the fruit tree wild;   45
  White hawthorn, and the pastoral eglantine;°   sweetbriar
    Fast fading violets covered up in leaves;
      And mid-May's eldest child,
The coming musk-rose, full of dewy wine,
  The murmurous haunt of flies on summer eves.   50

6

Darkling° I listen; and for many a time   in darkness
  I have been half in love with easeful Death,
Called him soft names in many a muséd rhyme,
  To take into the air my quiet breath;
Now more than ever seems it rich to die,   55
  To cease upon the midnight with no pain,
    While thou art pouring forth thy soul abroad
      In such an ecstasy!
Still wouldst thou sing, and I have ears in vain—
  To thy high requiem become a sod.   60

7

Thou wast not born for death, immortal Bird!
  No hungry generations tread thee down;
The voice I hear this passing night was heard
  In ancient days by emperor and clown:
Perhaps the selfsame song that found a path   65
  Through the sad heart of Ruth, when, sick for home,
    She stood in tears amid the alien corn;°

---

[32] **Bacchus . . . pards**   *the god of wine and revelry and the leopards who drew his chariot.*

The same that ofttimes hath
Charmed magic casements, opening on the foam
   Of perilous seas, in faery lands forlorn.   70

8

Forlorn! the very word is like a bell
   To toll me back from thee to my sole self!
Adieu! the fancy cannot cheat so well
   As she is famed to do, deceiving elf.
Adieu! adieu! thy plaintive anthem fades   75
   Past the near meadows, over the still stream,
      Up the hill side; and now 'tis buried deep
         In the next valley-glades:
Was it a vision, or a waking dream?
   Fled is that music:—Do I wake or sleep?   80

                    (1819, 1820)

Ode on a Grecian Urn

1

Thou still unravished bride of quietness,
   Thou foster child of silence and slow time,
Sylvan° historian, who canst thus express   woodland
   A flowery tale more sweetly than our rhyme:
What leaf-fringed legend haunts about thy shape   5
   Of deities or mortals, or of both,
      In Tempe or the dales of Arcady?°
   What men or gods are these? What maidens loath?
What mad pursuit? What struggle to escape?
      What pipes and timbrels? What wild ecstasy?   10

2

Heard melodies are sweet, but those unheard
   Are sweeter; therefore, ye soft pipes, play on;
Not to the sensual ear, but, more endeared,
   Pipe to the spirit ditties of no tone:
Fair youth, beneath the trees, thou canst not leave   15
   Thy song, nor ever can those trees be bare;
      Bold Lover, never, never canst thou kiss,
Though winning near the goal—yet, do not grieve;
      She cannot fade, though thou hast not thy bliss,
   Forever wilt thou love, and she be fair!   20

"Ode on a Grecian Urn"   [7]*Tempe . . . Arcady*   *in Greece, beautiful rural regions.*   [66-67]*Ruth . . . corn*
a Biblical heroine who worked in the harvest fields in a foreign land.

3

Ah, happy, happy boughs! that cannot shed
   Your leaves, nor ever bid the Spring adieu;
And, happy melodist, unweariéd,
   Forever piping songs forever new;
More happy love! more happy, happy love!   25
   Forever warm and still to be enjoyed,
      Forever panting, and forever young;
All breathing human passion far above,
   That leaves a heart high-sorrowful and cloyed,
      A burning forehead, and a parching tongue.   30

4

Who are these coming to the sacrifice?
   To what green altar, O mysterious priest,
Lead'st thou that heifer lowing at the skies,
   And all her silken flanks with garlands dressed?
What little town by river or sea shore,   35
   Or mountain-built with peaceful citadel,
      Is emptied of this folk, this pious morn?
And, little town, thy streets forevermore
   Will silent be; and not a soul to tell
      Why thou art desolate, can e'er return.   40

5

O Attic shape! Fair attitude! with brede°   woven pattern
   Of marble men and maidens overwrought,°   ornamented
With forest branches and the trodden weed;
   Thou, silent form, dost tease us out of thought
As doth eternity: Cold Pastoral!   45
   When old age shall this generation waste,
      Thou shalt remain, in midst of other woe
   Than ours, a friend to man, to whom thou say'st,
"Beauty is truth, truth beauty,"—that is all
   Ye know on earth, and all ye need to know.

(1819, 1820)

ELIZABETH BARRETT BROWNING
[1806–1861]

How do I love thee? Let me count the ways

How do I love thee? Let me count the ways.
I love thee to the depth and breadth and height
My soul can reach, when feeling out of sight
For the ends of Being and ideal Grace.
I love thee to the level of everyday's   5
Most quiet need, by sun and candle-light.
I love thee freely, as men strive for Right;
I love thee purely, as they turn from Praise.
I love thee with the passion put to use
In my old griefs, and with my childhood's faith.   10
I love thee with a love I seemed to lose
With my lost saints—I love thee with the breath,
Smiles, tears, of all my life!—and, if God choose,
I shall but love thee better after death.

(1850)

EDGAR ALLAN POE
[1809–1849]

To Helen

Helen, thy beauty is to me
  Like those Nicean barks° of yore,   ships
That gently, o'er a perfumed sea,
  The weary, way-worn wanderer bore
  To his own native shore.   5

On desperate seas long wont to roam,
  Thy hyacinth hair,° thy classic face,
Thy Naiad° airs have brought me home
  To the glory that was Greece
And the grandeur that was Rome.   10

Lo! in yon brilliant window-niche
  How statue-like I see thee stand!
  The agate lamp within thy hand,
Ah! Psyche from the regions which
  Are Holy Land!   15

(1831, 1845)

"To Helen" [7]**hyacinth hair** *allusion to the curled hair of the slain youth Hyacinthus, beloved of Apollo.*
[8]**Naiad** *water nymph.*

The Raven

Once upon a midnight dreary, while I pondered, weak and weary,
Over many a quaint and curious volume of forgotten lore—
While I nodded, nearly napping, suddenly there came a tapping,
As of some one gently rapping, rapping at my chamber door—
" 'Tis some visiter," I muttered, "tapping at my chamber door—   5
    Only this and nothing more."

Ah, distinctly I remember it was in the bleak December;
And each separate dying ember wrought its ghost upon the floor.
Eagerly I wished the morrow;—vainly I had sought to borrow
From my books surcease of sorrow—sorrow for the lost Lenore—   10
For the rare and radiant maiden whom the angels name Lenore—
    Nameless *here* for evermore.

And the silken, sad, uncertain rustling of each purple curtain
Thrilled me—filled me with fantastic terrors never felt before;
So that now, to still the beating of my heart, I stood repeating   15
" 'Tis some visiter entreating entrance at my chamber door—
Some late visiter entreating entrance at my chamber door;—
    This it is and nothing more."

Presently my soul grew stronger; hesitating then no longer,
"Sir," said I, "or Madam, truly your forgiveness I implore;   20
But the fact is I was napping, and so gently you came rapping,
And so faintly you came tapping, tapping at my chamber door,
   That I scarce was sure I heard you"—here I opened wide the door;—
    Darkness there and nothing more.

Deep into that darkness peering, long I stood there wondering,
    fearing,   25
Doubting, dreaming dreams no mortal ever dared to dream before;
But the silence was unbroken, and the stillness gave no token,
And the only word there spoken was the whispered word, "Lenore!"
This I whispered, and an echo murmured back the word, "Lenore!"
    Merely this and nothing more.   30

Back into the chamber turning, all my soul within me burning,
Soon again I heard a tapping somewhat louder than before.
"Surely," said I, "surely that is something at my window lattice;
Let me see, then, what thereat is, and this mystery explore—
Let my heart be still a moment and this mystery explore;—   35
    'Tis the wind and nothing more!"

Open here I flung the shutter, when, with many a flirt and flutter,
In there stepped a stately Raven of the saintly days of yore;

Not the least obeisance made he; not a minute stopped or stayed he;
But, with mien of lord or lady, perched above my chamber door— 40
Perched upon a bust of Pallas° just above my chamber door—
    Perched, and sat, and nothing more.

Then this ebony bird beguiling my sad fancy into smiling,
By the grave and stern decorum of the countenance it wore,
"Though thy crest be shorn and shaven, thou," I said, "art sure no craven, 45
Ghastly grim and ancient Raven wandering from the Nightly shore—
Tell me what thy lordly name is on the Night's Plutonian° shore!"
    Quoth the Raven "Nevermore."

Much I marvelled this ungainly fowl to hear discourse so plainly,
Though its answer little meaning—little relevancy bore; 50
For we cannot help agreeing that no living human being
Ever yet was blessed with seeing bird above his chamber door—
Bird or beast upon the sculptured bust above his chamber door,
    With such name as "Nevermore."

But the Raven, sitting lonely on the placid bust, spoke only 55
That one word, as if his soul in that one word he did outpour.
Nothing farther then he uttered—not a feather then he fluttered—
Till I scarcely more than muttered "Other friends have flown before—
On the morrow *he* will leave me, as my Hopes have flown before."
    Then the bird said "Nevermore." 60

Startled at the stillness broken by reply so aptly spoken,
"Doubtless," said I, "what it utters is its only stock and store
Caught from some unhappy master whom unmerciful Disaster
Followed fast and followed faster till his songs one burden bore—
Till the dirges of his Hope that melancholy burden bore 65
    Of 'Never—nevermore.'"

But the Raven still beguiling my sad fancy into smiling,
Straight I wheeled a cushioned seat in front of bird, and bust and door;
Then, upon the velvet sinking, I betook myself to linking
Fancy unto fancy, thinking what this ominous bird of yore— 70
What this grim, ungainly, ghastly, gaunt, and ominous bird of yore
    Meant in croaking "Nevermore."

Thus I sat engaged in guessing, but no syllable expressing
To the fowl whose fiery eyes now burned into my bosom's core;
This and more I sat divining, with my head at ease reclining 75
On the cushion's velvet lining that the lamp-light gloated o'er,
But whose velvet-violet lining with the lamp-light gloating o'er,
    She shall press, ah, nevermore!

"The Raven"   **41 Pallas**   *Pallas Athena, patron goddess of Athens.*   **47 Plutonian**   *Pluto, god of the underworld.*

Then, methought, the air grew denser, perfumed from an unseen censer
Swung by seraphim whose foot-falls tinkled on the tufted floor.   80
"Wretch," I cried, "thy God hath lent thee—by these angels he hath sent thee
Respite—respite and nepenthe from thy memories of Lenore;
Quaff, oh quaff this kind nepenthe and forget this lost Lenore!"
    Quoth the Raven "Nevermore."

"Prophet!" said I, "thing of evil!—prophet still, if bird or devil!—   85
Whether Tempter sent, or whether tempest tossed thee here ashore,
Desolate yet all undaunted, on this desert land enchanted—
Oh this home by Horror haunted—tell me truly, I implore—
Is there—*is* there balm in Gilead?—tell me—tell me, I implore!"
    Quoth the Raven "Nevermore."   90

"Prophet!" said I, "thing of evil!—prophet still, if bird or devil!
By that Heaven that bends above us—by that God we both adore—
Tell this soul with sorrow laden if, within the distant Aidenn,
It shall clasp a sainted maiden whom the angels name Lenore—
Clasp a rare and radiant maiden whom the angels name Lenore."   95
    Quoth the Raven "Nevermore."

"Be that word our sign of parting, bird or fiend!" I shrieked, upstarting—
"Get thee back into the tempest and the Night's Plutonian shore!
Leave no black plume as a token of that lie thy soul hath spoken!
Leave my loneliness unbroken!—quit the bust above my door!   100
Take thy beak from out my heart, and take thy form from off my door!"
    Quoth the Raven "Nevermore."

And the Raven, never flitting, still is sitting, *still* is sitting
On the pallid bust of Pallas just above my chamber door;
And his eyes have all the seeming of a demon's that is dreaming,   105
And the lamp-light o'er him streaming throws his shadow on the floor;
And my soul from out that shadow that lies floating on the floor
    Shall be lifted—nevermore!

(1845)

ALFRED, LORD TENNYSON
[1809–1892]

Ulysses°

It little profits that an idle king,
By this still hearth, among these barren crags,
Matched with an aged wife, I mete and dole
Unequal laws unto a savage race,
That hoard, and sleep, and feed, and know not me.   5
I cannot rest from travel; I will drink
Life to the lees. All times I have enjoyed
Greatly, have suffered greatly, both with those
That loved me, and alone; on shore, and when
Through scudding drifts the rainy Hyades°   10
Vext the dim sea. I am become a name;
For always roaming with a hungry heart
Much have I seen and known—cities of men
And manners,° climates, councils, governments,   customs
Myself not least, but honored of them all,—   15
And drunk delight of battle with my peers,
Far on the ringing plains of windy Troy.
I am a part of all that I have met;
Yet all experience is an arch wherethrough
Gleams that untraveled world whose margin fades   20
For ever and for ever when I move.
How dull it is to pause, to make an end,
To rust unburnished, not to shine in use!
As though to breathe were life! Life piled on life
Were all too little, and of one to me   25
Little remains; but every hour is saved
From that eternal silence, something more,
A bringer of new things; and vile it were
For some three suns to store and hoard myself,
And this gray spirit yearning in desire   30
To follow knowledge like a sinking star,
Beyond the utmost bound of human thought.
    This is my son, mine own Telemachus,
To whom I leave the scepter and the isle,
Well-loved of me, discerning to fulfill   35
This labor, by slow prudence to make mild
A rugged people, and through soft degrees

"Ulysses"   *according to Dante (in* The Inferno, *Canto 26) Ulysses, having been away for ten years during the Trojan War, is restless upon returning to his island kingdom of Ithaca, and he persuades a band of followers to accompany him on a journey.*   [10]*Hyades*   *a constellation of stars whose rising with the sun forecasts rain.*

Subdue them to the useful and the good.
Most blameless is he, centered in the sphere
Of common duties, decent° not to fail   proper   40
In offices° of tenderness, and pay   duties
Meet° adoration to my household gods,   appropriate
When I am gone. He works his work, I mine.
    There lies the port; the vessel puffs her sail;
There gloom the dark, broad seas. My mariners,   45
Souls that have toiled, and wrought, and thought with me,
That ever with a frolic welcome took
The thunder and the sunshine, and opposed
Free hearts, free foreheads—you and I are old;
Old age hath yet his honor and his toil.   50
Death closes all; but something ere the end,
Some work of noble note, may yet be done,
Not unbecoming men that strove with gods.
The lights begin to twinkle from the rocks;
The long day wanes; the slow moon climbs; the deep   55
Moans round with many voices. Come, my friends,
'Tis not too late to seek a newer world.
Push off, and sitting well in order smite
The sounding furrows; for my purpose holds
To sail beyond the sunset, and the baths   60
Of all the western stars, until I die.
It may be that the gulfs will wash us down;
It may be we shall touch the Happy Isles,°
And see the great Achilles, whom we knew.
Though much is taken, much abides; and though   65
We are not now that strength which in old days
Moved earth and heaven, that which we are, we are,
One equal temper of heroic hearts,
Made weak by time and fate, but strong in will
To strive, to seek, to find, and not to yield.   70

                                                                        (1842)

The Eagle

FRAGMENT

He clasps the crag with crooked hands;
Close to the sun in lonely lands,
Ringed with the azure world, he stands.

The wrinkled sea beneath him crawls;
He watches from his mountain walls,   5
And like a thunderbolt he falls.

                                                                        (1851)

63**Happy Isles**   *the abode after death of those favored by the gods.*

ROBERT BROWNING
[1812–1889]

Soliloquy of the Spanish Cloister

1

Gr–r–r—there go, my heart's abhorrence!
    Water your damned flower-pots, do!
If hate killed men, Brother Lawrence,
    God's blood,° would not mine kill you!
What? your myrtle-bush wants trimming?   5
    Oh, that rose has prior claims—
Needs its leaden vase filled brimming?
    Hell dry you up with its flames!

2

At the meal we sit together:
    Salve tibi!° I must hear   10
Wise talk of the kind of weather,
    Sort of season, time of year:
Not a plenteous cork-crop: scarcely
    Dare we hope oak-galls,° *I doubt:*
What's the Latin name for "parsley"?   15
    What's the Greek name for Swine's Snout?

3

Whew! We'll have our platter burnished,
    Laid with care on our own shelf!
With a fire-new spoon we're furnished,
    And a goblet for ourself,   20
Rinsed like something sacrificial
    Ere 'tis fit to touch our chaps—
Marked with L for our initial!
    (He–he! There his lily snaps!)

4

Saint, forsooth! While brown Dolores   25
    Squats outside the Convent bank
With Sanchicha, telling stories,
    Steeping tresses in the tank,
Blue-black, lustrous, thick like horsehairs,

"Soliloquy of the Spanish Cloister"   [4]**God's blood** *an oath.*   [10]***Salve tibi*** *Hail to thee!*   [14]*oak-*
galls *growths produced on oak leaves by gallflies.*

—Can't I see his dead eye glow,   30
Bright as 'twere a Barbary corsair's?°
    (That is, if he'd let it show!)

5

When he finishes refection,°   dinner
    Knife and fork he never lays
Cross-wise, to my recollection,   35
    As do I, in Jesu's praise.
I the Trinity illustrate,
    Drinking watered orange-pulp—
In three sips the Arian° frustrate;
    While he drains his at one gulp.   40

6

Oh, those melons? If he's able
    We're to have a feast! so nice!
One goes to the Abbot's table,
    All of us get each a slice.
How go on your flowers? None double?   45
    Not one fruit-sort can you spy?
Strange! And I, too, at such trouble,
    Keep them close-nipped on the sly!

7

There's a great text in Galatians,°
    Once you trip on it, entails   50
Twenty-nine distinct damnations,
    One sure, if another fails:
If I trip him just a-dying,
    Sure of heaven as sure can be,
Spin him around and send him flying   55
    Off to hell, a Manichee?°

8

Or, my scrofulous French novel
    On grey paper with blunt type!
Simply glance at it, you grovel
    Hand and foot in Belial's gripe:°   60
If I double down its pages

"Soliloquy of the Spanish Cloister"   31*Barbary corsair's   pirate's.*   39*Arian   Arius, a fourth-century heretic, denied the doctrine of the Trinity.*   49*Galatians   a New Testament epistle of St. Paul; see chapter 5, 14–15 and 16–24.*   56*Manichee   the Manichean heresy divided the world into two equally powerful forces of darkness (evil) and light (good).*   60*Belial's gripe   in the devil's grip.*

At the woeful sixteenth print,
When he gathers his greengages,
  Ope a sieve and slip it in't?

9

Or, there's Satan! one might venture   65
  Pledge one's soul to him, yet leave
Such a flaw in the indenture
  As he'd miss till, past retrieve,
Blasted lay that rose-acacia
  We're so proud of! *Hy, Zy, Hine*° . . .   70
'St, there's vespers! *Plena gratiâ*°
Ave, Virgo!° Gr-r-r—you swine!

(1842)

WALT WHITMAN
[1819–1892]

A noiseless patient spider

A noiseless patient spider,
I mark'd where on a little promontory it stood isolated,
Mark'd how to explore the vacant vast surrounding,
It launch'd forth filament, filament, filament, out of itself,
Ever unreeling them, ever tirelessly speeding them.   5

And you O my soul where you stand,
Surrounded, detached, in measureless oceans of space,
Ceaselessly musing, venturing, throwing, seeking the spheres to connect them,
Till the bridge you will need be form'd, till the ductile anchor hold,
Till the gossamer thread you fling catch somewhere, O my soul.   10

(1881)

Crossing Brooklyn Ferry

1

Flood-tide below me! I see you face to face!
Clouds of the west—sun there half an hour high—I see you also face to face.
Crowds of men and women attired in the usual costumes, how curious you are to me!

---

[70] **Hy, Zy, Hine** *an incantation.*   [71] **Plena gratiâ** *Full of grace.*   [72] **Ave, Virgo** *Hail Virgin (reverses the opening words of the Ave Maria).*

On the ferry-boats the hundreds and hundreds that cross, returning home, are more
    curious to me than you suppose,
And you that shall cross from shore to shore years hence are more to me, and more
    in my meditations, than you might suppose.   5

2

The impalpable sustenance of me from all things at all hours of the day,
The simple, compact, well-join'd scheme, myself disintegrated, every one
    disintegrated yet part of the scheme,
The similitudes of the past and those of the future,
The glories strung like beads on my smallest sights and hearings, on the walk in the
    street and the passage over the river,
The current rushing so swiftly and swimming with me far away,   10
The others that are to follow me, the ties between me and them,
The certainty of others, the life, love, sight, hearing of others.
Others will enter the gates of the ferry and cross from shore to shore,
Others will watch the run of the flood-tide,
Others will see the shipping of Manhattan north and west, and the heights of
    Brooklyn to the south and east,   15
Others will see the islands large and small;
Fifty years hence, others will see them as they cross, the sun half an hour high,
A hundred years hence, or ever so many hundred years hence, others will see them,
Will enjoy the sunset, the pouring-in of the flood-tide, the falling-back to the sea of
    the ebb-tide.

3

It avails not, time nor place—distance avails not,   20
I am with you, you men and women of a generation, or ever so many generations
    hence,
Just as you feel when you look on the river and sky, so I felt,
Just as any of you is one of a living crowd, I was one of a crowd,
Just as you are refresh'd by the gladness of the river and the bright flow, I was
    refresh'd,
Just as you stand and lean on the rail, yet hurry with the swift current, I stood yet
    was hurried,   25
Just as you look on the numberless masts of ships and the thick-stemm'd pipes of
    steamboats, I look'd.

I too many and many a time cross'd the river of old,
Watched the Twelfth-month° sea-gulls, saw them high in the air floating   December
    with motionless wings, oscillating their bodies,
Saw how the glistening yellow lit up parts of their bodies and left the rest in strong
    shadow,
Saw the slow-wheeling circles and the gradual edging toward the south,   30
Saw the reflection of the summer sky in the water,

Had my eyes dazzled by the shimmering track of beams,
Look'd at the fine centrifugal spokes of light round the shape of my head in the
    sunlit water,
Look'd on the haze on the hills southward and south-westward,
Look'd on the vapor as it flew in fleeces tinged with violet,   35
Look'd toward the lower bay to notice the vessels arriving,
Saw their approach, saw aboard those that were near me,
Saw the white sails of schooners and sloops, saw the ships at anchor,
The sailors at work in the rigging or out astride the spars,
The round masts, the swinging motion of the hulls, the slender serpentine   40
    pennants,
The large and small steamers in motion, the pilots in their pilot-houses,
The white wake left by the passage, the quick tremulous whirl of the wheels,
The flags of all nations, the falling of them at sunset,
The scallop-edged waves in the twilight, the ladled cups, the frolicsome crests and
    glistening,
The stretch afar growing dimmer and dimmer, the gray walls of the granite
    storehouses by the docks,   45
On the river the shadowy group, the big steam-tug closely flank'd on each side by
    the barges, the hay-boat, the belated lighter,
On the neighboring shore the fires from the foundry chimneys burning high and
    glaringly into the night,
Casting their flicker of black contrasted with wild red and yellow light over the tops
    of houses, and down into the clefts of streets.

4

These and all else were to me the same as they are to you,
I loved well those cities, loved well the stately and rapid river,   50
The men and women I saw were all near to me,
Others the same—others who look back on me because I look'd forward to them,
(The time will come, though I stop° here to-day and to-night.)   stay

5

What is it then between us?
What is the count of the scores or hundreds of years between us?   55

Whatever it is, it avails not—distance avails not, and place avails not,
I too lived, Brooklyn of ample hills was mine,
I too walk'd the streets of Manhattan island, and bathed in the waters around it,
I too felt the curious abrupt questionings stir within me,
In the day among crowds of people sometimes they came upon me,   60
In my walks home late at night or as I lay in my bed they came upon me,
I too had been struck from the float forever held in solution,
I too had receiv'd identity by my body,
That I was I knew was of my body, and what I should be I knew I should be of my
    body.

6

It is not upon you alone the dark patches fall,   65
The dark threw its patches down upon me also,
The best I had done seem'd to me blank and suspicious,
My great thoughts as I supposed them, were they not in reality meager?
Nor is it you alone who know what it is to be evil,
I am he who knew what it was to be evil,   70
I too knitted the old knot of contrariety,
Blabb'd, blush'd, resented, lied, stole, grudg'd,
Had guile, anger, lust, hot wishes I dared not speak,
Was wayward, vain, greedy, shallow, sly, cowardly, malignant,
The wolf, the snake, the hog, not wanting in me,   75
The cheating look, the frivolous word, the adulterous wish, not wanting,
Refusals, hates, postponements, meanness, laziness, none of these wanting,
Was one with the rest, the days and haps of the rest,
Was call'd by my nighest name by clear loud voices of young men as they saw me
      approaching or passing,
Felt their arms on my neck as I stood, or the negligent leaning of their flesh against
      me as I sat,   80
Saw many I loved in the street or ferry-boat or public assembly, yet never told them
      a word,
Lived the same life with the rest, the same old laughing, gnawing, sleeping,
Play'd the part that still looks back on the actor or actress,
The same old role, the role that is what we make it, as great as we like,
Or as small as we like, or both great and small.   85

7

Closer yet I approach you,
What thought you have of me now, I had as much of you—I laid in my stores in
      advance,
I consider'd long and seriously of you before you were born.

Who was to know what should come home to me?
Who knows but I am enjoying this?   90
Who knows, for all the distance, but I am as good as looking at you now, for all you
      cannot see me?

8

Ah, what can ever be more stately and admirable to me than mast-hemm'd
      Manhattan?
River and sunset and scallop-edg'd waves of flood-tide?
The sea-gulls oscillating their bodies, the hay-boat in the twilight, and the belated
      lighter?
What gods can exceed these that clasp me by the hand, and with voices I love call
      me promptly and loudly by my nighest name as I approach?   95

What is more subtle than this which ties me to the woman or man that looks in my
    face?
Which fuses me into you now, and pours my meaning into you?

We understand then do we not?
What I promis'd without mentioning it, have you not accepted?
What the study could not teach—what the preaching could not accomplish is
    accomplish'd, is it not?   100

9

Flow on, river! flow with the flood-tide, and ebb with the ebb-tide!
Frolic on, crested and scallop-edg'd waves!
Gorgeous clouds of the sunset! drench with your splendor me, or the men and
    women generations after me!
Cross from shore to shore, countless crowds of passengers!
Stand up, tall masts of Manhattan! stand up, beautiful hills of Brooklyn!   105
Throb, baffled and curious brain! throw out questions and answers!
Suspend here and everywhere, eternal float of solution!
Gaze, loving and thirsting eyes, in the house or street or public assembly!
Sound out, voices of young men! loudly and musically call me by my nighest name!
Live, old life! play the part that looks back on the actor or actress!   110
Play the old role, the role that is great or small according as one makes it!
Consider, you who peruse me, whether I may not in unknown ways be looking
    upon you;
Be firm, rail over the river, to support those who lean idly, yet haste with the hasting
    current;
Fly on, sea birds! fly sideways, or wheel in large circles high in the air;
Receive the summer sky, you water, and faithfully hold it till all downcast eyes have
    time to take it from you!   115
Diverge, fine spokes of light, from the shape of my head, or any one's head, in the
    sunlit water!
Come on, ships from the lower bay! pass up or down, white-sail'd schooners, sloops,
    lighters!
Flaunt away, flags of all nations! be duly lower'd at sunset!
Burn high your fires, foundry chimneys! cast black shadows at nightfall! cast red and
    yellow light over the tops of the houses!
Appearances, now or henceforth, indicate what you are,   120
You necessary film, continue to envelop the soul,
About my body for me, and your body for you, be hung our divinest aromas,
Thrive, cities—bring your freight, bring your shows, ample and sufficient rivers,
Expand, being than which none else is perhaps more spiritual,
Keep your places, objects than which none else is more lasting.   125

You have waited, you always wait, you dumb, beautiful ministers,
We receive you with free sense at last, and are insatiate henceforward,
Not you any more shall be able to foil us, or withhold yourselves from us,

We use you, and do not cast you aside—we plant you permanently within us,
We fathom you not—we love you—there is perfection in you also,   130
You furnish your parts toward eternity,
Great or small, you furnish your parts toward the soul.

                                                                (1856)

MATTHEW ARNOLD
[1822–1888]

Dover Beach

The sea is calm tonight.
The tide is full, the moon lies fair
Upon the straits; on the French coast the light
Gleams and is gone; the cliffs of England stand,
Glimmering and vast, out in the tranquil bay.   5
Come to the window, sweet is the night-air!
Only, from the long line of spray
Where the sea meets the moon-blanched land,
Listen! you hear the grating roar
Of pebbles which the waves draw back, and fling,   10
At their return, up the high strand,
Begin, and cease, and then again begin,
With tremulous cadence slow, and bring
The eternal note of sadness in.

Sophocles long ago   15
Heard it on the Aegean,° and it brought
Into his mind the turbid ebb and flow
Of human misery; we
Find also in the sound a thought,
Hearing it by this distant northern sea.   20

The Sea of Faith
Was once, too, at the full, and round earth's shore
Lay like the folds of a bright girdle furled.
But now I only hear
Its melancholy, long, withdrawing roar,   25
Retreating, to the breath
Of the night-wind, down the vast edges drear
And naked shingles of the world.

"Dover Beach"   ¹⁶*Aegean*   *See Sophocles,* Antigone, *ll. 732–736 in* Literature: Reading Fiction, Poetry, and Drama, Compact Edition.

Ah, love, let us be true
To one another! for the world, which seems   30
To lie before us like a land of dreams,
So various, so beautiful, so new,
Hath really neither joy, nor love, nor light,
Nor certitude, nor peace, nor help for pain;
And we are here as on a darkling plain   35
Swept with confused alarms of struggle and flight,
Where ignorant armies clash by night.

LEWIS CARROLL (CHARLES LUTWIDGE DODGSON)
[1832–1898]

Jabberwocky

'Twas brillig, and the slithy toves
   Did gyre and gimble in the wabe:
All mimsy were the borogoves,
   And the mome raths outgrabe.

"Beware the Jabberwock, my son!   5
   The jaws that bite, the claws that catch!
Beware the Jubjub bird, and shun
   The frumious Bandersnatch!"

He took his vorpal sword in hand:
   Long time the manxome foe he sought—   10
So rested he by the Tumtum tree,
   And stood awhile in thought.

And, as in uffish thought he stood,
   The Jabberwock, with eyes of flame,
Came whiffling through the tulgey wood,   15
   And burbled as it came!

One, two! One, two! And through and through
   The vorpal blade went snicker-snack!
He left it dead, and with its head
   He went galumphing back.   20

"And hast thou slain the Jabberwock?
   Come to my arms, my beamish boy!
O frabjous day! Callooh! Callay!"
   He chortled in his joy.

'Twas brillig, and the slithy toves   25
    Did gyre and gimble in the wabe:
All mimsy were the borogoves,
    And the mome raths outgrabe.

(1871)

THOMAS HARDY
[*1840–1928*]

The Ruined Maid

"O'Melia, my dear, this does everything crown!
Who could have supposed I should meet you in Town?
And whence such fair garments, such prosperi-ty?"
"O didn't you know I'd been ruined?" said she.

"You left us in tatters, without shoes or socks,   5
Tired of digging potatoes, and spudding up docks;
And now you've gay bracelets and bright feathers three!"
"Yes: that's how we dress when we're ruined," said she.

"At home in the barton° you said 'thee' and 'thou,'   farm
And 'thik oon,' and 'theäs oon,' and 't'other'; but now   10
Your talking quite fits 'ee for high compa-ny!"
"Some polish is gained with one's ruin," said she.

"Your hands were like paws then, your face blue and bleak
But now I'm bewitched by your delicate cheek,
And your little gloves fit as on any la-dy!"   15
"We never do work when we're ruined," said she.

"You used to call home–life a hag-ridden dream,
And you'd sigh, and you'd sock; but at present you seem
To know not of megrims° or melancho-ly!"   low spirits
"True. One's pretty lively when ruined," said she.   20

"I wish I had feathers, a fine sweeping gown,
And a delicate face, and could strut about Town!"
"My dear—a raw country girl, such as you be,
Cannot quite expect that. You ain't ruined," said she.

(1898)

Channel Firing

That night your great guns, unawares,
Shook all our coffins as we lay,
And broke the chancel window-squares,
We thought it was the Judgment-day

And sat upright. While drearisome   5
Arose the howl of wakened hounds:
The mouse let fall the altar-crumb,
The worms drew back into the mounds,

The glebe° cow drooled. Till God called, "No;   small field
It's gunnery practice out at sea   10
Just as before you went below;
The world is as it used to be:

"All nations striving strong to make
Red war yet redder. Mad as hatters
They do no more for Christés sake   15
Than you who are helpless in such matters.

"That this is not the judgment-hour
For some of them's a blessed thing,
For if it were they'd have to scour
Hell's floor for so much threatening. . . .   20

"Ha, ha. It will be warmer when
I blow the trumpet (if indeed
I ever do; for you are men,
And rest eternal sorely need)."

So down we lay again. "I wonder,   25
Will the world ever saner be,"
Said one, "than when He sent us under
In our indifferent century!"

And many a skeleton shook his head.
"Instead of preaching forty year,"   30
My neighbor Parson Thirdly said,
"I wish I had stuck to pipes and beer."

Again the guns disturbed the hour,
Roaring their readiness to avenge,
As far inland as Stourton Tower,   35
And Camelot, and starlit Stonehenge.°

(1914)

"Channel Firing" ³⁶**Stonehenge** *a circular grouping of stone monuments near Salisbury, England, dating back to the Bronze Age.*

Afterwards

When the Present has latched its postern° behind my tremulous stay,
    And the May month flaps its glad green leaves like wings,
Delicate-filmed as new-spun silk, will the neighbours say,
    "He was a man who used to notice such things"?

If it be in the dusk when, like an eyelid's soundless blink,   5
    The dewfall-hawk comes crossing the shades to alight
Upon the wind-warped upland thorn, a gazer may think,
    "To him this must have been a familiar sight."

If I pass during some nocturnal blackness, mothy, and warm,
    When the hedgehog travels furtively over the lawn,   10
One may say, "He strove that such innocent creatures should come to no harm,
    But he could do little for them; and now he is gone."

If, when hearing that I have been stilled at last, they stand at the door,
    Watching the full-starred heavens that winter sees,
Will this thought rise on those who will meet my face no more,   15
    "He was one who had an eye for such mysteries"?

And will any say when my bell of quittance° is heard in the gloom
    And a crossing breeze cuts a pause in its outrollings,
Till they rise again, as they were a new bell's boom,
    "He hears it not now, but used to notice such things"?   20

(1928)

GERARD MANLEY HOPKINS
[1844–1889]

God's Grandeur

The world is charged with the grandeur of God.
    It will flame out, like shining from shook foil;°
    It gathers to a greatness, like the ooze of oil
Crushed.° Why do men then now not reck his rod?
Generations have trod, have trod, have trod;   5
    And all is seared with trade; bleared, smeared with toil;
    And wears man's smudge and shares man's smell: the soil
Is bare now, nor can foot feel, being shod.

"Afterwards" ¹**postern** *gate.*   ¹⁷**bell of quittance** *death bell.*   "God's Grandeur" ²**foil** *gold or tinsel foil.*   ⁴**Crushed** *as when olives are crushed for their oil.*

And for all this, nature is never spent;
    There lives the dearest freshness deep down things;   10
And though the last lights off the black West went
    Oh, morning, at the brown brink eastward, springs—
Because the Holy Ghost over the bent
    World broods with warm breast and with ah! bright wings.

(1877, 1895)

The Windhover°

TO CHRIST OUR LORD

I caught this morning morning's minion,° king-   *darling*
   dom of daylight's dauphin,° dapple-dawn-drawn Falcon, in his   *prince*
      riding
   Of the rolling level underneath him steady air, and striding
High there, how he rung upon the rein of a wimpling° wing   *rippling*
In his ecstasy! then off, off forth on swing,   5
   As a skate's heel sweeps smooth on a bow-bend: the hurl and gliding
   Rebuffed the big wind. My heart in hiding
Stirred for a bird,—the achieve of, the mastery of the thing!

Brute beauty and valour and act, oh, air, pride, plume, here
   Buckle! AND the fire that breaks from thee then, a billion
Times told lovelier, more dangerous, O my chevalier!°   *knight* 10

   No wonder of it: shéer plód makes plough down sillion°   *furrow*
Shine, and blue-bleak embers, ah my dear,
   Fall, gall themselves, and gash gold-vermilion.

(1877, 1918)

Pied° Beauty   *variegated*

Glory be to God for dappled things—
   For skies of couple-colour as a brinded° cow;   *brindled, streaked*
     For rose-moles all in stipple upon trout that swim;
Fresh-firecoal chestnut-falls°; finches' wings;
   Landscape plotted and pieced—fold, fallow, and plough;   5
    And áll trádes, their gear and tackle and trim.°   *equipment*
All things counter, original, spare,° strange;   *unusual*
   Whatever is fickle, freckled (who knows how?)
    With swift, slow; sweet, sour; adazzle, dim;
He fathers-forth whose beauty is past change: 10
                 Praise him.

(1877, 1918)

"The Windhover"   *a kestrel, a kind of falcon.*   "Pied Beauty"   [4]**chestnut-falls** *roasted chestnuts stripped of their husks.*

Spring and Fall:
to a Young Child

Márgarét, áre you grieving
Over Goldengrove unleaving?
Leáves, like the things of man, you
With your fresh thoughts care for, can you?
Áh! ás the heart grows older   5
It will come to such sights colder
By and by, nor spare a sigh
Though worlds of wanwood leafmeal lie;
And yet you *will* weep and know why
Now no matter, child, the name: 10
Sórrow's spríngs áre the same.
Nor mouth had, no nor mind, expressed
What heart heard of, ghost guessed:
It ís the blight man was born for,
It is Márgarét you mourn for.   15

A. E. HOUSMAN
[1859–1936]

When I was one-and-twenty

When I was one-and-twenty
    I heard a wise man say,
'Give crowns and pounds and guineas
    But not your heart away;
Give pearls away and rubies   5
    But keep your fancy free.'
But I was one-and-twenty,
    No use to talk to me.

When I was one-and-twenty
    I heard him say again,   10
'The heart out of the bosom
    Was never given in vain;
'Tis paid with sighs a plenty
    And sold for endless rue.'
And I am two-and-twenty,   15
    And oh, 'tis true, 'tis true.

(1896)

To an Athlete Dying Young

The time you won your town the race
We chaired you through the market-place;
Man and boy stood cheering by,
And home we brought you shoulder-high.

To-day, the road all runners come,   5
Shoulder-high we bring you home,
And set you at your threshold down,
Townsman of a stiller town.

Smart lad, to slip betimes away
From fields where glory does not stay   10
And early though the laurel grows
It withers quicker than the rose.

Eyes the shady night has shut
Cannot see the record cut,
And silence sounds no worse than cheers   15
After earth has stopped the ears:

Now you will not swell the rout
Of lads that wore their honours out,
Runners whom renown outran
And the name died before the man.   20

So set, before its echoes fade,
The fleet foot on the sill of shade,
And hold to the low lintel up
The still-defended challenge-cup.

And round that early-laurelled head   25
Will flock to gaze the strengthless dead
And find unwithered on its curls
The garland briefer than a girl's.

(1896)

WILLIAM BUTLER YEATS
[1865–1939]

The Second Coming°

Turning and turning in the widening gyre°   spiral
The falcon cannot hear the falconer;
Things fall apart; the center cannot hold;
Mere anarchy is loosed upon the world,
The blood-dimmed tide is loosed, and everywhere   5
The ceremony of innocence is drowned;
The best lack all conviction, while the worst
Are full of passionate intensity.

Surely some revelation is at hand;
Surely the Second Coming is at hand;   10
The Second Coming! Hardly are those words out
When a vast image out of *Spiritus Mundi*°
Troubles my sight: somewhere in sands of the desert
A shape with lion body and the head of a man,
A gaze blank and pitiless as the sun,   15
Is moving its slow thighs, while all about it
Reel shadows of the indignant desert birds.
The darkness drops again; but now I know
That twenty centuries of stony sleep
Were vexed to nightmare by a rocking cradle,   20
And what rough beast, its hour come round at last,
Slouches towards Bethlehem to be born?

                                                                   (1921)

The Wild Swans at Coole

The trees are in their autumn beauty,
The woodland paths are dry,
Under the October twilight the water
Mirrors a still sky;
Upon the brimming water among the stones   5
Are nine-and-fifty swans.

The nineteenth autumn has come upon me
Since I first made my count;
I saw, before I had well finished,
All suddenly mount   10

"The Second Coming"   *the title alludes to the prophesied return of Jesus Christ and also to the beast of the*
Apocalypse. See Matthew 24 and Revelation.   [12]*Spiritus Mundi   for Yeats, a common storehouse of images, a*
communal human memory.

And scatter wheeling in great broken rings
Upon their clamorous wings.

I have looked upon those brilliant creatures,
And now my heart is sore.
All's changed since I, hearing at twilight,   15
The first time on this shore,
The bell-beat of their wings above my head,
Trod with a lighter tread.

Unwearied still, lover by lover,
They paddle in the cold   20
Companionable streams or climb the air;
Their hearts have not grown old;
Passion or conquest, wander where they will,
Attend upon them still.

But now they drift on the still water,   25
Mysterious, beautiful;
Among what rushes will they build,
By what lake's edge or pool
Delight men's eyes when I awake some day
To find they have flown away?   30

(1917)

Leda and the Swan°

A sudden blow: the great wings beating still
Above the staggering girl, her thighs caressed
By the dark webs, her nape caught in his bill,
He holds her helpless breast upon his breast.

How can those terrified vague fingers push   5
The feathered glory from her loosening thighs?
And how can body, laid in that white rush,
But feel the strange heart beating where it lies?

A shudder in the loins engenders there
The broken wall, the burning roof and tower   10
And Agamemnon dead.
                              Being so caught up,
So mastered by the brute blood of the air,
Did she put on his knowledge with his power
Before the indifferent beak could let her drop?   15

(1928)

"Leda and the Swan"   *Zeus, in the guise of a swan, raped Leda, Queen of Sparta. Helen, their daughter, married Menelaus, King of Sparta, but ran off with Paris, son of Priam, King of Troy. A ten-year siege of Troy by the Greeks ensued to bring Helen back.*

Sailing to Byzantium°

1

That is no country for old men. The young
In one another's arms, birds in the trees
—Those dying generations—at their song,
The salmon-falls, the mackerel-crowded seas,
Fish, flesh, or fowl, commend all summer long   5
Whatever is begotten, born, and dies.
Caught in that sensual music all neglect
Monuments of unaging intellect.

2

An aged man is but a paltry thing,
A tattered coat upon a stick, unless   10
Soul clap its hands and sing, and louder sing
For every tatter in its mortal dress,
Nor is there singing school but studying
Monuments of its own magnificence;
And therefore I have sailed the seas and come   15
To the holy city of Byzantium.

3

O sages standing in God's holy fire
As in the gold mosaic of a wall,
Come from the holy fire, perne° in a gyre,°   descend/spiral
And be the singing-masters of my soul.   20
Consume my heart away; sick with desire
And fastened to a dying animal
It knows not what it is; and gather me
Into the artifice of eternity.

4

Once out of nature I shall never take   25
My bodily form from any natural thing,
But such a form as Grecian goldsmiths make
Of hammered gold and gold enameling
To keep a drowsy Emperor awake;
Or set upon a golden bough to sing   30
To lords and ladies of Byzantium
Of what is past, or passing, or to come.

(1927)

"Sailing to Byzantium"   *Byzantium was the capital of the eastern Roman Empire and an important center of art and architecture.*

EDWIN ARLINGTON ROBINSON
[1869–1935]

Richard Cory

Whenever Richard Cory went down town,
We people on the pavement looked at him:
He was a gentleman from sole to crown,
Clean favored and imperially slim.

And he was always quietly arrayed,   5
And he was always human when he talked;
But still he fluttered pulses when he said,
"Good-morning," and he glittered when he walked.

And he was rich—yes, richer than a king—
And admirably schooled in every grace: 10
In fine, we thought that he was everything
To make us wish that we were in his place.

So on we worked, and waited for the light,
And went without the meat and cursed the bread;
And Richard Cory, one calm summer night,   15
Went home and put a bullet through his head.

PAUL LAURENCE DUNBAR
[1872–1906]

We wear the mask

We wear the mask that grins and lies,
It hides our cheeks and shades our eyes—
This debt we pay to human guile;
With torn and bleeding hearts we smile,
And mouth with myriad subtleties.   5

Why should the world be over-wise,
In counting all our tears and sighs?
Nay, let them only see us, while
     We wear the mask.

We smile, but, O great Christ, our cries
To thee from tortured souls arise.   10
We sing, but oh the clay is vile
Beneath our feet, and long the mile;
But let the world dream otherwise,
    We wear the mask!

                                                    (1896)

WALLACE STEVENS
[1879–1955]

Thirteen Ways of Looking at a Blackbird

1

Among twenty snowy mountains,
The only moving thing
Was the eye of the blackbird.

2

I was of three minds,
Like a tree   5
In which there are three blackbirds.

3

The blackbird whirled in the autumn winds.
It was a small part of the pantomime.

4

A man and a woman
Are one.   10
A man and a woman and a blackbird
Are one.

5

I do not know which to prefer,
The beauty of inflections
Or the beauty of innuendoes,   15
The blackbird whistling
Or just after.

6

Icicles filled the long window
With barbaric glass.
The shadow of the blackbird   20
Crossed it to and fro.
The mood
Traced in the shadow
An indecipherable cause.

7

O thin men of Haddam,   25
Why do you imagine golden birds?
Do you not see how the blackbird
Walks around the feet
Of the women about you?

8

I know noble accents   30
And lucid, inescapable rhythms;
But I know, too,
That the blackbird is involved
In what I know.

9

When the blackbird flew out of sight,   35
It marked the edge
Of one of many circles.

10

At the sight of blackbirds
Flying in a green light,
Even the bawds of euphony   40
Would cry out sharply.

11

He rode over Connecticut
In a glass coach.
Once, a fear pierced him,
In that he mistook   45
The shadow of his equipage
For blackbirds.

12

The river is moving.
The blackbird must be flying.

13

It was evening all afternoon.   50
It was snowing
And it was going to snow.
The blackbird sat
In the cedar-limbs.

(1923)

WILLIAM CARLOS WILLIAMS
[1883–1963]

Spring and All

By the road to the contagious hospital
under the surge of the blue
mottled clouds driven from the
northeast—a cold wind. Beyond, the
waste of broad, muddy fields   5
brown with dried weeds, standing and fallen
patches of standing water
the scattering of tall trees

All along the road the reddish
purplish, forked, upstanding, twiggy   10
stuff of bushes and small trees
with dead, brown leaves under them
leafless vines—

Lifeless in appearance, sluggish
dazed spring approaches—   15

They enter the new world naked,
cold, uncertain of all
save that they enter. All about them
the cold, familiar wind—

Now the grass, tomorrow   20
the stiff curl of wildcarrot leaf
One by one objects are defined—
It quickens: clarity, outline of leaf

But now the stark dignity of
entrance—Still, the profound change   25
has come upon them: rooted, they
grip down and begin to awaken

(1923)

Danse Russe

If when my wife is sleeping
and the baby and Kathleen
are sleeping
and the sun is a flame-white disc
in silken mists   5
above shining trees,—
if I in my north room
dance naked, grotesquely
before my mirror
waving my shirt round my head   10
and singing softly to myself:
"I am lonely, lonely.
I was born to be lonely,
I am best so!"
If I admire my arms, my face,   15
my shoulders, flanks, buttocks
against the yellow drawn shades,—

Who shall say I am not
the happy genius of my household?

(1917)

EZRA POUND
[1885–1972]

The River-Merchant's Wife: A Letter°

While my hair was still cut straight across my forehead
Played I about the front gate, pulling flowers.
You came by on bamboo stilts, playing horse,
You walked about my seat, playing with blue plums.
And we went on living in the village of Chōkan: 5
Two small people, without dislike or suspicion.

"The River-Merchant's Wife"   *Pound translated and adapted this poem from the Chinese. Rihaku is the Japanese name for the Chinese poet, Li T'ai Po, who wrote the poem that Pound adapted.*

At fourteen I married My Lord you.
I never laughed, being bashful.
Lowering my head, I looked at the wall.
Called to, a thousand times, I never looked back.   10

At fifteen I stopped scowling,
I desired my dust to be mingled with yours
Forever and forever and forever.
Why should I climb the look out?

At sixteen you departed,   15
You went into far Ku-tō-en, by the river of swirling eddies,
And you have been gone five months.
The monkeys make sorrowful noise overhead.

You dragged your feet when you went out.
By the gate now, the moss is grown, the different mosses,   20
Too deep to clear them away!
The leaves fall early this autumn, in wind.
The paired butterflies are already yellow with August

Over the grass in the West garden;
They hurt me. I grow older.   25
If you are coming down through the narrows of the river Kiang,
Please let me know before hand,
And I will come out to meet you
                    As far as Chō-fū-Sa.

                    by Rihaku

                                                              (1916)

MARIANNE MOORE
[1887–1972]

Poetry

I, too, dislike it: there are things that are important beyond all this fiddle.
    Reading it, however, with a perfect contempt for it, one discovers in
    it after all, a place for the genuine.
        Hands that can grasp, eyes
        that can dilate, hair that can rise   5
            if it must, these things are important not because a

high-sounding interpretation can be put upon them but because they are
  useful. When they become so derivative as to become unintelligible,
  the same thing may be said for all of us, that we
    do not admire what   10
    we cannot understand: the bat
      holding on upside down or in quest of something to

eat, elephants pushing, a wild horse taking a roll, a tireless wolf under
  a tree, the immovable critic twitching his skin like a horse that feels
    a flea, the base-
  ball fan, the statistician—   15
    nor is it valid
      to discriminate against "business documents and

school-books"; all these phenomena are important. One must make a distinction
  however: when dragged into prominence by half poets, the result is not poetry,
  nor till the poets among us can be   20
    "literalists of
    the imagination"—above
      insolence and triviality and can present

for inspection, "imaginary gardens with real toads in them," shall we have
  it. In the meantime, if you demand on the one hand,   25
  the raw material of poetry in
    all its rawness and
    that which is on the other hand
      genuine, you are interested in poetry.

(1921)

T. S. ELIOT
[1888–1965]

The Love Song of J. Alfred Prufrock

S'io credesse che mia risposta fosse
A persona che mai tornasse al mondo,
Questa fiamma staria senza più scosse.
Ma perciocche giammai di questo fondo
Non tornò vivo alcun, s'i'odo il vero,
Senza tema d'infamia ti rispondo.°

"The Love Song of J. Alfred Prufrock" *epigraph from Dante's Inferno, canto XXVII, 61–66. The words are spoken by Guido da Montefeltro when asked to identify himself: "If I thought my answer were given to anyone who could ever return to the world, this flame would shake no more; but since none ever did return above from this depth, if what I hear is true, without fear of infamy I answer thee."*

Let us go then, you and I,
When the evening is spread out against the sky
Like a patient etherized upon a table;
Let us go, through certain half-deserted streets,
The muttering retreats   5
Of restless nights in one-night cheap hotels
And sawdust restaurants with oyster-shells:
Streets that follow like a tedious argument
Of insidious intent
To lead you to an overwhelming question . . .   10
Oh, do not ask, "What is it?"
Let us go and make our visit.

In the room the women come and go
Talking of Michelangelo.

The yellow fog that rubs its back upon the window-panes   15
The yellow smoke that rubs its muzzle on the window-panes
Licked its tongue into the corners of the evening,
Lingered upon the pools that stand in drains,
Let fall upon its back the soot that falls from chimneys,
Slipped by the terrace, made a sudden leap,   20
And seeing that it was a soft October night,
Curled once about the house, and fell asleep.

And indeed there will be time
For the yellow smoke that slides along the street,
Rubbing its back upon the window-panes;   25
There will be time, there will be time
To prepare a face to meet the faces that you meet;
There will be time to murder and create,
And time for all the works and days of hands
That lift and drop a question on your plate;   30
Time for you and time for me,
And time yet for a hundred indecisions,
And for a hundred visions and revisions,
Before the taking of a toast and tea.

In the room the women come and go   35
Talking of Michelangelo.

And indeed there will be time
To wonder, "Do I dare?" and, "Do I dare?"
Time to turn back and descend the stair,
With a bald spot in the middle of my hair—   40
(They will say: "How his hair is growing thin!")
My morning coat, my collar mounting firmly to the chin,
My necktie rich and modest, but asserted by a simple pin—

(They will say: "But how his arms and legs are thin!")
Do I dare 45
Disturb the universe?
In a minute there is time
For decisions and revisions which a minute will reverse.

For I have known them all already, known them all:
Have known the evenings, mornings, afternoons, 50
I have measured out my life with coffee spoons;
I know the voices dying with a dying fall
Beneath the music from a farther room.
　　So how should I presume?

And I have known the eyes already, known them all— 55
The eyes that fix you in a formulated phrase,
And when I am formulated, sprawling on a pin,
When I am pinned and wriggling on the wall,
Then how should I begin
To spit out all the butt-ends of my days and ways? 60
　　And how should I presume?

And I have known the arms already, known them all—
Arms that are braceleted and white and bare
(But in the lamplight, downed with light brown hair!)
Is it perfume from a dress 65
That makes me so digress?
Arms that lie along a table, or wrap about a shawl.
　　And should I then presume?
　　And how should I begin?

Shall I say, I have gone at dusk through narrow streets 70
And watched the smoke that rises from the pipes
Of lonely men in shirt-sleeves, leaning out of windows? . . .

I should have been a pair of ragged claws
Scuttling across the floors of silent seas.
　　　　　　. . . . .
And the afternoon, the evening, sleeps so peacefully! 75
Smoothed by long fingers,
Asleep . . . tired . . . or it malingers,
Stretched on the floor, here beside you and me.
Should I, after tea and cakes and ices,
Have the strength to force the moment to its crisis? 80
But though I have wept and fasted, wept and prayed,
Though I have seen my head (grown slightly bald) brought in upon a platter,°

---

⁸²**head . . . platter**　*John the Baptist was beheaded at the order of King Herod to please his wife and daughter. See Matthew 14:1–11.*

I am no prophet—and here's no great matter;
I have seen the moment of my greatness flicker,
And I have seen the eternal Footman hold my coat, and snicker,   85
And in short, I was afraid.

And would it have been worth it, after all,
After the cups, the marmalade, the tea,
Among the porcelain, among some talk of you and me,
Would it have been worth while,   90
To have bitten off the matter with a smile,
To have squeezed the universe into a ball
To roll it toward some overwhelming question,
To say: "I am Lazarus,° come from the dead,
Come back to tell you all, I shall tell you all"—   95
If one, settling a pillow by her head,
   Should say: "That is not what I meant at all.
   That is not it, at all."

And would it have been worth it, after all,
Would it have been worth while,   100
After the sunsets and the dooryards and the sprinkled streets,
After the novels, after the teacups, after the skirts that trail along the floor—
And this, and so much more?—
It is impossible to say just what I mean!
But as if a magic lantern threw the nerves in patterns on a screen: 105
Would it have been worth while
If one, settling a pillow or throwing off a shawl,
And turning toward the window, should say:
   "That is not it at all,
   That is not what I meant, at all."   110
     . . . . .

No! I am not Prince Hamlet, nor was meant to be;
Am an attendant lord, one that will do
To swell a progress, start a scene or two,
Advise the prince; no doubt, an easy tool,
Deferential, glad to be of use,   115
Politic, cautious, and meticulous;
Full of high sentence,° but a bit obtuse;   sententiousness
At times, indeed, almost ridiculous—
Almost, at times, the Fool.

I grow old . . . I grow old . . .   120
I shall wear the bottoms of my trousers rolled.

Shall I part my hair behind? Do I dare to eat a peach?

[94]*Lazarus* *Jesus raised him from the dead. See John 11:1–44.*

I shall wear white flannel trousers, and walk upon the beach.
I have heard the mermaids singing, each to each.

I do not think that they will sing to me. 125

I have seen them riding seaward on the waves
Combing the white hair of the waves blown back
When the wind blows the water white and black.
We have lingered in the chambers of the sea
By sea-girls wreathed with seaweed red and brown 130
Till human voices wake us, and we drown.

(1917)

JOHN CROWE RANSOM
[1888–1974]

Piazza Piece

—I am a gentleman in a dustcoat trying
To make you hear. Your ears are soft and small
And listen to an old man not at all,
They want the young men's whispering and sighing.
But see the roses on your trellis dying 5
And hear the spectral singing of the moon;
For I must have my lovely lady soon,
I am a gentleman in a dustcoat trying.

—I am a lady young in beauty waiting
Until my truelove comes, and then we kiss. 10
But what grey man among the vines is this
Whose words are dry and faint as in a dream?
Back from my trellis, Sir, before I scream!
I am a lady young in beauty waiting.

(1927)

VICENTE HUIDOBRO
[1892–1948]

Ars Poetica°   The art of poetry

Let poetry be like a key
Opening a thousand doors.
A leaf falls; something flies by;

Let all the eye sees be created
And the soul of the listener tremble.   5

Invent new worlds and watch your word;
The adjective, when it doesn't give life, kills it.
We are in the age of nerves.
The muscle hangs,
Like a memory, in museums;   10
But we are not the weaker for it:
True vigor
Resides in the head.

Oh Poets, why sing of roses!
Let them flower in your poems;   15

For us alone
Do all things live beneath the Sun.

The poet is a little God.

TRANSLATED BY DAVID M. GUSS

(1932)

ARCHIBALD MACLEISH
[1892–1982]

Ars Poetica

A poem should be palpable and mute
As a globed fruit,

Dumb
As old medallions to the thumb,

Silent as the sleeve-worn stone   5
Of casement ledges where the moss has grown—

A poem should be wordless
As the flight of birds.

A poem should be motionless in time
As the moon climbs,   10

Leaving, as the moon releases
Twig by twig the night-entangled trees,

Leaving, as the moon behind the winter leaves,
Memory by memory the mind—

A poem should be motionless in time   15
As the moon climbs.

A poem should be equal to:
Not true.

For all the history of grief
An empty doorway and a maple leaf.   20

For love
The leaning grasses and two lights above the sea—

A poem should not mean
But be.

(1926)

WILFRED   OWEN
[1893–1918]

Dulce et Decorum Est°

Bent double, like old beggars under sacks,
Knock-kneed, coughing like hags, we cursed through sludge,
Till on the haunting flares we turned our backs
And towards our distant rest began to trudge.
Men marched asleep. Many had lost their boots   5
But limped on, blood-shod. All went lame; all blind;
Drunk with fatigue; deaf even to the hoots
Of tired, outstripped Five-Nines that dropped behind.

Gas! GAS! Quick, boys!—An ecstasy of fumbling,
Fitting the clumsy helmets just in time;   10
But someone still was yelling out and stumbling
And flound'ring like a man in fire or lime . . .
Dim, through the misty panes and thick green light,
As under a green sea, I saw him drowning.

"Dulce et Decorum Est"   *"It is sweet and fitting to die for one's country." See the last two lines, which are from*
Horace, Odes, *III, ii. 13.*

In all my dreams, before my helpless sight,   15
He plunges at me, guttering, choking, drowning.
If in some smothering dreams you too could pace
Behind the wagon that we flung him in,
And watch the white eyes writhing in his face,
His hanging face, like a devil's sick of sin;   20
If you could hear, at every jolt, the blood
Come gargling from the froth-corrupted lungs,
Obscene as cancer, bitter as the cud
Of vile, incurable sores on innocent tongues,—
My friend, you would not tell with such high zest   25
To children ardent for some desperate glory,
The old Lie: *Dulce et decorum est*
Pro patria mori.

(1920)

E. E. CUMMINGS
[1894–1962]

anyone lived in a pretty how town

anyone lived in a pretty how town
(with up so floating many bells down)
spring summer autumn winter
he sang his didn't he danced his did.

Women and men(both little and small)   5
cared for anyone not at all
they sowed their isn't they reaped their same
sun moon stars rain

children guessed(but only a few
and down they forgot as up they grew   10
autumn winter spring summer)
that noone loved him more by more

when by now and tree by leaf
she laughed his joy she cried his grief
bird by snow and stir by still   15
anyone's any was all to her

someones married their everyones
laughed their cryings and did their dance

(sleep wake hope and then)they
said their nevers they slept their dream 20

stars rain sun moon
(and only the snow can begin to explain
how children are apt to forget to remember
with up so floating many bells down)

one day anyone died i guess 25
(and noone stooped to kiss his face)
busy folk buried them side by side
little by little and was by was

all by all and deep by deep
and more by more they dream their sleep 30
noone and anyone earth by april
wish by spirit and if by yes.

Women and men(both dong and ding)
summer autumn winter spring
reaped their sowing and went their came 35
sun moon stars rain

(1940)

i thank You God for most this amazing

i thank You God for most this amazing
day:for the leaping greenly spirits of trees
and a blue true dream of sky; and for everything
which is natural which is infinite which is yes

(i who have died am alive again today, 5
and this is the sun's birthday; this is the birth
day of life and of love and wings:and of the gay
great happening illimitably earth)

how should tasting touching hearing seeing
breathing any—lifted from the no 10
of all nothing—human merely being
doubt unimaginable You?

(now the ears of my ears awake and
now the eyes of my eyes are opened)

(1950)

JEAN TOOMER
[1894–1967]

Song of the Son

Pour, O pour, that parting soul in song,
O pour it in the saw-dust glow of night,
Into the velvet pine-smoke air tonight,
And let the valley carry it along,
And let the valley carry it along.   5

O land and soil, red soil and sweet-gum tree
So scant of grass, so profligate of pines,
Now just before an epoch's sun declines
Thy son, in time, I have returned to thee,
Thy son, I have in time returned to thee.   10

In time, for though the sun is setting on
A song-lit race of slaves, it has not set;
Though late, O soil it is not too late yet
To catch thy plaintive soul, leaving, soon gone,
Leaving, to catch thy plaintive soul soon gone.   15

O Negro slaves, dark-purple ripened plums,
Squeezed, and bursting in the pine-wood air,
Passing, before they stripped the old tree bare
One plum was saved for me, one seed becomes

An everlasting song, a singing tree,   20
Carolling softly souls of slavery,
All that they were, and that they are to me,—
Carolling softly souls of slavery.

                                                                    (1922)

Reapers

Black reapers with the sound of steel on stones
Arc sharpening scythes. I see them place the hones
In their hip-pockets as a thing that's done,
And start their silent swinging, one by one.
Black horses drive a mower through the weeds,   5
And there, a field rat, startled, squealing bleeds,
His belly close to ground. I see the blade,
Blood-stained, continue cutting weeds and shade.

                                                                    (1923)

W. H. AUDEN
[1907–1973]

The Unknown Citizen

(To JS/07/M/378 This Marble Monument Is Erected by the State)

He was found by the Bureau of Statistics to be
One against whom there was no official complaint,
And all the reports on his conduct agree
That, in the modern sense of an old-fashioned word, he was a saint,
For in everything he did he served the Greater Community.   5
Except for the War till the day he retired
He worked in a factory and never got fired
But satisfied his employers, Fudge Motors Inc.
Yet he wasn't a scab or odd in his views,
For his Union reports that he paid his dues,   10
(Our report on his Union shows it was sound)
And our Social Psychology workers found
That he was popular with his mates and liked a drink.
The Press are convinced that he bought a paper every day
And that his reactions to advertisements were normal in every way.   15
Policies taken out in his name prove that he was fully insured,
And his Health-card shows he was once in hospital but left it cured.
Both Producers Research and High-Grade Living declare
He was fully sensible to the advantages of the Installment Plan
And had everything necessary to the Modern Man,   20
A phonograph, a radio, a car and a frigidaire.
Our researchers into Public Opinion are content
That he held the proper opinions for the time of year;
When there was peace, he was for peace; when there was war, he went.
He was married and added five children to the population,   25
Which our Eugenist says was the right number for a parent of his generation.
And our teachers report that he never interfered with their education.

Was he free? Was he happy? The question is absurd:
Had anything been wrong, we should certainly have heard.

(1940)

In Memory of W. B. Yeats

[d. January 1939]

1

He disappeared in the dead of winter:
The brooks were frozen, the air-ports almost deserted,
And snow disfigured the public statues;
The mercury sank in the mouth of the dying day.
O all the instruments agree   5
The day of his death was a dark cold day.

Far from his illness
The wolves ran on through the evergreen forests,
The peasant river was untempted by the fashionable quays;
By mourning tongues   10
The death of the poet was kept from his poems.

But for him it was his last afternoon as himself,
An afternoon of nurses and rumours;
The provinces of his body revolted,
The squares of his mind were empty,   15
Silence invaded the suburbs,
The current of his feeling failed: he became his admirers.

Now he is scattered among a hundred cities
And wholly given over to unfamiliar affections;
To find his happiness in another kind of wood   20
And be punished under a foreign code of conscience.
The words of a dead man
Are modified in the guts of the living.

But in the importance and noise of to-morrow
When the brokers are roaring like beasts on the floor of
    the Bourse,°   stock exchange   25
And the poor have the sufferings to which they are fairly accustomed,
And each in the cell of himself is almost convinced of his freedom;
A few thousand will think of this day
As one thinks of a day when one did something slightly unusual.

O all the instruments agree   30
The day of his death was a dark cold day.

2

You were silly like us: your gift survived it all;
The parish of rich women, physical decay,

Yourself; mad Ireland hurt you into poetry.
Now Ireland has her madness and her weather still, 35
For poetry makes nothing happen: it survives
In the valley of its saying where executives
Would never want to tamper; it flows south
From ranches of isolation and the busy griefs,
Raw towns that we believe and die in; it survives, 40
A way of happening, a mouth.

3

Earth, receive an honoured guest;
William Yeats is laid to rest:
Let the Irish vessel lie
Emptied of its poetry. 45

Time that is intolerant
Of the brave and innocent,
And indifferent in a week
To a beautiful physique,

Worships language and forgives 50
Everyone by whom it lives;
Pardons cowardice, conceit,
Lays its honours at their feet.

Time that with this strange excuse
Pardoned Kipling° and his views, 55
And will pardon Paul Claudel,°
Pardons him for writing well.

In the nightmare of the dark°
All the dogs of Europe bark,
And the living nations wait, 60
Each sequestered in its hate;

Intellectual disgrace
Stares from every human face,
And the seas of pity lie
Locked and frozen in each eye. 65

Follow, poet, follow right
To the bottom of the night,
With your unconstraining Voice
Still persuade us to rejoice;

"In Memory of W. B. Yeats"   [55]*Kipling*   *Rudyard Kipling (1865–1936), English writer with imperialistic views.*   [56]*Paul Claudel*   *French Catholic writer (1868–1955) of extreme political conservatism.*   [58]*the dark*   *World War II broke out a few months after Auden wrote this poem.*

With the farming of a verse   70
Make a vineyard of the curse,
Sing of human unsuccess
In a rapture of distress;

In the deserts of the heart
Let the healing fountain start,   75
In the prison of his days
Teach the free man how to praise.

                                                        (1940)

THEODORE ROETHKE
[*1908–1963*]

Elegy for Jane

MY STUDENT, THROWN BY A HORSE

I remember the neckcurls, limp and damp as tendrils;
And her quick look, a sidelong pickerel smile;
And how, once startled into talk, the light syllables leaped for her,
And she balanced in the delight of her thought,
A wren, happy, tail into the wind,   5
Her song trembling the twigs and small branches.
The shade sang with her;
The leaves, their whispers turned to kissing;
And the mold sang in the bleached valleys under the rose.

Oh, when she was sad, she cast herself down into such a pure depth,   10
Even a father could not find her:
Scraping her cheek against straw;
Stirring the clearest water.

My sparrow, you are not here,
Waiting like a fern, making a spiny shadow   15
The sides of wet stones cannot console me,
Nor the moss, wound with the last light.

If only I could nudge you from this sleep,
My maimed darling, my skittery pigeon.
Over this damp grave I speak the words of my love: 20
I, with no rights in this matter,
Neither father nor lover.

                                                        (1953)

E L I Z A B E T H   B I S H O P
[*1911–1979*]

Sestina

September rain falls on the house.
In the failing light, the old grandmother
sits in the kitchen with the child
beside the Little Marvel Stove,
reading the jokes from the almanac,   5
laughing and talking to hide her tears.

She thinks that her equinoctial tears
and the rain that beats on the roof of the house
were both foretold by the almanac,
but only known to a grandmother.   10
The iron kettle sings on the stove.
She cuts some bread and says to the child,

It's time for tea now; but the child
is watching the teakettle's small hard tears
dance like mad on the hot black stove,   15
the way the rain must dance on the house.
Tidying up, the old grandmother
hangs up the clever almanac

on its string. Birdlike, the almanac
hovers half open above the child,   20
hovers above the old grandmother
and her teacup full of dark brown tears.
She shivers and says she thinks the house
feels chilly, and puts more wood in the stove.

It was to be, says the Marvel Stove.   25
I know what I know, says the almanac.
With crayons the child draws a rigid house
and a winding pathway. Then the child
puts in a man with buttons like tears
and shows it proudly to the grandmother.   30

But secretly, while the grandmother
busies herself about the stove,
the little moons fall down like tears
from between the pages of the almanac

into the flower bed the child 35
has carefully placed in the front of the house.

Time to plant tears, says the almanac.
The grandmother sings to the marvelous stove
and the child draws another inscrutable house.

(1965)

MAY SWENSON
[1913–1989]

Women

Women   Or they
   should be   should be
    pedestals   little horses
     moving   those wooden
      pedestals   sweet
       moving   oldfashioned
        to the   painted
         motions   rocking
        of men   horses

        the gladdest things in the toyroom.

       The   feelingly
      pegs   and then
    of their   unfeelingly
   ears   To be
  so familiar   joyfully
  and dear   ridden
  to the trusting   rockingly
  fists   ridden until
To be chafed   the restored

egos dismount and the legs stride away

Immobile   willing
  sweetlipped   to be set
  sturdy   into motion
  and smiling   Women
   women   should be
    should always   pedestals
    be waiting   to men

(1970)

WILLIAM STAFFORD
[*b. 1914*]

Traveling through the dark

Traveling through the dark I found a deer
dead on the edge of the Wilson River road.
It is usually best to roll them into the canyon:
that road is narrow; to swerve might make more dead.

By glow of the tail-light I stumbled back of the car   5
and stood by the heap, a doe, a recent killing;
she had stiffened already, almost cold.
I dragged her off; she was large in the belly.

My fingers touching her side brought me the reason—
her side was warm; her fawn lay there waiting,   10
alive, still, never to be born.
Beside that mountain road I hesitated.

The car aimed ahead its lowered parking lights;
under the hood purred the steady engine.
I stood in the glare of the warm exhaust turning red;   15
around our group I could hear the wilderness listen.

I thought hard for us all—my only swerving—,
then pushed her over the edge into the river.

(1957)

DYLAN THOMAS
[*1914–1953*]

Fern Hill

Now as I was young and easy under the apple boughs
About the lilting house and happy as the grass was green,
    The night above the dingle starry,
        Time let me hail and climb
      Golden in the heydays of his eyes,   5
And honored among wagons I was prince of the apple towns
And once below a time I lordly had the trees and leaves
        Trail with daisies and barley
      Down the rivers of the windfall light.

And as I was green and carefree, famous among the barns   10
About the happy yard and singing as the farm was home,
    In the sun that is young once only,
        Time let me play and be
     Golden in the mercy of his means,
And green and golden I was huntsman and herdsman, the calves   15
Sang to my horn, the foxes on the hills barked clear and cold,
       And the sabbath rang slowly
    In the pebbles of the holy streams.

All the sun long it was running, it was lovely, the hay
Fields high as the house, the tunes from the chimneys, it was air   20
    And playing, lovely and watery
      And fire green as grass.
   And nightly under the simple stars
As I rode to sleep the owls were bearing the farm away,
All the moon long I heard, blessed among stables, the night-jars   25
    Flying with the ricks, and the horses
      Flashing into the dark.

And then to awake, and the farm, like a wanderer white
With the dew, come back, the cock on his shoulder: it was all
    Shining, it was Adam and maiden,   30
      The sky gathered again
   And the sun grew round that very day.
So it must have been after the birth of the simple light
In the first, spinning place, the spellbound horses walking warm
    Out of the whinnying green stable   35
      On to the fields of praise.

And honored among foxes and pheasants by the gay house
Under the new made clouds and happy as the heart was long,
    In the sun born over and over,
      I ran my heedless ways,   40
    My wishes raced through the house high hay
And nothing I cared, at my sky blue trades, that time allows
In all his tuneful turning so few and such morning songs
    Before the children green and golden
      Follow him out of grace,   45

Nothing I cared, in the lamb white days, that time would take me
Up to the swallow thronged loft by the shadow of my hand,
    In the moon that is always rising,
      Nor that riding to sleep
   I should hear him fly with the high fields   50
And wake to the farm forever fled from the childless land.
Oh as I was young and easy in the mercy of his means,

> Time held me green and dying
> Though I sang in my chains like the sea.

(1946)

Do not go gentle into that good night

Do not go gentle into that good night,
Old age should burn and rave at close of day;
Rage, rage against the dying of the light.

Though wise men at their end know dark is right,
Because their words had forked no lightning they   5
Do not go gentle into that good night.

Good men, the last wave by, crying how bright
Their frail deeds might have danced in a green bay,
Rage, rage against the dying of the light.

Wild men who caught and sang the sun in flight,   10
And learn, too late, they grieved it on its way,
Do not go gentle into that good night.

Grave men, near death, who see with blinding sight
Blind eyes could blaze like meteors and be gay,
Rage, rage against the dying of the light.   15

And you, my father, there on the sad height,
Curse, bless, me now with your fierce tears, I pray.
Do not go gentle into that good night.
Rage, rage against the dying of the light.

(1952)

G W E N D O L Y N   B R O O K S
[*b. 1917*]

the mother

Abortions will not let you forget.
You remember the children you got that you did not get,
The damp small pulps with a little or with no hair,
The singers and workers that never handled the air.
You will never neglect or beat   5

Them, or silence or buy with a sweet.
You will never wind up the sucking-thumb
Or scuttle off ghosts that come.
You will never leave them, controlling your luscious sigh,
Return for a snack of them, with gobbling mother-eye. 10

I have heard in the voices of the wind the voices of my dim killed children.
I have contracted. I have eased
My dim dears at the breasts they could never suck.
I have said, Sweets, if I sinned, if I seized
Your luck 15
And your lives from your unfinished reach,
If I stole your births and your names,
Your straight baby tears and your games,
Your stilted or lovely loves, your tumults, your marriages, aches, and your deaths,
If I poisoned the beginnings of your breaths,
Believe that even in my deliberateness I was not deliberate. 20
Though why should I whine,
Whine that the crime was other than mine?—
Since anyhow you are dead.
Or rather, or instead,
You were never made. 25

But that too, I am afraid,
Is faulty: oh, what shall I say, how is the truth to be said?
You were born, you had body, you died.
It is just that you never giggled or planned or cried.
Believe me, I loved you all. 30
Believe me, I knew you, though faintly, and I loved, I loved you
All.

(1945)

First fight. Then fiddle

First fight. Then fiddle. Ply the slipping string
With feathery sorcery; muzzle the note
With hurting love; the music that they wrote
Bewitch, bewilder. Qualify to sing
Threadwise. Devise no salt, no hempen thing 5
For the dear instrument to bear. Devote
The bow to silks and honey. Be remote
A while from malice and from murdering.
But first to arms, to armor. Carry hate
In front of you and harmony behind. 10
Be deaf to music and to beauty blind.

Win war. Rise bloody, maybe not too late
For having first to civilize a space
Wherein to play your violin with grace.

(1945)

LAWRENCE FERLINGHETTI
[*b. 1919*]

Constantly Risking Absurdity

Constantly risking absurdity
                    and death
      whenever he performs
               above the heads
                      of his audience   5

    the poet like an acrobat
               climbs on rime
           to a high wire of his own making
and balancing on eyebeams
             above a sea of faces   10
      paces his way
         to the other side of day
  performing entrechats

          and sleight-of-foot tricks
and other high theatrics   15

          and all without mistaking
     any thing
        for what it may not be
  For he's the super realist
          who must perforce perceive   20
     taut truth
        before the taking of each stance or step
  in his supposed advance
        toward that still higher perch
where Beauty stands and waits   25
          with gravity
           to start her death-defying leap

   And he
     a little charleychaplin man

who may or may not catch   30
her fair eternal form
              spreadeagled in the empty air
     of existence

                                                    (1958)

RICHARD WILBUR
[*b. 1921*]

The Death of a Toad

A toad the power mower caught,
Chewed and clipped off a leg, with a hobbling hop has got
     To the garden verge, and sanctuaried him
     Under the cineraria leaves, in the shade
          Of the ashen heartshaped leaves, in a dim,   5
               Low, and a final glade.

The rare original heartsblood goes,
Spends on the earthen hide, in the folds and wizenings, flows
     In the gutters of the banked and staring eyes. He lies
     As still as if he would return to stone,   10
          And soundlessly attending, dies
               Toward some deep monotone,

Toward misted and ebullient seas
And cooling shores, toward lost Amphibia's emperies.
     Day dwindles, drowning, and at length is gone   15
     In the wide and antique eyes, which still appear
          To watch, across the castrate lawn,
               The haggard daylight steer.

                                                    (1956)

PHILIP LARKIN
[*b. 1922*]

A Study of Reading Habits

When getting my nose in a book
Cured most things short of school,
It was worth ruining my eyes

To know I could still keep cool,
And deal out the old right hook   5
To dirty dogs twice my size.

Later, with inch-thick specs,
Evil was just my lark:
Me and my cloak and fangs
Had ripping times in the dark.   10
The women I clubbed with sex!
I broke them up like meringues.

Don't read much now: the dude
Who lets the girl down before
The hero arrives, the chap   15
Who's yellow and keeps the store,
Seem far too familiar. Get stewed:
Books are a load of crap.

(1964)

ROSARIO CASTELLANOS
[1925–1974]

Chess

Because we were friends and sometimes loved each other,
perhaps to add one more tie
to the many that already bound us,
we decided to play games of the mind.

We set up a board between us;   5
equally divided into pieces, values,
and possible moves.
We learned the rules, we swore to respect them,
and the match began.

We've been sitting here for centuries, meditating   10
ferociously
how to deal the one last blow that will finally
annihilate the other one forever.

TRANSLATED BY MAUREEN AHERN

(1988)

GALWAY KINNELL
[*b. 1927*]

Saint Francis and the Sow

The bud
stands for all things,
even for those things that don't flower,
for everything flowers, from within, of self-blessing;
though sometimes it is necessary   5
to reteach a thing its loveliness,
to put a hand on its brow
of the flower
and retell it in words and in touch
it is lovely   10
until it flowers again from within, of self-blessing;
as Saint Francis°
put his hand on the creased forehead
of the sow, and told her in words and in touch
blessings of earth on the sow, and the sow   15
began remembering all down her thick length,
from the earthen snout all the way
through the fodder and slops to the spiritual curl of the tail,
from the hard spininess spiked out from the spine
down through the great broken heart   20
to the sheer blue milken dreaminess spurting and shuddering
from the fourteen teats into the fourteen mouths sucking and
    blowing beneath them:
the long, perfect loveliness of sow.

(1980)

JAMES WRIGHT
[*b. 1927*]

Lying in a Hammock at William Duffy's Farm in Pine Island, Minnesota

Over my head, I see the bronze butterfly,
Asleep on the black trunk,

"Saint Francis and the Sow"   [12] **Saint Francis**   *Saint Francis of Assisi (1182–1226) was famed for his love of all creation, especially animals.*

Blowing like a leaf in green shadow.
Down the ravine behind the empty house,
The cowbells follow one another   5
Into the distances of the afternoon.
To my right,
In a field of sunlight between two pines,
The droppings of last year's horses
Blaze up into golden stones.   10
I lean back, as the evening darkens and comes on.
A chicken hawk floats over, looking for home.
I have wasted my life.

(1963)

A Blessing

Just off the highway to Rochester, Minnesota,
Twilight bounds softly forth on the grass.
And the eyes of those two Indian ponies
Darken with kindness.
They have come gladly out of the willows   5
To welcome my friend and me.
We step over the barbed wire into the pasture
Where they have been grazing all day, alone.
They ripple tensely, they can hardly contain their happiness
That we have come.   10
They bow shyly as wet swans. They love each other.
There is no loneliness like theirs.
At home once more,
They begin munching the young tufts of spring in the darkness.
I would like to hold the slenderer one in my arms,   15
For she has walked over to me
And nuzzled my left hand.
She is black and white,
Her mane falls wild on her forehead,
And the light breeze moves me to caress her long ear   20
That is delicate as the skin over a girl's wrist.
Suddenly I realize
That if I stepped out of my body I would break
Into blossom.

(1963)

ANNE SEXTON
[1928–1974]

Two Hands

From the sea came a hand,
ignorant as a penny,
troubled with the salt of its mother,
mute with the silence of the fishes,
quick with the altars of the tides,　　　　　　　　　5
and God reached out of His mouth
and called it man.
Up came the other hand
and God called it woman.
The hands applauded.　　　　　　　　　10
And this was no sin.
It was as it was meant to be.

I see them roaming the streets:
Levi complaining about his mattress,
Sarah studying a beetle,　　　　　　　　　15
Mandrake holding his coffee mug,
Sally playing the drum at a football game,
John closing the eyes of the dying woman,
and some who are in prison,
even the prison of their bodies,　　　　　　　　　20
as Christ was prisoned in His body
until the triumph came.

Unwind, hands,
you angel webs,
unwind like the coil of a jumping jack,　　　　　　　　　25
cup together and let yourselves fill up with sun
and applaud, world,
applaud.

(1969)

A SELECTION OF CONTEMPORARY POEMS

DONALD HALL
[b. 1928]

My son, my executioner

My son, my executioner,
    I take you in my arms,
Quiet and small and just astir,
    And whom my body warms.

Sweet death, small son, our instrument   5
    Of immortality,
Your cries and hungers document
    Our bodily decay.

We twenty-five and twenty-two,
    Who seemed to live forever,   10
Observe enduring life in you
    And start to die together.

(1955)

GREGORY CORSO
[b. 1930]

Marriage

Should I get married? Should I be good?
Astound the girl next door with my velvet suit and faustus hood?°
Don't take her to movies but to cemeteries
tell all about werewolf bathtubs and forked clarinets
then desire her and kiss her and all the preliminaries   5
and she going just so far and I understanding why
not getting angry saying You must feel! It's beautiful to feel!
Instead take her in my arms lean against an old crooked tombstone
and woo her the entire night the constellations in the sky—

"Marriage" ²**faustus hood** *Dr. Faustus, German magician and astrologer (ca. 1480–1538) was reputed to have sold his soul to the Devil in exchange for knowledge and power.*

When she introduces me to her parents   10
back straightened, hair finally combed, strangled by a tie,
should I sit knees together on their 3rd degree sofa
and not ask Where's the bathroom?
How else to feel other than I am,
often thinking Flash Gordon soap—   15
O how terrible it must be for a young man
seated before a family and the family thinking
We never saw him before! He wants our Mary Lou!
After tea and homemade cookies they ask What do you do for a living?

Should I tell them? Would they like me then?   20
Say All right get married, we're losing a daughter
but we're gaining a son—
And should I then ask Where's the bathroom?

O God, and the wedding! All her family and her friends
and only a handful of mine all scroungy and bearded   25
just wait to get at the drinks and food—
And the priest! he looking at me as if I masturbated
asking me Do you take this woman for your lawful wedded wife?
And I trembling what to say say Pie Glue!
I kiss the bride all those corny men slapping me on the back   30
She's all yours, boy! Ha-ha-ha!
And in their eyes you could see some obscene honeymoon going on—
Then all that absurd rice and clanky cans and shoes
Niagara Falls! Hordes of us! Husbands! Wives! Flowers! Chocolates!
All streaming into cozy hotels   35
All going to do the same thing tonight

The indifferent clerk he knowing what was going to happen
The lobby zombies they knowing what
The whistling elevator man he knowing
The winking bellboy knowing   40
Everybody knowing! I'd be almost inclined not to do anything!
Stay up all night! Stare that hotel clerk in the eye!
Screaming: I deny honeymoon! I deny honeymoon!
running rampant into those almost climactic suites
yelling Radio belly! Cat shovel!   45
O I'd live in Niagara forever! in a dark cave beneath the Falls
I'd sit there the Mad Honeymooner
devising ways to break marriages, a scourge of bigamy
a saint of divorce—

But I should get married I should be good   50
How nice it'd be to come home to her
and sit by the fireplace and she in the kitchen

aproned young and lovely wanting my baby
and so happy about me she burns the roast beef
and comes crying to me and I get up from my big papa chair   55
saying Christmas teeth! Radiant brains! Apple deaf!
God what a husband I'd make! Yes, I should get married!
So much to do! like sneaking into Mr Jones' house late at night
and cover his golf clubs with 1920 Norwegian books
Like hanging a picture of Rimbaud° on the lawnmower   60
like pasting Tannu Tuva° postage stamps all over the picket fence
like when Mrs Kindhead comes to collect for the Community Chest
grab her and tell her There are unfavorable omens in the sky!
And when the mayor comes to get my vote tell him
When are you going to stop people killing whales!   65
And when the milkman comes leave him a note in the bottle
Penguin dust, bring me penguin dust, I want penguin dust—

Yet if I should get married and it's Connecticut and snow
and she gives birth to a child and I am sleepless, worn,
up for nights, head bowed against a quiet window, the past behind me,   70
finding myself in the most common of situations a trembling man
knowledged with responsibility not twig-smear nor Roman coin soup—
O what would that be like!
Surely I'd give it for a nipple a rubber Tacitus°
For a rattle a bag of broken Bach records   75
Tack Della Francesca° all over its crib
Sew the Greek alphabet on its bib
And build for its playpen a roofless Parthenon

No, I doubt I'd be that kind of father
Not rural not snow no quiet window   80
but hot smelly tight New York City
seven flights up, roaches and rats in the walls
a fat Reichian° wife screeching over potatoes Get a job!
And five nose running brats in love with Batman
And the neighbors all toothless and dry haired   85
like those hag masses of the 18th century
all wanting to come in and watch TV

The landlord wants his rent
Grocery store Blue Cross Gas & Electric Knights of Columbus
Impossible to lie back and dream Telephone snow, ghost parking—   90
No! I should not get married I should never get married!
But—imagine if I were married to a beautiful sophisticated woman

---

[60]**Rimbaud**   *Arthur Rimbaud (1854–1891), French poet.*   [61]**Tannu Tuva**   *a republic in Siberia, part of the* USSR.   [74]**Tacitus**   *Roman historian (A.D. 55–117).*   [76]**Della Francesca**   *Italian Renaissance painter (1420–1492).*   [83]**Reichian**   *follower of psychoanalyst Wilhelm Reich (1897–1957).*

tall and pale wearing an elegant black dress and long black gloves
holding a cigarette holder in one hand and a highball in the other
and we lived high up in a penthouse with a huge window   95
from which we could see all of New York and ever farther on clearer days
No, can't imagine myself married to that pleasant prison dream—
O but what about love? I forget love
not that I am incapable of love
it's just that I see love as odd as wearing shoes—   100
I never wanted to marry a girl who was like my mother
And Ingrid Bergman was always impossible
And there's maybe a girl now but she's already married
And I don't like men and—
but there's got to be somebody!   105
Because what if I'm 60 years old and not married,
all alone in a furnished room with pee stains on my underwear
and everybody else is married! All the universe married but me!

Ah, yet well I know that were a woman possible as I am possible
then marriage would be possible—   110
Like SHE° in her lonely alien gaud waiting her Egyptian lover
so I wait—bereft of 2,000 years and the bath of life.

(1960)

LINDA PASTAN
[b. 1932]

Ethics

In ethics class so many years ago
our teacher asked this question every fall:
if there were a fire in a museum
which would you save, a Rembrandt painting
or an old woman who hadn't many   5
years left anyhow? Restless on hard chairs
caring little for pictures or old age
we'd opt one year for life, the next for art
and always half-heartedly. Sometimes
the woman borrowed my grandmother's face   10
leaving her usual kitchen to wander
some drafty, half imagined museum.

---

[111] **SHE**   *the heroine of H. Rider Haggard's novel* She *(1887) who gains eternal youth by bathing in fire and who waits thousands of years for her lover's return.*

One year, feeling clever, I replied
why not let the woman decide herself?
Linda, the teacher would report, eschews   15
the burdens of responsibility.
This fall in a real museum I stand
before a real Rembrandt, old woman,
or nearly so, myself. The colors
within this frame are darker than autumn,   20
darker even than winter—the browns of earth,
though earth's most radiant elements burn
through the canvas. I know now that woman
and painting and season are almost one
and all beyond saving by children.   25

(1981)

S Y L V I A   P L A T H
[1932–1963]

Mirror

I am silver and exact. I have no preconceptions.
Whatever I see I swallow immediately
Just as it is, unmisted by love or dislike.
I am not cruel, only truthful—
The eye of a little god, four-cornered.   5
Most of the time I meditate on the opposite wall.
It is pink, with speckles. I have looked at it so long
I think it is a part of my heart. But it flickers.
Faces and darkness separate us over and over.

Now I am a lake. A woman bends over me,   10
Searching my reaches for what she really is.
Then she turns to those liars, the candles or the moon.
I see her back, and reflect it faithfully.
She rewards me with tears and an agitation of hands.
I am important to her. She comes and goes.   15
Each morning it is her face that replaces the darkness.
In me she has drowned a young girl, and in me an old woman
Rises toward her day after day, like a terrible fish.

AUDRE LORDE
[1934–1992]

Hanging Fire

I am fourteen
and my skin has betrayed me
the boy I cannot live without
still sucks his thumb
in secret   5
how come my knees are
always so ashy
what if I die
before morning
and mamma's in the bedroom   10
with the door closed.

I have to learn how to dance
in time for the next party
my room is too small for me
suppose I die before graduation   15
they will sing sad melodies
but finally
tell the truth about me
There is nothing I want to do
and too much   20
that has to be done
and momma's in the bedroom
with the door closed.

Nobody even stops to think
about my side of it   25
I should have been on Math Team
my marks were better than his
why do I have to be
the one
wearing braces   30
I have nothing to wear tomorrow
will I live long enough
to grow up
and momma's in the bedroom
with the door closed.   35

(1978)

LUCILLE CLIFTON
[*b. 1936*]

Homage to My Hips

these hips are big hips.
they need space to
move around in.
they don't fit into little
petty places. these hips   5
are free hips.
they don't like to be held back.
these hips have never been enslaved,
they go where they want to go
they do what they want to do.   10
these hips are mighty hips.
these hips are magic hips.
i have known them
to put a spell on a man and
spin him like a top!   15

(1972)

MARGE PIERCY
[*b. 1936*]

A Work of Artifice

The bonsai tree
in the attractive pot
could have grown eighty feet tall
on the side of a mountain
till split by lightning.   5
But a gardener
carefully pruned it.
It is nine inches high.
Every day as he
whittles back the branches   10
the gardener croons,
It is your nature
to be small and cozy,
domestic and weak;
how lucky, little tree,   15

to have a pot to grow in.
With living creatures
one must begin very early
to dwarf their growth:
the bound feet,   20
the crippled brain,
the hair in curlers,
the hands you
love to touch.

(1973)

MARGARET ATWOOD
[b. 1939]

This Is a Photograph of Me

It was taken some time ago.
At first it seems to be
a smeared
print: blurred lines and grey flecks
blended with the paper;   5
then, as you scan
it, you see in the left-hand corner
a thing that is like a branch: part of a tree
(balsam or spruce) emerging
and, to the right, halfway up   10
what ought to be a gentle
slope, a small frame house.

In the background there is a lake,
and beyond that, some low hills.

(The photograph was taken   15
the day after I drowned.

I am in the lake, in the center
of the picture, just under the surface.

It is difficult to say where
precisely, or to say   20
how large or small I am:
the effect of water
on light is a distortion

but if you look long enough,
eventually   25
you will be able to see me.)

                                                                        (1966)

RAYMOND CARVER
[*1939–1988*]

Photograph of My Father in His Twenty-second Year

October. Here in this dank, unfamiliar kitchen
I study my father's embarrassed young man's face.
Sheepish grin, he holds in one hand a string
of spiny yellow perch, in the other
a bottle of Carlsbad beer.   5

In jeans and denim shirt, he leans
against the front fender of a 1934 Ford.
He would like to pose bluff and hearty for his posterity,
wear his old hat cocked over his ear.
All his life my father wanted to be bold.   10

But the eyes give him away, and the hands
that limply offer the string of dead perch
and the bottle of beer. Father, I love you,
yet how can I say thank you, I who can't hold my liquor either,
and don't even know the places to fish?   15

                                                                        (1988)

SEAMUS HEANEY
[*b. 1939*]

Mid-Term Break

I sat all morning in the college sick bay
Counting bells knelling classes to a close.
At two o'clock our neighbors drove me home.

In the porch I met my father crying—
He had always taken funerals in his stride—   5
And Big Jim Evans saying it was a hard blow.

The baby cooed and laughed and rocked the pram
When I came in, and I was embarrassed
By old men standing up to shake my hand

And tell me they were "sorry for my trouble,"   10
Whispers informed strangers I was the eldest,
Away at school, as my mother held my hand

In hers and coughed out angry tearless sighs.
At ten o'clock the ambulance arrived
With the corpse, stanched and bandaged by the nurses.   15

Next morning I went up into the room. Snowdrops
And candles soothed the bedside; I saw him
For the first time in six weeks. Paler now,

Wearing a poppy bruise on his left temple,
He lay in the four foot box as in his cot.   20
No gaudy scars, the bumper knocked him clear.

A four foot box, a foot for every year.

                                                    (1966)

Digging

Between my finger and my thumb
The squat pen rests; snug as a gun.

Under my window, a clean rasping sound
When the spade sinks into gravelly ground:
My father, digging. I look down   5

Till his straining rump among the flowerbeds
Bends low, comes up twenty years away
Stooping in rhythm through potato drills
Where he was digging.

The coarse boot nestled on the lug, the shaft   10
Against the inside knee was levered firmly.
He rooted out tall tops, buried the bright edge deep
To scatter new potatoes that we picked
Loving their cool hardness in our hands.

By God, the old man could handle a spade.   15
Just like his old man.

My grandfather cut more turf in a day
Than any other man on Toner's bog.
Once I carried him milk in a bottle
Corked sloppily with paper. He straightened up   20
To drink it, then fell to right away

Nicking and slicing neatly, heaving sods
Over his shoulder, going down and down
For the good turf. Digging.

The cold smell of potato mould, the squelch and slap   25
Of soggy peat, the curt cuts of an edge
Through living roots awaken in my head.
But I've no spade to follow men like them.

Between my finger and my thumb
The squat pen rests.   30
I'll dig with it.

(1966)

NIKKI GIOVANNI
[*b. 1943*]

Ego Tripping

(THERE MAY BE A REASON WHY)

I was born in the congo
I walked to the fertile crescent and built
          the sphinx
I designed a pyramid so tough that a star
          that only glows every one hundred years falls   5
          into the center giving divine perfect light
I am bad

I sat on the throne
          drinking nectar with allah
I got hot and sent an ice age to europe   10
          to cool my thirst
My oldest daughter is nefertiti
          the tears from my birth pains
          created the nile
I am a beautiful woman   15

I gazed on the forest and burned
   out the sahara desert
   with a packet of goat's meat
   and a change of clothes
I crossed it in two hours   20
I am a gazelle so swift
   so swift you can't catch me

   For a birthday present when he was three
I gave my son hannibal an elephant
   He gave me rome for mother's day   25
My strength flows ever on

My son noah built new/ark and
I stood proudly at the helm
   as we sailed on a soft summer day
I turned myself into myself and was   30
   jesus
   men intone my loving name
   All praises All praises
I am the one who would save

I sowed diamonds in my back yard   35
My bowels deliver uranium
   the filings from my fingernails are
   semi-precious jewels
   On a trip north
I caught a cold and blew   40
My nose giving oil to the arab world
I am so hip even my errors are correct
I sailed west to reach east and had to round off
   the earth as I went
   The hair from my head thinned and gold was laid   45
   across three continents
I am so perfect so divine so ethereal so surreal
I cannot be comprehended
   except by my permission

I mean . . . I . . . can fly   50
   like a bird in the sky . . .

          (1970)

SHARON OLDS
[b. 1942]

Size and Sheer Will

The fine, green pajama cotton,
washed so often it is paper-thin and
iridescent, has split like a sheath
and the glossy white naked bulbs of
Gabriel's toes thrust forth like crocus   5
this early Spring. The boy is growing
as fast as he can, elongated
wrists dangling, lean meat
showing between the shirt and the belt.
If there were a rack to stretch himself, he would   10
strap his slight body to it.
If there were a machine to enter,
skip the next ten years and be
sixteen immediately, this boy would
do it. All day long he cranes his   15
neck, like a plant in the dark with a single
light above it, or a sailor under
tons of green water, longing
for the surface, for his rightful life.

(1975)

CHRISTINE KANE MOLITO
[b. 1977]

Partial Reflections in Black & Blue

FOR PJL

I looked at you, looking at me
and wondered
do you see me fading?
When you looked straight
into my blue eyes   5
straight through—into the part of me
only you my dear are allowed to see,
did you notice the fade to grey?

Remember you loved me first
when my black hair was long
and my blue eyes bright.

JANE KENYON
[1947–1995]

Notes from the Other Side

I divested myself of despair
and fear when I came here.

Now there is no more catching
one's own eye in the mirror,

there are no bad books, no plastic, 5
no insurance premiums, and of course

no illness. Contrition
does not exist, nor gnashing

of teeth. No one howls as the first
clod of earth hits the casket. 10

The poor we no longer have with us.
Our calm hearts strike only the hour,

and God, as promised, proves
to be mercy clothed in light.

(1990)

YUSEF KOMUNYAKAA
[b. 1947]

Facing It

My black face fades,
hiding inside the black granite.
I said I wouldn't,
dammit: No tears.
I'm stone. I'm flesh. 5
My clouded reflection eyes me
like a bird of prey, the profile of night
slanted against morning. I turn
this way—the stone lets me go.

I turn that way—I'm inside   10
the Vietnam Veterans Memorial
again, depending on the light
to make a difference.
I go down the 58,022 names,
half-expecting to find   15
my own in letters like smoke.
I touch the name Andrew Johnson;
I see the booby trap's white flash.
Names shimmer on a woman's blouse
but when she walks away   20
the names stay on the wall.
Brushstrokes flash, a red bird's
wings cutting across my stare.
The sky. A plane in the sky.
A white vet's image floats   25
closer to me, then his pale eyes
look through mine. I'm a window.
He's lost his right arm
inside the stone. In the black mirror
a woman's trying to erase names: 30
No, she's brushing a boy's hair.

(1988)

NEAL BOWERS
[b. 1948]

Driving Lessons

I learned to drive in a parking lot
on Sundays, when the stores were closed—
slow maneuvers out beyond the light-poles,
no destination, just the ritual of clutch and gas,
my father clenching with the grinding gears,   5
finally giving up and leaving my mother
to buck and plunge with me and say,
repeatedly, "Once more. Try just once more."

She walked out on him once
when I was six or seven, my father   10
driving beside her, slow as a beginner,
pleading, my baby brother and I
crying out the windows, "Mama, don't go!"
It was a scene to break your heart

or make you laugh—those wailing kids,   15
a woman walking briskly with a suitcase,
the slow car following like a faithful dog.

I don't know why she finally got in
and let us take her back
to whatever she had made up her mind to leave;   20
but the old world swallowed her up
as soon as she opened that door,
and the other life she might have lived
lay down forever in its dark infancy.

Sometimes, when I'm home, driving   25
through the old neighborhoods, stopping
in front of each little house we rented,
my stillborn other life gets in,
the boy I would have been if
my mother had kept on walking.   30
He wants to be just like her,
far away and gone forever, wants
me to press down on the gas;
but however fast I squeal away,
the shaggy past keeps loping behind,   35
sniffing every turn.

When I stop in the weedy parking lot,
the failed stores of the old mall
make a dark wall straight ahead;
and I'm alone again, until my parents get in,   40
unchanged after all these years,
my father, impatient, my mother
trying hard to smile, waiting for me
to steer my way across this emptiness.

                                                                    (1992)

KRAFT ROMPF
[b. 1948]

Waiting Table

To serve, I wait and pluck
the rose, brush crumbs, carry

madly trays of oysters and
Bloody Marys. Swinging through

doors, I hear them: mouths   5
open, eyes bugging, choking;

they beat a white clothed
table for caffeine piping

hot and sweet, sweet sugar.
Oh, I should pour it in   10

their eyes! And set their
tongues afire. How the chef

understands when I order
tartare and shout, "Let them

eat it raw!" Oh I would stuff   15
their noses with garlic

and the house pianist
could play the Hammer March

on their toes. But for a
tip—for a tip, for a tip   20

I would work so very, very
hard, and so gladly let

them shine into my soul,
and bow to them and laugh

with them and sing. I would   25
gladly give them everything.

(1978)

JIMMY SANTIAGO BACA
[b. 1952]

from *Meditations on the South Valley*

XVII

I love the wind
when it blows through my barrio.
It hisses its snake love
down calles de polvo,
and cracks egg-shell skins   5
of abandoned homes.
Stray dogs find shelter
along the river,
where great cottonwoods rattle
like old covered wagons,   10
stuck in stagnant waterholes.
Days when the wind blows
full of sand and grit,
men and women make decisions
that change their whole lives.   15
Windy days in the barrio
give birth to divorce papers
and squalling separation. The wind tells us
what others refuse to tell us,
informing men and women of a secret,   20
that they move away to hide from.

(1979)

RITA DOVE
[b. 1952]

Canary

FOR MICHAEL S. HARPER

Billie Holiday's burned voice
had as many shadows as lights,
a mournful candelabra against a sleek piano,
the gardenia her signature under that ruined face.

(Now you're cooking, drummer to bass,   5
magic spoon, magic needle.

Take all day if you have to
with your mirror and your bracelet of song.)

Fact is, the invention of women under siege
has been to sharpen love in the service of myth. 10

If you can't be free, be a mystery.

(1989)

J U D I T H   O R T I Z   C O F E R
[b. 1952]

The Idea of Islands

The place where I was born,
that mote in a cartographer's eye,
interests you?
Today Atlanta is like a port city
enveloped in mist. The temperature 5
is plunging with the abandon
of a woman rushing to a rendezvous.
Since you ask, things were simpler
on the island. Food and shelter
were never the problem. Most days, 10
a hat and a watchful eye were all
one needed for protection, the climate being
rarely inclement. Fruit could be plucked
from trees languishing under the weight
of their own fecundity. The thick sea 15
spewed out fish that crawled into the pots
of women whose main occupation was to dress
each other's manes with scarlet hibiscus,
which as you may know, blooms
without restraint in the tropics. 20
I was always the ambitious one, overdressed
by my neighbors' standards, and unwilling
to eat mangoes three times a day.
In truth, I confess to spending my youth
guarding the fire by the beach, waiting 25
to be rescued from the futile round
of paradisial life.
How do I like the big city?
City lights are just as bright
as the stars that enticed me then; 30

the traffic ebbs and rises like the tides
and in a crowd,
everyone is an island.

(1989)

ALBERTO RIOS
[b. 1952]

A Dream of Husbands

Though we thought it, Doña Carolina did not die.
She was too old for that nonsense, and too set.
That morning she walked off just a little farther
into her favorite dream, favorite but not nice
so much, not nice and not bad, so it was not death.   5
She dreamed the dream of husbands
and over there she found him after all the years.
Cabrón, she called him, *animal,* very loud
so we could hear it, for us it was a loud truck
passing, or thunder, or too many cats, very loud   10
for having left her for so long and so far. Days now
her voice is the squeak of the rocking chair
as she complains, we hear it, it will not go
not with oils or sanding or shouts back at her.
But it becomes too the sound a spoon makes, her old   15
very large wooden spoon as it stirs a pot of soup.
Dinnertimes, we think of her, the good parts, of her
cooking, we like her best then, even the smell of her.
But then, *cabrones* she calls us, *animales,* irritated,
from over there, from the dream, they come, her words   20
they are the worst sounds of the street in the night
so that we will not get so comfortable about her,
so comfortable with her having left us
we thinking that her husband and her long dream
are so perfect, because no, they are not, not so much,   25
she is not so happy this way, not in this dream,
this is not heaven, don't think it. She tells us this,
sadness too is hers, a half measure, sadness at having
no time for the old things, for rice, for chairs.

(1985)

GERTRUDE SCHNACKENBERG
[*b. 1952*]

Signs

Threading the palm, a web of little lines
Spells out the lost money, the heart, the head,
The wagging tongues, the sudden deaths, in signs
We would smooth out, like imprints on a bed,

In signs that can't be helped, geese heading south,   5
In signs read anxiously, like breath that clouds
A mirror held to a barely open mouth,
Like telegrams, the gathering of crowds—

The plane's X in the sky, spelling disaster:
Before the whistle and hit, a tracer flare;   10
Before rubble, a hairline crack in plaster
And a housefly's panicked scribbling on the air.

(1982)

GARY SOTO
[*b. 1952*]

Behind Grandma's House

At ten I wanted fame. I had a comb
And two Coke bottles, a tube of Bryl-creem.
I borrowed a dog, one with
Mismatched eyes and a happy tongue,
And wanted to prove I was tough   5
In the alley, kicking over trash cans,
A dull chime of tuna cans falling.
I hurled light bulbs like grenades
And men teachers held their heads,
Fingers of blood lengthening   10
On the ground. I flicked rocks at cats,
Their goofy faces spurred with foxtails.
I kicked fences. I shooed pigeons.
I broke a branch from a flowering peach

And frightened ants with a stream of spit.   15
I said *"Chale,"* "In your face," and "No way
Daddy-O" to an imaginary priest
Until grandma came into the alley,
Her apron flapping in a breeze,
Her hair mussed, and said, "Let me help you,"   20
And punched me between the eyes.

                                                                        (1985)

LOUISE ERDRICH
[b. 1954]

Indian Boarding School: The Runaways

Home's the place we head for in our sleep.
Boxcars stumbling north in dreams
don't wait for us. We catch them on the run.
The rails, old lacerations that we love,
shoot parallel across the face and break   5
just under Turtle Mountains. Riding scars
you can't get lost. Home is the place they cross.

The lame guard strikes a match and makes the dark
less tolerant. We watch through cracks in boards
as the land starts rolling, rolling till it hurts   10
to be here, cold in regulation clothes.
We know the sheriff's waiting at midrun
to take us back. His car is dumb and warm.
The highway doesn't rock, it only hums
like a wing of long insults. The worn-down welts   15
of ancient punishments lead back and forth.

All runaways wear dresses, long green ones,
the color you would think shame was. We scrub
the sidewalks down because it's shameful work.
Our brushes cut the stone in watered arcs   20
and in the soak frail outlines shiver clear
a moment, things us kids pressed on the dark
face before it hardened, place, remembering
delicate old injuries, the spines of names and leaves.

                                                                        (1984)

Critical Theory: Approaches to the Analysis and Interpretation of Literature

READING FOR ANALYSIS

EMILY DICKINSON
[1830–1886]

I'm "wife"—I've finished that—
That other state—
I'm Czar—I'm "Woman" now—
It's safer so—

How odd the Girl's life looks
Behind this soft Eclipse—
I think that Earth feels so
To folks in Heaven—now—

This being comfort—then
That other kind—was pain—
But why compare?
I'm "Wife"! Stop there!

THE CANON AND THE CURRICULUM

Interpreting literature is an art and a skill that readers develop with experience and practice. Regular reading of stories, poems, plays, and essays will give you opportunities to become a skillful interpreter. Simply reading the literary works, however, is not enough, not if you wish to participate in the invigorating critical conversations teachers and other experienced readers bring to their discussion of literature. To develop a sense of the interpretive possibilities of literary works, you will need to know something of the various critical perspectives that literary critics use to analyze and interpret literature. This chapter introduces you to a number of major critical perspectives, including historical, biographical, psychological, and sociological approaches (among others), each of which approaches the study of literature a different way.

This discussion of critical perspectives aims to provide you with a set of ideas about how literature can be analyzed and interpreted. It is not designed to explain the history of literary criticism. Nor is its goal to convert you to a particular critical approach. Neither has any attempt been made to present the intricacies and variations in interpretive analysis developed by proponents of the various critical perspectives. And although you will find in this chapter discussions of ten critical perspectives, still other approaches to literary interpretation are available, both older ones that have currently declined in use and newer approaches that are still emerging.

Before considering the first of our critical perspectives, that of formalist criticism, we should review some basic questions currently being debated, sometimes heatedly, throughout the educational establishment. You may have already heard about the controversy surrounding the literary "canon" or list of works considered suitable for study in a university curriculum. There is now considerable disagreement about just what books should be read in college courses, why they should be read, and how they should be read. As a way of putting the ten critical perspectives in context, we will take up each of these questions in a brief overview of the current debate about the university literature curriculum.

What We Read

The notion of a literary canon or collection of accepted books derives from the idea of a biblical canon—those books accepted as official scriptures. A scriptural canon contains those works deemed to represent the moral standards and religious beliefs of a particular group, Jews for example, or Muslims, Hindus, or Christians. A canon of accepted works also contains, by implication, its obverse or flip side—that some works are excluded from the canon. Just as certain works, such as the

Book of Maccabees, were not accepted into the Hebrew Scriptures and the Gospel of Thomas was denied entry into the Christian New Testament, not every book or literary work written can become part of an officially sanctioned literary canon or a university curriculum. Certain works inevitably will be omitted while others just as necessarily are selected for inclusion. The central question revolves around which works should be included in the canon, and why.

As you may know, certain "classics" for a long time have dominated the canon of literature for study in university courses—epic poems by Homer and Dante, for example, plays by Ibsen and Shakespeare, poems by writers from many countries, but especially those from Europe and America, novels such as Charles Dickens's *Great Expectations,* Jane Austen's *Pride and Prejudice,* Mark Twain's *The Adventures of Huckleberry Finn*, Emily Brontë's *Wuthering Heights,* and many others. In the last two decades, however, there has been a movement to alter the canon of classical works, most of which have been written by white males of European ancestry, in the more or less distant past. Some of the changes in what we read have come from adding works by writers long omitted, such as those by minority writers—African Americans, Native Americans, Asian Americans, and other writers from around the world beyond Europe, those from Australia, India, and Africa, for example. The works added by minority writers have been largely, though not exclusively, modern and contemporary ones.

Still other changes in the literary canon have come from the rediscovery or recovery of older works, many from the Renaissance and the nineteenth century, especially works by women, which had for a long time been considered unworthy of serious study and of inclusion in college literature curricula. Such works were considered not to have withstood the test of time, lasting decades or centuries, as have the classics. What needs to be remembered, however, is that "time" is an abstraction that itself accomplishes nothing. It is, rather, individuals throughout time who make the choices about which books are to be taught in schools and universities. And it is people today of both genders and of various cultures, races, ethnicities, and sexual dispositions who are debating not only what works should be part of the canon of literature but whether the very idea of a canon is viable at all. In other words, what is a canon for? Is a literary canon inevitable? Is it even necessary?

Why We Read

These changes in what we read are related to a debate about why we read. Classic novels and plays, stories and poems have long been read because the lessons they are presumed to teach are considered valuable. The meanings of certain American canonical works, for example, have been viewed as educationally and morally good for readers to assimilate, largely because the works are believed to reflect values central to the American way of life. They reflect values relating to the importance of friendship, responsible behavior, and hard work, for example, or values relating to decency, justice, and fair play. Of course, other works accepted into the literary canon taught in American colleges and universities do not reflect such views, both works written by American writers and works by writers of other nationalities and literary traditions, many of which are included in this book.

It is certainly the case that regardless of the language(s) and tradition(s) represented by a canon of literary works, those works are often canonized because they are believed to perpetuate a tradition of moral beliefs, cultural attitudes, and social dispositions. What is interesting to note, however, is that canonical literary works of many traditions and genres—Henrik Ibsen's *A Doll House,* for example, or Emily Dickinson's lyric poems—disrupt and run counter to many traditional literary, social, religious, and cultural values. And works such as Shakespeare's tragedies and Keats's and Wordsworth's poetry harbor ideas and attitudes about which common readers and professional critics have long disagreed, a disagreement that derives partly from varying critical perspectives used to interpret the works and partly from their richness and complexity, which makes it impossible to say once and for all just what those enticing and intellectually provocative works mean.

Another reason for the continuity of the traditional canon is that it is easier to preserve the status quo than to initiate change. Change is neither welcomed nor embraced, even when it is inevitable. Moreover, later generations read the books of former ones because earlier generations want their descendants to read and value what they read and valued. Those earlier generations have the power to enforce such a decision since they hold the positions of authority in schools and on councils that design curricula and create reading lists for school programs and university courses.

Today, however, many of these assumptions have been reevaluated by teachers and critics from a wide range of political persuasions. With the demographic changes that have been occurring in educational institutions in the past quarter century have come additional reasons for reading. Minority groups that now form a significant population in university classrooms, minority teachers, younger faculty raised in a much altered political environment, large numbers of women faculty—all insist on the need for multiple perspectives, varying voices, different visions of experience. They argue that literary works should be read to challenge conventional ways of behaving and orthodox ways of thinking. (Some educators say that there is nothing new in this, and that, in fact, traditional canonical works have long been read this way.) For some of these other readers, however, literature exists less for moral instruction or cultural education than to help inaugurate political and social change, a view that is less widely endorsed than the view that literary works should invite critical scrutiny and stimulate questioning and debate.

How We Read

That brings us to the important question of how we read. Just how do we read? Do we simply "just read"? And if we do, then what do we mean by "just reading"? Most often just reading means something on the order of reading for pleasure, without worrying about analysis and interpretation. From the standpoint of more analytical reading, "just reading" refers to interpreting the words on the page, making sense of them in a way that seems reasonable.

But a number of assumptions lie behind this notion. One such assumption is that the meaning of a literary work is available to anyone willing to read it carefully. Another is that literary works contain layers or levels of meaning, that they have to be analyzed to understand their complex meanings. Still another is that although different readers all bring their unique experience as members of particular genders, races, religions, and nationalities to their interpretation of literary works, they finally understand the meaning of those works in the same way. In this view, literary works such as *Hamlet* or *The Scarlet Letter* mean the same thing to every reader.

Each of these assumptions, however, has been challenged by literary theorists in the past two decades, to the extent that many serious readers find them untenable. It doesn't take long, for example, to realize that though we share some understanding of Shakespeare's play or Hawthorne's novel, we invariably see different things in them and see them differently. The differences we make of literary works and the different ways we understand them are related to the varying assumptions about literature and life that we bring to our reading. The different ways these assumptions have been modified and the different emphases and focuses serious readers and literary critics bring to bear on literary works can be categorized according to various approaches or critical perspectives. Ten critical perspectives are here presented, though others could be added. These ten, however, reflect critical positions that many academic readers find useful, whether they are reading works new to the canon or older established ones.

For each critical perspective you will find an overview that introduces the critical approach, an application of the critical perspective to the Emily Dickinson poem reprinted at the beginning of this chapter, and a list of questions you can use to apply the critical perspective to other literary works. A set of selected readings concludes each section.

Think of these ten critical perspectives as a kind of critical smorgasbord, a set of intellectual dishes you can sample and taste. Those you find most appealing you may wish to partake of more heartily, partly by applying them in your own analytical writing, partly by reading from the list of selected books. Or your instructor may encourage you to work with ones he or she believes are especially valuable. The important thing to realize, however, is that you always interpret a literary work from a theoretical standpoint, however hidden or implicit it may be. Understanding the assumptions and procedures of the various theoretical perspectives is crucial for understanding what you are doing when you interpret literature, how you do it, and why you do it that way.

In his lively book introducing college students to literary theory, *Falling Into Theory* (1994), David H. Richter of Queens College CUNY summarizes the important issues concerning literary studies today in a series of provocative questions. Richter organizes his questions according to the categories I have borrowed from him for this introductory overview: *why we read, what we read, how we read*. Keep Richter's guiding questions in mind as you read the discussion of the various critical perspectives.

> *Why we read*. What is the place of the humanities and literary studies in society? Why should we study literature? Why do we read?
> *What we read*. What is literature and who determines what counts as literature? Is there a core of "great books" that every student should read? What is the relationship of literature by women and minority groups to the canon? Are criteria of quality universal, or are literary values essentially political?
> *How we read*. How do we and how should we read texts? Does meaning reside in the author, the text, or the reader? To what degree is the meaning of a text fixed? What ethical concerns do we bring to texts as readers, and how do these concerns reshape the texts we read? What do we owe the text and what does it owe us? How do the politics of race and gender shape our reading of texts? Do political approaches to literature betray or shed light on them?

Canon and Curriculum: Selected Readings

To learn more about the controversy surrounding the literary canon and the college English curriculum, the following books provide a variety of perspectives on the issues.

Alter, Robert. *The Pleasures of Reading in an Ideological Age*. 1989.
Atlas, James. *The Battle of the Books*. 1990.
D'Souza, Dinesh. *Illiberal Education: The Politics of Sex and Race on Campus*. 1991.
Eagleton, Terry. *Literary Theory: An Introduction*. 1983.
Graff, Gerald. *Beyond the Culture Wars*. 1992.
Greenblatt, Stephen, and Giles Gunn. *Redrawing the Boundaries: The Transformation of English and American Literary Studies*. 1992.
Kimball, Roger. *Tenured Radicals: How Politics Has Corrupted Higher Education*. 1990.
Lauter, Paul. *Canons and Contexts*. 1991.
Lentricchia, Frank. *Criticism and Social Change*. 1983.
Levine, George et al. *Speaking for the Humanities*. 1989.
Richter, David. *Falling Into Theory*. 1994.
Scholes, Robert. *Textual Power*. 1985.

FORMALIST PERSPECTIVES

An Overview of Formalist Criticism

Formalist critics view literature as a distinctive art, one that uses the resources of language to shape experience, communicate meaning, and express emotion.

Formalists emphasize the form of a literary work to determine its meaning, focusing on literary elements such as plot, character, setting, diction, imagery, structure, and point of view. Approaching literary works as independent systems with interdependent parts, formalists typically subordinate biographical information or historical data in their interpretations. Underlying formalist critical perspectives is the belief that literary works are unified artistic wholes that can be understood by analyzing their parts.

According to the formalist view, the proper concern of literary criticism is with the work itself rather than with literary history, the life of the author, or a work's social and historical contexts. For a formalist, the central meaning of a literary work is discovered through a detailed analysis of the work's formal elements rather than by going outside the work to consider other issues, whether biographical, historical, psychological, social, political, or ideological. Such additional considerations, from the formalist perspective, are extrinsic, or external, and are of secondary importance. What matters most to the formalist critic is how the work comes to mean what it does—how its resources of language are deployed by the writer to convey meaning. Implicit in the formalist perspective, moreover, is that readers can indeed determine the meanings of literary works—that literature can be understood and its meanings clarified.

Two other tenets of formalist criticism deserve mention: (1) that a literary work exists independent of any particular reader—that is, that a literary work exists outside of any reader's re-creation of it in the act of reading; (2) that the greatest literary works are "universal," their wholeness and aesthetic harmony transcending the specific particularities they describe.

The primary method of formalism is a close reading of the literary text, with an emphasis, for example, on a work's use of metaphor or symbol, its deployment of irony, its patterns of image or action. Lyric poetry lends itself especially well to the kinds of close reading favored by formalist critics because its language tends to be more compressed and metaphorical than the language of prose—at least as a general rule. Nonetheless, formal analysis of novels and plays can also focus on close reading of key passages (the opening and closing chapters of a novel, for example, or the first and last scenes of a play, or a climactic moment in the action of drama, poetry, or fiction). In addition, formalist critics analyze the large-scale structures of longer works, looking for patterns and relationships among scenes, actions, and characters.

One consistent feature of formalist criticism is an emphasis on tension and ambiguity. Tension refers to the way elements of a text's language reflect conflict and opposition. Ambiguity refers to the ways texts remain open to more than a single, unified, definitive interpretation. Both tension and ambiguity as elements of formalist critical approaches were picked up and elaborated to serve different interpretive arguments by critics employing the methodologies of structuralism and deconstruction.

In Chapter Three, "Elements of Poetry," "Diction," you will find techniques of formal analysis applied to Wordsworth's diction in "I wandered lonely as a cloud," which is analyzed to show how Wordsworth's language relates to the image patterns he creates and how diction and imagery contribute to the poem's meaning.

Thinking from a Formalist Perspective

A formalist critic reading Emily Dickinson's "I'm 'wife'" would note its neat division into three stanzas and consider the focus of each. A formalist perspective would consider why, in fact, the poem is cast in three stanzas and not one or two, four, or six. A consideration of the relationship between form and meaning might help readers notice how the poem's rhyme scheme and its sentence patterns reinforce or subvert its stanza organization.

Other considerations formalist critics would be likely to raise about the poem might include the connotations of "Czar" for the speaker. Of particular importance in this regard would be the language used to describe the "Girl's life" in the second stanza, especially how it is described as existing behind a "soft Eclipse." Readers following a formalist agenda might also question how the slant rhymes of the poem contribute to its idea and its effect.

Such questions, however, are only a starting point toward a formal analysis of Dickinson's poem.

A CHECKLIST OF FORMALIST CRITICAL QUESTIONS

1. How is the work structured or organized? How does it begin? Where does it go next? How does it end? What is the work's plot? How is its plot related to its structure?
2. What is the relationship of each part of the work to the work as a whole? How are the parts related to one another?
3. Who is narrating or telling what happens in the work? How is the narrator, speaker, or character revealed to readers? How do we come to know and understand this figure?
4. Who are the major and minor characters, what do they represent, and how do they relate to one another?
5. What are the time and place of the work—its setting? How is the setting related to what we know of the characters and their actions? To what extent is the setting symbolic?
6. What kind of language does the author use to describe, narrate, explain, or otherwise create the world of the literary work? More specifically, what images, similes, metaphors, symbols appear in the work? What is their function? What meanings do they convey?

Formalist Criticism: Selected Readings

Brooks, Cleanth. *The Well Wrought Urn: Studies in the Structure of Poetry.* 1947.
Burke, Kenneth. *Counterstatement.* 1930.
Eliot, T. S. *Selected Essays.* 1932.
Empson, William. *Seven Types of Ambiguity.* 1930.
Ransom, John Crowe. *The New Criticism.* 1941.
Wellek, Rene, and Austin Warren. *Theory of Literature.* 1949, 1973.

Wimsatt, W. K. *The Verbal Icon*. 1954.

BIOGRAPHICAL PERSPECTIVES

An Overview of Biographical Criticism

To what extent a writer's life should be brought to bear on an interpretation of his or her work has long been a matter of controversy. Some critics insist that biographical information at best distracts from and at worst distorts the process of analyzing, appreciating, and understanding literary works. These critics believe that literary works must stand on their own, stripped of the facts of their writers' lives.

Against this view, however, can be placed one that values the information readers gain from knowing about writers' lives. Biographical critics argue that there are essentially three kinds of benefits readers acquire from using biographical evidence for literary interpretation: (1) readers understand literary works better since the facts about authors' experiences can help readers decide how to interpret those works; (2) readers can better appreciate a literary work for knowing the writer's struggles or difficulties in creating it; and (3) readers can better assess writers' preoccupations by studying the ways they modify and adjust their actual experience in their literary works.

Knowing, for example, that Shakespeare was an actor who performed in the plays he wrote provides an added dimension to our appreciation of his genius. It also might invite us to look at his plays from the practical standpoint of a performer rather than merely from the perspective of an armchair reader, a classroom student, or a theatergoer. Or understanding the more circumscribed life led by poet Emily Dickinson may bear on our reading of her work. Considering biographical information and using it to analyze the finished literary work can be illuminating rather than distracting or distorting. Thinking about the different alternative titles a writer may have considered can also lead readers to focus on different aspects of a work, especially to emphasize different incidents and to value the viewpoints of different characters. As with any critical approach, however, a biographical perspective should be used judiciously, keeping the focus on the literary work and using the biographical information to clarify understanding and to develop an interpretation.

A biographical critic can focus on a writer's works not only to enhance understanding of them individually but also to enrich a reader's understanding of the artist. In an essay on the relations between literature and biography, Leon Edel, author of an outstanding biography of Henry James, suggests that what the literary biographer seeks to discover about the subject are his or her characteristic ways of thinking, perceiving, and feeling that may be revealed more honestly and thoroughly in the writer's work than in his or her conscious nonliterary statements. In addition, what we learn about writers from a judicious study of their work can also be linked with an understanding of the writer's world, and thus serve as a bridge to an appreciation of the social and cultural contexts in which the writer lived.

Thinking from a Biographical Perspective

Of biographical interest regarding Dickinson's "I'm 'wife'" is the fact that Dickinson never married. A critic with a biographical bent might see in this early poem themes and concerns that became important preoccupations for the poet, issues of gender and power, concerns about the relationship between men and women in marriage, both a marriage she may have wanted for herself and the marriage of her brother, a marriage that some biographers argue was a disappointment to her, though one she initially encouraged. Biographical questions of interest would focus on whether Dickinson's poem was based on her own experience, perhaps on frustrated hopes, or whether it was simply a metaphor she played with poetically to deflect the circumstances of everyday reality.

A CHECKLIST OF BIOGRAPHICAL CRITICAL QUESTIONS

1. What influences—persons, ideas, movements, events—evident in the writer's life does the work reflect?
2. To what extent are the events described in the work a direct transfer of what happened in the writer's actual life?
3. What modifications of the actual events has the writer made in the literary work? For what possible purposes?
4. Why might the writer have altered his or her actual experience in the literary work?
5. What are the effects of the differences between actual events and their literary transformation in the poem, story, play, or essay?
6. What has the author revealed in the work about his or her characteristic modes of thought, perception, or emotion? What place does this work have in the artist's literary development and career?

Biographical Criticism: Selected Readings

Edel, Leon. *Henry James,* 5 vols. 1953–1972.
Farr, Judith. *The Passion of Emily Dickinson.* 1992.
Mariani, Paul. *William Carlos Williams: A New World Naked.* 1981.
Sewall, Richard B. *The Life of Emily Dickinson,* 2 vols. 1974.
Williams, William Carlos. *Autobiography.* 1951, 1967.
Wolff, Cynthia Griffin. *Emily Dickinson.* 1986.

HISTORICAL PERSPECTIVES

An Overview of Historical Criticism

Historical critics approach literature in two ways: (1) they provide a context of background information necessary for understanding how literary works were perceived in their time; (2) they show how literary works reflect ideas and attitudes of the time in which they were written. These two general approaches to historical criticism represent methods and approaches that might be termed "old historicism" and "new historicism" respectively.

The older form of historical criticism, still in use today, insists that a literary work be read with a sense of the time and place of its creation. This is necessary, insist historical critics, because every literary work is a product of its time and its world. Understanding the social background and the intellectual currents of that time and that world illuminate literary works for later generations of readers.

Knowing something about the London of William Blake's time, for example, helps readers better appreciate and understand the power of Blake's protest against horrific social conditions and the institutions of church and state Blake held responsible for permitting such conditions to exist. In his poem "London," Blake refers to chimney sweepers, who were usually young children small enough to fit inside a chimney, and whose parents sent them to a kind of work that drastically curtailed not only their childhood but also their lives.

Thinking from a New Historicist Perspective

Like earlier historical approaches, a more contemporary approach identified as "new historicism" considers historical contexts of literary works essential for understanding them. A significant difference, however, between earlier historical criticism and new historicism is the newer variety's emphasis on analyzing historical documents with the same intensity and scrutiny given foregrounded passages in the literary works to be interpreted. In interpreting Dickinson's "I'm 'wife'" new historicist critics would concern themselves with diaries of women written during the early 1860s, when the poem was written. The diaries would be read to ascertain prevailing cultural attitudes about middle-class marriage. In addition, new historicist critics might also typically compare prevailing cultural attitudes about this issue today with those of the times in which the poem was written. In fact, one common strategy of new historicist critics is to compare and contrast the language of contemporaneous documents and literary works to reveal hidden assumptions, biases, and cultural attitudes that relate the two kinds of texts, literary and documentary, usually to demonstrate how the literary work shares the cultural assumptions of the document.

An important feature of new historicist criticism is its concern with examining the power relations of rulers and subjects. A guiding assumption among many new historicist critics is that texts, not only literary works but also documents, diaries, records, even institutions such as hospitals and prisons, are ideological products culturally constructed from the prevailing power structures that dominate particular societies. Reading a literary work from a new historicist perspective thus becomes an exercise in uncovering the conflicting and subversive perspectives of the marginalized and suppressed, as, for example, the vision and values of the speaker in Dickinson's "I'm 'wife,'" whose perspectives tend to be undervalued because she is female.

While appropriating some of the methods of formalist and deconstructive critics, new historicists differ from them in a number of important ways. Most importantly, unlike critics who limit their analysis of a literary work to its language and structure, new historicists spend more time analyzing nonliterary texts from the same time in which the literary work was written. New historicists, however, do apply the close reading strategies of formalist and deconstructive perspectives, but their goal is not, like the formalists, to show how the literary work manifests universal values or how it is unified. Nor is the new historicist goal to show how the text undermines and contradicts itself, an emphasis of deconstructive perspectives. Instead, new historicists analyze the cultural context embedded in the literary work and explain its relationship with the network of the assumptions and beliefs that inform social institutions and cultural practices prevalent in the historical period when the literary work was written. Finally, it is important to note that for new historicist critics, history does not provide mere "background" against which to study literary works, but is, rather, an equally important "text," one that is ultimately inseparable from the literary work, which inevitably reveals the conflicting power relations that underlie all human interaction, from the small-scale interactions with families to the large-scale interactions of social institutions.

One potential danger of applying historical perspectives to literature is that historical information and documents may be foregrounded and emphasized so heavily that readers lose sight of the literary work the historical approach is designed to illuminate. When the prism of history is used to clarify and explain elements of the literary work, however, whether in examining intellectual currents, describing social conditions, or presenting cultural attitudes, readers' understanding of literary works can be immeasurably enriched. The challenge for historical understanding, whether one uses the tools of the older historicist tradition or the methods of the new historicism, is to ascertain what the past was truly like, how its values are inscribed in its cultural artifacts, including its literature. Equally challenging is an exploration of the question, What was it possible to think or do at a particular moment of the past, including possibilities that may no longer be available to those living today?

A CHECKLIST OF HISTORICAL AND NEW HISTORICIST CRITICAL QUESTIONS

1. When was the work written? When was it published? How was it received by the critics and the public? Why?
2. What does the work's reception reveal about the standards of taste and value during the time it was published and reviewed?
3. What social attitudes and cultural practices related to the action of the work were prevalent during the time the work was written and published?
4. What kinds of power relations does the work describe, reflect, or embody?
5. How do the power relations reflected in the literary work manifest themselves in the cultural practices and social institutions prevalent during the time the work was written and published?

6. What other types of historical documents, cultural artifacts, or social institutions might be analyzed in conjunction with particular literary works? How might a close reading of such a nonliterary "text" illuminate those literary works?
7. To what extent can we understand the past as it is reflected in the literary work? To what extent does the work reflect differences from the ideas and values of its time?

Historical and New Historicist Criticism: Selected Readings

Dollmore, Jonathan, and Alan Sinfield. *Political Shakespeare.* 1985.
Geertz, Clifford. *The Interpretation of Cultures.* 1973.
Greenblatt, Stephen. *Learning to Curse: Essays in Early Modern Culture.* 1990.
Greenblatt, Stephen. *Marvellous Possessions.* 1991.
Kenner, Hugh. *The Pound Era.* 1971.
Levinson, Marjorie, et al. *Rethinking Historicism.* 1989.
Veeser, H. Aram. *The New Historicism.* 1989.
Veeser, H. Aram. *The New Historicism: A Reader.* 1994.

PSYCHOLOGICAL PERSPECTIVES

An Overview of Psychological Criticism

Psychological criticism approaches a work of literature as the revelation of its author's mind and personality. Psychological critics see literary works as intimately linked with their author's mental and emotional characteristics. Critics who employ a psychological perspective do so to explain how a literary work reflects its writer's consciousness and mental world, and they use what they know of writers' lives to explain features of their work. Some psychological critics are more interested in the creative processes of writers than in their literary works; these critics look into literary works for clues to a writer's creative imagination. Other psychological critics wish to study not so much a writer's creative process as his or her motivations and behavior; these critics may study a writer's works along with letters and diaries to better understand not just what a writer has done in life but why the writer behaved in a particular manner. Still other critics employ methods of Freudian psychoanalysis to understand not only the writers themselves, such as Shakespeare or Kafka, but the literary characters they create, Iago, for example, or Gregor Samsa.

Psychoanalytic criticism derives from Freud's revolutionary psychology in which he developed the notion of the "unconscious" along with the psychological mechanisms of "displacement," "condensation," "fixation," and "manifest and latent" dream content. Freud posited an unconscious element of the mind below consciousness, just beneath awareness. According to Freud, the unconscious harbors forbidden wishes and desires, often sexual, that are in conflict with an individual's or society's moral standards. Freud explains that although the individual represses or "censors" these unconscious fantasies and desires, they become "displaced" or distorted in dreams and other forms of fantasy, which serve to disguise their real meaning.

The disguised versions that appear in a person's conscious life are considered to be the "manifest" content of the unconscious wishes that are their "latent" content, which psychoanalytic critics attempt to discover and explain. Psychoanalytic critics rely heavily on symbolism to identify and explain the meaning of repressed desires, interpreting ordinary objects such as clocks and towers and natural elements such as fire and water in ways that reveal aspects of a literary character's sexuality. These critics also make use of other psychoanalytic concepts and terms such as "fixation," or "obsessive compulsion," attaching to feelings, behaviors, and fantasies that individuals presumably outgrow yet retain in the form of unconscious attractions.

Among the most important of the categories derived from Freud that psychoanalytic critics employ are those Freud used to describe mental structures and dynamics. Freud recognized three types of mental functions, which he designated the "id," the "ego," and the "superego." Freud saw the id as the storehouse of desires, primarily libidinal or sexual, but also aggressive and possessive. He saw the superego as the representative of societal and parental standards of ethics and morality. And he saw the ego as the negotiator between the desires and demands of the id and the controlling and constraining force of the superego, all influenced further by an individual's relationship with other people in the contexts of actual life. These few but important psychoanalytic concepts have been put to varied uses by critics with a wide range of psychological approaches.

Thinking from a Psychoanalytic Perspective

We can use a psychoanalytic perspective to make a few observations about the marital situation described in Dickinson's "I'm 'wife.'" Dickinson's speaker seems to fulfill a socially sanctioned role as "wife." What is interesting from a psychoanalytic standpoint, however, is the way she subverts that role by comparing herself to a "Czar," a powerful emperor, which seems to conflict with her role as "wife" and "Woman." Moreover, the speaker's comparison between the "Girl's life" and the wife's, which is elaborated with the analogy of differences experienced between those on Earth and in Heaven, can be seen as a displacement of her poetic ambition onto the image of a wife, which the speaker endows with spiritual and temporal powers.

A CHECKLIST OF PSYCHOLOGICAL CRITICAL QUESTIONS

1. What connections can you make between your knowledge of an author's life and the behavior and motivations of characters in his or her work?
2. How does your understanding of the characters, their relationships, their actions, and their motivations in a literary work help you better understand the mental world and imaginative life, or the actions and motivations, of the author?

3. How does a particular literary work—its images, metaphors, and other linguistic elements—reveal the psychological motivations of its characters or the psychological mindset of its author?
4. To what extent can you employ the concepts of Freudian psychoanalysis to understand the motivations of literary characters?
5. What kinds of literary works and what types of literary characters seem best suited to a critical approach that employs a psychological or psychoanalytical perspective? Why?
6. How can a psychological or psychoanalytic approach to a particular work be combined with an approach from another critical perspective—for example, that of biographical or formalist criticism, or that of feminist or deconstructionist criticism?

Psychological and Psychoanalytic Criticism: Selected Readings

Bloom, Harold. *The Anxiety of Influence.* 1973.
Chodorow, Nancy. *Feminism and Psychoanalytic Theory.* 1990.
Crews, Frederick. *Skeptical Engagements.* 1986.
Felman, Soshana. *Jacques Lacan and the Adventure of Insight.* 1987.
Freud, Sigmund. *The Interpretation of Dreams.* 1900.
Freud, Sigmund. *Introductory Lectures on Psychoanalysis.* 1917–1918.
Freud, Sigmund. *New Introductory Lectures on Psychoanalysis.* 1933.
Hoffman, Frederick J. *Freudianism and the Literary Mind.* 1957.
Holland, Norman. *The Dynamics of Literary Response.* 1968.
Manheim, Leonard, and Eleanor Manheim, eds. *Hidden Patterns: Studies in Psychoanalytic Literary Criticism.* 1966.
Mitchell, Juliet. *Psychoanalysis and Feminism.* 1975.
Nelson, Benjamin, ed. *Sigmund Freud on Creativity and the Unconscious.* 1958.
Skura, Meredith. *The Literary Use of the Psychoanalytic Process.* 1981.
Trilling, Lionel. *The Opposing Self.* 1955.
Wilson, Edmund. *The Wound and the Bow.* 1941.
Wright, Elizabeth, ed. *Psychoanalytic Criticism.* 1984.

SOCIOLOGICAL PERSPECTIVES

An Overview of Sociological Criticism

Like historical and biographical critics, sociological critics argue that literary works should not be isolated from the social contexts in which they are embedded. And also like historical critics, especially those who espouse new historicist perspectives, sociological critics emphasize the ways power relations are played out by varying social forces and institutions. Sociological critics focus on the values of a society and how those values are reflected in literary works. At one end of the sociological critical spectrum, literary works are treated simply as documents that either embody social conditions or are a product of those conditions. Critics employing a sociological perspective study the economic, political, and cultural issues expressed in literary works as those issues are reflected in the societies in which the works were produced.

A sociological approach to the study of Shakespeare's *Othello* could focus on the political organization of the Venetian state as depicted in the play and its relation to the play's depiction of authority, perhaps considering as well the breakdown of authority in the scenes set in Cyprus. Another sociological perspective might focus on the play's economic aspects, particularly how money and influence are used to manipulate others. Still other sociological issues that could be addressed include the role of women in the play and the issue of Othello's race. How, for example, does Shakespeare portray the power relations between Othello and Desdemona, Iago and Emilia, Cassio and Bianca? To what extent is each of these women's relationship with men considered from an economic standpoint? Or, to what extent is Othello's blackness a factor in his demise, or is his race a defining characteristic in other characters' perceptions of him?

Two significant trends in sociological criticism have had a decisive impact on critical theory: Marxist criticism and feminist criticism. Proponents of each of these critical perspectives have used some of the tools of other critical approaches such as the close reading of the formalists and deconstructionists and the symbolic analysis of the psychoanalytic critics to espouse their respective ideologies in interpreting literature.

Marxist Critical Perspectives

In the same way that many psychoanalytic critics base their approach to literature on the theoretical works of Sigmund Freud, Marxist critics are indebted to the political theory of Karl Marx and Friedrich Engels. Marxist critics examine literature for its reflection of how dominant elite and middle-class/bourgeois values lead to the control and suppression of the working classes. Marxist critics see literature's value in promoting social and economic revolution, with works that espouse Marxist ideology serving to prompt the kinds of economic and political changes that conform to Marxist principles. Such changes would include the overthrow of the dominant capitalist ideology and the loss of power by those with money and privilege. Marxist criticism is concerned both with understanding the role of politics, money, and power in literary works, and with redefining and reforming the way society distributes its resources among the classes. Fundamentally, the Marxist ideology looks toward a vision of a world not so much where class conflict has been minimized but one in which classes have disappeared altogether.

Marxist critics generally approach literary works as products of their era, especially as influenced, even determined by the economic and political ideologies that prevail at the time of their composition. The literary work is considered a "product" in relation to the actual economic and social conditions that exist at either the time of the work's composition or the time and place of the action it describes.

A CHECKLIST OF MARXIST CRITICAL QUESTIONS

1. What social forces and institutions are represented in the work? How are these forces portrayed? What is the author's attitude toward them?
2. What political economic elements appear in the work? How important are they in determining or influencing the lives of the characters?
3. What economic issues appear in the course of the work? How important are economic facts in influencing the motivation and behavior of the characters?
4. To what extent are the lives of the characters influenced or determined by social, political, and economic forces? To what extent are the characters aware of these forces?

Marxist Criticism: Selected Readings

Baxandall, Lee, and Stefan Morawski, eds. *Marx and Engels on Literature and Art.* 1973.
Benjamin, Walter. *Illuminations.* 1968.
Eagleton, Terry. *Marxism and Literary Criticism.* 1976.
Jameson, Fredric. *Marxism and Form.* 1971.
Lukacs, George. *Realism in Our Time.* 1972.
Trotsky, Leon. *Literature and the Revolution.* 1924.
Williams, Raymond. *Marxism and Literature.* 1977.

Feminist Critical Perspectives

Feminist criticism, like Marxist and new historicist criticism, examines the social and cultural aspects of literary works, especially for what those works reveal about the role, position, and influence of women. Like other socially minded critics, feminist critics consider literature in relation to its social, economic, and political contexts, and indeed look to analyze its social, economic, and political content. Feminist critics also typically see literature as an arena to contest for power and control, since as sociological critics, feminist critics also see literature as an agent for social transformation.

Moreover, feminist critics seek to redress the imbalance of literary study in which all important books are written by men or the only characters of real interest are male protagonists. Feminist critics have thus begun to study women writers whose works have been previously neglected. They have begun to look at the way feminine consciousness has been portrayed in literature written by both women and men. And they have begun to change the nature of the questions asked about literature that reflect predominantly male experience. In these and other ways feminist critical perspectives have begun to undermine the patriarchal or masculinist assumptions that have dominated critical approaches to literature until relatively recently. Feminist perspectives only began to be raised in literary circles with Virginia Woolf's *A Room of One's Own* (1929), which describes the difficult conditions under which women writers of the past had to work, and with Simone de Beauvoir's *The Second Sex* (1949), which analyzes the biology, psychology, and sociology of women and their place, role, and influence in Western culture.

In his influential and widely used *Glossary of Literary Terms,* M. H. Abrams identifies four central tenets of much feminist criticism, summarized in the following list.

> 1. Western civilization is pervasively patriarchal (ruled by the father)—that is, it is male-centered and controlled, and is organized and conducted in such a way as to subordinate women to men in all cultural domains: familial, religious, political, economic, social, legal, and artistic.
> 2. The prevailing concepts of *gender*—of the traits that constitute what is masculine and what is feminine—are largely, if not entirely, cultural constructs that were generated by the omnipresent patriarchal biases of our civilization.
> 3. This patriarchal (or "masculinist," or "androcentric") ideology pervades those writings which have been considered great literature, and which until recently have been written almost entirely by men for men.
> 4. The traditional aesthetic categories and criteria for analyzing and appraising literary works . . . are in fact infused with masculine assumptions, interests, and ways of reasoning, so that the standard rankings, and also the critical treatments, of literary works have in fact been tacitly but thoroughly gender-biased.★

It should be noted, however, that Abrams's list, though helpful, tends to blur distinctions among the many different varieties of feminist criticism as currently practiced. Thus the ways these assumptions are reflected in feminist criticism vary enormously from the reader-response approaches used by feminist critics, such as Judith Fetterley and Elizabeth Flynn, to the cultural studies approaches used by Jane Tompkins and Eve Kosovsky Sedgwick, to the Lacanian psychoanalytic approaches employed by Helene Cixous and Julia Kristeva. It would be better to think of feminist criticism in the plural as the criticism of feminists rather than to envision it as a singular monolithic entity.

Thinking from a Feminist Perspective

In applying the perspective of feminist criticism to "I'm 'wife,'" we might consider the way the roles of woman and wife are suggested in the poem. A feminist reading would be alert for other signs of power contestation in the poem, why for example the speaker compares herself to a "Czar," and what that means in terms of her ability to exert her will and control her destiny. Feminist readers would also ask what the masculine term "Czar" signifies in the poem, and whether there is a feminine counterpart.

★M. H. Abrams. *A Glossary of Literary Terms,* 6th ed., 1993, pp. 234–35.

Feminist readers might also interrogate the poem to ask why the state of wifehood brings "comfort" and "That other" state—of girlhood—"was pain." They would probe beyond the text of the poem to consider the extent to which such differences in experience and feeling obtained in marriages during Dickinson's lifetime, thus sharing an interest with new historicist critics. Moreover, they might also wonder whether the poem's abrupt ending "I'm 'Wife'! Stop there!" with its insistent tone might not mask an undercurrent of fear or powerlessness.

A CHECKLIST OF FEMINIST CRITICAL QUESTIONS

1. To what extent does the representation of women (and men) in the work reflect the place and time in which the work was written?
2. How are the relations between men and women, or those between members of the same sex, presented in the work? What roles do men and women assume and perform and with what consequences?
3. Does the author present the work from within a predominantly male or female sensibility? Why might this have been done, and with what effects?
4. How do the facts of the author's life relate to the presentation of men and women in the work? To their relative degrees of power?
5. How do other works by the author correspond to this one in their depiction of the power relationships between men and women?

Feminist Criticism: Selected Readings

Baym, Nina. *Woman's Fiction.* 1978.
Buck, Claire. *The Bloomsbury Guide to Women's Literature.* 1992.
Cixous, Helene. *The Laugh of the Medusa.* 1976.
Fetterley, Judith. *The Resisting Reader.* 1978.
Gallop, Jane. *The Daughter's Seduction: Feminism and Psychoanalysis.* 1982.
Gates, Henry L., Jr. *Reading Black, Reading Feminist.* 1990.
Gilbert, Sandra, and Susan Gubar. *The Madwoman in the Attic.* 1979.
Heilbrun, Carolyn. *Toward a Recognition of Adrogyny.* 1973.
Moers, Ellen. *Literary Women.* 1976.
Rich, Adrienne. *On Lies, Secrets, and Silence.* 1980.
Ruthven, K. K. *Feminist Literary Studies: An Introduction.* 1984.
Schweickart, Patricinio, and Elizabeth Flynn. *Gender and Reading.* 1986.
Showalter, Elaine. *A Literature of Their Own.* 1977.
Showalter, Elaine. *The New Feminist Criticism.* 1986.
Smith, Barbara. *Toward a Black Feminist Criticism.* 1977.

READER-RESPONSE PERSPECTIVES

An Overview of Reader-Response Criticism

Reader-response criticism raises the question of where literary meaning resides—in the literary text, in the reader, or in the interactive space between text and reader. Reader-response critics differ in the varying degrees of subjectivity they allow into their theories of interpretation. Some, like David Bleich, see the literary text as a kind of mirror in which readers see themselves. In making sense of literature, readers recreate themselves. Other reader-response critics, like Wolfgang Iser, focus on the text rather than on the feelings and reactions of the reader. Text-centered reader-response critics emphasize the temporal aspect of reading, suggesting that readers make sense of texts over time, moving through a text sentence by sentence, line by line, word by word, filling in gaps and making inferences about what is being implied by textual details as they read.

Still other reader-response critics like Norman Holland focus on the psychological dynamics of reading. Holland argues that every reader creates a specific identity theme unique to him or her self in reading any literary work. He suggests that to make sense of a literary work readers must find in it, or create through the process of reading it, their identity themes.

One of the earliest and most influential reader-response critics, Louise Rosenblatt, argues against placing too much emphasis on the reader's imagination, identity, or feelings in literary interpretation. Like Iser, Rosenblatt keeps the focus on the text, though she is more concerned than is Iser with the dynamic relationship between reader and text, since it is in that interrelationship that Rosenblatt believes literary meanings are made.

For Rosenblatt, as for other reader-response critics, the meaning of a literary work cannot exist until it is "performed" by the reader. Until then literary meaning is only potential. It becomes actual when readers realize its potential through their acts of reading, responding, and interpreting. As you might expect, reader-response critics respect not only the intellectual acts of analysis and comprehension that readers perform but also their subjective responses and their emotional apprehension of literary works.

One benefit of using reader-response perspectives to interpret literary works is that you begin with what is primary and basic—your initial reactions, your primary responses. Of course, as you read, you may change your mind about your reaction to a work. You may experience opposite or different feelings. Or you may make sense of the work differently because of discoveries you make later in the process of reading. What you read in the last chapter of a novel, for example, may change your understanding of what you read in the first chapter or in a middle chapter, which you had interpreted one way until you reached the end. What's important for reader-response critics is just this kind of active reading dynamic, in which a reader's changing ideas and feelings are foregrounded. These critics describe the recursiveness of the reading process, the way in which our minds anticipate what is coming in the text based on what we have already read and, simultaneously, the way we loop back retrospectively to reconsider earlier passages in light of later ones that we read. The literary text does not disappear for reader-response critics. Instead it becomes part of readers' experience as they make their way through it.

Reader-response criticism thus emphasizes process rather than product, an experience rather than an object, a shifting subjectivity rather than a static and objective text and meaning. For reader-response critics the text is not a "thing"; it does not stand still, for it lives only in its readers' imaginations. For these critics, then, literary works do not have an independent objective meaning that is true once and for all and that is identical for all readers. Instead, they argue that readers *make* meaning through their encounters with literary texts. And the meanings they make may be as varied as the individuals who read them.

Reader-response critics emphasize two additional points about the range and variety of readers' interpretations. First, an individual reader's interpretation of a work may change, in fact, probably will change over time. Reading Shakespeare's sonnets in high school can be a very different experience from reading them in college or later as an adult. Second, historically, readers from different generations and different centuries interpret books differently. The works say different things to readers of different historical eras based on their particular needs, concerns, and historical circumstances. In both the individual cases and the larger historical occasions, changes occur, changes that affect how individuals perceive, absorb, and understand what they read at different times of their lives.

The crucial thing for readers is to acknowledge their own subjectivity in the act of reading and to be aware that they come to literary works with a set of beliefs, ideas, attitudes, values—with all that makes them who and what they are. Being aware of our predispositions when we read can prevent our biases and prejudices from skewing our interpretations of literary works. At the same time, we need to pay attention to the details of the text. We cannot make words and sentences mean anything at all. There are limits and boundaries to what is acceptable, limits and boundaries that are subject to negotiation and debate. For most reader-response theorists, interpretation has both latitude and limits. Negotiating between them in a delicate balancing act allows readers to exercise their subjectivity while recognizing the significance of the words on the page.

Perhaps an analogy will clarify the double-sided nature of literary interpretation from a reader-response perspective, one that recognizes both the reader's freedom and the text's limits. You might think of a text as a musical score, one that is brought to life in performance. Readers make the potential meanings of a text come to life in much the same way that a musician brings a piece of music to life in performance. When musicians play a score or readers read a literary work, they cannot change the notes of the score or the words of the text. Both readers and musicians are limited by what is on the page. Yet there is room for differing interpretations and varied responses. Two interpretations of a literary work, like two musical performances, are likely to differ, sometimes in significant ways. The varying interpretations will be valid insofar as they respect the words or notes on the page, and insofar as they represent a reasonable and logically defensible approach to the work.

Thinking from a Reader–Response Perspective

In reading Dickinson's "I'm 'wife,'" reader-response critics might point to the way the poem's language associates "wife" with "Woman" and with "Czar" and invite readers to consider the extent to which these terms reflect their experience or understanding of marriage. They might ask whether the idea of marriage reflected in the poem reminds you of your own relatives' marriages, of the marriage of your parents. If so, why, a reader-response critic might ask, and, if not, why not?

Reader-response critics would also ask about readers' responses to the men who are implied but not explicitly named in the poem, and to the analogy made in the second stanza, which uses the contrast between Earth and Heaven to suggest a difference between the speaker's life before and after marriage. These critics might ask readers to explore their feelings about such an analogy and invite them to consider ways in which their own lives involve a difference such as that describing the speaker's before and after states. The emphases of reader-response critics essentially, then, would be two: (1) the reader's direct experience of the language and details of the poem in the process of reading it; (2) the reader's actual experience outside the poem which he or she brings to the reading and which is used to interpret it. Where formalist critics would play down this experiential connection to the poem and encourage readers to focus solely on the words on the page, reader-response critics want to extend the readers' perceptions about the poem and deepen their response to it by deliberately evoking actual experiences of readers that they can bring to bear on both their apprehension and their comprehension of the poem.

A CHECKLIST OF READER-RESPONSE CRITICAL QUESTIONS

1. What is your initial emotional response to the work? How did you feel upon first reading it?
2. Did you find yourself responding to it or reacting differently at any point? If so, why? If not, why not?
3. At what places in the text did you have to make inferences, fill in gaps, make interpretive decisions? On what bases did you make these inferential guesses?
4. How do you respond to the characters, the speaker, or the narrator? How do you feel about them? Why?
5. What places in the text caused you to do the most serious thinking? How did you put the pieces, sections, parts of the work together to make sense of it?
6. If you have read a work more than once, how has your second and subsequent readings differed from earlier ones? How do you account for those differences, or for the fact that there are no differences in either your thoughts or your feelings about the work?

Reader–Response Criticism: Selected Readings

Bleich, David. *Readings and Feelings.* 1975.
Bleich, David. *Subjective Criticism.* 1968.
Clifford, John, ed. *The Experience of Reading.* 1991.
Eco, Umberto. *The Open Work.* 1989.
Fish, Stanley. *Is There a Text in This Class?* 1980.
Freund, Elizabeth. *The Return of the Reader.* 1987.

Holland, Norman. *The Dynamics of Literary Response.* 1968.
Holland, Norman. *Poems in Persons.* 1973.
Iser, Wolfgang. *The Act of Reading.* 1978.
Mailloux, Steven. *Interpretive Conventions.* 1982.
Rabinowitz, Peter. *Before Reading.* 1987.
Rosenblatt, Louise. *Literature as Exploration.* 1939, 1975.
Rosenblatt, Louise. *The Reader, The Text, The Poem: A Transactional Theory of the Literary Work.* 1978.
Steig, Michael. *Stories of Reading.* 1989.
Suleiman, Susan R., and Inge Crosman, eds. *The Reader in the Text.* 1980.
Tompkins, Jane, ed. *Reader-Response Criticism.* 1980.
Wimmers, Inge Crosman. *Poetics of Reading.* 1988.

MYTHOLOGICAL PERSPECTIVES

An Overview of Mythological Criticism

In general terms a "myth" is a story that explains how something came to be. Every culture creates stories to explain what it considers important, valuable, and true. Thus the Greek myth of Persephone, who was kidnapped by Pluto, the god of the underworld, and allowed to return to her mother Demeter every year, explains the changes of the seasons. Or the Biblical story of Eve's temptation by the serpent in the book of Genesis, which concludes with God's curse of the serpent, explains, among other things, why snakes crawl on their bellies.

Myth criticism, however, is not concerned with stories that explain origins so much as those that provide universal story patterns that recur with regularity among many cultures and in many different times and places. The patterns myth critics typically identify and analyze are those that represent common, familiar, even universal human experiences, such as being born and dying, growing up and crossing the threshold into adulthood, going on a journey, engaging in sexual activity. These familiar patterns of human action and experience, however, are of interest to myth critics not primarily in and of themselves, but rather for how they represent religious beliefs, social customs, and cultural attitudes.

Birth, for example, is of interest as a symbolic beginning and death as a symbolic ending. A journey is a symbolic venturing out into the world to explore and experience what it has in store for the traveler. Sleeping and dreaming are not simply states of ordinary experience but symbolic modes of entrance into another realm and an envisioning of unusual and perhaps strange possibilities unimagined in waking life. So too with physical contests, sexual encounters, and other forms of experience, which many times are occasions for individuals to be tested, challenged, and perhaps initiated into an advanced or superior state of being—becoming a warrior, for example, a mother, a prophet, or a king.

Myth critics discover in literature of all times and places stories with basic patterns that can be explained in terms of *archetypes,* or universal symbols, which some mythological critics believe are part of every person's unconscious mind, a kind of a collective unconscious that each of us inherits by virtue of our common humanity. Besides the fundamental facts of human existence, other archetypes include typical literary characters such as the Don Juan or womanizer, the *femme fatale* or dangerous female, the trickster or con artist, the damsel in distress, the rebel, the tyrant, the hero, the betrayer. Creatures real and imaginary can also be archetypal symbols. The lion, for example, can represent strength, the eagle independence, the fox cunning, the unicorn innocence, the dragon destruction, the centaur the union of matter and spirit, animality and humanity, or even humanity and divinity.

It is on plot or the sequence of causally related incidents and actions, however, that myth criticism focuses most heavily. The archetypal images, creatures, and characters exist within stories that themselves exhibit patterns of recurrence. So, for example, there are stories of the arduous quest fraught with perils which a protagonist must survive, perhaps to rescue an innocent victim, perhaps to prove superior courage or morality, perhaps to save others from destruction. There are stories of vengeance, of death and rebirth, of resurrection, of transformation from one state of being into another, stories of enlightenment, of devastation, of lost paradises. Many such stories can be found in the religious literature of cultures around the world. The Bible, for example, contains stories of creation (Adam and Eve), fraternal rivalry and murder (Cain and Abel), destruction (Noah) and forgiveness (the ark and the covenant), wandering and enslavement (the exodus), death and resurrection (Jesus' life and ministry)—and so on. This list can be multiplied by consulting, for example, the Taoist and Confucian religious traditions of China, the Hindu traditions of India, the Buddhist traditions of Japan, and the Islamic tradition of the Middle East.

Myth critics approach the study of literary works and the study of a culture's myths in many ways. The Canadian critic Northrop Frye, for example, explains the traditional literary genres, including the novel, the drama, and epic, with reference to the recurrence in them of mythic patterns such as death and rebirth, departure and return, ignorance and insight. Frye, in fact, associates the genres of comedy, romance, tragedy, and irony or satire with the cycle of the seasons, each genre representing the natural events associated with a particular season (comedy with the fertility of spring, for example, and tragedy with the decline of the year in autumn). The French critic, Claude Lévi-Strauss, who employs the strategies of structuralist and semiotic analysis, treats cultural myths as signs whose meanings are not understood by the cultures that create those myths. His work is grounded in structural anthropology and owes much to the linguistic theory of Ferdinand de Saussure, who had a profound effect on the development of French and American structuralist perspectives on literary analysis and interpretation. And the American critic of popular culture, John Cawelti, to cite still another approach, analyzes the mythic impulse and mythic elements in forms of popular literature such as the western.

Thinking from a Mythological Perspective

What a mythological critic does with archetypal characters, stories, creatures, and even natural elements such as sun and moon, darkness and light, fire and water, is to link them up with one another, to see one literary work in relation to others of a similar type. Thus, for example, Hamlet's revenge of his father's death can be linked with myths from other cultures that include a son's avenging his father. Or the story of Hamlet can be linked with others in which the corruption poisoning a country has been eliminated through some action taken by the hero.

A myth critic might consider the role of Dickinson's "wife" and her rank as "Czar" in the poem "I'm 'wife'" in relation to prominent female characters from myth and legend, whether human or divine. Myth critics would probably take note too of the references to Heaven and Earth in developing an explanation of the transformation undergone by the speaker of the poem.

A CHECKLIST OF MYTHOLOGICAL CRITICAL QUESTIONS

1. What incidents in the work seem common or familiar enough as actions that they might be considered symbolic or archetypal? Are there any journeys, battles, falls, reversals of fortune?
2. What kinds of character types appear in the work? How might they be typed or classified?
3. What creatures, elements of nature, or man-made objects play a role in the work? To what extent might they be considered symbolic?
4. What changes do the characters undergo? How can those changes be characterized or named? To what might they be related or compared?
5. What religious or quasi-religious traditions with which you are familiar might the work's story, characters, elements, or objects be compared to or affiliated with? Why?

Mythological Criticism: Selected Readings

Bodkin, Maud. *Archetypal Patterns in Poetry.* 1934.
Campbell, Joseph. *The Hero with a Thousand Faces.* 1949.
Cawelti, John. *Adventure, Mystery, Romance.* 1976.
Chase, Richard. *Quest for Myth.* 1949.
Fiedler, Leslie. *Love and Death in the American Novel.* 1964.
Frazer, James G. *The Golden Bough,* rev. 1911.
Frye, Northrop. *Anatomy of Criticism.* 1957.
Graves, Robert. *The White Goddess.* 1948.
Jung, Carl Gustav. *Modern Man in Search of a Soul.* 1933.
Lévi-Strauss, Claude. *Structural Anthropology.* 1968.
Vickery, John B., ed. *Myth and Literature,* 1966.

STRUCTURALIST PERSPECTIVES

An Overview of Structuralist Criticism

It is important to distinguish the general meaning of "structure" as used by critics of varying persuasions from its use by adherents of structuralist criticism. In the traditional and most general sense, the word "structure" refers to the organization of a literary work—to its arrangement of incident and action (plot); its division into sections, chapters, parts, stanzas, and other literary units; its employment of repetition and contrast; its patterns of imagery (light and dark images, for example) and sound (its patterns of rhythm and rhyme).

For structuralist critics, however, the notion of "structure" has another meaning, one which derives from linguistics and anthropology and which refers to the systems of signs that designate meaning. To understand the structuralist perspective one needs to understand what structuralists mean by "signs" and how language is an arbitrary system of such signs. We can illustrate with a familiar example—the word "dog," which represents the four-legged animal many of us have as a pet. Why do the letters D-O-G, when put together, signify the creature who barks at the mail carrier and wags its tail while running off with our sneakers? The answer, of course, is because of a particular set of linguistic conventions that operate due to common usage and agreement. Such use and agreement, such a convention, however, is arbitrary. That is, it could have been otherwise. In fact, in languages such as French and Italian, the word "dog" means nothing. In those languages the furry four-footed barker is respectively *chien* (pronounced sheYEN) and *cane* (pronounced CAHnay), a word that looks like the English "cane," or walking stick, but which is a sign, in Italian, for what we call a dog.

But there is one additional linguistic element of importance—that of difference. We have just seen how the English word "cane" differs from the Italian *cane* and the French *chien* and how the two languages designate the faithful canine companion, perhaps named "Fido," in different ways. In both languages (as in all languages) words are differentiated from one another by sound and by spelling. Thus, in English C-A-N-E refers to a walking stick, but C-O-N-E and C-A-P-E to entirely different things. The same is true in Italian, where *cane,* our equivalent of dog, differs from *cani* (CAHknee), the Italian plural, meaning "dogs." This notion of difference is critical to the way structuralism analyzes systems of signs, for it is through differences that languages, literatures, and other social systems convey meaning.

One technique structuralist critics rely on heavily in analyzing difference is "binary opposition," in which a text's contrasting elements are identified and examined. In employing binary opposition as an analytical instrument, structuralist literary critics imitate what structural anthropologists do when they analyze societies to determine which of their social habits and customs are meaningful. The founder of structuralist anthropology, Claude Lévi-Strauss, an important influence on literary structuralism, has explained how a society's most important values can be deciphered by analyzing such binary oppositions as the distinction between "the raw and the cooked," which became a title for one of his books.

Structuralist critics find all kinds of opposition in literature, from small-scale elements, such as letters and syllables; through symbols, such as light and dark; to motions or directions (up and down), times (before and after), places (inside and outside), distances (far and near); to elements of plot and character, such as changes of feeling and reversals of fortune. Such differences are significant structural elements requiring interpretation, whether the differences are explicit or implicit, described or only hinted at.

Semiotics

Semiotics is the study of signs and sign systems; it is, more importantly, the study of codes, or the systems we use to understand the meaning of events and entities, including institutions and cultural happenings as well as verbal and visual texts—from poems to songs to advertisements, and more. Situated on the border between the humanities and the social and behavioral sciences, semiotics is concerned with how the workings of sign systems in various disciplines such as literature and psychology enable us to understand the richly textured significations of all kinds of cultural texts, from action films and television game shows and situation comedies to professional football games to parades and fourth of July celebrations; from religious rituals such as bar mitzvahs and marriage ceremonies to social occasions such as annual company picnics and New Year's parties.

Although semiotic perspectives derive from the theoretical foundations of structuralist and poststructuralist thought, semiotics does not limit itself to the goals and methods of those critical approaches. And though semiotic analysis is sometimes presented in logical symbols and mathematical terminology, it is not restricted to those forms of language. In fact, one of the strengths of a semiotic perspective is its ability to analyze the ways various discourses convey meaning, whether these discourses employ words or communicate, as does fashion, for example, by means of other signs and symbols.

Thinking from a Structuralist Perspective

We can analyze virtually anything from a structuralist perspective—a baseball or football game, an aerobics class, a restaurant menu or a three-course dinner, fashion shows, movies, MTV videos, newspaper cartoons. The possibilities are endless, and, in fact, one critic, Roland Barthes in his book *Mythologies,* has provided a series of brilliant structuralist analyses of foods, fashions, and sports, including wrestling.

Fairy tales and folktales have been a popular source of interpretations for structuralist critics, for such basic stories contain plots and character elements that lend themselves well to binary analysis, and they often reveal much about the values of the cultures that created them. Think of Cinderella, for example, and how she exists in opposition to her stepsisters (she is beautiful while they are ugly; she is poor while they are rich; she is a servant, they her masters). Remember how she loses one slipper while retaining the other, how her coach turns into a pumpkin and her footmen into mice (or is it the other way around)? Difference functions throughout the story on many levels, including the all-important one of the reversal of her fortune with that of her stepsisters and of a prince replacing her nasty stepmother as her future companion. You may also wish to consider books and movies that make use of the "Cinderella plot," where a metaphorical Prince Charming rescues a poor common girl from an oppressive and unhappy life. The films *An Officer and a Gentleman* and *Pretty Woman* provide two examples.

Dickinson's "I'm 'wife'" invites structuralist analysis as well. Not only do the poem's first and last lines begin with the words "I'm 'wife,'" which gives the poem something of a circular movement, but the term "Girl's life" is contrasted with the words "wife" and "Woman," and the state of being "wife" is set off against "That other state," which is unnamed but implied. In addition there is a contrast between "comfort" and "pain" and another posited between "Earth" and "Heaven." All these oppositions would be viewed by structuralist critics as key elements of signification.

A CHECKLIST OF STRUCTURALIST CRITICAL QUESTIONS

1. What are the elements of the work—words, stanzas, chapters, parts, for example— and how can these be seen as revealing "difference"?
2. How do the characters, narrators, speakers, or other voices heard in the work reveal difference?
3. How do the elements of the work's plot or overall action suggest a meaningful pattern? What changes, adjustments, transformations, shifts of tone, attitude, behavior, or feeling do you find?
4. How are the work's primary images and events related to one another? What elements of differentiation exist, and what do they signify?
5. What system of relationships governs the work as a whole?
6. What system of relations could be used to link this work with others of its kind? With different kinds of things with which it shares some similarities?

Structuralist Criticism: Selected Readings

Barthes, Roland. *Elements of Semiology.* 1967.
Culler, Jonathan. *Structuralist Poetics.* 1975.
Genette, Gerard. *Figures.* 1966.
Hawkes, Terence. *Structuralism and Semiotics.* 1977.
Lévi-Strauss, Claude. *The Raw and the Cooked.* 1966.
Macksey, Richard, and Eugenio Donato, eds. *The Structuralist Controversy.* 1970.
Scholes, Robert. *Semiotics and Interpretation.* 1982.
Scholes, Robert. *Structuralism in Literature: An Introduction.* 1974.
Smith, Barbara Herrnstein. *On the Margins of Discourse.* 1978.
Todorov, Tzvetan. *The Poetics of Prose,* trans. 1977.

DECONSTRUCTIVE PERSPECTIVES

An Overview of Deconstructive Criticism

Deconstruction arose as a further development of structuralism. Like structuralist critics, deconstructive critics look for opposition in literary works (and in other kinds of "texts" such as films, advertisements, and social institutions, including schools and hospitals). Like structuralism, deconstruction emphasizes difference, or the structure of constituent opposition in a text or any signifying system (for example, male/female, black/white, animate/inanimate). For deconstructionist critics, any meaning is constructed as the result of an opposition, which can be read as ideologically grounded. This is the case with the use of language itself, which creates meaning by opposition (the difference in meaning between the English words "cap" and "cup," for example, is based on a difference between their middle letters). The difference is significant as the words refer to different things.

Deconstruction differs from structuralism, however, in describing at once both a pair of equally valid conflicting oppositions, and in identifying a prevailing ideology that needs to be subverted, undermined, challenged, or otherwise called into question—an ideological view, for example, that suggests that one race or gender is superior to another, or a conviction that the poor are happy with their lot. We can distinguish the more explicitly politicized type of deconstruction, "deconstructionist criticism," from a less politically animated type, "deconstructive criticism," in which the ideological impulse is implicit rather than explicit, latent rather than overtly expressed.

Through a careful analysis of a text's language, deconstructive critics unravel the text by pointing to places where it is ambivalent, contradictory, or otherwise ambiguous. Critics who employ deconstruction as a critical method actually would say that the text deconstructs itself, and that critics do not deconstruct the text so much as show how the text contradicts itself and thereby dismantles itself. They would argue that the contradictions found in any verbal text are inherent in the nature of language, which functions as a system of opposition or differences. And since language itself is radically oppositional and thereby inherently ideological, then all discourse is, first, oppositional and hence subject to deconstruction, and, second, ideological, and indicative of power differentiation. In addition, deconstructionist critics also posit the existence of absent textual qualities or characteristics by suggesting that these absent elements have been suppressed by the dominant ideology that controls the apparent meaning of the work.

Deconstructionist critics operate on the premise that language is irretrievably self-contradictory and self-destroying. They argue that since language is unstable, it cannot be controlled by writers. As a result, literary works mean more than their authors are aware of, and their meanings are as unstable as the language of which they are constructed. The aim of deconstructive analysis is to demonstrate the instability of language in texts, thereby revealing how a text's conflicting forces inevitably destroy its apparently logical or meaningful structure and how its apparently clear meaning splits into contradictory, incompatible, and ultimately undecidable possibilities.

Deconstructionist criticism favors terms like "unmasking," "unraveling," "recovering," "suppression," and "contradiction." Unlike formalist criticism, which it resembles in its scrupulous attention to textual detail and its insistence on analyzing the text as a self-contained world, deconstructionist criticism attempts to dismantle the literary work and show that it does not mean what it appears to mean. Deconstructionist criticism includes a penchant for showing how literary texts "subvert" and "betray" themselves, an elevation of criticism to an equal stature with literary creation, and its radical skepticism about the ability of language to communicate anything except contradictions.

A crucial notion for deconstructionist criticism is that of difference, or "différence," as the seminal deconstructionist philosopher and critic Jacques Derrida spells it. By différence, Derrida means to suggest both the usual meaning of difference (dissimilarity) and the additional idea of deferral, both derived from the two meanings of the French verb "différer," which means "to differ" and "to defer" or "postpone." The kind of difference meant by Derrida is, specifically, a deferral of meaning that is never completed or finished because a spoken utterance or a written text means whatever it means as a function of differences among its elements. The result is that its meaning cannot be established as single or determinate. Meaning, thus, is indefinitely postponed, endlessly deferred.

This kind of playing with language is further exemplified by Derrida's explanation of the "self-effacing trace," his notion that a network of differences of meaning is implied even though those differences are not actually present in an utterance or a text. The explicit meaning, which is present, carries with it "traces" of the absent implied meanings, which for ideological reasons are suppressed, though other implications are "there" as inescapable alternative possibilities because they can be construed or imagined.

Thinking from a Deconstructive Perspective

A deconstructive analysis of Dickinson's "I'm 'wife'" would include consideration of the binary oppositions noted in the discussion of "Thinking from a Structuralist Perspective" mentioned earlier. The deconstructive strategy would be to show how the terms "wife," "Woman," "Czar," and "Girl's life" cancel each other out so that a single determinate meaning of the poem is impossible to establish. Deconstructionist critics would, in addition, attempt to show how the poem's inherent contradictions privilege one pair of terms, "wife" for example, over "Girl['s]," while undermining the apparent authority and privileged status of "wife" and the state to which it refers. They would also consider absent terms suggested but not stated directly, such as "Husband."

A CHECKLIST OF DECONSTRUCTIVE CRITICAL QUESTIONS

1. What oppositions exist in the work? Which of the two opposing terms of each pair is the privileged or more powerful term? How is this shown in the work?
2. What textual elements (descriptive details, images, incidents, passages) suggest a contradiction or alternative to the privileged or more powerful term?
3. What is the prevailing ideology or set of cultural assumptions in the work? Where are these assumptions most evident?
4. What passages of the work most reveal gaps, inconsistencies, or contradictions?
5. How stable is the text? How decidable is its meaning?

Deconstructive Criticism: Selected Readings

Attridge, Derek, ed. *Acts of Literature.* 1992.
Bloom, Harold, ed. *Deconstruction and Criticism.* 1979.
Culler, Jonathan. *On Deconstruction.* 1982.
de Man, Paul. *Allegories of Reading.* 1979.
Derrida, Jacques. *Writing and Difference.* 1978.
Johnson, Barbara. *A World of Difference.* 1987.
Norris, Christopher. *Deconstruction: Theory and Practice.* 1982.
Scholes, Robert. *Protocols of Reading.* 1989.
Taylor, Mark C., ed. *Deconstruction in Context.* 1986.

CULTURAL STUDIES PERSPECTIVES

An Overview of Cultural Studies

The term "cultural studies" indicates a wide range of critical approaches to the study of literature and society. It is a kind of umbrella term that not only includes approaches to the critical analysis of society such as Marxism, feminism, structuralism, deconstruction, and new historicism, but also refers to a wide range of interdisciplinary studies, including women's studies, African-American studies, Asian, Native American, Latino studies, and other types of area studies.

Like deconstruction, feminism, and new historicism, cultural studies perspectives are multidisciplinary. These and other forms of cultural criticism typically include the perspectives of both humanistic disciplines, such as literature and art, and the social and behavioral sciences, such as anthropology, economics, and psychology. The idea of cultural studies, however, is broader than any of the particular critical perspectives described in this chapter. Cultural studies are not restricted, for example, to structuralist or deconstructionist critical procedures, nor are they solely concerned with feminist issues or Marxist causes.

As a critical perspective in the late twentieth century, cultural studies employs a definition of culture that differs from two other common ways of considering it. Traditionally, and especially from the perspective of anthropology, culture has been considered as the way of life of a people, including its customs, beliefs, and attitudes, all of which cohere in a unified and organic way of life. This traditional anthropological notion has coexisted with another idea, one of culture as representing the best that a civilization has produced—in its institutions, its political and philosophical thought, its art, literature, music, architecture and other lasting achievements.

Both of these ways of viewing culture are contested by the newer forms of cultural studies, which look not at the stable coherences of a society or a civilization's history, but at its dissensions and conflicts. For the newer versions of cultural criticism, the unifying concerns and values of older forms of cultural study are suspect, largely because they avoid issues of political and social inequality. In fact, one way of viewing the current debate over the humanities described in an earlier section of this chapter, "The Canon and the Curriculum," is as a conflict between the older view of cultural studies that emphasizes a kind of normative national cultural consensus, and newer versions, which challenge such norms and values and question the very idea of cultural consensus. Moreover, the different goals and procedures of these contrasting cultural studies perspectives, along with the differences among the critical perspectives described earlier, powerfully illustrate how nearly everything now associated with literate culture has become contested. These areas of contestation include not only the meaning of "culture," but the meaning of teaching, learning, reading, and writing, along with notions of text, author, meaning, criticism, discipline, and department. Cultural studies perspectives breach the traditional understanding of these terms, in the process redrawing the boundaries that formerly separated them.

The notion of boundaries, in fact, is one of the more helpful metaphors for thinking about the new cultural studies. That some new emergent critical schools overlap or that critical perspectives may combine forces suggests how disciplinary borders are being crossed and their boundaries reconfigured. In addition to crossing geographical and intellectual boundaries (as well as those between high and popular culture), the new cultural studies also envision a plurality of cultures rather than seeing "Culture" with a capital "C" as singular, monolithic, or universal.

Thinking from a Cultural Studies Perspective

In considering literary works and other kinds of canonical and noncanonical texts from the various standpoints of cultural studies, it is important to note that no single approach, method, or procedure prevails. There is, then, no single "cultural studies" perspective on Dickinson's "I'm 'wife.'" Rather there are various ways of thinking about the cultural and social issues embedded in this work. Some of these issues have been raised in the explanations of feminist, Marxist, new historicist, structuralist, and deconstructionist critical perspectives.

One additional cultural studies perspective that has recently gained prominence is that of *gender criticism,* more specifically gay and lesbian studies. Gender criticism and studies overlap, to some extent, with feminist critical perspectives. In addition to studying the relations between and among men, gender criticism also explores such intra-gender issues of women as lesbian sexuality and female power relations.

One of the central problems of gender studies is the way gender is defined. To what extent, for example, does gender overlap with sex? To what extent is gender a cultural category and sex a biological one? To what extent do the language of sexuality used in the past and the current uses of both "sex" and "gender" as categories reflect biological, psychological, and socially constructed elements of sexual difference? Related to these overlapping questions are others, especially considerations of what some gender critics see as heterosocial or heterosexist bias in the very concept of gender and gender relations.

Gender critics share with adherents of other socially oriented perspectives a concern for analyzing power relations and for discerning ways in which homophobic discourse and attitudes prevail in society at large. Through analysis of various forms of historical evidence and through acts of political agency, gender critics have challenged perspectives that view homosexual acts and unions as "sinful" or "diseased." They have questioned the way AIDS has been represented in the mainstream media and have opened up discussion about what constitutes such apparently familiar notions as "family," "love," and "sexual identity."

A CHECKLIST OF GENDER STUDIES CRITICAL QUESTIONS

1. What kinds of sexual identity, behavior, and attitudes are reflected in the work? Is there any overtly or covertly expressed view of homosexuality or lesbianism?
2. To what extent does the work accommodate, describe, or exemplify same-sex relationships? To what extent are same-sex sexual relationships either in the foreground or background of the work?
3. With what kinds of social, economic, and cultural privileges (or lack thereof) are same-sex unions or relationships depicted? With what effects and consequences?

Cultural Studies: Selected Readings

Butler, Judith. *Gender Trouble.* 1989.
Comley, Nancy, and Robert Scholes. *Hemingway's Genders.* 1994.
Giroux, Henry. *Border Crossings.* 1992.
Gunn, Giles. *The Culture of Criticism and the Criticism of Culture.* 1987.
Sedgwick, Eve Kosofsky. *Between Men: English Literature and Male Homosexual Desire.* 1985.
Sedgwick, Eve Kosofsky. *Epistemology of the Closet.* 1990.
Tompkins, Jane. *Sensational Designs: The Cultural Work of American Fiction 1790–1860.* 1985.
Torgovnick, Marianna DeMarco. *Crossing Ocean Parkway.* 1994.

USING CRITICAL PERSPECTIVES AS HEURISTICS

One of your more difficult decisions regarding critical theory will be in choosing a critical perspective that is suitable and effective in analyzing a particular literary work. You might be able to offer, for example, a Marxist, deconstructionist, or feminist reading of "Humpty Dumpty" or "Little Bo Peep," even though these nursery rhymes may not be conventionally approached from any of those critical perspectives. You will need to decide whether one of those approaches offers a richer yield than a more traditional approach, such as formalism or myth criticism. The same is true of your approach to Dickinson's "I'm 'wife.'" Although it has been analyzed in this chapter from ten critical perspectives, you probably found that certain critical perspectives made a better interpretive fit than others for Dickinson's poem.

Another thing to remember is that you can combine critical perspectives. There is no rule of interpretation that says you must limit yourself to the language and method of a single critical approach or method. You may wish, for example, to combine formalist and structural perspectives in analyzing "I'm 'wife,'" while also raising feminist critical questions in your interpretation. Or you may wish to combine new historicist critical concerns with those of a biographical, psychological, or structuralist approach. In some ways, in fact, various concerns of the critical perspectives explained in this chapter overlap. Feminists raise historical questions as well as psychological and biographical ones. Reader-response critics attend to structuralist and formalist issues. And new historicist critics may employ formalist or deconstructionist methods of close reading.

A danger in using any critical approach to literature is that literary texts are read with an eye toward making them conform to a particular critical theory rather than using that critical theory to illuminate the text. In the process, critics may distort the text of a literary work by quoting from it selectively or by ignoring aspects of it that do not fit their theoretical approach or conform to their interpretive perspective. Some critics, moreover, apply their favorite critical perspective in a mechanical way, so that every work of literature is read with an eye toward proving the same ideological point, regardless of how important the issue is in one work as compared with another. Or critics may put all works of literature through an identical ideological meat grinder with every work emerging ground into the same kind of critical hamburger.

The various critical perspectives you have been learning about should be used as ways to think about literary works rather than as formulas for grinding out a particular kind of interpretation. Try to see the various critical perspectives as interpretive possibilities, as intellectual vistas that open up literary works rather than as stultifying formulas that limit what can be seen in them. Try, as well, to experience the element of intellectual playfulness, the imaginative energy and resourcefulness used in thinking with and through these critical perspectives.

Perhaps the best way to consider these and other critical perspectives is as *heuristics*, or methods for generating ideas, in this case, ideas about literature. A heuristic often takes the form of a set of questions. Writers and speakers use a sequence of questions to think through a topic in preparation for writing or speaking about it. Greek and Roman rhetoricians developed heuristics for generating ideas and for developing and organizing their thinking by using sets of questions that would enable them to think through a subject from a variety of perspectives. They used questions that invited comparison and contrast, definition and classification, analysis and division of a topic.

You can do the same with the critical perspectives described in this chapter. Instead of the classical questions that encourage comparison or causal analysis, use the questions that accompany each of the critical perspectives. Rather than deciding at first just which critical perspective is best suited to your chosen literary work, jot down answers to the questions for each of the approaches. As you think and write, you will begin to see which critical perspectives yield the most helpful ideas, which, that is, prompt your best thinking. In the course of using the critical questions to stimulate your thinking, you will also decide whether to use one critical perspective or to combine a few. You will also decide what you wish to say about the work. And you will begin to discover why you see it as you do, what you value in it, and how you can substantiate your way of seeing and experiencing it.

In addition, try to consider these critical perspectives as opportunities to engage in a play of mind. Viewing a literary work (or other cultural artifact) from a variety of critical perspectives will enable you to see more of its possibilities of signification. It will also give you a chance to live inside a variety of critical methods, to put on a number of different critical hats. Try to enjoy the experience.

CHAPTER NINE

Writing with Sources

WHY DO RESEARCH ABOUT LITERATURE?

One reason to do research about the literary works you read and study is to understand them better. Another is to see how they have been interpreted over the years, perhaps even centuries, since they were written. Moreover, scholars who have devoted their lives to the study of particular authors, periods, and genres can provide insights that can enrich your understanding and deepen your appreciation of literature.

Reading and studying literature in an academic environment also often requires research. You may be required to read books and articles about an author or a work, using your research in an essay on a literary topic. This is a fairly standard requirement in both general introductory literature courses and in more specialized courses for literature majors.

Even if research on the literature you read is not a requirement, you may find that what others who have read the same works have to say provides a stimulus for your own ideas. For example, you can use *The Humanities Index,* the *MLA Bibliography,* or your library's computerized catalog (see "Using Computerized Databases" in this chapter) to find articles about many of the selections in this book. You can also use *The New York Times Index* and *Book Review Digest* to find reviews of collections of short stories, essays, poems, or plays.

Locate several articles or reviews on a work you have read and, as you read them, notice when you have a particularly strong reaction. You may disagree with what you read, you may be surprised by a new point of view, or you may find your own opinions reinforced in a way you had not expected. You may find that one or more of the works consulted provides the spark for a fully developed essay of your own.

Research materials consist of two general kinds: primary sources and secondary sources. *Primary sources* are firsthand accounts, such as historical documents, diaries, journals, letters, and original literary works, including novels, stories, poems, plays, and essays. Primary sources constitute raw evidence you can use for your research paper. *Secondary sources* are materials written about primary sources. Secondary sources include critical writing that expresses opinions, draws conclusions, or explains an issue. Secondary sources include books, articles, pamphlets, and reviews.

CLARIFYING THE ASSIGNMENT

It is critical that you understand thoroughly the requirements of the assignment. Does your instructor expect you to write a three-page paper or a twenty-page paper—or, as is more likely, something in between? Are you expected to type your paper double-spaced? Are you required to use primary sources, secondary sources, or both? How many words, how many pages, and how many sources are required?

Are you expected to focus on a single work using only one or two sources, on a single work using multiple sources, on multiple works by an author—or something else? Are you expected to document your sources and to provide a list of works you cite in the paper? Be sure that you clarify the specific requirements of the assignment.

SELECTING A TOPIC

Instructors sometimes provide topics, either by assigning everyone the same topic (or some variation of it) or by giving individual students assigned topics of their own. If that is your situation, you can skip down to the next section on finding and using sources. Most often, however, you will need to choose your own topic for a paper utilizing literary research.

You can do a number of things to simplify the task of finding a topic. First, ask your instructor for suggestions. Second, look over your class notes and your reading notes for key points of emphasis, recurrent concerns, and interesting questions and ideas. Third, talk with other students, both with your classmates and with students who have already written papers for the course you are taking. Fourth, you can consult other sources with information about the author and work (or works) you will be writing about. Any or all of these can provide guidance and suggestions about viable topics for your paper.

A *viable topic* is one you can manage in the allotted number of pages required for the assignment. It should also be a topic you can say something about in detail and with specificity. Once you have settled on a topic, it's a good idea to clear it with your instructor. Once your instructor sees what you're interested in, he or she can help you shape the topic, perhaps by narrowing or broadening it in ways that might make it more manageable or potentially more interesting, or both.

You can also get ideas for topics by consulting the ideas for writing suggestions in Chapter Five, where you will find additional guidelines for writing about literary works. As a general guideline for all literary papers, however, try to turn your topic into a question that your research paper answers. This question need not be explicit in your topic, but it should emerge in the opening paragraphs of your paper, either explicitly or implicitly, as you present your thesis. When you read the student papers later in this chapter, notice how the focused topics lead naturally into a manageable thesis, allowing for specific observations to be developed into a cogent argument.

FINDING AND USING SOURCES

Researchers have a number of tools available for finding secondary sources—critical studies of authors, analyses of their works, and relevant biographical, social, and historical background material. Your school library's computer databases of books and articles provide comprehensive listings of such sources. But even before tapping into those databases you can consult books in the library reference room as a preliminary step. General reference works about literature can give you an overview of an author's life and work, an introduction to a genre, such as tragedy or epic, or an understanding of a critical approach, such as new historicism, or provide some other kind of generalized prelude to the more focused search you will undertake once you have refined your topic and decided how to proceed with your research.

Works you may find helpful as preliminary guides to literary research include the following:

Columbia Literary History of the United States. Ed. Emory Elliot et al. New York: Columbia University Press, 1988.

An Encyclopedia of Continental Women Writers. Ed. Karharina Wilson. 2 vols. New York: Garland, 1991.

Encyclopedia of World Literature in the Twentieth Century. Ed. Leonard S. Klein. 5 vols. Rev. ed. New York: Continuum, 1983–1984.

European Writers. George Stade and William T. Jackson. 7 vols. New York: Macmillan, 1983–1985.

Longman Companion to Twentieth-Century Literature. Ed. A. C. Ward. 3rd ed. New York: Longman, 1981.

MLA International Bibliography. Available on line and on CD-ROM. New York: MLA, 1921–.

The New Cambridge Bibliography of English Literature. 5 vols. Cambridge: Cambridge UP, 1967–1977.

The New Guide to Modern World Literature. Ed. Martin Seymour-Smith. 4 vols. New York: Peter Bedrick Books, 1985.

The New Princeton Encyclopedia of Poetry and Poetics. Ed. Alex Preminger and T.V.F. Brogan. Princeton: Princeton UP, 1993.

The Oxford History of English Literature. 13 vols. Oxford: Oxford UP, 1945–.

A Research Guide for Undergraduate Students: English and American Literature. By Nancy L. Baker. 2nd ed. New York: MLA, 1985.

Research Guide to Biography and Criticism: Literature. Ed. Walton Beacham. 2 vols. Osprey, FL: Beacham, 1985.

You can find some or all of these sources in the reference sections of many college libraries.

USING COMPUTERIZED DATABASES

You may have access to your university library with a link from your room, your home, your residence hall, or your school's computer center. You may also be able to access the library's holdings through computer terminals located in the library proper. One of the first things you should do is learn how to use the library's computerized catalog to access bibliographic information. You can get a friend to help you. You can get assistance from the library staff. Your school may even provide formal instructions in use of their online services.

All online catalogs are organized in a similar way. The information that is retrieved and displayed on the computer screen depends on the format you use in making your request. Most programs offer at least three search options: author, title, and subject. For example, suppose you know that you want to write about Ernest Hemingway. You don't have a precise topic in mind, and want to consult some books *about* Ernest Hemingway. To find out what books the library has about Hemingway, you would search for "Hemingway, Ernest," as subject. (The program will give you on-screen instructions on how to start the search.) Following is what one university library's online catalog lists for Hemingway as subject:

1. Hemingway, Ernest 1898		1 entry
2. Hemingway, Ernest 1899–1961		52 entries
3. Hemingway, Ernest 1899–1961	Appreciation	1 entry
4. Hemingway, Ernest 1899–1961	Appreciation—Germany	1 entry
5. Hemingway, Ernest 1899–1961	Bibliography	10 entries
6. Hemingway, Ernest 1899–1961	Biography	12 entries
7. Hemingway, Ernest 1899–1961	Juvenile letters	1 entry
8. Hemingway, Ernest 1899–1961	Biography—Marriage	4 entries

Notice that category 2 includes fifty-two items. Since the category has no heading, to determine the kinds of books included within it, you would press 2 and scan the listings. If you press 8, Biography—Marriage, four listings appear:

1. Along with Youth	Griffin, Peter
2. Hadley	Diliberto, Gioia
3. The Hemingway Women	Kert, Bernice
4. How It Was	Hemingway, Mary Welsh

If you want more data on one of these books, press the appropriate number. You will be provided with information about the length and size of the book, its publication date, and location. Most systems also provide information about the book's availability.

In browsing in one of these books about Hemingway's personal life, you might get an idea for a research paper that focuses on the home life depicted in "Soldier's Home." Reading that story in the context of secondary biographical sources would be one way to gain added insight into the story. Another would be to consult critical secondary sources that are less biographical than analytical and interpretive. Here you would return to that large category of 52 items and begin scanning for titles that appeared promising. One such recent title is Paul Smith's *A Reader's Guide to the Short Stories of Ernest Hemingway* (Boston: G. K. Hall, 1989). After locating a few such sources, you are ready to read and take notes as you work toward refining your topic and developing a thesis for your paper.

USING THE INTERNET FOR RESEARCH

Through the Internet you can connect to the World Wide Web (WWW), a system of linked electronic documents. Navigating the WWW involves connecting to electronic pathways within and between Web pages and Web sites. Accessing various Web sites for information requires either a specific Internet address or use of a search engine, such as Yahoo or InfoSeek, which allows you to enter key words for the topic you wish to research.

To make use of the Internet for your literary research, follow these guidelines:

• Link your computer to the Internet, open your web browser, and call up the browser's home page.
• Go to the browser's search options and select a search engine.
• Enter the words you want to search (key words for your topic).
• Survey the list of "hits" the search engine provides.
• Click on any related hyperlinks that seem interesting.
• Skim each site and download those that appear promising. (Store their addresses for future use.)

Using the Internet for research can be fun. But it can also prove a formidable challenge. One problem you may confront is a large number of hits or potential sources. Deciding which of these are of most value requires careful analysis. This is due largely to the openness of the World Wide Web. Since anyone can put up a Web site and place any information on that site, you cannot be certain that the site's information is accurate, current, or unbiased.

Therefore, you must evaluate Internet sources for their reliability. You can use the following guidelines to do so.

• Consider the source of the electronic information you discover. Consider the credentials of the source provider. Is the source maintained by a reputable provider, such as a university or corporation?
• Compare your electronic sources with your print sources. Evaluate your electronic sources for range and depth as well as accuracy and currency of information.

• Ask yourself whether you are sufficiently confident of the source's reliability to cite it in your research paper.

For guidance in documenting electronic sources, see pp. 375–377.

DEVELOPING A CRITICAL PERSPECTIVE

How can you use outside critical sources to develop a critical perspective? Let us say, for example, that you are required to write a five- or six-page paper analyzing and interpreting a particular literary work. Let us speculate further that you are required to read and cite in your paper two or three outside sources. And let us also imagine that you have been asked to select critical sources that provide different interpretive perspectives on the work you will be writing about. What will you do? How will you go about writing this paper?

One technique useful for writing critical papers is quoting key passages and commenting on their significance or validity. In writing a paper about Hemingway's "Soldier's Home," for example, you could (and perhaps should) quote a bit of the story directly. Or you might select a few such passages for direct quotation. Of more importance than your apt selection of such passages, however, is the way you relate them in your comments explaining their significance. The way to get a start on this crucial process is record the relevant passages verbatim and practice commenting on their significance. These comments will provide the germ from which your paper will grow.

In using outside critical sources you will find yourself usually doing one of two things. Either you will agree with the critic and use his or her comments to bolster your interpretation. Or you will disagree and take exception to the critic's ideas by arguing against them in your paper. Both are acceptable ways to proceed. In fact, given a requirement to include more than two sources, it is highly unlikely that you will agree entirely with the positions taken in all of them. Thus even if you agree in part, you will need to make distinctions and to express qualified approval as you modify their viewpoints and express the reservations necessary to make them congruent with your own ideas.

DEVELOPING A THESIS

You should be able to state your thesis in a single direct sentence. Your thesis concentrates in a sentence nutshell what you wish to emphasize—your central idea, the point you wish to make about your topic. Your essay overall elaborates your thesis, providing evidence in the form of textual support.

In general, when you develop your thesis, try to make it as specific as you can. At the same time, try to avoid oversimplifying your idea by setting up mutually exclusive "black and white" categories. Introduce qualifying terms as necessary. Words such as "although," "however," "but," and "rather" suggest an approach that reflects thoughtful consideration of the issues.

Consider Lucienne Retelle's thesis as she analyzes Alice Walker's story "Everyday Use" in the context of a critical article she read about the work. Here is her thesis:

> In relating the story ["Everyday Use"] to the Biblical Prodigal Son, Patricia Kane shows thoughtfulness and insight; however, in her eagerness to expose what she sees as differences in male/female values, she demonstrates a superficial understanding of the Gospel parable and misses the central message: one of repentance and forgiveness.

Notice how Ms. Retelle takes issue with the critical perspective offered by Patricia Kane. She uses the critic's view as a springboard from which to launch her own analysis of the story as one whose central concerns are the prodigal son's repentance and his father's forgiveness. Her thesis is clear, direct, and specific. We know what she thinks. It remains for her to flesh out her interpretation and to refute Patricia Kane's argument.

DRAFTING AND REVISING

In writing your research paper, follow the guidelines for drafting and revising your paper just as you would for an interpretive paper in which you do not use secondary sources. Set aside sufficient time to work out the basic argument of your research paper. This will involve the extra time necessary for tracking down sources, taking notes, and reflecting on their significance for your overall argument.

In your preliminary draft you should try to articulate your argument without your sources. Get your ideas down as clearly as you can. Provide the textual support you need as evidence from the work(s) you are analyzing or otherwise discussing. Then write a second draft in which you incorporate the relevant sources either to support your idea or as representing antithetical views that you attempt to refute.

Leave time for a third draft in which you further refine your thinking, taking into consideration additional evidence you find in the text or in the secondary sources. Use this third draft also to provide precise documentation for your sources—accurate parenthetical citations and precise page references.

In general, approach the drafting of a research essay or paper as you would any other essay or assignment. Make sure you get your own ideas into the initial draft before you begin relying on your secondary sources. This is critical if you want to avoid letting your sources take over the voice and content of your research essay.

CONVENTIONS

In writing about literary works you need to observe a number of conventions, including those regarding quotations, verb tenses, manuscript form, and the strict avoidance of plagiarism.

Using Quotations

In writing about literature you will need to quote lines from poems, dialogue from plays and stories, and descriptive and explanatory passages from prose fiction and nonfiction. For quoted prose passages that exceed four typed lines in your paper, begin a new line and indent ten spaces from the left margin for each line of the quotation. This format, called block quotation, does not require quotation marks because the blocked passage is set off visually from the rest of your text.

   When quoting poetry, separate the lines of poetry with slashes. Include a space before and after each slash.

> Lorraine Hansberry derived the title of her best-known play, *A Raisin in the Sun,* from a poem by Langston Hughes. In "Dream Deferred," the speaker asks, "What happens to a dream deferred? / Does it dry up / like a raisin in the sun?"

Verb Tense Conventions in Literary Papers

In writing about literature, you will often need to describe a story, novel, poem, or play. In doing so you will use present tense, past tense, or both. In most instances, it is conventional to use present tense when describing what happens in a literary work. Consider the following examples:

> In Robert Hayden's "Those Winter Sundays," the speaker <u>reflects</u> on his father and <u>realizes</u> how much his father <u>loved</u> the family.

The present tense is used to describe the speaker's actions of reflecting and realizing. The past tense is used to describe the father's action, which occurred in the past, well before the speaker's present acts of reflecting and realizing.

> Ibsen's <u>A Doll House</u> <u>portrays</u> a conventional middle-class environment and a conventional middle-class family. In displaying a strong concern for money and for authority, Ibsen's characters <u>reveal</u> their middle-class values. Ibsen often <u>portrayed</u> characters with everyday problems of the middle class.

The verbs describing what the play does are in the present tense. Those describing what the dramatist did are in past tense.

Manuscript Form

In preparing your paper for submission, observe the following guidelines:

1. Type your essay double-spaced on 8 1/2-inch by 11-inch paper.
2. Leave 1-inch margins at the top and bottom, and on both sides.
3. Beginning in the upper-left corner 1 inch below the top and 1 inch from the left side, type the following on separate lines:
    (a) your name
    (b) your instructor's name
    (c) course title, number, and section
    (d) date
4. Double-space below the date and center your title. It is not necessary to put quotation marks around your title or to underline or italicize it. It is necessary to underline titles of books and plays used in your title. And it is necessary to put quotation marks around the titles of short stories, poems, and essays.
5. Be sure your printer's ink supply or your typewriter ribbon is adequate for clear, readable copy.
6. If your printer feeds connected sheets of paper, be sure to separate them before submitting your essay.
7. Number each page consecutively beginning with the second page, 1/2 inch from the upper-right corner.
8. Clip or staple the paper, making sure the pages are right side up and in the correct numerical order.

Plagiarism

Plagiarism is the act of using someone else's words, ideas, or organizational patterns without crediting the source. Plagiarism may be the result of careless note taking, or may be deliberate. To avoid plagiarism, it is necessary to clearly indicate what you have borrowed so your reader can distinguish your own language and ideas from those of your sources.

Research essays and papers written with little original thought and containing many long passages of quoted and summarized material strung together may include plagiarized words and ideas. Be sure to credit each source you use at the point of borrowing, even in the midst of a paragraph or the middle of a sentence. Be sure not only to acknowledge using the source but also, if you have used exact language from the source, to put quotation marks around the borrowed words and phrases—even if you have separated some of the borrowed material and interspersed your own language.

Plagiarism is a serious offense. A form of academic theft, plagiarism is not tolerated in colleges and universities. Some have stringent policies, including failure for the course in which the plagiarism occurs and even expulsion from school.

To avoid plagiarism observe the following guidelines in writing your research essays and papers.

• Develop your own ideas about the works you read. Keep notes of your ideas separate from the notes you take from sources.
• Jot the title, author, and page number of a source on the page or notecard you use for your notes pertaining to material from that source.
• Put quotation marks around quoted material you copy from sources into your notes.
• When you summarize and paraphrase a source, be sure to use your own words. Avoid having the source open before you when you summarize and paraphrase.
• If you introduce any quotations from a source into your summaries and paraphrases of them, put quotation marks around the quoted words and phrases.
• Make sure that your own ideas and your own voice are the controlling centers in your research essays and papers. Use your sources to support, illustrate, and amplify your own thinking presented in your own words.
• Observe the conventions for documentation provided in the following section of this book, in your college handbook, and in the *MLA Handbook for Writers of Research Papers,* 5th ed. (1999).

DOCUMENTING SOURCES

If you incorporate the work of others into your paper, it will be necessary to credit your sources through documentation. You should always provide source credit when quoting directly, paraphrasing (rewriting a passage in your own words), borrowing ideas, or picking up facts that aren't general knowledge.

By crediting your sources, you are participating honestly and correctly in shared intellectual activity. You are showing your reader that your knowledge of a text includes some insights into what others have thought and said about it. And you are assisting your reader, who may want to consult the sources that you found valuable.

Established conventions for documenting sources vary from one academic discipline to another. For research essays and papers in literature and language the preferred style is that of the Modern Language Association (MLA). MLA documentation style has established conventions for citing sources within the text of research essays, papers, and articles. It also has established conventions for the list of works you use in preparing your research writing—usually called "List of Works Cited" or "Works Cited."

In the current MLA style, parenthetical citations within the text indicate that a source has been used. These citations refer the reader to a reference list, which should start on a new page at the end of the paper. In the "alternate" or "old" MLA style, references are marked by raised numbers in the text that correspond to numbered notes either at the foot of the page (footnotes) or the end of the paper (endnotes). Both the reference list and the endnotes and footnotes contain bibliographic information about the sources; however, the arrangement, punctuation, and capitalization of the sources differs between the two reference styles.

New MLA Style: Parenthetical Citations Paired with a Reference List

When you refer to a specific section of a work in the body of your paper, provide your reader with the author and page numbers of your source. Place the page numbers in parentheses, and add the author's name if it isn't contained in your sentence.

> According to Lawrence Lipking (30–39), a poet's life involves much more than his or her literal biography.

> A recent critic argues that a poet's life involves much more than his or her literal biography (Lipking 30–39).

If your paper includes two or more works by the same author, add the title of the work before the page number(s). The following are examples of other kinds of citations commonly found in literature papers.

A work in an anthology:

> Bacon's "Of Revenge" affords us a glimpse at his view of human nature: "There is no man doth a wrong for the wrong's sake, but thereby to purchase himself profit, or pleasure, or honor, or the like" (1565).

(The author and title of the anthologized selection should be listed in the *Works Cited*.)

A classic verse play or poem:

> "She loved me for the dangers I had passed," recounts Othello, "And I loved her that she did pity them" (I.iii.166–67).

(Act, scene, and line numbers are used instead of page numbers. Arabic numbers may also be used for the act and scene.)

> Tennyson's Ulysses compares a dull existence to a dull sword when he says: "How dull it is to pause, to make an end, / To rust unburnished, not to shine in use!" (22–23).

(Line numbers are used instead of page numbers. Note the use of a slash [/] to indicate the end of a line.)

Styling a Works Cited List

The items in a works cited list should be alphabetically arranged. The following are typical kinds of entries for a literature paper.
    A book by a single author:

> Lipking, Lawrence. *The Life of the Poet: Beginning and Ending Poetic Careers.* Chicago: U of Chicago P, 1981.

(The second line is indented five spaces.)
    An article in a book:

> Williams, Sherley Anne. "The Black Musician: The Black Hero as Light Bearer." *James Baldwin: A Collection of Critical Essays.* Ed. Kenneth Kinnamon. Englewood Cliffs, NJ: Prentice-Hall, 1974. 147-54.

(The page numbers "147-54" refer to the entire article. References to specific pages would appear in parenthetical citations.)
    A journal article:

> Walker, Janet. "Hardy's Somber Lyrics." *Poetry* 17 (1976): 25-39.

(The article appeared in issue 17 of the journal *Poetry.* The page numbers refer to the entire article.)
    A work in an anthology:

> Bacon, Francis. "Of Revenge." *Literature: Reading Fiction, Poetry, Drama, and the Essay.* 2nd ed. Ed. Robert DiYanni. New York: McGraw-Hill, 1990. 1565-1655.

(The page numbers refer to the entire essay.)
    Cite the anthology itself if you are using more than one selection from it. The selections can simply be cited without repeating the anthology title and publication data.

> DiYanni, Robert, ed. *Literature: Reading Fiction, Poetry, Drama, and the Essay.* 4th ed. New York: McGraw-Hill, 1998.
> Tennyson, Alfred, Lord. "Ulysses." DiYanni. 649-50.

    A multivolume work; a second edition:

> Daiches, David. *A Critical History of English Literature.* 2nd ed.
> 2 vols. New York: Ronald, 1970.

A translation:

> Auerbach, Erich. *Mimesis: The Representation of Reality in Western
> Literature.* Trans. Willard Trask. Princeton: Princeton UP,
> 1953.

Alternate MLA Style: Note Numbers Paired with Endnotes/Footnotes

Using Note Numbers

Raised note numbers, in consecutive order, follow the quotation or informa-
tion being cited. They belong *after* all punctuation, except a dash.

> "She loved me for the dangers I had passed," recounts Othello,
> "And I loved her that she did pity them."[1]

If you include several quotations from the same text in your paper, you may
switch to parenthetical citations after the first note. This will reduce the num-
ber of footnotes or endnotes.

> Emilia tells Desdemona that jealousy is "a monster begot upon
> itself, born on itself" (III.iv.155-56).

Using Endnotes/Footnotes

Each raised note number corresponds to a footnote or endnote. The only dif-
ference between footnotes and endnotes is their placement in the paper. Foot-
notes appear at the bottom of the page on which the reference occurs:
quadruple-space between the last line of text and the first note. Endnotes are
grouped together on a separate page immediately following the last page of
text.

The following are the same sources given above, but now in endnote form.
Note that specific page references are given for each entry; these page refer-
ences would be contained in parentheses in new MLA style.

> [1]Lawrence Lipking, *The Life of the Poet: Beginning and Ending
> Poetic Careers* (Chicago: U of Chicago P, 1981) 30-39.
> [2]Sherley Anne Williams, "The Black Musician: The Black
> Hero as Light Bearer," in *James Baldwin: A Collection of Critical Es-*

says, ed. Kenneth Kinnamon (Englewood Cliffs, NJ: Prentice-Hall, 1974) 147.

[3]Janet Walker, "Hardy's Somber Lyrics," *Poetry* 17 (1976): 35.

[4]Francis Bacon, "Of Revenge," *Literature: Reading Fiction, Poetry, Drama, and the Essay,* 2nd ed., ed. Robert DiYanni (New York: McGraw-Hill, 1990) 1565–66.

[5]David Daiches, *A Critical History of English Literature,* 2nd ed., 2 vols. (New York: Ronald, 1970) 2: 530.

[6]Erich Auerbach, *Mimesis: The Representation of Reality in Western Literature,* trans. Willard Trask (Princeton: Princeton UP, 1953) 77.

Noting Subsequent References

It is usually enough simply to list the author's name and the appropriate page(s) in subsequent references to a source.

[7]Lipking 98.

DOCUMENTING ELECTRONIC SOURCES

The MLA Handbook for Writers of Research Papers, 5th ed., distinguishes electronic citation forms according to whether the material is available on a CD-ROM or whether it is available online. Because electronic media are continually changing, the details of citations may evolve even as the basic needs for citing references remain the same.

Source on CD-ROM

Citations for electronic sources are distinguished according to whether the material was published once, like a book, or whether it is published in regularly updated periodical form.

CD Produced as a One-Time Publication

Author's name followed by the title underlined or italicized; editor, compiler, or translator if relevant. Publication medium; edition, release, or version if relevant; place of publication; name of publisher; date of publication.

> French, William P., ed. *Database of African-American Poetry, 1760–1900.* CD-ROM. Alexandria, VA: Chadwyck-Healy, 1995.

If you wish to cite part of a work, place quotation marks around the part or section you cite. Underline or italicize the title of the work as a whole. If you are not provided with an author, begin your citation with the title.

"Modernism." *The Oxford English Dictionary.* 2nd ed. CD-ROM.
Oxford: Oxford UP, 1992.

CD Updated Periodically

Author or institution name followed by a period. Article's title and original
date or inclusive dates in quotation marks. Database name underlined followed
by type of source (CD, for example). Locator and provider or the vendor of the
database if available; date of publication.

Smith, Dinitia. "Hollywood Adopts the Canon." *New York Times*
10 Nov. 1996: D4. *New York Times Ondisc.* CD-ROM.
UMI–Proquest. Dec. 1996.

If you cite a CD-ROM multidisk publication, include the total number of
disks if you use them all, or the disk number(s) for the one(s) you wish to cite.

Patrologia Latina Database. CD-ROM. 5 discs. Alexandria, VA:
Chadwyck-Healey, 1995.

Online Sources

When citing Internet sources include the Internet address or URL (uniform
resource locator) in angle brackets < >. Provide the entire address, including
the access-mode identifier (http, ftp, gopher, telnet, news).

Online Scholarly Project or Reference Database

Title underlined or italicized; editor if given followed by electronic publication
information, date or latest update, and name of sponsoring institution if pro-
vided. Date of access and electronic address in angle brackets.

African American Women Writers of the Nineteenth Century. Ed.
Thomas P. Lukas. 1999. Digital Schomburg, New York
Public Library. 11 May 1999
<http.//digital.nypl.org/schomburg/writers_aal9/>.

Online Professional or Personal Site

Name of person who created the site, title of site underlined or italicized; if no
title is given, provide a title such as Home Page. Name of institution or organ-
ization associated with the site, date of access, and electronic address.

Pace University Home Page. Pace. 3 Dec. 1998
<http://www.pace.edu/>.

Online Book

Author's name, title underlined or italicized; name of editor, compiler, or translator if relevant. City of publication, publisher, year of publication. Date of access and electronic address.

> Alice Dunbar-Nelson. *The Goodness of St. Rocque and Other Stories.* New York: Dodd, Mead, 1899. *African American Women Writers of the Nineteenth Century.* Ed. Thomas P. Lukas. 1999. Digital Schomburg, New York Public Library. 11 May 1999
> <http://digilib.nypl.org/dynaweb/
> digs-f/wwm976/@Generic_BookView>.

Online Periodical Article

Author, title of article, title of journal or magazine, volume, number, year, and date for scholarly journal; date for magazine; electronic address.

Scholarly Journal

> Pereira, Edimilson de Almeida. "Survey of African-Brazilian Literature." *Callaloo* 18.4 (1995): 875–80. 11 Apr. 1997
> <http://muse.jhu.edu/journals/callaloo/vol8/18.4de_
> almeida_pereira9.html>.

Magazine

> Landsburg, Steven E. "Who Shall Inherit the Earth?" *Slate* 1 May 1997. 2 May 1997 <http://slate.com/Economics/97-
> 05-01/Economics.asp>.

A STUDENT PAPER INCORPORATING RESEARCH

Jean-Marie Salvia
Mrs. Fitzgerald
April 10, 1999

The Dark Woods of Robert Frost

Many people question the paths they have chosen in life. They often
wonder whether they had made the right decisions and ask: Am I the
person I want to be? What do I believe in? Am I honest with myself?
Robert Frost's poems raise similar questions. In many of his works,
Frost challenges his inner desires, stands up to various
temptations, and questions his place in the society in which he
lives. The imagery of dark trees and woods in poems such as "The
Road Not Taken," "Into My Own," "Stopping by Woods on a Snowy
Evening," and "Come In" introduces the poet's questions and suggests
Frost's ongoing struggle with his innermost thoughts and feelings.

   The speaker in a Frost poem is often found at the edge of a forest that
beckons him into its mysterious unknown. The speaker must choose between
the spiritual journey that the woods offer and the unappealing society
that surrounds the trees. He desires the solitude and tranquility of the
forest, but more often than not, Frost's speaker chooses not to venture
into the unknown. Frost shows desire for the inner self and the spiritual
solitude the woods have to offer, but he does not always adhere to these.
"Into My Own" suggests Frost's longing for the darkest woods, and he
chooses to travel into these woods in "The Road Not Taken"; however, in
the other two poems, Frost suppresses his desire and decides not to travel
into the woods. Though he finds the woods alluring, he has societal
responsibilities.

   In the poem "The Road Not Taken," the speaker "faces a dilemma of
choosing between the unknown, represented by wild nature, or mundane life,
represented by a clearing or town" ("Robert Frost"). When confronted by
two "diverging roads," the speaker clearly chooses to take the path less
traveled, or the unknown. He understands that he will not be able to come
back and take the other, and will sigh when he tells his tale; however, he
presses on down the less traveled road, leading into the dark woods.
Critic John Ogilvie agrees: "The two roads that 'diverged in a yellow
wood' represent a critical choice between two ways of life. The poet takes
'the one less traveled by,' the lonelier road, which, we can presume,
leads deeper into the wood. . . . " (69).

   Frost's speaker retreats from the beaten path in "The Road Not Taken" to
the wilderness of "Into My Own." In this poem, the speaker expresses a
wish that the deep woods that now confront him stretch endlessly out
toward the edge of doom (Barry 147). The speaker wants to lose himself in
the infinite depths of such a forest, but questions if it is wise. As he
ponders his decision, the speaker asks, "Who will miss me here?" and

wonders if he should be taken by death. The tone of the poem suggests a "wished-for freedom to retreat into the vastness of those dark trees," where the poet will not encounter the exposed, man-made world of open land and highways. He is identified with "coming into his own." For this, he is willing to forsake everything that is dear (Ogilvie 70). The ideas present in "Into My Own" are significant because they suggest that the poem contains "Frost's statement of how he would submerge himself in nature and find strength to hold the ideas and principles he had evolved" (Sutton 124). Though a decision to enter the dark woods and give up life as men know it is not made, readers see Frost's struggle with this idea in later poems.

In "Stopping by Woods on a Snowy Evening," the speaker still does not make a decision concerning his entrance into the woods, but readers can see that he is clearly leaning in one direction. This poem is also about the spell of the woods and the speaker's attraction to the deep darkness. The forest may be more attractive in "Stopping by Woods" because it appears to be much darker; it is the "darkest evening of the year" (8). However, it seems as though the speaker "turns away from nature, [and] he chooses the world of humanity. The woods are dark and Frost's [speaker] decides the better journey is to the light of town" (French 161). He chooses to venture into town because he feels it is the right choice; he has "promises to keep" (14). Human obligations and responsibilities must take precedence. Peter Poland agrees, noting that "the narrator of 'Stopping by Woods' realizes how dangerously alluring the woods are. He realizes that he has 'promises to keep,' that he can not 'sleep' in the face of his societal obligations, and so he shortly turns homeward" (96). Though it seems as though some form of conclusion is made in "Stopping by Woods," it is important to note that the speaker never leaves the setting. He stands still, mesmerized by the infinite darkness, and fades out, repeating the last thought: "And miles to go before I sleep / And miles to go before I sleep" (15–16).

"Come In," another poem that focuses on an implicit "death wish," further entices the speaker to enter the forest. The song of the thrush beckons the speaker to enter the woods. Yet he takes a strong stance and convinces himself that he has not been asked to "come in": "would not come in / I meant not even if asked, / And I hadn't been" (18–20). The difference with this later poem is that the speaker is significantly in control of the temptation and notices the limitations of the darkness. This control may be noted in the rhyme and meter of the poem. In the first stanza, the words shift away from the overall scheme, creating great emotional tension. This aspect shows that the poet (and, thus, the speaker) is in control of himself and his situation. He does not get carried away by the poetry in the scene. Frost has come to a realization that the dark woods, though fascinating, must remain a mystery. He has chosen the other road and must stay on his path.

Like his poems' speakers, Robert Frost questions the life choices he has made. He has decided to take the road "less traveled by," and therefore, must deal with the attractions and temptations it offers alone. While the "speaker of 'Into My Own' indulges the temptation with grandiose self-dramatization, [the speaker] in 'Stopping by Woods' rejects it with a certain self-righteousness. In 'Come In' he is more assured" (Barry 27). In each poem, the dark woods and trees are fascinating, but Frost belongs to a different world. Like most of us, the speakers choose to overcome their darkest desires to abandon civilization and remain in established society.

Works Cited

Barry, Elaine. *Robert Frost.* New York: Frederick Ungar, 1973.

French, Robert W. "Robert Frost and the Darkness of Nature." *The English Record* 29.1 (1978): 2–5.

Ogilvie, John T. "From Woods to Stars: A Pattern of Imagery in Robert Frost's Poetry." *South Atlantic Quarterly* 58.1 (1959): 64–76.

Poland, Peter D. "Frost's 'Neither Out Far Nor In Deep.'" *The Explicator* 52.2 (1994): 95–6.

"Robert Frost." *Contemporary Literary Criticism Select.* Gale Literary Dababases. The Gale Group, 1999. 11 May 1999 <http://www.nypl.org/branch/resources/egaleliterary.html>.

Sutton, William A. *Newdick's Season of Frost: An Interrupted Biography of Robert Frost.* Albany: State University of New York Press, 1976.

Writers' Lives

M A R G A R E T   A T W O O D
(b. 1939)

Margaret Atwood, one of Canada's foremost writers, was born in Ottawa. She graduated from the University of Toronto and received an M.A. from Radcliffe College in 1962. The recipient of many awards and fellowships, Atwood has won international acclaim for her critical writing and fiction. One of her most widely known novels, *The Handmaid's Tale,* which was made into a film, describes life in a future world where women suffer severe repression. Her numerous stories, novels, and poems are complemented by her editorial and critical work, which includes the *Oxford Book of Canadian Verse.*

W. H. A U D E N
(1907–1973)

Wystan Hugh Auden was born in England but emigrated to America in 1939, becoming a U.S. citizen in 1946. As a young English poet his early work reflected Marxist and Freudian thinking as well as a droll wit. His later work revealed a more conservative political strain and a Christian sympathy. Auden was a prolific editor, anthologist, and translator as well as one of the twentieth century's most renowned poets.

ELIZABETH BISHOP
(1911–1979)

Elizabeth Bishop was born and raised in Worcester, Massachusetts. As a consequence of her father's early death and her mother's mental illness, Bishop, at age six, went to live with her grandmother in Nova Scotia. After graduating from boarding school and Vassar College, she moved to Key West, Florida, and then to Brazil, where she lived for fifteen years. Returning to the United States, she taught at the University of Washington and at Harvard. She published her first volume of poems, *North and South,* in 1946 and later won both the Pulitzer prize and the National Book Award. Her last collection, *Complete Poems 1927–1979,* won the National Book Critics Circle Award.

WILLIAM BLAKE
(1757–1827)

William Blake was born in London and was apprenticed to an engraver there at the age of fourteen. At age twenty-two Blake entered the Royal Academy as an engraving student, but clashes over artistic differences precipitated his return to private study of such Renaissance masters as Raphael, Durer, and Michelangelo. A revolutionary at heart, Blake moved in a circle of radical thinkers including William Godwin, Thomas Paine, and Mary Wollstonecraft. His poems, which he published himself, and for which he supplied engravings and water colors, include *Songs of Innocence* (1789), *Songs of Experience* (1794), and the prophetic *Marriage of Heaven and Hell* (1790), among others. His work is visionary and unconventional.

ROBERT BROWNING
(1812–1889)

Robert Browning was born in a London suburb and educated primarily through reading in his father's extensive library. Browning's first poems were printed in his early twenties, but he did not achieve fame as a poet until he was in his fifties. Browning was married to the poet Elizabeth Barrett, with whom he lived in Italy, returning to England after her death. The work that made him famous, *The Ring and The Book* (1868–69), which is based on a seventeenth-century Roman murder trial, represents the poetic form for which he is best known—the dramatic monologue. The form weds the character revelations of drama with the lyricism of poetry. Among Browning's most successful examples of the genre is "My Last Duchess."

RAYMOND CARVER
(1939–1988)

Originally from Oregon where he was raised in a working-class milieu, Raymond Carver lived in Washington and spent much of his life in California. After working at a series of low-paying odd jobs, Carver worked as an editor and as a college teacher at the University of California at Berkeley, the University of Iowa, the University of Texas at El Paso, and Syracuse University. Carver's fictional mentors include James Joyce, Ernest Hemingway, and above all, Anton Chekhov, whose stories Carver admired above those of all other writers. His best stories are lean and spare and touch deeply on central human problems.

E. E. CUMMINGS
(1894–1962)

Edward Estlin Cummings was born in Cambridge, Massachusetts. After attending Harvard University, he joined the Red Cross Ambulance Corps in France during World War I. Comments critical of the French army in his letters got him imprisoned, but he was released after four months. His poems, which began appearing in the 1920s, are identifiable by their unusual typography and punctuation. In addition to poetry, Cummings wrote essays and a novel, *The Enormous Room,* based on his experiences in France. He also produced graphic art, including paintings.

JOHN DONNE
(1572–1631)

John Donne was both a poet and a prelate, who made his name as a preacher at St. Paul's Cathedral in London. Before his conversion from Roman Catholicism to Anglicanism and his ordination as an Anglican priest, Donne wrote worldly love lyrics at the court of Queen Elizabeth I. His poems, which circulated in manuscript, were justly famous, and were later collected under the title *Songs and Sonnets.* Donne's poetry is justly celebrated for its striking and unusual imagery, its strong and direct language, and its probing analyses of the experiences of religious faith and doubt and of secular and sacred love.

T. S. ELIOT
(1888–1965)

Thomas Stearns Eliot was born in St. Louis, Missouri, but moved to England in 1914 and became a British citizen in 1927. Though he had been raised in the southwestern United States, Eliot traced his family's roots to New England, where he vacationed. He studied at the Sorbonne in Paris and at Merton College, Oxford, England. Instead of pursuing an academic life, Eliot turned to business and poetry, working as a clerk for Lloyd's Bank of London and as editor and director of the London publishing house Faber and Faber, all the while writing the poems that were to make him famous. The most explosive of these was *The Waste Land,* which burst upon the literary scene in 1922, becoming for a long time the most famous modern poem in English. Earlier, Eliot had written "The Love Song of J. Alfred Prufrock," a dramatic monologue that portrays the life of a timid, inhibited man.

LAWRENCE FERLINGHETTI
(b. 1919)

Lawrence Ferlinghetti was both a poet and a publisher who founded the City Lights bookstore in San Francisco, the country's first paperback bookstore. He also edited City Lights Books, a feature of the San Francisco poetry revival of the 1950s. Along with Allen Ginsberg, whose poem "Howl" he published, which led to his being charged with obscenity, Ferlinghetti was a central figure in the group of writers known as the "Beats." His poetry often centers on political concerns and typically reflects anti-bourgeois tendencies and attitudes. His best-known volume, however, *A Coney Island of the Mind* (1958), contains his more lyrical and freely imaginative poems.

THOMAS HARDY
(1840–1928)

Thomas Hardy, English Victorian novelist and poet, was born in Dorsetshire, the region of England he later called Wessex in his novels. Hardy trained as an architect and began to practice in 1867, but he soon turned his attention to writing, initially poetry, then fiction, for which he became famous. His first published poetry, however, was not available until 1898, when *Wessex Poems* appeared, after he had given up his career as the novelist who had penned *Jude the Obscure* and *Tess of the D'Urbervilles.* Hardy's poetry ranges widely in style and form, as he experimented with image and idiom throughout his thirty-year career as a poet.

SEAMUS HEANEY
(b. 1939)

Seamus Heaney was born and raised in Northern Ireland, an area torn for decades by political, religious, and civil strife. He was educated at Queens College, Belfast, where he later taught. His first collection of poetry, *Death of a Naturalist* (1966), led a new generation of Irish poets in civil war–torn Northern Ireland. His poems, which touch on themes of nature and history as well as politics, are among the most celebrated of the century, as Heaney has been hailed as the successor to William Butler Yeats as the most important Irish poet of the later modern era.

GEORGE HERBERT
(1593–1633)

George Herbert, English poet and Anglican priest, after serving as a University of Cambridge orator, became a parson in charge of a country parish. His prose work, *The Country Parson,* was recognized as a valuable source of wise guidance for devout and useful Christian living. His poetry, collected after his death by his friend Nicholas Ferrar, was printed in 1633 as *The Temple.* Herbert's poems, while ranging widely in imagery like those of his contemporary John Donne, offer a more homely and familiar window on religious experience.

ROBERT HERRICK
(1591–1674)

Robert Herrick is an English poet best known for his pastoral and love lyrics. Herrick attended Cambridge University and became an Anglican cleric in 1627. Though a clergyman, Herrick was a lover of London's society of poets and wits, who initially regarded his work in rural England as a form of exile. Herrick was a classicist, who was influenced by his Roman predecessors. His verse is formal and refined. His best-known poem, "To the Virgins, to Make Much of Time," celebrates the theme of *carpe diem,* or seize the day.

GERARD MANLEY HOPKINS
(1844–1889)

Gerard Manley Hopkins was an English poet gifted not only in his poetic resourceful-
ness but also in music and art. Hopkins was born in Essex, outside London. As a stu-
dent at Oxford University he studied classic Greek and Roman literature. At the age
of twenty-two Hopkins converted from Anglicanism to Roman Catholicism and be-
came a Jesuit priest. He spent several years in working-class parishes until he was ap-
pointed Professor of Greek at University College in Dublin in 1877. His poetry is
distinguished by an intricate form of rhythm, which he called "sprung rhythm" and by
an intense musicality.

A. E. HOUSMAN
(1859–1936)

Alfred Edward Housman, British poet and scholar, was an eminent classical scholar and
translator and a professor of Latin at Cambridge University from 1911 to 1936. He
achieved general fame with his book *A Shropshire Lad* (1896), a collection of poems
that stressed the brevity and fragility of youth and love. His lyrics, which celebrate na-
ture, are set against the background of the English countryside and reveal the influence
of English ballads and classical verse. Among his most famous poems are "When I Was
One-and-Twenty" and "To an Athlete Dying Young."

BEN JONSON
(1573–1637)

Ben Jonson was born and educated in London, where he received a strong grounding
in classical Greek and Latin. He worked as a bricklayer and a soldier before becoming
a playwright and poet. Jonson was famed for his wit and his ability to engage others in
contests of poetry, and he was well known at The Mermaid Tavern in London for the
weekly literary discussions, during which he would match wits with rival poets, in-
cluding William Shakespeare. Jonson's followers called themselves the "tribe of Ben" in
his honor. He was crowned as the first poet Laureate of England in 1619.

JOHN KEATS
(1795–1821)

John Keats, who was born in London, experienced the loss of both his parents when he was still a child. After being apprenticed to a medical doctor, Keats received his own license to practice medicine, but gave up that career for poetry. At an early age Keats was stricken with tuberculosis, and he went to Italy in the hope of regaining his health. He died in Rome at the age of twenty-five, but not before producing a small but significant body of enduring poems, including the great "Ode to a Nightingale" and "Ode on a Grecian Urn."

BOB McKENTY
(b. 1935)

Bob McKenty is a retired businessman who worked for many years for the Equitable Life Assurance Company as a computer specialist. He has written light verse for as long as he can remember, getting serious about humor some years ago when he established a newsletter of light verse entitled *Lighten Up!* He lives happily in Matawan, New Jersey, with his wife, Mary.

JOHN MILTON
(1608–1674)

John Milton was born to be a poet. He was educated under private tutors at home before entering St. Paul's School and Cambridge University, where he studied Greek and Latin and mastered modern languages in his spare time. He then spent five years of independent study followed by a two-year tour of Europe all in preparation for his vocation as a poet. During the Puritan Interregnum, Milton served as a secretary to Oliver Cromwell, who ran the Commonwealth until the restoration of the English kings. Milton's poetry is vastly learned and heavily allusive, especially in his long magisterial epic poems *Paradise Lost* and *Paradise Regained*. But Milton also wrote a number of memorable poems on a smaller scale, including some of the finest sonnets in English.

EDGAR ALLAN POE
(1809–1849)

Edgar Allan Poe was born in Boston, and orphaned at the age of two and adopted by a wealthy family. Poe was forced to make his own way, however, after causing a breach with his family during his later school years. He supported himself as a literary editor and a writer, producing *Tales of the Grotesque and Arabesque* (1840) and *The Raven and Other Poems* (1845). Poe is best known for his stories of horror and of crime and detection. A great influence on the French symbolist poets and unique among the American writers of his day, Poe was, after his death, the subject of a malicious biography, which strove to link his life with his brilliantly grotesque literary creations.

ALEXANDER POPE
(1688–1744)

Alexander Pope was born a Roman Catholic at a time when England was violently anti-Catholic and was educated largely at home. A childhood accident deformed his spine and retarded his physical growth, which led the young Alexander Pope to pursue a bookish life. He was a skillful poet early on, having written his *Pastorals* by the age of sixteen. In his mid-twenties he translated Homer's *Iliad* and *Odyssey,* edited Shakespeare's plays, and published *An Essay on Criticism,* a highly regarded work of critical thought in poetic form. Pope is best known, however, for his witty and satirical poems written in heroic couplets, *The Dunciad* and *The Rape of the Lock.*

ADRIENNE RICH
(b. 1929)

Adrienne Rich was born in Baltimore. She attended Radcliffe College, publishing her first book of poems, *A Change of World* (1951), while a student there. After studying at Oxford University, she married an economist and raised a family of sons, before becoming radicalized and emerging as a lesbian-feminist political activist. She has taught at a number of colleges and universities, including Brandeis, Smith, Douglass, Columbia, and the City College of New York. She has published prose as well as poetry, with *Of Woman Born* (1976) and *On Lies, Secrets and Silence,* two of her more important works. Her poetry continues to receive a wide readership as Rich herself remains a highly influential figure in feminist circles.

E. A. ROBINSON
(1869–1935)

Edwin Arlington Robinson was raised in Gardiner, Maine, the "Tilbury Town" of such poems as "Miniver Cheevy" and "Richard Cory." He attended Harvard for two years, but had to leave because of the failure of his father's lumber business. Widely read in English and American literature, Robinson was drawn to the dark vision of novelist and poet Thomas Hardy, whose starkness of perspective can be detected in some of Robinson's ironic poems. Robinson won three Pulitzer prizes, with special acknowledgment of the success of his dramatic monologues.

THEODORE ROETHKE
(1908–1963)

Theodore Roethke was born in Saginaw, Michigan, where his father oversaw a substantial greenhouse. After attending the University of Michigan and Harvard University, Roethke taught poetry at a number of schools before settling at the University of Washington. His influence extended to other poets, who studied with him there, including James Wright. Roethke's first book of poems, *Open House* (1941), shows his extensive knowledge of flowers and vegetation. His second volume, *The Lost Son* (1948), includes the lyric "My Papa's Waltz." He earned a Pulitzer prize in 1953 for *The Waking.*

ANNE SEXTON
(1928–1974)

Anne Sexton was born and raised in Massachusetts, where she later worked in the Boston literary milieu. She taught creative writing at a number of universities, and was recognized early on as a poet of considerable talent and raw power. She suffered from mental illness and depression, experiences which are reflected in her work. Before taking her own life at age forty-six, Sexton published *Live or Die* (1966), which was awarded the Pulitzer prize for poetry.

WILLIAM SHAKESPEARE
(1564–1616)

William Shakespeare was born and raised, lived and died, in Stratford-on-Avon, a country town nearly a hundred miles outside London. Although Shakespeare is best known as a playwright, considered by many to be the greatest dramatist that ever lived, he was also a gifted poet, both in the songs and speeches from his plays and in his narrative poems *Venus and Adonis* (1593) and *The Rape of Lucrece* (1594). Shakespeare's *Sonnets,* composed between 1593 and 1601 and published in 1609, remain the height of achievement in this genre. Their densely metaphorical language, their formal elegance, and their psychological penetration make them among Shakespeare's finest poetic accomplishments.

WALLACE STEVENS
(1879–1955)

Wallace Stevens was born in Reading, Pennsylvania, and studied at Harvard before taking a law degree from New York University. For nearly forty years Stevens was associated with the Hartford Accident and Indemnity Company, where he became a vice president. In college Stevens wrote poetry and served as president of the literary magazine and the literary society. During his years of practicing law and working as an insurance industry executive, Stevens wrote and published many poems. His first volume, *Harmonium,* was published in 1923. His *Collected Poems* (1955) won both the Pulitzer prize and the National Book Award.

MAY SWENSON
(1919–1989)

May Swenson was born in Utah of Swedish parents, and moved to New York City after attending college. She performed editorial jobs and taught poetry while writing her own poems and winning awards for them. Her first book, *A Cage of Spines* (1958), was followed by *Half Sun Half Sleep* (1967), which includes witty descriptions of life in New York City along with translations from six Swedish poets. Swenson was a poetic experimenter who played with poetic forms, as in her shaped verse, exemplified by "Women."

ALFRED, LORD TENNYSON
(1809–1892)

Alfred, Lord Tennyson, one of the best known and liked Victorian poets, became Poet Laureate in 1850. His early poetry is influenced by the English Romantic poets, especially by John Keats. Among his more highly recognized work is the twelve-part narrative poem, *Idylls of the King,* based on King Arthur and his Round Table, which occupied Tennyson from 1859 to 1888. Tennyson, however, is justly honored as a lyric poet of exquisite musicality and deep feeling as exemplified by his long elegiac poem, *In Memoriam* (1850), inspired by the death of his friend Arthur Hallam.

DYLAN THOMAS
(1914–1953)

Dylan Thomas was born in coastal Wales, the son of an English teacher. His poetry, which centers on themes of birth and death, innocence, childhood, and sex, reflects his Welsh heritage and his rural upbringing. Thomas lacked a university education and thus instead of supporting himself and his family by teaching, he made broadcasts for BBC radio and went on extended poetry reading tours in the United States, where he was a wildly popular figure, with a reputation for being a prodigious drinker as well as a fine performer of poems. His handful of highly regarded poems is complemented by some memorable short stories and a play for voices, *Under Milk Wood* (1954).

WALT WHITMAN
(1819–1892)

Walt Whitman was born in Huntington, New York, and was educated in the Brooklyn public schools. In his youth he worked successively as an office boy and clerk for a doctor, lawyer, and printer. After teaching school from 1836 to 1841, he began a journalistic career, which involved, at various stages, writing, typesetting, and editing the *Brooklyn Daily Eagle* and *Daily Times,* among other newspapers. During the Civil War, Whitman served as a nurse and worked briefly as a clerk in the Bureau of Indian Affairs. His wide range of experiences is reflected in his deeply democratic vision in poems remarkable for their formal freedom, their freshness of idiom, and their profound compassion.

WILLIAM CARLOS WILLIAMS
(1883–1963)

William Carlos Williams, poet, novelist, short-story writer, was born in Rutherford, New Jersey, where, after earning an M.D., he pursued a medical career as a pediatrician. In the early years of his medical practice there was little time for writing, so Williams concentrated on short forms. His poetic output, which was both innovative and prodigious, was part of a modernist literary revolution that sent poetry in new directions. His fiction is collected in *Making Light of It, The Knife of the Times,* and *The Farmer's Daughter and Other Stories.*

WILLIAM WORDSWORTH
(1770–1850)

William Wordsworth was born in the Lake District of northern England, which is central to many of his poems. Along with Samuel Taylor Coleridge, Wordsworth was the earliest and most influential of the English Romantic poets. With Coleridge, he published *Lyrical Ballads* (1798), which essentially launched the Romantic movement in England, calling for a poetry written in a language really used by common people and about matters reflective of everyday life. Wordsworth's sister Dorothy was a constant companion and inspiration. It was from her notebook entries that he later culled the details for his poem "I wandered lonely as a cloud." As with much of Wordsworth's poetry, this lyric reflects his deep love of nature, his vision of a unified world, and his celebration of the power of memory and imagination.

JAMES WRIGHT
(1927–1980)

James Wright was born in Martins Ferry, Ohio, and received his Ph.D. at the University of Washington, where he studied with Theodore Roethke. In 1966, he began teaching at Hunter College in New York, where he taught until his death. In addition to his own poetry, which first appeared in the volume *A Green Wall* (1957) and was last collected in *Above the River: The Complete Poems* (1990), Wright was also a translator of the works of Cesar Valejo, Pablo Neruda, and George Trakl.

WILLIAM BUTLER YEATS
(1865–1939)

William Butler Yeats was born in Dublin, Ireland, son of the well-known Irish painter, John Butler Yeats. W. B. Yeats himself studied painting for three years, and art would become one of the three dominant themes in his poetry, along with Irish nationalism and the occult. Yeats's interest in Irish folklore was reflected in his early poetry and in the plays he wrote based on Irish legend, especially about Cuchulain. His occult interests appear in his book *The Celtic Twilight* (1893) and *The Secret Rose* (1897). His love for things Irish is revealed throughout his work, which spans a period of nearly half a century, during which he reinvented himself as a poet numerous times, and developed a range of varying styles, voices, and perspectives. Yeats is generally considered the greatest Irish poet of the twentieth century and one of the finest poets of modern times.

Glossary

Allegory   A symbolic narrative in which the surface details imply a secondary meaning. Allegory often takes the form of a story in which the characters represent moral qualities.

Alliteration   The repetition of consonant sounds, especially at the beginning of words.

Anapest   Two unaccented syllables followed by an accented one, as in cŏmprĕheńd or iňtĕrveńe.

Antagonist   A character or force against which a main character struggles.

Assonance   The repetition of similar vowel sounds in a sentence or a line of poetry as in "I rose and told him of my woe."

Aubade   A love lyric in which the speaker complains about the arrival of the dawn, when he must part from his lover.

Ballad   A narrative poem written in four-line stanzas, characterized by swift action and narrated in a direct style.

Blank verse   A line of poetry or prose in unrhymed iambic pentameter.

Caesura   A strong pause within a line of verse.

Character   An imaginary person that lives in a literary work. Literary characters may be major or minor, static or dynamic.

Characterization   The means by which writers present and reveal character.

Closed form   A type of form or structure in poetry characterized by regularity and consistency in such elements as rhyme, line length, and metrical pattern.

Connotation   The personal and emotional associations called up by a word that go beyond its dictionary meaning.

Convention   A customary feature of a literary work such as the use of rhyme in a sonnet.

Couplet   A pair of rhymed lines that may or may not constitute a separate stanza in a poem.

Dactyl   A stressed syllable followed by two unstressed ones, as in flút-tĕr-ĭng or blúe-bĕr-r̆y.

Denotation   The dictionary meaning of a word.

Dialogue   The conversation of characters in a literary work.

Diction   The selection of words in a literary work.

Dramatic monologue   A type of poem in which a speaker addresses a silent listener.

Elegy   A lyric poem that laments the dead.

Elision   The omission of an unstressed vowel or syllable to preserve the meter of a line of poetry.

Enjambment   A run-on line of poetry in which logical and grammatical sense carries over from one line into the next. An enjambed line differs from an end-stopped line in which the grammatical and logical sense is completed within the line. In the opening lines of Robert Browning's "My Last Duchess," for example, the first line is end-stopped and the second enjambed:

> That's my last Duchess painted on the wall,
> Looking as if she were alive. I call
> That piece a wonder, now. . . .

Epic   A long narrative poem that records the adventures of a hero. Epics typically chronicle the origins of a civilization and embody its central values.

Epigram   A brief witty poem, often satirical.

Falling meter   Poetic meters such as trochaic and dactylic that move or fall from a stressed to an unstressed syllable.

Figurative language   A form of language use in which writers and speakers convey something other than the literal meaning of their words. See *hyperbole, metaphor, metonymy, simile, synecdoche,* and *understatement.*

Foot   A metrical unit composed of stressed and unstressed syllables. For example, an *iamb* or *iambic foot* is represented by ˘ ´, that is, an unaccented syllable followed by an accented one.

Free verse   Poetry without a regular pattern of meter or rhyme.

Hyperbole   A figure of speech involving exaggeration.

Iamb   An unstressed syllable followed by a stressed one, as in tŏdáy.

Image   A concrete representation of a sense impression, a feeling, or an idea. Imagery refers to the pattern of related details in a work.

Imagery   The pattern of related comparative aspects of language in a literary work.

Irony   A contrast or discrepancy between what is said and what is meant or between what happens and what is expected to happen. In verbal irony characters say the opposite of what they mean. In irony of circumstance or situation the opposite of what is expected happens. In dramatic irony a character speaks in ignorance of a situation or event known to the audience or to other characters.

Literal language   A form of language in which writers and speakers mean exactly what their words denote.

Lyric poem   A type of poem characterized by brevity, compression, and the expression of feeling.

Metaphor   A comparison between essentially unlike things without a word such as *like* or *as*. An example: "My love is a red, red rose."

Meter   The measured pattern of rhythmic accents in poems.

Metonymy   A figure of speech in which a closely related term is substituted for an object or idea. An example: "We have always remained loyal to the crown."

Monologue   A speech by one character.

Narrative poem   A poem that tells a story.

Narrator   The voice and implied speaker of a fictional work, to be distinguished from the actual living author.

Octave   An eight-line unit, which may constitute a stanza or a section of a poem, as in the octave of a sonnet.

Ode   A long, stately poem in stanzas of varied length, meter, and form. Usually a serious poem on an exalted subject.

Onomatopoeia   The use of words to imitate the sounds they describe. Words such as *buzz* and *crack* are onomatopoetic.

Open form   A type of structure or form in poetry characterized by freedom from regularity and consistency in such elements as rhyme, line length, and metrical pattern.

Parody   A humorous, mocking imitation of a literary work.

Personification   The endowment of inanimate objects or abstract concepts with animate or living qualities. An example: "The yellow leaves flaunted their color gaily in the wind."

Plot   The unified structure of incidents in a literary work.

Point of view   The angle of vision from which a story is narrated.

Protagonist   The main character of a literary work.

Quatrain   A four-line stanza in a poem.

Rhetorical question   A question to which an overt answer is not expected. Writers use rhetorical questions to set up an explanation they are about to provide and to trigger a reader's mental response.

Rhyme   The matching of final vowel or consonant sounds in two or more words.

Rhythm   The recurrence of accent or stress in lines of verse.

Rising meter   Poetic meters such as iambic and anapestic that move or ascend from an unstressed to a stressed syllable.

Romance   A type of narrative fiction or poem in which adventure is a central feature and in which an idealized vision of reality is presented.

Satire   A literary work that criticizes human misconduct and ridicules vices, stupidities, and follies.

Sestet   A six-line unit of verse constituting a stanza or section of a poem; the last six lines of an Italian sonnet.

Sestina   A poem of thirty-nine lines written in iambic pentameter. Its six-line stanzas repeat in an intricate and prescribed order the six last words of each line in the opening stanza. After the sixth stanza there is a three-line *envoi* (or envoy) which uses the six repeating words, two to a line.

Setting   The time and place of a literary work that establish its context.

Simile   A figure of speech involving a comparison between unlike things using *like, as,* or *as though*. An example: "My love is like a red, red rose."

Soliloquy   A speech in a play which is meant to be heard by the audience but not by other characters on the stage. If there are no other characters present the soliloquy represents the character's thinking aloud.

Sonnet   A fourteen-line poem in iambic pentameter. The *Shakespearean* or *English sonnet* is arranged as three quatrains and a couplet, rhyming *abab cdcd efef gg*. The *Petrarchan* or *Italian sonnet* divides into two parts: an eight-line octave and a six-line sestet, rhyming *abba abba cde cde* or *abba abba cd cd cd*.

Spondee   A metrical foot represented by two stressed syllables such as kníck-knáck.

Stanza   A division or unit of a poem that is repeated in the same form—with similar or identical patterns of rhyme and meter.

Structure   The design or form of a literary work.

Style   The way an author chooses words, arranges them in sentences or in lines of dialogue or verse, and develops ideas and actions *with* description, imagery, and other literary techniques.

Subject   What a story or play is about; to be distinguished from plot and theme.

Subplot   A subsidiary or subordinate or parallel plot in a play or story that coexists with the main plot.

Symbol   An object or action in a literary work that means more than itself, that stands for something beyond itself.

Synecdoche   A figure of speech in which a part is substituted for the whole. An example: "Lend me a hand."

Syntax   The grammatical order of words in a sentence or line of verse or dialogue.

Tempo   The variation in pace in which a scene is acted.

Tercet   A three-line stanza.

Theme   The idea of a literary work abstracted from its details of language, character, and action, and cast in the form of a generalization.

Tone   The implied attitude of a writer toward the subject and characters of a work.

Understatement   A figure of speech in which a writer or speaker says less than what he or she means; the converse of exaggeration.

Villanelle   A nineteen-line lyric poem that relies heavily on repetition. The first and third lines alternate throughout the poem, which is structured in six stanzas—five tercets and a final quatrain.

Acknowledgments

Poetry

MARGARET ATWOOD "This Is a Photograph of Me" from *The Circle Game* by Margaret Atwood, 1965. Reprinted with the permission of Stoddart Publishing Co., Limited, Don Mills, Ontario, Canada.

W. H. AUDEN "The Unknown Citizen," "Museé des Beaux Arts," and "In Memory of W. B. Yeats" from *W. H. Auden: Collected Poems* by W. H. Auden, edited by Edward Mendelson. Copyright © 1940 and renewed 1968 by W. H. Auden. Reprinted by permission of Random House, Inc.

JIMMY SANTIAGO BACA "Section XVII from Meditations on the South Valley" by Jimmy Santiago Baca, from *Martin and Meditations on The South Valley*. Copyright © 1987 by Jimmy Santiago Baca. Reprinted by permission of New Directions Publishing Corp.

ELIZABETH BISHOP "First Death in Nova Scotia" and "Sestina" from *The Complete Poems 1927–1979* by Elizabeth Bishop. Copyright © 1979, 1983 by Alice Helen Methfessel. Reprinted by permission of Farrar, Straus and Giroux, LLC.

NEAL BOWERS "Driving Lessons" by Neal Bowers as appeared in *Shenandoah*, 42:2 (Summer 1992), pp. 42–43. Reprinted by permission of the author.

GWENDOLYN BROOKS "the mother" and "First fight. Then fiddle." from *Blacks* by Gwendolyn Brooks.

RAYMOND CARVER "Photograph of My Father in His Twenty-second Year" by Raymond Carver, © 1984 by Raymond Carver; © 1988 by Tess Gallagher. Reprinted by permission of ICM. All rights reserved.

ROSARIO CASTELLANOS "Chess" as translated by Maureen Ahern from *A Rosario Castellanos Reader* by Rosario Castellanos, edited by Maureen Ahern, translated by Maureen Ahern and others. Copyright © 1988. By permission of Maureen Ahern, Fondo de Cultura Economica and the University of Texas Press.

C.P. CAVAFY "The City" by C.P. Cavafy from *Collected Poems, Revised Edition,* translated by Edmund Keeley and Philip Sherrard. Copyright © 1992 by Edmund Keeley and Philip Sherrard. Reprinted by permission of Princeton University Press.

HELEN CHASIN "The Word *Plum*" From *Coming Close and Other Poems* by Helen Chasin, 1968. Reprinted by permission of Yale University Press.

LUCILLE CLIFTON   "Homage to My Hips" by Lucille Clifton. Copyright © 1980 by The University of Massachusetts Press. First appeared in *Two-Headed Woman,* published by the University of Massachusetts Press. Now appears in *Good Woman: Poems and a Memoir 1969–1980,* published by BOA Editions, Ltd. Reprinted by permission of Curtis Brown, Ltd.

JUDITH ORTIZ COFER   "The Idea of Islands" by Judith Ortiz Cofer is reprinted with permission from the publisher of *Terms of Survival* (Houston: Arte Publico Press—University of Houston, 1987).

GREGORY CORSO   "Marriage" by Gregory Corso, from *The Happy Birthday of Death.* Copyright © 1960 by New Directions Publishing Corp. Reprinted by permission of New Directions Publishing Corp.

E.E. CUMMINGS   "I(a," "Me up at does," "anyone lived in a pretty how town," "[Buffalo Bill's,]" and "i thank You God for most this amazing" from *Complete Poems: 1904–1962* by E.E. Cummings, edited by George J. Firmage. Copyright 1923, 1925, 1926, 1931, 1935, 1938, 1939, 1940, 1944, 1945, 1946, 1947, 1948, 1949, 1950, 1951, 1952, 1953, 1954, © 1955, 1956, 1957, 1958, 1959, 1960, 1961, 1962, 1963, 1966, 1967, 1968, 1972, 1973, 1974, 1975, 1976, 1977, 1978, 1979, 1980, 1981, 1982, 1983, 1984, 1985, 1986, 1987, 1988, 1989, 1990, 1991, by the Trustees for the E.E. Cummings Trust. Copyright © 1973, 1976, 1978, 1979, 1981, 1983, 1985, 1991 by George James Firmage. Reprinted by permission of Liveright Publishing Corporation.

EMILY DICKINSON   "Because I Could Not Stop for Death," #712, "I'm 'wife'—I've finished that," #199, "I taste a liquor never brewed," #214, "I like a look of Agony," #241, "Wild Nights—Wild Nights!" #249, "There's a certain Slant of light," #258, "I felt a Funeral, in my Brain," #280, "Some keep the Sabbath going to Church," #328, "I dreaded that first Robin, so," #348, "Much Madness is divinest Sense," #435, "I died for Beauty—but was scarce," #449, "I heard a Fly buzz—when I died," #465, "The Heart asks Pleasure—first," #536, "Pain—has an Element of Blank," #650, "Remorse—is Memory—awake," #744, "I like to see it lap the Miles," #585, "The Bustle in a House," #1078, "The last Night that She lived," #1100, "A narrow Fellow in the Grass," #986, "Further in Summer than the Birds," #1068, "A Route of Evanescence," #1463, "Apparently with no surprise," #1624, "My life closed twice before its close," #1732, "The Soul Selects her own Society," #303, "The Wind begun to knead the Grass" and "Wind begun to rock the Grass," #824, "Crumbling is not an instant's Act," #997, and Poems #632, #650, by Emily Dickinson. Reprinted by permission of the publishers and the Trustees of Amherst College from *The Poems of Emily Dickinson,* Thomas H. Johnson, ed., Cambridge, Mass.: The Belknap Press of Harvard University Press, Copyright © 1951, 1955, 1979, 1983 by the President and Fellows of Harvard College. "Tell all the Truth but tell it slant," #1129, and "I'm 'wife'—I've finished that," #199 by Emily Dickinson. Reprinted by permission of the publisher from *The Passion of Emily Dickinson* by Judith Farr, Cambridge, Mass.: Harvard University Press, Copyright © 1997 by the President and Fellows of Harvard College. "After great pain, a formal feeling comes," #341, by Emily Dickinson. "We grow accustomed to the Dark," #419, by Emily Dickinson. "There is a pain—so utter," #599, by Emily Dickinson. "My Life had stood—a Loaded Gun," #754, by Emily Dickinson. "I cannot dance upon my toes," #326, by Emily Dickinson.

HILDA DOOLITTLE   "Heat, part II of Garden" by H.D., from *Collected Poems, 1912–1944.* Copyright © 1982 by The Estate of Hilda Doolittle. Reprinted by permission of New Directions Publishing Corp.

RITA DOVE   "Canary" from *Grace Notes* by Rita Dove. Copyright © 1989 by Rita Dove. Reprinted by permission of the author and W.W. Norton & Company, Inc.

T.S. ELIOT   "Journey of the Magi" from *Collected Poems 1909–1962* by T.S. Eliot, copyright 1936 by Harcourt Brace & Company, copyright © 1964, 1963 by T.S. Eliot, reprinted by permission of the publisher, and Faber and Faber, Ltd. "The Love Song of J. Alfred

Prufrock" by T.S. Eliot from *Collected Poems 1909–1962* by T.S. Eliot. Reprinted by permission of Faber and Faber Ltd.

LOUISE ERDRICH "Indian Boarding School: The Runaways" from *Jacklight* by Louise Erdrich.

ROBERT FAGLES "The Starry Night" by Robert Fagles from *I, Vincent: Poems from the Pictures of Van Gogh* by Robert Fagles. Reprinted by permission of Professor Robert Fagles.

LAWRENCE FERLINGHETTI "Constantly Risking Absurdity" by Lawrence Ferlinghetti from *A Coney Island of the Mind*. Copyright © 1958 by Lawrence Ferlinghetti. Reprinted by permission of New Directions Publishing Corp. "Short Story on a Painting of Gustav Klimt" by Lawrence Ferlinghetti, from *Endless Life*. Copyright © 1976 by Lawrence Ferlinghetti. Reprinted by permission of New Directions Publishing Corp.

ROBERT FROST "Dust of Snow," "Stopping by Woods on a Snowy Evening," "The Silken Tent," "The Span of Life," "Fire and Ice," "For Once, Then, Something," "Two Look at Two," "Once by the Pacific," "Acquainted with the Night," "Tree at My Window," "Departmental," "Desert Places," "Design," "Provide, Provide," "The Most of It," "Sentence Sounds," "The Figure a Poem Makes," "The Road Not Taken," "Mowing," "Mending Wall," "Birches," and "Putting in the Seed" from *The Poetry of Robert Frost* by Robert Frost. "The Unmade Word," "The Tuft of Flowers," "Home Burial," and "Hyla Brook" from *Collected Poems, Prose, and Plays by Robert Frost*. Reprinted by permission of the Executor of the Robert Frost Estate.

DAVID GEWANTER Goya's "The Third of May, 1808" by David Gewanter. Copyright 1997 by The University of Chicago. All rights reserved. Reprinted by permission.

NIKKI GIOVANNI "Ego Tripping" from *The Women And The Men* by Nikki Giovanni. Copyright © 1970, 1974, 1975 by Nikki Giovanni. By permission of William Morrow and Company, Inc.

ROBERT GRAVES "Symptoms of Love" by Robert Graves from *Collected Poems* by Robert Graves, 1975. Reprinted by permission of Carcanet Press Limited.

DONALD HALL "My son, my executioner" by Donald Hall. Copyright Donald Hall. Reprinted by permission of the author.

GARY LAYNE HATCH "Terrier Torment: or Mr. Hopkins and His Dog" by Gary Layne Hatch, 1995. Reprinted by permission of the author.

ROBERT HAYDEN "Those Winter Sundays" copyright © 1966 by Robert Hayden, from *Angle of Ascent: New and Selected Poems* by Robert Hayden. Reprinted by permission of Liveright Publishing Corporation.

SEAMUS HEANEY "Mid-Term Break" and "Digging" from *Open Ground: Selected Poems 1966–1996* by Seamus Heaney. Reprinted by permission of Farrar, Straus and Giroux, LLC.

E. WARD HERLANDS "When Edward Hopper Was Painting" by E. Ward Herlands, *Midstream* 37:4 (May 1991). Reprinted by permission of the author.

GERARD MANLEY HOPKINS "Carrion Comfort" from *Poems of Gerard Manley Hopkins*. Oxford University Press.

A. E. HOUSMAN "When I was one-and-twenty" and "To an Athlete Dying Young" from "A Shropshire Lad," Authorized Edition, from *The Collected Poems of A. E. Housman*. copyright 1939, 1940, © 1965 by Holt, Rinehart and Winston. Copyright © 1967, 1968 by Robert E. Symons. Reprinted by permission of Henry Holt and Co., Inc.

LANGSTON HUGHES "Dream Deferred," "Same in Blues," "Dream Boogie," "The Negro Speaks of Rivers," "Mother to Son," "I, Too," "My People," "The Weary Blues," "Young Gal's Blues," "Morning After," "Trumpet Player," "Madam and the Rent Man," "Theme for English B," "Aunt Sue's Stories," "Let America Be America Again," by Langston Hughes. From *Collected Poems* by Langston Hughes. Copyright © 1994 by the Estate of Langston Hughes. Reprinted by permission of Alfred A. Knopf Inc.

VICENTE HUIDOBRO "Ars Poetica" by Vicente Huidobro, translation by David M. Guss, from *The Selected Poems of Vicente Huidobro*. Copyright © 1963 by Empreza Editoria

Zig Zag, S.A., © 1981 by David M. Guss. Reprinted by permission of New Directions Publishing Corp.

JANE KENYON   "Notes from the Other Side" copyright 1996 by the Estate of Jane Kenyon. Reprinted from *Otherwise: New & Selected Poems* with the permission of Graywolf Press, Saint Paul, Minnesota.

GALWAY KINNELL   "Saint Francis and the Sow" from *Three Books* by Galway Kinnell. Copyright © 1993 by Galway Kinnell. Previously published in *Mortal Acts, Mortal Words* (1980). Reprinted by permission of Houghton Mifflin Co. All rights reserved.

KENNETH KOCH   "Variations on a Theme by William Carlos Williams" by Kenneth Koch. Copyright © by Kenneth Koch, 1994. Reprinted by permission of the author.

YUSEF KOMUNYAKAA   "Facing It" from *Dien Cai Dau* © 1988 by Yusef Komunyakaa, Wesleyan University Press by permission of University Press of New England.

JOSEPH LANGLAND   "Hunters in the Snow: Breughel" from *The Greed Town* by Joseph Langland, Scribners, 1956.

PHILIP LARKIN   "A Study of Reading Habits" from *Collected Poems* by Philip Larkin. Reprinted by permission of Faber and Faber Ltd.

D.H. LAWRENCE   "The Piano" and "Piano" by D.H. Lawrence from *The Complete Poems of D.H. Lawrence* by D.H. Lawrence, edited by V. de Sola Pinto & F.W. Roberts. Copyright © 1964, 1971 by Angelo Ravagli and C.M. Weekley, Executors of the Estate of Frieda Lawrence Ravagli. Used by permission of Viking Penguin, a division of Penguin Putnam Inc.

DENISE LEVERTOV   "O Taste and See" by Denise Levertov, from *Poems 1960–1967.* Copyright © 1964 by Denise Levertov. Reprinted by permission of New Directions Publishing Corp.

AUDRE LORDE   "Hanging Fire" from *The Black Unicorn* by Audre Lorde. Copyright © 1978 by Audre Lorde. Reprinted by permission of W.W. Norton & Company, Inc.

ARCHIBALD MACLEISH   "Ars Poetica" from *Collected Poems 1917–1982* by Archibald MacLeish. Copyright © 1982 by The Estate of Archibald MacLeish. Reprinted by permission of Houghton Mifflin Company. All rights reserved.

BOB MCKENTY   "Snow on Frost" and "Adam's Song" by Bob McKenty, 1993. Reprinted by permission of the author.

PETER MEINKE   "Advice to My Son" from *Liquid Paper: New and Selected Poems* by Peter Meinke, © 1991. Reprinted by permission of the University of Pittsburgh Press.

CHRISTINE KANE MOLITO   "Partial Reflections in Black & Blue" by Christine Kane Molito. Reprinted by permission of the author.

MARIANNE MOORE   "Poetry" Reprinted with the permission of Simon & Schuster from *The Collected Poems of Marianne.* Copyright 1935 by Marianne Moore; copyright renewed © 1963 by Marianne Moore and T.S. Eliot.

HOWARD MOSS   "Shall I Compare Thee to a Summer's Day?" from *A Swim Off the Rocks* by Howard Moss. Reprinted by permission of the Executor for Howard Moss.

SHARON OLDS   "Size and Sheer Will" from *The Dead And The Living* by Sharon Olds. Copyright © 1983 by Sharon Olds. Reprinted by permission of Alfred A. Knopf, Inc.

WILFRED OWEN   "Dulce et Decorum Est" by Wilfred Owen, from *The Collected Poems of Wilfred Owen.* Copyright © 1963 by Chatto & Windus, Ltd. Reprinted by permission of New Directions Publishing Corp.

LINDA PASTAN   "Ethics" from *Waiting For My Life* by Linda Pastan. Copyright © 1981 by Linda Pastan. Reprinted by permission of W.W. Norton & Company, Inc.

MARGE PIERCY   "A Work of Artifice" from *Circles On The Water* by Marge Piercy. Copyright © 1982 by Marge Piercy. Reprinted by permission of Alfred A. Knopf, Inc.

SYLVIA PLATH   "Mirror" by Sylvia Plath. Copyright © 1963 by Ted Hughes. From *The Collected Poems of Sylvia Plath,* edited by Ted Hughes. Reprinted by permission of Harper-Collins Publishers, and Faber and Faber Ltd.

EZRA POUND   "The River-Merchant's Wife: A Letter" by Ezra Pound from *Personae*. Copyright © 1926 by Ezra Pound. Reprinted by permission of New Directions Publishing Corp.

JACQUES PRÉVERT   "Family Portrait" by Jacques Prévert translated by Harriet Zinnes.

JOHN CROWE RANSOM   "Piazza Piece" from *Selected Poems* by John Crowe Ransom. Copyright 1927 by Alfred A. Knopf, Inc., and renewed 1955 by John Crowe Ransom. Reprinted by permission of the publisher.

HENRY REED   "Naming of Parts" from *A Map of Verona* by Henry Reed.

ADRIENNE RICH   "Aunt Jennifer's Tigers" and "Rape" from *The Fact of A Doorframe: Poems Selected and New 1950–1984* by Adrienne Rich. Copyright © 1984 by Adrienne Rich. Copyright © 1975, 1978 by W.W. Norton & Company, Inc. Copyright © 1981 by Adrienne Rich. Reprinted by permission of the author and W.W. Norton & Company, Inc.

ALBERTO RIOS   "A Dream of Husbands" by Alberto Rios from *Whispering to Fool the Wind*.

THEODORE ROETHKE   "Elegy for Jane," copyright 1950 by Theodore Roethke, "My Papa's Waltz," copyright 1942 by Hearst Magazines, Inc., "The Waking," copyright 1953 by Theodore Roethke, from *The Collected Poems of Theodore Roethke* by Theodore Roethke. Used by permission of Doubleday, a division of Random House Inc.

KRAFT ROMPF   "Waiting Table" by Kraft Rompf. Reprinted by permission of the author.

NATALIE SAFIR   "Matisse's Dance" by Natalie Safir.

GERTRUDE SCHNACKENBERG   "Signs" from *The Lamplit Answer* by Gertrude Schnackenberg. Copyright © 1985 by Gertrude Schnackenberg. Reprinted by permission of Farrar, Straus and Giroux, LLC.

ANNE SEXTON   "Her Kind" from *To Bedlam and Part Way Back* by Anne Sexton. Copyright © 1960 by Anne Sexton, © renewed 1988 by Linda G. Sexton. "The Starry Night" from *All My Pretty Ones* by Anne Sexton. Copyright © 1962 by Anne Sexton, © renewed 1990 by Linda G. Sexton. "Two Hands" from *The Awful Rowing Toward God* by Anne Sexton. Copyright © 1975 by Loring Conant, Jr., Executor of the Estate of Anne Sexton. Reprinted by permission of Houghton Mifflin Co. All rights reserved.

LOUIS SIMPSON   "The Battle" reprinted by permission of Louis Simpson from *Good News of Death and Other Poems*. Copyright © 1955 by Louis Simpson.

STEVIE SMITH   "Mother, Among the Dustbins" by Stevie Smith, from *Collected Poems of Stevie Smith*. Copyright © 1972 by Stevie Smith. Reprinted by permission of New Directions Publishing Corp.

Critical Perspective

EMILY DICKINSON   From "On 'Wild Nights'" by Judith Farr. Reprinted by permission of the publisher from *The Passion of Emily Dickinson* by Judith Farr, Cambridge, Mass.: Harvard University Press, Copyright © 1997 by the President and Fellows of Harvard College.

JUDITH FARR   "On 'Wild Nights'" from *The Passion of Emily Dickinson*. Reprinted by permission of the publishers. Harvard University Press. Cambridge, Mass. Copyright © 1992 by the President and Fellows of Harvard College.

ROBERT FROST   From "The Unmade Word" by Robert Frost from *Collected Poems, Prose, and Plays* by Robert Frost. Reprinted by permission of the Executor of the Robert Frost Estate.

HELEN McNEIL   Excerpt from *Emily Dickinson* by Helen McNeil, 1986. Reprinted by permission of Virago Press.

RICHARD POIRIER   From "On 'Stopping by Woods'" and "On 'Mending Wall'" from *Robert Frost: The Work of Knowing* edited by Richard Poirier. Copyright © 1977 by Richard Poirier. Used by permission of Oxford University Press, Inc.

WILLIAM PRITCHARD From *Frost: A Literary Life Reconsidered* edited by William Pritchard. Copyright © 1984 by William Pritchard. Used by permission of Oxford University Press, Inc.

ALLEN TATE "Dickinson and Knowledge" and "On 'Because I Could Not Stop for Death'" from "Emily Dickinson" from *Collected Essays* by Allen Tate, Swallow, 1959. Reprinted by permission of Mrs. Helen Tate.

YVOR WINTERS "Robert Frost: or, the Spiritual Drifter as Poet" by Yvor Winters from *The Function of Criticism*. Reprinted with the permission of Ohio University Press/Swallow Press, Athens, Ohio.

Poems and Paintings

VINCENT VAN GOGH *The Starry Night,* photograph © 1997 the Museum of Modern Art, New York.

EDWARD HOPPER *Sunday,* photograph © 1997 the Museum of Modern Art, New York.

HENRI MATISSE *Dance (First Version),* © 1998 Succession H. Matisse, Paris/Artists Rights Society (ARS), New York. Photograph © 1997 the Museum of Modern Art, New York.

PABLO PICASSO *Girl with a Mandolin (Fanny Tellier),* © 1998 Estate of Pablo Picasso/Artists Rights Society (ARS). New York. Photograph © 1997 the Museum of Modern Art, New York.

PABLO PICASSO *Still Life with Pitcher, Bowl, & Fruit,* © 1998 Estate of Pablo Picasso/Artists Rights Society (ARS), New York.

Index

of Authors, Titles, and First Lines

Selection titles appear in italics, and first lines of poems appear in roman type. Page numbers in roman type indicate the opening page of a selection; italic numbers indicate discussion. Bold page numbers indicate complete sections on specific authors.

Abortions will not let you forget, 297
A broken ALTAR, Lord, They servant rears, 225
Ackerman, Amanda
  The Sad World of "London," 130
Acquainted with the Night, 18, 166, 184
Adam's Curse, 91
Adam's Song, 70
Advice to My Son, 49, 50–51
The Aeneid, 15, 15
After great pain, a formal feeling comes, 153
Afterwards, 266
The Altar, 225
Among twenty snow mountains, 274
An ant on the tablecloth, 185
A narrow Fellow in the Grass, 140, 159
A noiseless patient spider, 257
Anonymous
  Barbara Allan, 16, 210
  Edward, Edward, 16, 212
  Western Wind, 25

anyone lived in a pretty how town, 286
A poem should be palpable and mute, 284
Apparently with no surprise, 162
Arnold, Matthew
  Dover Beach, 262
A Route of Evanescence, 162
Ars Poetica (Huidobro), 283
Ars Poetica (MacLeish), 284
A sudden blow: the great wings beating still, 271
As virtuous men pass mildly away, 220
A sweet disorder in the dress, 34
A toad the power mower caught, 300
At ten I wanted fame, 325
Atwood, Margaret, 381
  This Is a Photograph of Me, 312
Auden, W. H., *381*
  In Memory of W. B. Yeats, 290
  The Unknown Citizen, 289
Aunt Jennifer's Tigers, 10, 11
Aunt Jennifer's tigers prance across a screen, 11

Aunt Sue has a head full of stories, 206
Aunt Sue's Stories, 206
Avenge, O Lord, thy slaughtered saints, whose bones, 226
A wayward crow, 104

Ballad of the Landlord, 193–194, 207
Barbara Allan, 16, 210
Barksdale, Richard K.
  On Hughes's "Ballad of the Landlord," 193
Batter my heart, three-personed God, 223
The Battle, 47
Because I could not stop for Death, 53, *146–147*
Because we were friends and sometimes loved each other, 301
Behind Grandma's House, 325
Behold her, single in the field, 233
La Belle Dame sans Merci, 17, 243

Bent double, like old beggars under sacks, 285
Between my finger and my thumb, 314
Billie Holiday's burned voice, 322
Birches, 165, 177
Bishop, Elizabeth, *382*
   First Death in Nova Scotia, 36, 37–39
   Sestina, 18, 293
Black reapers with the sound of steel on stones, 288
Blake, William, *382*
   The Clod & the Pebble, 229
   The Garden of Love, 231
   The Lamb, 230
   London, 92, 93–95, 129–133, 337
   A Poison Tree, 52
   The Tyger, 230
A Blessing, 303
Bowers, Neal
   Driving Lessons, 319
Bradstreet, Anne
   To My Dear and Loving Husband, 227
Brooks, Gwendolyn
   First fight. Then fiddle, 298
   the mother, 297
Browning, Elizabeth Barrett
   How do I love thee? Let me count the ways, 249
Browning, Robert, *382*
   Meeting at Night, 40
   My Last Duchess, 21, 23
   Soliloquy of the Spanish Cloister, 255
Buffalo Bill's, 84, *84–85*
Burns, Robert
   A Red, Red Rose, 232
Busy old fool, unruly sun, 56
By June our brook's run out of song and speed, 181
Byron, Lord (George Gordon)
   The Destruction of Sennacherib, 77
   She walks in beauty, 239
By the road to the contagious hospital, 276

Canary, 322
The Canonization, 219
Carrion Comfort, 101
Carroll, Lewis (Charles Lutwidge Dodgson)
   Jabberwocky, 263
Carver, Raymond, *383*
   Photograph of My Father in His Twenty-second Year, 313
Castellanos, Rosario
   Chess, 301

Cavafy, C. P.
   The City, 88
Channel Firing, 265
Chasin, Helen
   The Word "Plum," 70
Chess, 301
The City, 88
Clifton, Lucille
   Homage to My Hips, 311
The Clod & the Pebble, 229
Cofer, Judith Ortiz
   The Idea of Islands, 323
Coleridge, Samuel Taylor
   Kubla Khan, 238
Come In, 378–380
Come live with me and be my love (Marlowe), 216
Come live with me and be my love (McKenty), 70
Composed upon Westminster Bridge, September 3, 1802, 234
A Considerable Speck, 165
Constantly risking absurdity, 299
Corso, Gregory
   Marriage, 305
Crane, Stephen
   War is Kind, 20, 21
Crossing Brooklyn Ferry, 257
Crumbling is not an instant's Act, 64, 89, *90*
cummings, e. e., *383*
   anyone lived in a pretty how town, 286
   Buffalo Bill's, 84, *84–85*
   i thank You God for most this amazing, 287
   l (a, 83, *83–84*
   Me up at does, *58,* 61, *127*

The Dance, 85
Danse Russe, 277
Dante
   Divine Comedy, 15
The Dark Woods of Robert Frost, 378
Death, be not proud, though some have callèd thee, 222
The Death of a Toad, 300
Delight in Disorder, 34
Departmental, 165, 185
Desert Places, 165, 186
Design, 166, 187
The Destruction of Sennacherib, 77
Dickinson, Emily, **137–162**
   After great pain, a formal feeling comes, 153
   Apparently with no surprise, 162
   Because I could not stop for Death, 53, *146–147*

Dickinson, Emily *(Cont.)*
   The brain is wider than the sky, 149, 157
   The Bustle in a House, *140,* 160
   Crumbling is not an instant's Act, *64, 89, 90*
   Further in Summer than the Birds, 160
   The Heart asks Pleasure—first, 156
   I cannot dance upon my Toes, 141
   I died for Beauty—but was scarce, 155
   I dreaded that first Robin, so, 153
   I felt a Funeral, in my Brain, 152
   I heard a Fly buzz—when I died, 155
   I like a look of Agony, 150
   I like to see It lap the Miles, 156
   I'm "wife"—I've finished that, 149, 327, *334, 336, 337, 340, 344, 347–348, 351, 353–354, 356, 358, 360*
   I taste a liquor never brewed, 150
   The last Night that She lived, 160
   Much Madness is divinest Sense, 154
   My life closed twice before its close, 162
   My Life had stood—a Loaded Gun, 158
   A narrow Fellow in the Grass, *140,* 159
   Pain has an element of blank, *147–148,* 148, 157
   Remorse—is Memory—awake, 158
   A Route of Evanescence, 162
   Some keep the Sabbath going to Church, 152
   The Soul selects her own Society, 142, 149
   Tell all the Truth but tell It slant, *140,* 161
   There is a pain—so utter, 157
   There's a certain Slant of light, 151
   We grow accustomed to the Dark, 154
   Wild Nights—Wild Nights!, *144–146,* 151
   The Wind begun to knead the Grass, 96
   The Wind begun to rock the Grass, 97
   Zero at the Bone, 140

Dickinson and Knowledge, 143

Dickinson's Method, 147

Digging, 314

Divine Comedy, 15

Does the road wind up-hill all the way?, 51

Donne, John, *383*
  Batter my heart, three-personed God, 223
  The Canonization, 219
  Death, be not proud, though some have called thee, 222
  The Flea, 221
  Hymn to God the Father, 44
  Song, 218
  The Sun Rising, 17, 56, *57–58, 72*
  A Valediction: Forbidding Mourning, 220

Do Not Go Gentle into that Good Night, *18,* 297

Do not weep, maiden, for war is kind, 20

The Double-Play, 45

Dove, Rita
  Canary, 322

Dover Beach, 262

Dream Boogie, 195, 203

Dream Deferred, 196

A Dream of Death, 95

A Dream of Husbands, 324

Drink to me only with thine eyes, 224

Driving Lessons, 319

Droning a drowsy syncopated tune, 200

Dulce et Decorum Est, 285

Dunbar, Paul Laurence
  We wear the mask that grins and lies, 273

During Wind and Rain, 67

Dust of Snow, 103

The Eagle, 254

Earth has not anything to show more fair, 234

Edward, Edward, 16, 212

Ego Tripping, 315

Elegy for Jane, 292

Eliot, T. S., *384*
  The Love Song of J. Alfred Prufrock, 58, 279

Emanuel, James A.
  On "Trumpet Player," 195

Erdrich, Louise
  Indian Boarding School: The Runaways, 326

An Essay on Man, *58,* 229

Ethics, 308

The Eve of St. Agnes, 91–92

Facing It, 318

Family Portrait, 27

Farewell, thou child of my right hand, and joy, 223

Farr, Judith
  On "Wild Nights," 145

Ferlinghetti, Lawrence, *384*
  Constantly risking absurdity, 299

Fern Hill, 295

Fire and Ice, 182

First Death in Nova Scotia, 36, *37–39*

First fight. Then fiddle, 298

First fight. Then fiddle. Ply the slipping string, 298

Five years have passed; five summers, with the length, 234

The Flea, 221

Flood-tide below me! I see you face to face!, 257

For God's sake hold your tongue, and let me love, 219

For Once, Then, Something, 182

From the sea came a hand, 304

Frost, Robert, **163–188,** *378–380*
  Acquainted with the Night, 18, 166, 184
  Birches, 165, 177
  Come In, *378–380*
  A Considerable Speck, 165
  Departmental, 165, 185
  Desert Places, 165, 186
  Design, 166, 187
  Dust of Snow, 103
  For Once, Then, Something, 182
  Fire and Ice, 182
  Home Burial, 165, 178
  Hyla Brook, 181
  Mending Wall, 165, 172–173, 176
  The Most of It, 165, 188
  Mowing, 166, 174
  Into My Own, 378–380
  Once by the Pacific, 166, 169, 184
  Provide, Provide, 165, 187
  Putting in the Seed, 166, 181
  The Road Not Taken, 52, 165, 378–380
  The Silken Tent, 58, 60, 127, 165
  The Span of Life, 72
  Stopping by Woods on a Snowy Evening, 5, 6–8, 9–10, 36, 55–56, 63, 63–65, 73–74, 75, 89, 165, 170–172, 378–380
  Tree at My Window, 165, 184
  The Tuft of Flowers, 165, 174
  Two Look at Two, 165, 183

Further in Summer than the Birds, 160

The Garden of Love, 231

Gather ye rosebuds while ye may, 224

Giovanni, Nikki
  Ego Tripping, 315

Glory be to God for dappled things, 267

Go, and catch a falling star, 218

God's Grandeur, 266

Good morning, daddy!, 195, 203

Graves, Robert
  Symptoms of Love, 125, 125–126

Gr-r-r—there go, my heart's abhorrence!, 255

H. D. (Hilda Doolittle)
  Heat, 40, 126

"Had he and I but met, 59

Had we but world enough, and time, 227

Hall, Donald
  My son, my executioner, 305

Hanging Fire, 310

Hardy, Thomas, *41, 384*
  Afterwards, 266
  Channel Firing, 265
  The Man He Killed, 58, 59
  Neutral Tones, 41, 126
  The Ruined Maid, 264
  During Wind and Rain, 67

Hatch, Gary Layne
  Terrier Torment; or, Mr. Hopkins and his Dog, 101

Hayden, Robert
  Those Winter Sundays, 2, 2–5, 9–10, 19–20, 36, 55, 88, 124

Heaney, Seamus, *385*
  Digging, 314
  Mid-Term Break, 313

Heat, 40, 126

He clasps the crag with crooked hands, 254

He disappeared in the dead of winter, 290

Helen, thy beauty is to me, 249

Helmet and rifle, pack and overcoat, 47

Herbert, George, *385*
  The Altar, 225
  Virtue, 53

Her Kind, 78

Herrick, Robert, *385*
  Delight in Disorder, 34
  Upon Julia's Clothes, 224

Herrick, Robert (*Cont.*)
  *To the Virgins, to Make Much of
    Time,* 224
He saw her from the bottom of
  the stairs, 178
He thought he kept the universe
  alone, 188
He was found by the Bureau of
  Statistics to be, 289
Holland, Norman
  Reading Frost, 169
Homage to My Hips, 311
Home Burial, 165, 178
Homer
  Iliad, 15
Home's the place we head for in
  our sleep, 326
Hopkins, Gerard Manley, *386*
  Carrion Comfort, 101
  God's Grandeur, 266
  Pied Beauty, 267
  Spring and Fall, 268
  Thou art indeed just, Lord,
    24, *58*
  In the Valley of the Elwy, 65,
    65–66, 74
  The Windhover, 267
Housman, A. E., *386*
  To an Athlete Dying Young, 269
  When I was one-and-twenty,
    268
How do I love thee? Let me count
  the ways, 249
Hughes, Langston, **188–208**
  Aunt Sue's Stories, 206
  Ballad of the Landlord,
    193–194, 207
  Dream Boogie, 195, 203
  Dream Deferred, 196
  I, Too, 199
  Let America Be America Again,
    208
  *Madam and the Rent
    Man,* 204
  Morning After, 201
  Mother to Son, 198
  My People, 199
  The Negro Speaks of Rivers,
    194–195, 198
  Same in Blues, 197
  Theme for English B, 205
  A Toast to Harlem, 190
  Trumpet Player, 195–196, 202
  The Weary Blues, 200
  Young Gal's Blues, 200
*Hughes and the Evolution of
  Consciousness in Black
  Poetry,* 192
Huidobro, Vicente
  Ars Poetica, 283
Hyla Brook, 181
Hymn to God the Father, 44

I am a gentleman in a dustcoat
  trying, 283
I am fourteen, 310
I am silver and exact, 309
I cannot dance upon my Toes, 141
I caught this morning morning's
  minion, 267
I chopped down the house that
  you had been saving to live in
  next summer, 100
The Idea of Islands, 323
I died for Beauty—but was
  scarce, 155
I divested myself of despair, 318
I dreaded that first Robin, so, 153
I dreamed that one had died in a
  strange place, 95
If all the world and love were
  young, 215
I felt a Funeral, in my Brain, 152
If ever two were one, then surely
  we, 227
I found a dimpled spider, fat and
  white, 187
If when my wife is sleeping, 277
I have been one acquainted with
  the night, 184
I have eaten the plums, 99
I have gone out, a possessed
  witch, 78
I heard a Fly buzz—when I
  died, 155
I know that I shall meet my
  fate, 60
I learned to drive in a parking
  lot, 319
Iliad, 15
I like a look of Agony, 150
I like to see it lap the Miles, 156
I love the wind, 322
I met a traveler from an antique
  land, 240
I'm gonna walk to the
  graveyard, 200
I'm "wife"—I've finished that,
  149, *327, 334, 336, 337, 340,
  344, 347–348, 351, 353–354,
  356, 358, 360*
In Breughel's great picture, The
  Kermess, 85
*Indian Boarding School: The
  Runaways,* 326
In ethics class so many years
  ago, 308
In his sea lit, 45
In Memory of W. B. Yeats, 290
In the cold, cold parlor, 36
In the Orchard, 23, 126
In the Valley of the Elwy, 65,
  65–66, 74
Into My Own, 378–380
In Xanadu did Kubla Khan, 238

I remember a house where all
  were good, 65
I remember the neckcurls, limp
  and damp as tendrils, 292
*An Irish Airman Foresees His Death,
  58,* 60
I said to my baby, 197
I sat all morning in the college
  sick bay, 313
I sing of warfare and a man at
  war, 15
I taste a liquor never brewed, 150
i thank You God for most this
  amazing, 287
'I thought you loved me.' 'No, it
  was only fun.,' 23
It is a beauteous evening, calm
  and free, 33
It little profits that an idle
  king, 253
I, Too, 199
I, too, dislike it: there are things
  that are important beyond all
  this fiddle, 278
I, too, sing America, 199
It was in and about the Martinmas
  time, 210
It was taken some time ago, 312
I've known rivers, 197
I wake to sleep, and take my
  waking slow, 87
I wandered lonely as a cloud, 29,
  30–31, 42–43, 56, 76–77
I wander thro' each charter'd
  street, 93
I wander thro' each dirty street, 92
I was angry with my friend, 52
I was born in the congo, 315
I was so sick last night I, 201
I went to the Garden of Love, 231
I went to turn the grass once after
  one, 174
I will arise and go now, and go to
  Innisfree, 39

Jabberwocky, 263
Jemie, Onwuchekwa
  *Hughes and the Evolution of
    Consciousness in Black
    Poetry,* 192
  *On "The Negro Speaks of
    Rivers,"* 194
Jonson, Ben, *386*
  On My First Son, 223
  Song: To Celia, 224
Just off the highway to Rochester,
  Minnesota, 303

Keats, John, *387*
  La Belle Dame sans Merci,
    17, 243

Keats, John (*Cont.*)
  The Eve of St. Agnes, 91–92
  On First Looking into Chapman's
    Homer, 81, 81–82
  Ode on a Grecian Urn, 247
  Ode to a Nightingale, 17, 245
  When I have fears that I may
    cease to be, 243
Kenyon, Jane
  Notes from the Other Side, 318
Kinnell, Galway
  Saint Francis and the Sow, 302
Know then thyself, presume not
  God to scan, 229
Koch, Kenneth
  Variations on a Theme by William
    Carlos Williams, 100
Komunyakaa, Yusef
  Facing It, 318
Kubla Khan, 238

The Lake Isle of Innisfree, 39
The Lamb, 230
Landlord, landlord, 207
Langston Hughes as Folk Poet, 191
Larkin, Philip
  A Study of Reading Habits, 300
Lawrence, D. H.
  The Piano, 97
  Piano, 98
Leda and the Swan, 271
Let America Be America
  Again, 208
Let me not to the marriage of
  true minds, 217
Let poetry be like a key, 283
Let us go then, you and I, 280
Levertov, Denise
  O Taste and See, 86
Lines (composed above Tintern
  Abbey), 234
Little Lamb, who made thee?, 230
London, 92, 93–95, 129–133, 337
Lorde, Audre
  Hanging Fire, 310
Love and forgetting might have
  carried them, 183
Love is a universal migraine, 125
Love seeketh not Itself to
  please, 229
The Love Song of J. Alfred Prufrock,
  58, 279
Lying in a Hammock at William
  Duffy's Farm in Pine Island,
  Minnesota, 302

McKenty, Bob, *387*
  Adam's Song, 70
  Snow on Frost, 104
MacLeish, Archibald
  Ars Poetica, 284

McNeil, Helen
  Dickinson's Method, 147
  Madam and the Rent Man, 204
  The Man He Killed, 58, 59
Márgáret, áre you grieving, 268
Mark but this flea, and mark in
  this, 221
Marlowe, Christopher
  The Passionate Shepherd to His
    Love, 216
Marriage, 305
Marvell, Andrew
  To His Coy Mistress, 227
Meditations on the South
  Valley, 322
Meeting at Night, 40
Meinke, Peter
  Advice to My Son, 49, 50–51
Mending Wall, 165, 172–173, 176
Me up at does, *58, 61, 127*
Mid-Term Break, 313
Milton, John, *387*
  On the Late Massacre in
    Piedmont, 58, 226
  Paradise Lost, 15, 16
  When I consider how my light
    is spent, 226
Miniver Cheevy, 32
Miniver Cheevy, child of
  scorn, 32
Mirror, 127–129, 309
Molito, Christine Kane
  Partial Reflections in Black &
    Blue, 317
Moore, Marianne
  Poetry, 278
Morning After, 201
Moss, Howard
  Shall I compare thee to a summer's
    day?, 103
The Most of It, 165, 188
the mother, 297
Mother, Among the Dustbins, 62
Mother, among the dustbins and
  the manure, 62
Mother to Son, 198
Mowing, 166, 174
Much have I traveled in the realms
  of gold, 81
Much Madness is divinest
  Sense, 154
My black face fades, 318
My heart aches, and a drowsy
  numbness pains, 245
My Last Duchess, 21, 23
My life closed twice before its
  close, 162
My Life had stood—a Loaded
  Gun, 158
My mistress' eyes are nothing like
  the sun, 218

My Papa's Waltz, 12, 13–14, 19,
  28–29, 64, 88
My People, 199
My son, my executioner, 305

Naming of Parts, 26, 126
The Negro Speaks of Rivers,
  194–195, 198
Neutral Tones, 41, 126
Notes from the Other Side, 318
Not, I'll not, carrion comfort,
  Despair, not feast on thee, 101
Now as I was young and easy
  under the apple boughs, 295
The Nymph's Reply to the
  Shepherd, 215

October. Here in this dank,
  unfamiliar kitchen, 313
Ode on a Grecian Urn, 247
Ode to a Nightingale, 17, 245
Ode to the West Wind, 240
Of man's first disobedience, and
  the fruit, 16
Olds, Sharon
  Size and Sheer Will, 317
O'Melia, my dear, this does
  everything crown!, 264
O my luve's like a red, red
  rose, 232
On "Because I Could Not Stop for
  Death," 146
Once by the Pacific, 166, 169, 184
Once upon a midnight dreary,
  while I pondered, weak and
  weary, 250
l (a, 83, *83–84*
One day I wrote her name upon
  the strand, 214
On First Looking into Chapman's
  Homer, 81, 81–82
On Hughes's "Ballad of the
  Landlord," 193
On "Mending Wall," 172
On My First Son, 223
On "Stopping by Woods on a Snowy
  Evening (Poirier), *171*
On "Stopping by Woods"
  (Pritchard), *170–172*
On the Collar of a Dog, 17
On the Late Massacre in Piedmont,
  58, 226
On "The Negro Speaks of
  Rivers," 194
On "Trumpet Player," 195
On "Wild Nights," 145
O Taste and See, 86
Others taunt me with having
  knelt at well-curbs, 182
Over my head, I see the bronze
  butterfly, 302

Owen, Wilfred
   Dulce et Decorum Est, 21, 285
O what can ail thee, Knight at
   arms, 243
O wild West Wind, thou breath of
   Autumn's being, 243
O wind, rend open the heat, 40
Ozymandias, 240

Pain has an element of blank,
   147–148, 148, 157
Paradise Lost, 15, 16
Partial Reflections in Black & Blue,
   317
The Passionate Shepherd to His
   Love, 216
Pastan, Linda
   Ethics, 308
Photograph of My Father in His
   Twenty-second Year, 313
The Piano, 97
Piano, 98
Piazza Piece, 283
Pied Beauty, 267
Piercy, Marge
   A Work of Artifice, 127, 311
Plath, Sylvia
   Mirror, 127–129, 309
Poe, Edgar Allan, *388*
   To Helen, 127, 249
   The Raven, 63, 250
Poetry, 278
Poirier, Richard
   On *"Mending Wall,"* 172
   On *"Stopping by Woods on a*
      Snowy Evening, 171
A Poison Tree, 52
Pope, Alexander, *388*
   from *An Essay on Man, 58,* 229
   On *the Collar of a Dog,* 17
   Sound and Sense, 68
Pound, Ezra
   The River-Merchant's Wife: A
      Letter, 277
Pour, O pour, that parting soul in
   song, 288
Prévert, Jacques
   Family Portrait, 27
Pritchard, William
   On *"Stopping by Woods,"*
      170–172
Provide, Provide, 165, 187
Put, stay put, Terrier Torment,
   Heel! I'll put on thee—, 101
Putting in the Seed, 166, 181

Raleigh, Sir Walter
   The Nymph's Reply to the
      Shepherd, 215
Rampersad, Arnold
   Langston Hughes as Folk Poet, 191

Ransom, John Crowe
   Piazza Piece, 283
Rape, 34
The Raven, 63, 250
Reading Frost, 169
Reapers, 288
A Red, Red Rose, 232
The Red Wheelbarrow, 79
Reed, Henry
   Naming of Parts, 26, 126
Reflections on Sylvia Plath's
   "Mirror," 128
Remorse—is Memory—
   awake, 158
Rich, Adrienne, *388*
   Aunt Jennifer's Tigers, 10, 11
   Rape, 34
Richard Cory, 273
Rios, Alberto
   A Dream of Husbands, 324
The Road Not Taken, 52, 165,
   378–380
Robert Frost: Or, the Spiritual Drifter
   as Poet, 173
Robinson, Edwin Arlington, *389*
   Miniver Cheevy, 32
   Richard Cory, 273
Roethke, Theodore, *389*
   Elegy for Jane, 292
   My Papa's Waltz, 12, 13–14,
      19, 28–29, 64, 88
   The Waking, 18, 87
Rompf, Kraft
   Waiting Table, 321
Rossetti, Christina
   Up-Hill, 51
   The Ruined Maid, 264

The Sad World of "London," 130
Sailing to Byzantium, 272
Saint Francis and the Sow, 302
Salvia, Jean-Marie
   The Dark Woods of Robert
      Frost, 378
Same in Blues, 197
Santiago Baca, Jimmy
   from *Meditations on the South*
      Valley, 322
Sappho
   To me he seems like a god, 209
Schnackenberg, Gertrude
   Signs, 325
The Second Coming, 270
September rain falls on the
   house, 293
Sestina, 18, 293
Sexton, Anne, *389*
   Her Kind, 78
   Two Hands, 304
Shakespeare, William, *390*
   Let me not to the marriage of
      true minds, 217

Shakespeare, William *(Cont.)*
   My mistress' eyes are nothing
      like the sun, 218
   Shall I compare thee to a
      summer's day?, 102
   That time of year thou may'st
      in me behold, *36, 43,*
      43–44, 65, 73, 74, 80, 80
   Th' expense of spirit in a waste
      of shame, 217
   When, in disgrace with fortune
      and men's eyes, 216
Shall I compare thee to a summer's
   day? (Moss), 103
Shall I compare thee to a
   summer's day?
   (Shakespeare), 102
She is as in a field a silken tent, 60
Shelley, Percy Bysshe
   Ode to the West Wind, 240
   Ozymandias, 240
She walks in beauty, like the
   night, 239
Should I get married? Should I
   get good?, 305
Signs, 325
The Silken Tent, 58, 60, 127, 165
Simpson, Louis
   The Battle, 47
Size and Sheer Will, 317
Smith, Stevie
   Mother, Among the Dustbins, 62
Snow falling and night falling fast,
   oh, fast, 186
Snow on Frost, 104
Softly, in the dusk, a woman is
   singing to me, 98
Soliloquy of the Spanish Cloister, 255
The Solitary Reaper, 233
Some keep the Sabbath going to
   Church, 152
Some say the world will end in
   fire, 182
Somewhere beneath that piano's
   superb sleek black, 97
so much depends, 79
Song, 218
Song: To Celia, 224
Song of the Son, 288
Soto, Gary
   Behind Grandma's House, 325
Sound and Sense, 68
The Span of Life, 72
Spenser, Edmund
   One day I wrote her name
      upon the strand, 214
Spring and All, 276
Spring and Fall, 268
Stafford, William
   Traveling through the dark I
      found a deer, 295
Stepkowski, Jennifer
   Reflections on Sylvia Plath's
      "Mirror," 128

Stevens, Wallace, *390*
  Thirteen Ways of Looking at a
    Blackbird, 274
Stopping by Woods on a Snowy
  Evening, 5, *6–8, 9–10, 36,*
  55–56, 63, 63–65, 73–74, 75,
  89, 165, 170–172, 378–380
Stuart, Muriel
  In the Orchard, 23, *126*
A Study of Reading Habits, 300
Sundays too my father got up
  early, 2, 124
The Sun Rising, 17, 56, *57–58, 72*
Sweet day, so cool, so calm, so
  bright, 53
Swenson, May, *390*
  The Universe, 69
  Women, 294
Symptoms of Love, 125, *125–126*

Tate, Allen
  On "Because I Could Not Stop for
    Death," 146
  Dickinson and Knowledge, 143
Tell all the Truth but tell It slant,
  140, 161
Tennyson, Alfred, Lord, *391*
  The Eagle, 254
  Ulysses, 253
Terrier Torment; or, Mr. Hopkins and
  his Dog, 101
That is no country for old
  men, *272*
That night your great guns,
  unawares, 265
That's my last Duchess painted on
  the wall, 21
That time of year thou may'st in
  me behold, *36, 43, 43–44, 65,*
  73, 74, 80, 80
The Assyrian came down like the
  wolf on the fold, 77
The bonsai tree in the attractive
  pot, 311
The brain is wider than the sky,
  149, 157
The bud stands for all things, 302
The Bustle in a House,
  140, 160
Th' expense of spirit in a waste of
  shame, 217
The fine, green pajama
  cotton, 317
The gray sea and the long black
  land, 40
The Heart asks Pleasure—
  first, 156
The instructor said, 205
The last Night that She lived, 160
Theme for English B, 205
The mother knits, 27

The Negro With the trumpet at
  his lips, 202
The night is beautiful, 199
The old dog barks backward
  without getting up, 72
The place where I was
  born, 323
There is a cop who is both
  prowler and father, 34
There is a pain—so utter, 157
The rent man knocked, 204
There's a certain Slant of
  light, 151
There was never a sound beside
  the wood but one, 174
The sea is calm tonight, 262
these hips are big hips, 311
The shattered water made a misty
  din, 184
The Soul selects her own Society,
  142, 149
The time you won your town the
  race, 269
The trees are in their autumn
  beauty, 270
The trick is, to live your days, 49
The way a crow, 103
The whiskey on your breath, 12
The Wind begun to knead the
  Grass, 96
The Wind begun to rock the
  Grass, 97
The witch that came (the
  withered hag), 187
The word *plum* is delicious, 70
The world is charged with the
  grandeur of God, 266
The world is not with us
  enough, 86
The world is too much with
  us, 232
They flee from me, 213
They flee from me, that sometime
  did me seek, 213
They sing their dearest songs, 67
Thirteen Ways of Looking at a
  Blackbird, 274
This Is a Photograph of Me, 312
This Is Just to Say, 99
Thomas, Dylan, *391*
  Do Not Go Gentle into that
    Good Night, *18, 297*
  Fern Hill, 295
Those Winter Sundays, 2, *2–5,*
  9–10, 19–20, 36, 55, 88, 124
Thou art indeed just, Lord, 24, *58*
Thou art indeed just, Lord, if I
  contend, 24
Though we thought it, Doña
  Carolina did not die, 324
Thou still unravished bride of
  quietness, 247

Threading the palm, a web of little
  lines, 325
To an Athlete Dying Young, 269
A Toast to Harlem, 190
Today we have naming of parts, 26
To Helen, 127, 249
To His Coy Mistress, 227
To me he seems like a god, 209
To My Dear and Loving
  Husband, 227
Toomer, Jean
  Reapers, 288
  Song of the Son, 288
To serve, I wait and pluck, 321
To the Virgins, to Make Much of
  Time, 224
Traveling through the dark I
  found a deer, 295
Tree at My Window, 165, 184
Tree at my window, window
  tree, 184
True ease in writing comes from
  art, not chance, 68
Trumpet Player, 195–196, 202
The Tuft of Flowers, 165, 174
Turning and turning in the
  widening gyre, 270
'Twas brillig and the slithy
  toves, 263
Two Hands, 304
Two Look at Two, 165, 183
Two roads diverged in a yellow
  wood, 52
The Tyger, 230
Tyger! Tyger! burning bright, 230

Ulysses, 253
The Universe, 69
The Unknown Citizen, 289
Up-Hill, 51
Upon Julia's Clothes, 224

A Valediction: Forbidding
  Mourning, 220
Variations on a Theme by William
  Carlos Williams, 100
Virgil
  The Aeneid, 15, 15
Virtue, 53

Waiting Table, 321
The Waking, 18, 87
Wallace, Robert
  The Double-Play, 45
War is Kind, 20, 21
The Weary Blues, 200
We basically don't know where
  we came from before birth, 317

We grow accustomed to the
   Dark, 154
Well, son, I'll tell you, 198
Western Wind, 25
Western wind, when will thou
   blow, 25
We stood by a pond that winter
   day, 41
We wear the mask that grins and
   lies, 273
What happens to a dream
   deferred?, 196
What is it about, 69
Whenas in silks my Julia goes, 224
Whenever Richard Cory went
   down town, 273
When getting my nose in a book,
   300
When I consider how my light
   is spent, 226
When I have fears that I may cease
   to be, 243
When I heard the learn'd
   astronomer, *56, 64, 75–76,*
   82, 82
When, in disgrace with fortune
   and men's eyes, 216
When I see birches bend to left
   and right, 177
When I was one-and-twenty, 268
When the Present has latched its
   postern behind my tremulous
   stay, 266
While my hair was still cut straight
   across by forehead, 277
Whitman, Walt, *391*
   Crossing Brooklyn Ferry, 257
   A noiseless patient spider, 257
   When I heard the learn'd
      astronomer, *56, 65, 75–76,*
      82, 82

Who says you're like one of the
   dog days?, 103
Whose woods these are I think I
   know, 5
"Why does your brand sae drap
   wi' bluid, 212
Wilbur, Richard
   The Death of a Toad, 300
Wild Nights—Wild Nights!,
   144–146, 151
The Wild Swans at Coole, 270
Williams, William Carlos, *392*
   The Dance, 85
   Danse Russe, 277
   The Red Wheelbarrow, 79
   Spring and All, 276
   This Is Just to Say, 99
Wilt thou forgive that sin where I
   begun, 44
The Windhover, 267
Winters, Yvor
   *Robert Frost: Or, the Spiritual
      Drifter as Poet,* 173
Woman should be pedestals, 294
Woman to Child, 48
Women, 294
The Word "Plum," 70
Wordsworth, William, *392*
   *Composed upon Westminster
      Bridge, September 3,
      1802,* 234
   It is a beauteous evening, 33
   I wandered lonely as a cloud,
      *29, 30–31, 42–43, 56,
      76–77*
   Lines (composed above Tintern
      Abbey), 234
   The Solitary Reaper, 233
   The world is too much with
      us, 232

A Work of Artifice, 127, 311
Wright, James, *392*
   A Blessing, 303
   *Lying in a Hammock at William
      Duffy's Farm in Pine Island,
      Minnesota,* 302
Wright, Judith
   Woman to Child, 48
Wyatt, Thomas
   They flee from me, 213

Yeats, William Butler, *393*
   Adam's Curse, 91
   A Dream of Death, 95
   *An Irish Airman Foresees His
      Death, 58, 60*
   The Lake Isle of Innisfree, 39
   Leda and the Swan, 271
   Sailing to Byzantium, 272
   The Second Coming, 270
   The Wild Swans at Coole, 270
You come to fetch me from my
   work tonight, 181
Young Gal's Blues, 200
You said: "I'll go to another
   country, go to another
   shore, 88
You who were darkness warmed
   my flesh, 48

Zero at the Bone, 140